Applied Social Psychology

Applied social psychology combines the science of social psychology with the practical application of solving social problems that exist in the real world. This exciting new textbook provides a thorough explanation of how social psychologists can contribute to the understanding and management of different social problems. A highly prestigious team of contributors from across Europe and the United States illustrate how social psychological theories, research methods and intervention techniques can be successfully applied to social problems encountered in the fields of physical and mental health, integration and immigration issues, gender issues, organizational issues, economic behaviour, political behaviour, environmental behaviour and education. Each field studied features an overview of important problems, the role of human behaviour in these problems, the factors influencing relevant behaviour, and effective ways to change this behaviour. This is an essential volume for all undergraduate and graduate students studying applied social psychology.

LINDA STEG is Associate Professor in Environmental Psychology at the University of Groningen.

ABRAHAM P. BUUNK is Academy Professor on behalf of the Royal Netherlands Academy of Arts and Sciences and Professor of Evolutionary Social Psychology at the University of Groningen.

TALIB ROTHENGATTER is Professor of Applied Psychology at the University of Groningen.

Applied Social Psychology

Understanding and Managing Social Problems

Edited by

Linda Steg, Abraham P. Buunk and
Talib Rothengatter

CAMBRIDGE
UNIVERSITY PRESS

CAMBRIDGE UNIVERSITY PRESS
Cambridge, New York, Melbourne, Madrid, Cape Town, Singapore, São Paulo, Delhi

Cambridge University Press
The Edinburgh Building, Cambridge CB2 8RU, UK

Published in the United States of America by Cambridge University Press, New York

www.cambridge.org
Information on this title: www.cambridge.org/9780521690058

First published 2008

Printed in the United Kingdom at the University Press, Cambridge

A catalogue record for this publication is available from the British Library

ISBN 978-0-521-86979-9 hardback
ISBN 978-0-521-69005-8 paperback

Contents

List of figures	*page*	xi
List of tables		xiv
List of boxes		xv
List of contributors		xvii
Acknowledgements		xix

1 Introduction to applied social psychology	1
LINDA STEG AND TALIB ROTHENGATTER	
Introduction: social problems and human cognition and behaviour	1
Definition of applied social psychology	4
Correspondence between basic and applied social psychology	8
Developing and testing theories	8
Basic and applied social psychology as science	9
Goals of science	11
Causes of behaviour and cognitions	12
Features of applied social psychology	15
The role of personal values	15
The use of multiple theories, intervention techniques and research methods	17
Interdisciplinary research	18
Field settings	19
Social utility	20
Roles of applied social psychologists	22
Overview of the book	24
2 The USE of theory in applied social psychology	28
P. WESLEY SCHULTZ AND MICA ESTRADA-HOLLENBECK	
Introduction	28
The role of theory in the field of applied social psychology	29
Theories, principles and constructs	32
Social-psychological theories	35
Social thinking	35
Social influence	39
Social relationships	42

Things to consider when using theory in applied work   47
    How basic, applied and use-inspired researchers
        develop theory   49

3   Applications of social psychology to increase the impact of
    behaviour-focused intervention   57
    PHILIP K. LEHMAN AND E. SCOTT GELLER

Introduction   57
A behaviour-analysis approach to intervention   57
Behavioural intervention strategies   59
    Antecedent strategies   59
    Consequence strategies   62
Enhancing interventions through social influence   67
    Consistency   67
    Authority   75
    Liking   76
    Reciprocity   77
    Scarcity   79

4   Research designs in applied social psychology   87
    MELISSA BURKLEY AND HART BLANTON

Research designs in applied social psychology   87
    Selecting a research method   87
True experiments: maximizing precision   89
    Defining features of true experiments   89
    Advantages of true experiments   90
    Disadvantages of true experiments   94
    Minimizing the disadvantages of true experiments   95
Correlational research: generalizing to situations   97
    Defining features of correlational research   97
    Advantages of correlational research   99
    Disadvantages of correlational research   99
    Minimizing the disadvantages of correlational studies   100
Quasi-experiments: compromising between precision and
    generalizability to situations   103
    Defining features of quasi-experimental research   103
    Advantages of quasi-experimental research   106
    Disadvantages of quasi-experimental research   107
Survey research: generalizing to people   107
    Defining features of survey research   108
    Advantages of survey research   110
    Disadvantages of survey research   110
    Minimizing disadvantages of survey research   111

5 Social psychology and economic behaviour: heuristics and
  biases in decision making and judgement   117
  W. FRED VAN RAAIJ

  Introduction   117
    Economic theory of utility maximization   117
    Anomalies   118
    Social-psychological factors   119
  Personal, social and situational reference   119
    Personal reference   119
    Social reference   120
    Situational reference   121
  Loss aversion   122
    Introduction   122
    Endowment effect   130
    Status-quo bias   131
    Sunk-costs effect   132
  Time preference   133
  Towards a new 'rationality' of economic behaviour of consumers,
    investors and entrepreneurs   135
  Applied social psychology in context   136

6 Social psychology and immigration: relations between
  immigrants and host societies   141
  JAN PIETER VAN OUDENHOVEN, CHARLES JUDD AND
  COLLEEN WARD

  Introduction   141
  Migration and cultural diversity in the twenty-first century   141
  Acculturation theory and research   143
    One-dimensional models of acculturation   143
    Multidimensional models of acculturation   144
  Social-psychological theories and research   149
  Acculturation research and social-psychological theories   152
  Interventions   154
  Applied social psychology in context: the influence of globalization
    on host–immigrant relationships   155

7 Applying social psychology to the classroom   162
  PASCAL HUGUET AND HANS KUYPER

  Introduction   162
  Social comparison   163
    Upward social comparison in the classroom   165
  Students' 'Theories' of intelligence and academic self-concept   168
    Entity versus incremental theory of intelligence   168

Academic self-concept of failure and performance   169
Academic self-concept of success and the BFLPE   173
Stereotype threat: the role of negative stereotypes   175
Classroom climate   176
Applied social psychology in context   177
Final thoughts   178

8 Social psychology and environmental problems   184
LINDA STEG AND ROBERT GIFFORD

Introduction   184
Environmental influences on well-being and behaviour   185
Effects of behaviour on the environment   188
    Environmental problems and human behaviour   188
    Understanding environmental behaviour   189
    Promoting pro-environmental behaviour   198
Applied social psychology in context   201

9 Gender issues in work and organizations   206
TINEKE M. WILLEMSEN AND
ANNELIES E. M. VAN VIANEN

Introduction   206
Women and men at work   206
    Quantitative differences   206
    Qualitative differences   207
Early studies   207
Stereotyping men, women and jobs   208
Women's choices and decisions regarding jobs and careers   209
    Self-efficacy   210
    Outcome expectancies   210
Selection and assessment   211
    Gender typing of applicants and their behaviours   212
    Gender typing of jobs   213
Explaining the glass ceiling   213
    Gender typing of leadership and management   214
    Gender differences in leadership style and effectiveness   214
    Emergent leadership   215
Structure and culture of organizations   217
    Structure   217
    Organizational culture   218
Interventions   218
Applied social psychology in context: what other disciplines say
    about gender differences in work   220
    Economics: human capital theory   220
    Economics: statistical discrimination theory   221
    Sociology: socialization theory   221

10 **Social psychology of health and illness**   226
ARIE DIJKSTRA AND ALEXANDER ROTHMAN

Description of problems in the field   226
    The societal burden of unhealthy behaviours   226
    The societal burden of chronic illnesses   228
Contributions of social psychology to prevent and solve health
    problems   228
Understanding health and illness behaviours   229
    Motivation and self-efficacy expectations   229
    Initiation and implementation of behaviour   232
    Illness behaviour   233
    Stage models   235
    Research methods to assess changes over time   236
Promoting health behaviour   237
    Tailoring messages   238
    Framing messages   242
Applied social psychology in context   243

11 **Social psychology and mental health**   249
ABRAHAM P. BUUNK AND PIETERNEL DIJKSTRA

Introduction   249
Disturbed body image   249
    Gender differences in body image   251
    Consequences of disturbances in body image   252
    Theoretical explanations of disturbed body image   253
    Preventing body image disturbances   254
Depression   255
    Gender differences in depression   256
    Social comparison theory and depression   256
    Preventing depression   257
Relationship problems   259
    Attachment theory   260
    Attachment style and relationship quality   260
    Social exchange and interdependence theory   262
    Preventing relationship problems   264
Applied social psychology in context   266

12 **Social psychology and modern organizations: balancing
    between innovativeness and comfort**   271
KAREN VAN DER ZEE AND PAUL PAULUS

Introduction   271
Social context of modern organizations   271
Strengths of active exploration   273
Social identity theory   276

Dynamic organizational development: cohesion and
    locomotion goals   278
Interventions   281
  Promoting cohesion   281
  Promoting locomotion   282
  Flexibility in cohesion and locomotion   283
Applied social psychology in context   285

13   Social psychology and the study of politics   291
MARTIN ROSEMA, JOHN T. JOST AND
DIEDERIK A. STAPEL

Introduction   291
Political leadership   292
  'Big Five' personality factors   293
  Profiling political leaders   294
  Crisis decision making   296
  Groupthink   297
Voting behaviour   299
  To vote or not to vote?   299
  Theory of reasoned action   300
  The Michigan model of voting   303
  Online model of candidate evaluations   305
Ideology   307
  Has ideology come to an end?   307
  Ideology and values   308
  Prejudice   309
Applied social psychology in context   310

Index   316

Figures

1.1 Foot-in-the-door technique © George Wills   *page* 5
1.2 Cognitive dissonance reduction © George Wills   5
1.3 Inductive (left) and deductive (right) approach   6
2.1 Three functions of theories in applied social psychology (USE)   29
2.2 Three roles of theory in applied social psychology © George Wills   33
2.3 Quadrant model of scientific research (Stokes, D. (1997). *Pasteur's quadrant: Basic science and technological innovation.* Washington, DC: Brookings. Redrawn from p. 73.) 50
3.1 Polite prompts are usually more effective   60
3.2 A promise card can be used to encourage a number of behaviours   62
3.3 Negative consequences motivate, but don't make us happy © George Wills 64
3.4 Extrinsic rewards can stifle intrinsic motivation © George Wills   66
3.5 When peers perform, there's pressure to conform © George Wills   72
3.6 Similarity increases liking © George Wills   77
3.7 The reciprocity norm involves payback © George Wills   78
4.1 Three-horned dilemma: most research choices involve trade-offs © George Wills 88
4.2 Violent video games cause an increase in aggressive behaviour © George Wills 91
4.3 Confounds © George Wills   92
4.4 Effects of violent media preference and aggression during grade 3 and grade 13 (Eron *et al.*, 1972) 102
4.5 Effects of video game violence and gender on noise blast intensity (Bartholow & Anderson, 2002) 106
4.6 Context of survey research can impact the quality of the data © George Wills 111
5.1 Risk taking to avoid loss © George Wills   123
5.2 The value function of prospect theory   123
5.3 Less worry through mental accounting © George Wills   125
5.4 Segregation of gains   126
5.5 Integration of losses   127
5.6 Paying by credit card is less painful © George Wills   127
5.7 Integration of a loss with a larger gain   128
5.8 Segregation of a gain from a larger loss   128

6.1 One-dimensional model of acculturation   143
6.2 A two-dimensional model of acculturation strategies (Berry, 1997)   145
6.3 Integration © George Wills   146
6.4 Assimilation © George Wills   146
6.5 Separation © George Wills   147
6.6 Marginalization © George Wills   147
6.7 Liking (1 = little; 5 = much) of 'neighbours' dependent on
    nationality, religion and employment status (N = 2389)   150
7.1 Children doing a geometry or drawing test © George Wills   169
7.2 The complex figure used by Huguet *et al.* (2001)   170
7.3 Memory recall score of students (max. = 44 points) by task context
    and academic standing   171
7.4 The big-fish-little-pond effect (BFLPE): theoretical predictions
    (adapted from Marsh & Hau, 2003)   174
8.1 The level of noise annoyance depends on social-psychological
    factors © George Wills   186
8.2 World energy consumption by fuel type, 1970–2020
    (EIA, *International Energy Outlook 2001*)   189
8.3 Self-serving denial © George Wills   193
8.4 A schematic representation of the VBN theory of
    environmentalism (adapted from Stern, 2000)   194
9.1 Gender-role attitudes and subjective norms predicting career
    orientation and actual career. (Derived from Vincent, Peplau &
    Hill, 1998, p. 772.) The arrows reflect regression paths with
    standardized regression coefficients. The model could explain 42
    per cent of the variance in career orientation and 9 per cent of the
    variance in career behaviour 14 years later.   212
10.1 Percentages of healthy years lost caused by health-related
    behaviours and risk factors (World Health Organization, 2002)   227
10.2 Increasing self-efficacy © George Wills   232
10.3 A stage model of health behaviour change   236
10.4 Computer-tailored persuasion composes individualized output
    (on paper or on screen) based on an individual assessment.   239
10.5 Computer-tailored information © George Wills   239
11.1 Disturbed body image   250
11.2 Stimuli presented to the participants in Fallon and Rozin's study
    (1985)   251
11.3 Attachment theory: the four-group model of attachment   261
11.4 Preoccupied attachment style © George Wills   262
11.5 Relationship inequity © George Wills   264
12.1 Intercultural working environment © George Wills   273
12.2 Processes of cohesion and locomotion in organizations as a
    function of organizational and team context   280
13.1 The relevance of politics to the young   293

13.2 Psychological processes bring leaders support from their staff
       © George Wills   298
13.3 Why some people do not bother to vote © George Wills   300
13.4 Poster used to encourage people to vote   301
13.5 Canvassing by phone is not effective © George Wills   302
13.6 The Michigan model of voting   304
13.7 Candidate differences determine level of electoral turnout
       © George Wills   305

Tables

2.1 Summary of focus, examples and application of
social-psychological theories   *page* 36

3.1 Applications of social influence principles for behaviour-
focused intervention   81

4.1 Summary of the four research designs   88

5.1 Preference for a coffee mug or a piece of chocolate   131

5.2 Average amounts to delay and speed-up receiving a gift
certificate of $7   134

10.1 Changes in life expectancy in years to live by world region 227

12.1 Stages of cohesion and locomotion in groups   274

Boxes

1.1 Solving social problems via changing cognitions and behaviour   *page* 2
1.2 The power of situations: the Stanford prison experiment   13
1.3 City dwellers less friendly when many people are around   14
2.1 Knowledge is not enough: knowledge-deficit model of behaviour change   30
2.2 Applying the elaboration likelihood model to reduce HIV-risky behaviours   41
3.1 The hypocrisy effect: facilitating behaviour change with reminders of past failures   71
3.2 The social-norms approach to reducing college student drinking   74
4.1 Example of experimental research   90
4.2 Example of correlational research   98
4.3 Example of quasi-experimental research   105
4.4 Example of survey research   109
5.1 Applying research methods: choice prospects   118
5.2 Applying intervention strategies: Save More Tomorrow™   129
5.3 Research design on the endowment effect   130
6.1 Testing the theory: the similarity-attraction hypothesis   149
6.2 From theory to practice: how to promote a common ingroup identity   152
6.3 An innovative research method   153
7.1 Theory application: how to make use of social comparison principles   167
7.2 Application of a research technique   172
7.3 Application of a research method: should the two genders be separated in the school setting?   175
8.1 Applying research methods: social design saves pain and improves moods in hospitals   187
8.2 Applying theories: habit versus planned behaviour   197
8.3 Applying intervention strategies: effects of feedback on household gas use   199
9.1 Gender gaps: some statistics on women and men at work in the European Union   207
9.2 An application of the theory of reasoned action to women's career behaviour   211

9.3	Gender stereotypes and selection	213
9.4	A series of experiments to refine the theory on gender bias in evaluations	216
9.5	The evaluation of mentoring programmes	219
10.1	Sources of self-efficacy	231
10.2	Near real-time versus retrospective recall	237
10.3	Computer-tailored persuasive messages	241
11.1	Experiment: gender differences in weight dissatisfaction	251
11.2	Intervention: the 'Everybody's Different' programme	255
11.3	The theory of involuntary subordinate strategies	258
11.4	Experiment: temporarily alleviating depression	259
11.5	Assessing attachment style	263
11.6	Theory: individual differences in exchange orientation	265
12.1	Application of theory: a case example of principles from social identity theory	277
12.2	Interventions: application of structured brainstorming methods in practice	283
12.3	Research design: a case example of experimental evaluation of interventions	284
13.1	Prospect theory and the Cuban missile crisis	296
13.2	Effects of personal appeals on voter turnout	302
13.3	The dynamic information board	306

Contributors

HART BLANTON
Texas A & M University

MELISSA BURKLEY
Oklahoma State University

ABRAHAM P. BUUNK
University of Groningen, Department of Psychology

ARIE DIJKSTRA
University of Groningen, Department of Psychology

PIETERNEL DIJKSTRA

MICA ESTRADA-HOLLENBECK
California State University, Department of Psychology

E. SCOTT GELLER
Virginia Polytechnic Institute and State University

ROBERT GIFFORD
University of Victoria, Department of Psychology

PASCAL HUGUET
CNRS et Université de Provence, Laboratoire de Psychologie Cognitive

JOHN T. JOST
New York University, Department of Psychology

CHARLES JUDD
University of Colorado at Boulder, Department of Psychology

HANS KUYPER
University of Groningen, Institute for Educational Research

PHILIP K. LEHMAN
Virginia Polytechnic Institute and State University

PAUL PAULUS
University of Texas Arlington

MARTIN ROSEMA
University of Twente, Department of Political Science and Research Methods

TALIB ROTHENGATTER
University of Groningen, Department of Psychology

ALEXANDER ROTHMAN
University of Minnesota, Department of Psychology

P. WESLEY SCHULTZ
California State University, Department of Psychology

DIEDERIK A. STAPEL
Tilburg University, Tilburg Institute for Behavioural Economics Research

LINDA STEG
University of Groningen, Department of Psychology

KAREN VAN DER ZEE
University of Groningen, Department of Psychology

JAN PIETER VAN OUDENHOVEN
University of Groningen, Department of Psychology

W. FRED VAN RAAIJ
Tilburg University, Department of Social Sciences

ANNELIES E.M. VAN VIANEN
University of Amsterdam, Department of Psychology

COLLEEN WARD
Victoria University of Wellington, School of Psychology

TINEKE M. WILLEMSEN
Tilburg University, Department of Social Sciences

Acknowledgements

We express our gratitude to the following students from the Bachelor of Science in Psychology programme at the University of Groningen for carefully reviewing the draft chapters of this book: Gustaaf Bos, Leonie Bouwkamp, Rivka de Vries, Chanti Hazeleger, Menno Norden, Vivian Rhemrev, Thirza Troost, and Sebastiaan Wiering. Their comments have significantly improved this book.

1   Introduction to applied social psychology

LINDA STEG AND TALIB ROTHENGATTER

Introduction: social problems and human cognition and behaviour

Social psychology is a basic science aimed at understanding human social behaviour and the motivations, cognitions and emotions related to such behaviour. For example, social psychologists try to understand why people so easily give in to social pressure, why people often seem insensitive to the needs of others, why people become aggressive, why people like each other or why people are unhappy even though they seem to have everything going for them. Social psychology tries to build knowledge primarily through laboratory experiments, and therefore theories and findings from social psychology may sometimes seem remote from the actual problems in society. However, many, if not most, societal problems have social-psychological aspects, that is, they are rooted in behaviour or human cognitions. For example, integration problems may result from conflicts between groups and the inherent human tendency to favour one's own group, and traffic accidents are to a large extent caused by unsafe driving styles and the unrealistic perception that one is a better driver than most others. Moreover, health problems are related to unhealthy eating habits and a sense of not being able to control one's appetite, and environmental problems result in part from growing consumption levels and a tendency to pay attention only to one's immediate interests. Consequently, solutions and prevention of such problems require changes in attitudes, values, behaviour and lifestyles (Zimbardo, 2002). Social psychologists can play an important role in this respect. Box 1.1 illustrates how social problems may – at least partly – be managed via behavioural changes. This example demonstrates how social psychologists may help resolve social problems and highlights several issues that enhance the social utility of applied social psychological studies. First, in order to design effective solutions for social problems, we have to understand which behaviour causes the given problem. Applied scientists should focus on those aspects of a social problem where interventions would have the most impact in resolving these problems. In our example, speeding by moped riders was studied because moped riders are relatively often involved in traffic accidents, while, in turn, these traffic accidents appeared to be strongly related to speeding. Second, it is important to examine which factors influence the particular behaviour. Behaviour-change programmes

Box 1.1   Solving social problems via changing cognitions and behaviour

Social problem

The Province of Drenthe (in the north of the Netherlands) is concerned about traffic safety in the region. Researchers analysed the local traffic statistics, and found that moped riders are twenty-two times more likely to be involved in traffic accidents than average road users (including pedestrians), and forty times more likely than average car users. Based on this, they decided to develop a traffic safety programme aimed to increase the safety of moped riders. They first decided to commission a study in which they examined which factors underlie the high accident involvement of moped riders.

Which behaviour causes accidents?

The research team first examined which behaviour causes accident involvement of moped riders. It appeared that traffic accidents are especially related to traffic violations (e.g., speeding), and not to errors (e.g., by accident not giving priority) or lapses (e.g., not noticing a traffic light) made by moped riders. Therefore, the research team decided to focus on factors affecting traffic offences. More specifically, they decided to focus on speeding, because the survey study revealed that moped riders generally do not obey speed limits, and they are quite often fined for speeding. The research team assumed that speeding typically results from conscious decision making. Therefore, they based their study on a theoretical model that aims to explain planned behaviour that is under volitional control: the theory of planned behaviour (TPB) (Ajzen, 1991; see Chapter 2).

Factors influencing traffic violations

Following the TPB, the research team examined to what extent speeding was related to *attitudes* towards speeding (i.e., the degree to which a person has a favourable or an unfavourable evaluation or appraisal of speeding), *social norms* (i.e., the individual's perception of the extent to which important others would approve or disapprove of speeding) and *perceived behavioural control* (i.e., the perceived ease or difficulty of (not) speeding). It appeared that moped riders having positive attitudes and strong social norms towards speeding were more likely to violate speed limits than those with negative attitudes and weak social norms. Perceived behaviour control was not significantly related to speeding.

Policies to increase traffic safety

Based on these results, the research team concluded that traffic safety programmes could best focus on changing attitudes and social norms towards speeding. Among other things, they suggested stressing the risks associated with speeding, so as to make prevalent attitudes more negative. Although the study revealed that moped riders do acknowledge these risks, it appeared that these risks did not outweigh the advantages of traffic offences, such as feelings of freedom and the 'kick' out of not respecting the law. Also, the research team suggested presenting examples of youngsters who disapprove of speeding in information campaigns, so as to weaken social norms.

will be more effective to the extent to which they target important antecedents of behaviour. Thus, we need to understand which factors cause behaviour. Third, it is important to understand which intervention techniques are available to change behaviour, taking into account which behavioural antecedents are typically targeted by various intervention techniques. In our example, speeding appeared to be strongly related to attitudes and social norms. Thus, interventions should best focus on changing attitudes and social norms related to speeding, for example, by designing information campaigns that stress the risks associated with speeding. The involvement of applied social psychologists does not need to stop here. Applied social psychologists can also play an important role in evaluating the effects of interventions, by examining to what extent interventions indeed change behaviour and the underlying determinants, and whether social problems are indeed resolved. This will not only reveal whether intervention programmes are successful, but also how they may be improved. Moreover, evaluation studies provide unique opportunities to test social psychological theories in real-life settings.

In sum, applied scientists should focus their efforts on aspects of a social problem where they would have the most impact in improving the relevant problems. This basic principle should be taken into account when deciding which problem to study (in our example: traffic safety of moped riders), which variables to concentrate on (in our example: causes of traffic violations) and the decision on what kind of interventions to use in managing the problem (in our example: changing attitudes and norms).

This book aims to provide an introduction to the contribution of social psychology to the understanding and managing of various social problems, and the methods used to achieve this. The book gives an overview of a wide range of social psychological theories, intervention techniques and research designs that can be applied to better understand and manage social problems. Moreover, the book aims to demonstrate how knowledge from social psychology has been applied in practice. When discussing the role of social psychologists in ameliorating social and practical problems, we highlight the role of human behaviour in various social problems, factors influencing such behaviour and effective ways to change the particular behaviour.

Definition of applied social psychology

Before elaborating on how social psychologists can contribute to resolving social problems, we will first define the field. Given the broad range of interests of social psychologists, as will become apparent from the second part of this book, it is not easy to provide a formal definition of social psychology. However, in general, social psychologists seek to acquire basic knowledge about how people think about, feel about, relate to and influence one another, and why they do so. Thus, **social psychology** may be defined as the scientific field that seeks to understand the nature and causes of individual behaviour and thought in social situations. This includes, for example, behaviour and thoughts related to helping, attraction, conflict, prejudice, self-esteem, group processes and social exclusion (Baron & Byrne, 2004).

Applied social psychology, in turn, may be defined as the systematic application of social psychological constructs, principles, theories, intervention techniques, research methods and research findings to understand or ameliorate social problems (Oskamp & Schultz, 1998). Constructs are the building blocks of psychological principles and theories. A **construct** refers to a clearly defined individual (psychological) characteristic that is generally latent and thus not directly observable, although it can be assessed through interviews or questionnaires. Examples are attitudes (i.e., whether one evaluates a topic positively or negatively), values (i.e., general beliefs about desirable behaviour or goals) or social norms (i.e., whether one's social group disapproves or approves of a particular behaviour).

A **principle** is a statement of how a psychological process works. Principles describe basic processes by which humans think, feel and act. Examples are:

- The *foot-in-the-door technique*, which involves making a small initial request, followed by a larger related request within a short period (Figure 1.1); generally, those who agreed to the small request are much more likely to comply with the larger request as well, as compared with those who were not asked to agree with a small request or to those who did not agree to the small request.
- *Cognitive dissonance*, which refers to the uncomfortable tension that can result from having two conflicting thoughts at the same time, or from engaging in behaviour that conflicts with one's beliefs or attitudes (Figure 1.2). When two cognitions (including beliefs, emotions, attitudes, behaviour) are incompatible, individuals try to reduce this dissonance by inventing new thoughts or beliefs, or by modifying existing beliefs.
- The *availability heuristic*, which refers to the tendency to judge the likelihood or frequency of an event by the ease with which relevant instances come to mind.

A **theory** is an integrated set of principles that describes, explains and predicts observed events. Theories provide explanations for our observations, and enable

Figure 1.1 *Foot-in-the-door technique*

Figure 1.2 *Cognitive dissonance reduction*

us to predict future events. A theory integrates various principles. An example is the theory of planned behaviour, described in Box 1.1. Theories are not facts or laws; the tenability of theories should be tested in practice. We elaborate on relevant theories, intervention techniques and research designs in Chapters 2, 3 and 4, respectively.

Basic and applied social psychology differ in two important respects.

1. Basic social psychologists are particularly interested in developing and test-ing theories, while applied social psychologists focus on understanding and resolving practical problems. Basic social psychologists may conduct stud-ies merely out of scientific curiosity about some phenomenon, while applied social psychologists are specifically trying to contribute towards solving social problems. In the end, applied social psychologists will focus their efforts on the improvement of people's quality of life. They do not necessarily have to con-duct studies themselves to learn more about phenomena causing the problems at hand. In some cases, available knowledge may be sufficient to plan interven-tions or social programmes that would ameliorate these problems. Does this imply that applied social psychologists do not contribute to the development of theories at all? No, it does not. Rather, theory development is not their main interest; it is not the primary reason that they do research.

2. Basic social psychologists tend to follow a **deductive approach**. They start with a particular theory, and examine to what extent the theory may be help-ful in understanding various types of social behaviour. In contrast, applied social psychologists tend to follow an **inductive approach**. They start from a specific social problem, and examine to what extent various theories may help to understand this specific problem, and which theory provides the best explanation of the particular behaviour causing the problems. This difference is illustrated in Figure 1.3.

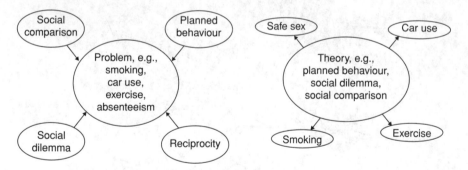

Figure 1.3 *Inductive (left) and deductive (right) approach*

Inductive perspective. An example of an inductive approach might be when under-standing why in a particular organization many people are often absent from work. We might examine this using the theory of planned behaviour, which would sug-gest that such behaviour reflects the lack of a negative attitude towards being absent, a lack of strong negative sanctions for such behaviour, and a feeling of not being able to go to work when one is not feeling well (Hopstaken, 1994). A social comparison perspective might suggest that people may often be absent from work because they think that they do so less often than others, or because they feel that they are treated worse than their colleagues (Geurts, Buunk & Schaufeli, 1994). A social dilemma perspective may suggest that people are absent from work because they do not feel responsible for their work, and feel their contribution to the organizational goals is negligible. According to reciprocity theory, people will often be absent when they feel they invest more in their work than they obtain in return. These explanations are not necessarily mutually exclusive, and may all contribute to the understanding of this or any other problem.

Deductive perspective. A researcher may be particularly interested in examining the extent to which a specific theory is successful in explaining various types of social behaviour. For example, the theory of planned behaviour (Ajzen, 1991) has been applied to understand a wide range of social behaviours, including low-fat diet consumption, drug and alcohol use, smoking, safe sex, recycling, mode choice and driving violations. A meta-analytic review revealed that TPB was quite successful in explaining this wide range of social behaviour, although the TPB is less successful in predicting observed behaviour compared to self-reported behaviour (see Armitage & Conner, 2001).

Of course, many scientists and many studies may be categorized as both basic and applied. Combining basic and applied work is quite valuable, since it demonstrates to what extent theories tested in experimental settings are valid in real-life situations as well. Thus, studies may be both theory oriented and problem oriented. First, so-called applied studies may sometimes lead to major theoretical breakthroughs. Second, so-called basic studies may be conducted in applied settings and make a major contribution to the insight in an applied problem. Both kinds of studies are highly valuable, since they reveal how social problems may be solved while at the same time they contribute to theory testing and building.

Theoretical breakthroughs in applied research. A good example is the work by Shelley Taylor and her colleagues on social comparison among women with breast cancer (Wood, Taylor & Lichtman, 1985). This research was undertaken in order to examine the psychological aspects of the strategies these women were using in coping with their disease. Unexpectedly, when asked how well they were coping with their problems compared with other women with breast cancer, 80 per cent of the women interviewed reported they were doing 'somewhat' or 'much' better than other women. Perhaps more important, an analysis of the comments that were made spontaneously by these women during the interview indicated that no matter how serious these women's problems were, they believed that there were others who were worse off. And if they did not know of any specific person who had been more seriously afflicted, they imagined others, or even fabricated a target, that is, they cognitively constructed a comparison target themselves. This study was of major theoretical importance because it suggested (1) that so-called *downward comparisons* (comparisons with others who were worse off) were very prevalent among people facing a threat; (2) that such comparisons did not necessarily involve contact with others, but could take the form of cognitively constructing others; and (3) that these comparisons seemed to help women with breast cancer cope by allowing them to feel better about themselves and their own situation (Buunk & Gibbons, 1997). It is also possible that, for these women, expressing these downward comparisons was a way of maintaining a positive view of themselves towards their environment to prevent being seen as a complainer.

Applied breakthroughs from basic research. Various experimental studies demonstrated that losses loom larger than gains (see Kahneman & Tversky, 1979). That is, individual preferences change when the same outcomes are framed as losses instead of gains. For example, subjects are likely to pay less to obtain a certain good (for instance, a mug) than when the demand for parting with the same good is at stake. The initial endowment (owning or not owning the good) serves as the reference point from which subjects value prospects. Buyers perceive the purchase of the good as a gain, while sellers perceive selling the same good as a loss. This phenomenon is called loss aversion: people dislike losses more than they like gains of the same size. Whether outcomes are considered as a loss or a gain depends on the reference point used. This finding is very important for practitioners. For example, it explains why consumers dislike deductibles, even though policies with high deductibles can offer considerable savings. Consumers probably frame deductibles as an extra loss. That is, consumers consider the costs of the insurance premium and the additional out-of-pocket costs of the deductible as two separate costs, and thus segregated losses. They pay the premium, but still have to cover part of the costs when they claim their expenses. To take another example, health messages can focus on the benefits of performing particular behaviour (a gain-framed appeal) or the costs of failing to perform this behaviour (a loss-framed appeal). Both appeals can have different effects on behaviour, as will be illustrated in Chapter 10.

Correspondence between basic and applied social psychology

Despite these differences, basic and applied psychology are similar in many ways. Both are interested in developing and testing theories, both use scientific methods, both are motivated by the same goals of science and both include similar factors predicting cognitions and behaviour in their studies. These common characteristics are discussed below.

Developing and testing theories

Basic as well as applied social psychologists are interested in testing theories (although it is generally not the primary interest of applied social psychologists). In fact, valid theories are very useful in solving social problems, as stressed in one of the most famous quotations by Kurt Lewin: 'There is nothing so practical as a good theory' (Lewin, 1951). Theories provide explanations for human behaviour. Theories are very useful for understanding causes of social problems, and may suggest techniques by which such problems can be solved, as is illustrated by the example in Box 1.1. More specifically, theories provide coherent frameworks for understanding behaviour that causes social problems. They help us to structure problem situations, and to find critical factors (such as attitudes or values) causing behaviour or cognitions. As such, theories provide ideas that guide our research and provide a direction that may yield solutions for social problems. Theories are very helpful in understanding and interpreting results of research. They help us to understand why and how things are related, and to identify where further research work is needed. Theories help us to develop interventions as well, by specifying variables or conditions that must be controlled or changed in order to reach our goals. This is illustrated in Box 1.1: the theory of planned behaviour was used to examine why moped riders violate traffic rules. It appeared that traffic violations were especially related to attitudes and social norms, which suggests that traffic safety among moped riders may be improved by highlighting the risks associated with speeding (and thus by making attitudes towards speeding less positive), or by targeting social norms, for example, by presenting examples of youngsters who disapprove of speeding in the media. Similarly, the study by Taylor and colleagues described above used social comparison theory to understand how women cope with breast cancer. Their study revealed that downward comparison (comparisons with those who are worse off) seemed to help women with breast cancer by allowing them to feel better about themselves and their own situation. This suggests that coping behaviour among women with breast cancer can be improved by providing breast cancer patients with examples of women who are worse off compared with themselves.

Theories do not only help applied social psychologists in carrying out their work. Applied social psychology can also contribute fruitfully to basic psychological principles, theories and intervention techniques, because studies in field settings provide the ultimate test of the validity of theories. Based on applied research, new questions may arise that necessitate adjustment of theories, or the development of new theories. For example in Chapter 5 van Raaij demonstrates that people tend to discount consequences that occur in the long term. People demand a high compensation for a delay in receiving money, and this compensation is typically higher than the interest rate. However, (applied) studies on environmental risks revealed that not all future consequences are discounted. In fact, environmental risks are not always considered to be more serious when they occur in the short term rather than in the distant future, and many people do not appear to discount future environmental risks at all (Gattig & Hendrickx, 2007). This suggests that discounting especially occurs in particular domains (for example, economic behaviour), and that people do not have a general tendency to value future consequences less.

Basic and applied social psychology as science

Both basic and applied social psychology are sciences. The term science refers to two things: (1) reliance on scientific methods, and (2) guidance by the core values of science.

Scientific methods are those methods that depend on empirical tests, that is, the use of systematic observations to evaluate propositions and ideas. An empirical test of an idea or proposition means, first of all, that studies are set up in a way that allows support or refutation of the idea being tested. Second, the study should be conducted in such a way as to enable other researchers to evaluate and replicate the research. Researchers adopt these scientific methods because 'common sense' is often unreliable and inconsistent. Moreover, many potential biases may influence our thoughts and make them unreliable. For example, one may have the impression that a lack of knowledge is the basic reason that many people eat too many fatty foods. However, a survey study in a representative sample of the population may uncover that most people know quite well how unhealthy such foods are, and that the major reason people do not refrain from eating them is that they feel they cannot control their appetite.

A core set of values should be adopted to qualify a study as scientific in nature. Four of these values are most important (Baron & Byrne, 2004):

- **Accuracy**: gather and evaluate information that is as carefully examined, precise, and error-free as possible, for example, researchers should develop reliable measures for their main constructs. Unreliable measures can lead to false conclusions of 'no effect'.
- **Objectivity**: minimize bias in obtaining and evaluating data, for example, researchers should make sure that their expectations do not affect the behaviour of subjects.
- **Scepticism**: accept findings as accurate only to the extent that they have been verified over and over again by the data, for example, outcomes of a single study may be caused by chance. Results should be replicated in various comparable studies to rule out the possibility of results that occur by chance only.
- **Open-mindedness**: accept evidence as valid, even if the evidence is not consistent with one's initial, and perhaps strongly held, beliefs and theories, for example, researchers should accept evidence refuting their theory, even though they may be very keen to demonstrate the validity of their theory.

Basic as well as applied social psychologists are committed to these values. Adherence to these values guarantees that research findings are a valid reflection of the phenomenon under study.

In addition, both basic and applied psychologists respect general ethical guidelines for psychologists, as proposed in the 'Ethical principles of psychologists and code of conduct' by the American Psychological Association (APA) (2003). These principles refer to ethical responsibilities of psychologists. Social psychologists should follow these general ethical standards in their work. Various general ethical standards and specific ethical responsibilities are listed, such as respect for people's rights and dignity, compliance with law, concern for others welfare, avoiding harm, avoiding sexual intimacies, maintaining confidentiality and integrity. Various other (national) psychological foundations publish their own codes of conduct, most of which are quite similar to the APA guidelines.

Some ethical precepts specifically concern social scientists, and refer to the way research should be conducted. Some important concerns of precepts are:

- *Deception*: deception of clients or research participants should be avoided whenever possible. Deception should only be used when it serves a higher desirable goal, which should be decided upon by ethics committees.
- *Informed consent*: research participants should be able to give meaningful informed consent to participate in the study. This implies that participants should be informed about the aim of the study and the impact the study may have on them.
- *Invasion of privacy*: the privacy of the participants should be respected. Personal details should be kept confidential.
- *Debriefing*: research participants should be debriefed as soon as possible after the research is completed in order to update them on the research, and deal with any misconceptions.

Goals of science

Another similarity between basic and applied social psychologists is that both are motivated by four main goals of science: description, prediction, causality and explanation. We define these goals below and illustrate them by considering the possible influence of social relationships on health.

Description refers to identifying and specifying the details and nature of a phenomenon. Often, different types of the phenomenon are distinguished, and the frequency of occurrence of the phenomenon is recorded. In the case of examining effects of social relationships on health, a researcher may record people's health status, and collect data on both physical and psychical health. The researcher may also record how many relationships people have with others. Accurate descriptions of phenomena provide an important first step towards understanding them, but not sufficient.

Prediction enhances understanding of phenomena, for example because it does reveal why people are healthy. Prediction requires knowing what factors are systematically related to the phenomenon of interest. Thus, to what extent the phenomenon being studied is correlated with various factors is examined. In our example, if people who have many social relationships appear to be healthier (which suggests that social relationships are positively related to health), we would understand that health can be predicted by the number of social relationships people have. However, we would still not be sure whether social relationships cause a better health status. A third factor could be responsible for existence of the relationship between health and the number of friends a person has. For example, self-confidence could influence both health and the number of social relationships. It could be that self-confident people are healthier, and are more successful in making friends. Alternatively, the number of social relationships an individual maintains may depend on health status, that is, healthier people may be more outgoing and make more friends.

Thus, identifying causes of a phenomenon is another important component of understanding: we need to determine **causality**. This means that we have to find out whether changes in one factor indeed cause changes in the other factor. By demonstrating that social relationships increase health, we could provide clear-cut suggestions to increase people's health.

A final component of understanding is **explanation**. Explanation implies the need to establish why a phenomenon or relationship occurs. Why would social relationships improve one's health status? Is it because people need social support in difficult times, because people need to relate to others or because of some other factor?

Causes of behaviour and cognitions

As mentioned above, both basic and applied social psychologists are primarily interested in understanding the many factors and conditions that affect the behaviour and thoughts of individuals concerning other people. Obviously, behaviour and thoughts are shaped by many different factors. In general, social psychologists take into account individual, social, situational, cultural and biological factors, as well as interactions between these factors.

Individual factors refer to interpersonal characteristics and processes. Individual differences may exist in cognitive processes and in the extent to which people engage in behaviour. For example, people who strongly value the environment may be more likely to recycle products than those who strongly value individual interests. Likewise, people with positive attitudes towards speeding are more likely to speed. And extroverts are more likely to have an active social life than introverts.

Social factors pertain to the effect of opinions and actions of other people on our behaviour and thoughts. We are often strongly affected by the actions and thoughts of other people, and by social situations. Imagine, for example, that you arrive at a pedestrian-crossing light. No traffic around at all. Will you cross the street if the light is red? Your reaction might be quite different when many people neglect the red light and cross the street to when many people are waiting for the traffic light to turn green. Fashion is another apt example of the influence of actions of other people on our behaviour and thoughts. For example, people wear specific clothing because many others or important role models wear such clothing. In addition, in many cases, we are affected by the physical appearance of others. Research has shown that we evaluate attractive and unattractive people differently. For example, physical beauty appears to influence how instructors are rated for teaching ability: instructors who ranked high on beauty also rated high on course evaluations (Hamermesh & Parker, 2005). Age, ethnicity, physical disabilities and gender may also affect how we approach and interact with others. For example, female motorists in distress receive more help than male motorists or male–female pairs (West, Whitney & Schnedler, 1975), particularly from young men driving alone.

The behaviour of individuals is strongly affected by social situation. The power of social influences has been demonstrated in many studies. In fact, some of the most classic and best-known studies in social psychology highlight the role of social influences on behaviour. For example, studies by Milgram (1974) revealed that many normal, healthy people complied with an experimenter's insistent directives to administer painful shocks to a learner (who happened to be an accomplice of the experimenter, and only pretended to receive the shocks) every time the learner made a mistake on a learning task. In another experiment, Asch (1955) demonstrated that many people went along with the erroneous judgements of others rather than publicly disagree with them, even though it was perfectly obvious that the others were wrong. Asch presented subjects with a very simple judgement task, to distinguish between the lengths of lines. In each case, the correct judgement was self-evident. Still, the vast majority of participants conformed at least in some instances. The Stanford prison experiment, conducted by Zimbardo and colleagues, is another classic demonstration of the power of social situations, see Box 1.2.

Box 1.2   The power of situations: the Stanford prison experiment

In 1971, 24 male college students volunteered to participate in a prison experiment conducted by Zimbardo and colleagues. Half of them, randomly selected, were assigned to be guards, the others to be prisoners. They were put into a 'mock' prison, that is, a functional simulation of a prison aimed to produce similar effects to those of a real prison. The guards were given no specific training on how to be guards. They were told only to do whatever they thought was necessary to maintain law and order in the prison. Thus, the guards made up their own set of rules. Initially, both the guards and prisoners were not completely into their roles. But things soon changed dramatically. Within a few days, most of those who played the role of guards transformed into brutal sadists, while most of those who played the role of prisoners transformed into abject, frightened and submissive men, some having severe mental symptoms. Guards began to harass and intimidate the prisoners, and started using psychological techniques to control them. For example, guards demanded push-ups from prisoners, prisoners were forced into solitary confinement, forced to clean toilets with a toothbrush and stripped naked. Guards were escalating their abuse of prisoners in the middle of the night when they thought no researchers were watching and the experiment was off. Interestingly, all participants stayed in character. Even the 'good' guards felt helpless to intervene. No one challenged the (arbitrary) rules set. Outsiders, such as parents who were allowed to visit their sons, and a priest who was consulted by the prisoners, did not call the rules into question either. Even the researcher himself (who played the role of prison superintendent) was absorbed in the experiment, and started thinking like a prison superintendent rather than a research psychologist. The experiment was planned to last two weeks. However, as the reactions of both groups were very intense, the experiment was broken off after six days.

This study clearly demonstrates that personal identities, long cherished values and morality may be seriously distorted as participants internalized situated identities in their assigned roles as prisoners and guards, respectively. Based on the experiment, the researchers concluded that many, perhaps most, people can be made to do almost anything by the strength of the situation they are put in, regardless of their morals, personal convictions and values. Zimbardo drew parallels between this experiment and real-life situations, such as the incidents in the Abu Ghraib prison in Iraq, where Iraqi prisoners were seriously abused by US guards in 2003 and 2004. More detailed information about the Stanford prison experiment can be found at www.prisonexp.org/.

Situational factors reflect contextual factors that may affect our behaviour and thoughts. The physical world may strongly affect our behaviour, thoughts and feelings. For example, the availability of recycling bins or curbside recycling programmes may strongly affect participation levels in recycling. Ambient temperature affects our behaviour. For example, we become more irritable and aggressive when ambient temperature is increasing (Bell, 2005). Furthermore, environmental stressors, such as noise or crowding, make us less helpful (see Box 1.3).

Box 1.3   City dwellers less friendly when many people are around

Social psychologist Robert Levine and colleagues conducted studies in 23 different cities in the world to assess how friendly city dwellers are. They pretended to be in need of help and observed whether they received help from city dwellers. For example, they dropped a pen, pretended to be blind or to have a broken leg, or dropped a stamped, addressed letter to see whether these were picked up and posted by city dwellers. They received twice as much help from residents of cities like Rio de Janeiro and Madrid compared with residents of Bangkok, Singapore, New York and Amsterdam.

Population density appeared to be a more important factor in determining helpful behaviour than were culture and ethnicity. People in sparsely populated cities appeared to be more helpful than those in densely populated cities. These results may be explained by the 'stimulus-overload theory', proposed by Stanley Milgram (1970). According to Milgram, residents of densely populated cities cope with the many people around them by keeping others at a distance and by ignoring incidents happening in the street. Thus, crowding makes people unfriendly (and not their personality). When people from New York or Amsterdam are on holiday in Rio, they are much friendlier, according to the researchers.

Cultural factors refer to cultural values that affect cognitions and behaviour. Culture may be defined as the system of shared meanings, perceptions and beliefs held by people belonging to a particular group (Smith & Bond, 1993). Our behaviour and thoughts are strongly affected by cultural norms, that is, social rules concerning how people should behave in specific situations. For example, cultural norms towards smoking have shifted rapidly during the last decades. About thirty years ago, it was quite common for people to smoke at work, in classrooms, at restaurants and in bars, while today smoking has been banned from public spaces in many countries around the world. To give another example: ideals of female beauty have shifted from rounded and curvy figures to thin figures, and dieting has become common practice for many women. Thus, cultural norms and values may strongly affect us.

Biological factors pertain to the effect of biological processes and genetic factors on our behaviour and thoughts. Evolutionary psychology suggests that we possess a large number of evolved psychological mechanisms that help us survive and reproduce. For instance, our preference for natural above urban landscapes has been explained by the fact that humans had to survive in natural landscapes for thousands of years, and consequently we still prefer such landscapes. Interestingly, there is some evidence that we particularly like landscapes with features of the savanna, the type of landscape in which mankind evolved (Ulrich, 1983). Similarly, mating preferences have been related to biological and genetic factors: we prefer characteristics in mates that are associated with reproductive capacity, that is, we find people more attractive if they have symmetrical facial structures and lustrous hair, while women with a relatively small waist-to-hip ratio are believed to be more attractive than those having a large waist-to-hip ratio (Buss, 1994).

Clearly, individual, social, situational, cultural and biological factors interact. For instance, whether individuals who strongly value the environment (an individual characteristic) recycle or not depends on the availability of recycling facilities (a situational factor).

Features of applied social psychology

We discussed two important features of applied social psychology: a drive to address social problems and, because of this, a tendency to follow an inductive approach. Both clearly illustrate that applied social psychologists are particularly trying to contribute towards solving social problems. We highlight below five other typical features of applied social psychology.

The role of personal values

Applied social psychology is not value free. The mere fact that applied social psychologists decide what problems and which target groups to study, and which changes should be realized, demonstrates that values do play an important role in applied social psychology. Applied social psychologists should be aware of their personal values, and the way their values may affect their work. In some cases, their values may conflict with values of other groups involved. For example, applied social psychologists may define unhealthy lifestyles, such as smoking, eating too much and malnutritious food, and exercising too little, as a social problem, but not everyone involved may agree with them. On the one hand, it may be argued that a healthy lifestyle should be promoted because smoking and obesity cause serious health problems, such as cancer, heart disease, high blood pressure and diabetes. Moreover, smoking and obesity are associated with high economic costs, related to the resources needed to diagnose and treat diseases caused by such unhealthy behaviour. Spending on smoking-related and obesity-related medical care accounts for a significant proportion of all private healthcare spending. Thus, taking this view, health and economic concerns call for the promotion of healthy lifestyles. On the other hand, some groups argue that the risks associated with unhealthy lifestyles are exaggerated and that an unhealthy lifestyle may even promote well-being. Moreover, these groups argue that the economic costs of unhealthy lifestyles are not as high as claimed by health movements. In general, smokers and people who are overweight die much earlier than non-smokers and people of average weight. Consequently, they will make claims on collective funds (such as healthcare or pensions) for a shorter time, and the net financial burden on society may not differ much from that of people with a healthy lifestyle. Moreover, liberals may argue that individual freedom and autonomy should be respected at any time. They would argue that whether one would like to smoke or drink is one's own responsibility. Which line of reasoning do you find most convincing? Would you impose your view upon others? In any case, you can surely imagine that social programmes will be received quite differently by groups favouring these different perspectives.

We have indicated that applied social psychologists focus their efforts on the improvement of people's quality of life. The conflict described above illustrates that not everyone may agree on what is qualified as fostering quality of life. Such disagreements are quite common, as we live in a pluralistic and multicultural society. Various groups may have quite different views on society and quality of life, depending on their own value system. Value systems of different groups are often incompatible, at least partially. Even on an individual level conflicts between values may occur. For example, we may strongly value freedom of choice, while at the same time we think some people should be restricted in their freedom of choice when they are a threat to other people's quality of life. Thus, we constantly have to choose between different values. To acknowledge this, applied social psychologists who aim to increase the quality of life in a specific problem area must start with determining their own value position. By explicating this position, they may increase understanding among those involved.

Although values influence which topics are being studied by applied social psychologists, they do not affect the methods used to study them. As indicated in the previous section, applied social psychologists are committed to a core set of scientific values (viz., accuracy, objectivity, scepticism and open-mindedness).

This implies that decisions about the validity of a theory or effectiveness of intervention programmes are made value free, that is, based on objective, empirical data.

The use of multiple theories, intervention techniques and research methods

Because applied social psychologists follow a problem-oriented, inductive approach, they typically do not apply single theories, intervention techniques or research methods. Various factors may cause a particular social problem. Consequently, a whole range of variables may be considered when trying to understand such problems. As each single theory typically focuses on a limited set of variables, problems may be better understood when studied from different theoretical perspectives. For example, students' educational performance may be related to many different factors, among which are intelligence, personality, self-esteem, attribution, prejudice, encouragements by parents and (teachers') expectations. These factors are being studied from different theoretical perspectives. Together, these perspectives provide a comprehensive overview of factors influencing performance in various situations, and, consequently, ways to improve performance of students. Of course, some theories may be more applicable than others, depending on the problem at hand. For example, social influences will probably be less influential when behaviour is anonymous. In this case, theories focusing on the role of social norms, such as the theory of normative conduct (Cialdini, Kallgren & Reno, 1991) may be less helpful in understanding behaviour. The theory of normative conduct contends that behaviour is influenced by injunctive norms (i.e., the extent to which behaviour is supposed to be commonly approved or disapproved of) as well as descriptive norms (i.e., the extent to which behaviour is perceived as common). The more salient a particular norm, the stronger it influences the relevant behaviour. On the other hand, theories on stereotyping are highly relevant when trying to understand discrimination against women or minority groups.

Similarly, some intervention techniques may be more appropriate in a given problem situation than others. In general, intervention techniques are more effective to the extent to which they specifically address those factors that contribute substantially to the particular problem behaviour, and those factors that can be improved. For example, providing teenagers with information about safe sex will hardly be effective if knowledge levels are already high. Likewise, information campaigns have limited effects if people see no opportunities to change their behaviour. For example, promoting public transport use by highlighting the advantages of using public transport will not be effective if no practicable public transport services are available. In contrast, when people are not familiar with the advantages of socially beneficial behaviour, information campaigns may be successful, and when lack of facilities prohibit specific behaviour, providing such facilities may be quite effective. Thus, one should know which factors cause or inhibit behaviour before designing intervention programmes to change behaviour.

In many cases, multiple research designs may be followed to study social problems. A priori, no research design is superior to others. In fact, as will be shown in Chapter 4, each research design has its strengths and weaknesses. Weaknesses of one research design may be compensated by another. For example, experimental studies are generally high in internal validity, as, when conducted properly, they enable us to draw firm conclusions on causal relationships between variables. However, as these studies tend to be conducted in artificial settings, external or ecological validity is less strong, that is, it may be hard to generalize results of such studies to real-life problems. In contrasts, the external validity of field studies is generally much higher, as these studies tend to be conducted in real-life settings. However, in many cases, internal validity is weaker, because in real-life settings there are many factors that may also influence behaviour that cannot be controlled by researchers, making it more difficult to draw clear conclusions on causality. Ideally, the same phenomenon is studied following different research designs, trying to replicate the findings over and over. By doing so, we will gain increasing assurance that our findings really reflect reality. Although experimental studies are important to test theories, studies in real-life settings provide crucial tests of the validity and strength of theories in practice.

Interdisciplinary research

Many societal problems are rooted in a wide range of factors, which are not solely social-psychological by nature. Economic, sociological, political and/or organizational factors, to name just a few, may play an important role. For example, political factors may prevent the solution of environmental problems caused by car use, that is, politicians may be reluctant to implement stringent (and effective) policies because they want to be re-elected. This necessitates social psychologists being informed on and aware of the research contributions and knowledge bases of other social science disciplines. In many cases, not only social science knowledge should be considered, but knowledge from a wide range of other disciplines should be taken into account as well. For example, when studying health behaviour and promoting healthy lifestyles, researchers should know about the health consequences of various types of behaviour. Similarly, when examining environmental behaviour, scholars should be acquainted with the environmental effects of behaviour in order to decide which behaviour could best be studied to reduce environmental problems. Based on this, applied social psychologists can decide which behaviours could best be studied (and changed) in order to reduce environmental problems. In the 1990s, many social psychologists studied factors affecting waste management and not energy consumption, while the latter is far more problematic from an environmental point of view. This implies that input may be needed from a wide range of sciences. Obviously, which disciplines it is relevant to consider depends on the problem at stake.

Of course, social psychologists cannot fully grasp relevant knowledge bases from all relevant disciplines. Luckily, they do not need to do so. Relevant knowledge can be applied by collaborating with scientists from other disciplines. Social psychologists should pursue multi- or interdisciplinary research and collaboration to take advantage of the knowledge and perspectives of other disciplines. For example, by working with medical doctors who are aiming to improve the quality of life of cancer patients, social psychologists may learn what the major physical consequences from various types of cancer are, and how these may affect individual quality of life. This can help social psychologists in developing their interventions more efficiently, addressing the particular problems that specific groups of patients experience.

Working in multi- or interdisciplinary settings is not easy. Different disciplines may use similar concepts for different phenomena, or different concepts for similar phenomena. For example, in psychology, a model usually refers to a conceptual model: a model explicates how different variables are mutually related. In contrast, in economics, a model typically refers to an arithmetical model, that is, a series of formulas which enable the researcher to actually predict or forecast behaviour. Members of multidisciplinary teams should acknowledge that each discipline has some unique contribution to offer. Usually it takes time to understand different viewpoints, and to appreciate each other's contribution. But in the end, multidisciplinary teams may outperform mono-disciplinary teams in many respects because they consider a broader range of factors that should be targeted to solve relevant social problems. After all, as behaviour is generally caused by multiple factors, changes in one factor may not be sufficient for problem solution. For example, if policy makers want to know to what extent road pricing will be effective in reducing car use, and, consequently, congestion problems, economists can examine which price level should be set, traffic engineers can study the effects of road traffic on the transport system and congestion levels, and social psychologists can explore to what extent road pricing would be acceptable to those involved, and how acceptability may be increased, as road-pricing policies will probably not be implemented if public resistance is large.

Field settings

From the above, it will not be a surprise that applied social psychologists are more likely to conduct research in field settings, that is, in natural settings where people live, work or recreate, than are basic social psychologists. This implies that applied social psychologists are less inclined to conduct true experiments, and are more apt to use quasi-experimental or correlational designs. As will be discussed in Chapter 4, such studies are generally high in external validity, meaning that, provided they are properly conducted, results may be more easily generalized to larger populations. However, it is less easy to infer causal relationships based on studies in applied settings. In many field settings, researchers are not able to control the many variables at stake, and, consequently, it is usually not possible to draw definite conclusions on which variables influence other variables.

This is not to say, however, that applied social psychologists do not conduct true experiments at all. As will be illustrated in the second part of this book, experimental studies may yield results with high practical value.

Social utility

Ultimately, applied social psychology aims to understand and solve social problems of different kinds and to increase quality of life, as will become apparent in the second part of this book. It is assumed that social problems may be reduced by changing people's attitudes, norms, values, perceptions, behaviours and lifestyles. This is the core subject of the field of social psychology. Thus, knowledge and methods of social psychology can be highly useful in achieving social goals.

We have already illustrated that the social utility of applied social psychology increases if scientists focus their efforts on those aspects of a social problem where they are likely to have the most impact in resolving the problem(s) at hand. This implies that they should consider which type of behaviour is most problematic, which factors are most influential in causing such behaviour and which strategies may be successfully applied to change them. For instance, when trying to reduce environmental impacts in households, scientists could better focus on reducing thermostat settings instead of reducing showering time, since the environmental impact of the former is much higher (Gatersleben, Steg & Vlek, 2002). Of course, the extent to which behaviour is amenable to change should be considered as well. Next, they should examine which factors are related to thermostat settings. After all, interventions will be more effective to the extent to which they target important antecedents of behaviour.

Another issue when considering social utility is the ratio of cost-effectiveness of interventions: Which results may we expect per euro, pound or dollar invested? For example, mass media campaigns are generally far less costly than individualized information. However, in general, individualized information tends to be more effective in changing behaviour than mass media campaigns, because the information can be tailored to the needs and preferences of individuals being targeted. In the end, individualized information may be more cost effective in as far as it would result in more significant changes in behaviour, and, consequently, the resolution of social problems. This clearly indicates that applied social scientists may need to develop quantitative estimates about the costs and expected benefits of interventions before they are implemented.

Applied researchers are especially keen on finding strong effects to guarantee the practical significance of their work. Thus, finding statistically significant results is not enough. In order to be useful in practice, results should be meaningful as well. It is often important to consider the *effect size*, that is, the strength of the association between two variables. For example, one may find in a large sample a significant correlation of .16 between a positive attitude towards smoking and the daily number of cigarettes smoked. However, this means that no more than 2.56 per cent of the variance in cigarette intake can be explained on the basis of the attitudes towards this behaviour (you compute the variance explained by computing the square of the univariate correlation). This is very little, considering that 97.44 per cent of the variance apparently depends on other factors. Nevertheless, the strength of the correlation and thus the amount of explained variance does not say everything. For example, even though the correlation between taking a low dose of aspirin and not getting a heart attack is only .034, which is considered extremely low by psychologists, it would mean that 34 people out of every 1000 would be saved from a heart attack if they used a low dose of aspirin on a daily basis (for an extensive treatment of these issues, see Rosenthal & DiMatteo, 2001).

Much applied research is conducted by order of a client or sponsoring agency. Not surprisingly, clients and sponsors want their problem to be solved within a specified period. In many cases, applied researchers have to meet strict deadlines in order to ensure that results are useful to clients or sponsors. Basic researchers tend to have much more freedom in the planning of their work, and usually do not face serious time constraints. This implies that applied scientists may have little time to think through their study design and results in much detail, as they have to make sure to deliver study outcomes in time. Moreover, applied social psychologists have less often the opportunity to develop new and possibly risky lines of research, as these may not yield results that are applicable in practice in the short term.

Applied social psychologists will increase the social utility of their work by clearly communicating the results of their work. These results should not be communicated only to fellow scientists, but to the public at large as well. Applied social-psychological studies are not primarily published in the general social-psychological journals that are particularly read by fellow scientists. You are more likely to find this work in specialized journals that focus on particular content areas, such as educational research, health behaviour, economic behaviour, environmental behaviour, traffic behaviour and gender issues. Furthermore, applied social psychological studies are often published in policy-oriented publications, targeting practitioners who may actually apply the knowledge. Although policy-oriented publications are generally valued less in the scientific community, they are highly important from a societal point of view. To increase the social utility of their work, applied social psychologists may try to communicate the implications of their findings to the public at large, for example, through non-technical journals, the mass media and popular lectures. This makes it necessary for applied social psychologists to communicate their work in an understandable way, thereby reducing unnecessary complexities in describing the research, and avoiding the use of technical jargon. Thus, they need to communicate their findings in clear and crisp language, without too many scientific terms. Social psychological concepts may be introduced, in as far as they clarify the analysis of the problem. For example, a concept like the bystander effect will be easily understood by an audience, and may put a problem in the right perspective. Explaining a term like self-efficacy may be necessary when presenting an intervention that is aimed at enhancing the control individuals experience over their situation. Knowledge will not be readily adopted and used when the public does not understand results of studies. Therefore, social scientists should carefully consider which information would be most useful for practitioners. This may differ from what is most significant from a scientific point of view. Policy makers are likely to be particularly interested in variables that can be readily manipulated through social programmes within a short-term frame. Also, policy makers tend to be more interested in descriptive results as compared with testing the validity of theoretical models.

Even though applied social scientists may have developed social programmes that are highly effective, there is no guarantee that these programmes will be actually implemented. Social programmes may not be feasible in practice. Policy makers have to deal with multiple interests, and have to reach compromises. Powerful lobbying organizations may seriously inhibit the implementation of social programmes that may have been highly successful in theory, thereby preventing the actual use of results from applied psychological research.

Roles of applied social psychologists

You are now familiar with the social utility of applied social psychology. Let us now consider possible roles scholars working in this field may fulfil. We distinguish three major roles for applied social psychologists: researcher, consultant and policy advisor.

Researcher

One obvious role of applied social psychologists is to conduct applied research. As indicated earlier in this chapter, in their research, applied social psychologists are not mainly interested in theory development and testing. They are particularly interested in contributing towards solving social problems. Applied social psychologists may do so in different ways. First, by studying the antecedents of behaviour that causes social problems. Understanding which factors cause a particular behaviour is highly relevant, because behaviour-change programmes will be more effective to the extent to which they target important antecedents of behaviour. For example, providing information on negative consequences of smoking will be especially effective when attitudes towards smoking are significantly related to smoking. Second, they may evaluate the effects of interventions on cognitions and behaviour. For example, an evaluation of a Dutch safe sex campaign revealed that this campaign successfully changed psychological variables targeted by the campaign, that is, the campaign resulted in more positive attitudes, social norms, perceived behaviour control and intentions towards safe sex (Yzer, Siero & Buunk, 2000). However, interventions are not always successful. In such cases, evaluation studies can indicate how to improve the effectiveness of such interventions. For example, information campaigns may not have been effective in changing attitudes and behaviour because people did not notice the information.

This implies that more effort should be made to get the attention of the public. Third, applied social psychologists can evaluate effects of interventions on social problems and individual quality of life, that is, did changes in cognitions and/or behaviour indeed resolve social problems, and did overall quality of life improve, as expected? Not only outcomes of interventions should be evaluated, but the process as well. Process evaluations may tell us much about what went wrong, and why. Both are important to examine the effectiveness of social programmes, and provide ways to enhance further programme effectiveness.

Of course, in principle, the way applied scientists conduct their studies does not differ from procedures followed by basic scientists. However, even when their research is not directly commissioned by an agency, applied scientists will, explicitly, consider the practical implications of their work. You may especially find researchers at universities, university colleges and research institutes established by governments.

Consultant

This is perhaps the most common role of applied social psychologist. In the role of consultant, applied social psychologists assist individuals, groups, organizations or communities to resolve particular problems they are facing. As such, applied social psychologists may be concerned with training and development, coaching, managing, marketing, public relations and communication. To give some specific examples, applied social psychologists may teach courses in social skills, negotiation or effective leadership, or they can coach employees and managers in order to increase their performance and well-being in professional and personal life. They can develop communication strategies, or design marketing strategies in order to promote specific products and services of those organizations. Also, the capacity of a consultant includes public relations; applied social psychologists can inform or influence potential customers or the public by means of advertisements, publicity, promotions and the like. Public relations officers are employed by business organizations, non-profit organizations, governmental agencies, politicians, or rich or famous people. The practice of public relations can serve various goals, including education, correcting a mistruth, building or improving an image, and securing a high (or low) profile for a particular organization, agency or person. Overall, as consultants, applied social psychologists assist or advise clients to improve their performance, appearance or quality of life.

Policy advisor

Applied social psychologists may be actively involved in policy making by public and governmental agencies or business or civic organizations. They can advise policy makers on ways to change cognitions and behaviour in order to improve or solve social problems of different kinds. Applied social psychologists may assist agencies and organizations in designing intervention programmes. For example, they can design information campaigns about safe sex, safe driving, energy conservation or company culture, to name just a few. As indicated earlier in this chapter, many social problems are rooted in a wide range of factors that are not only social-psychological by nature. As a consequence, in the role of policy advisor, applied social psychologists have to be able to successfully collaborate with scientists of other disciplines who are also involved in the policy-making processes. Thus, policy advisors should be able to work in interdisciplinary settings.

In practice, differences between these roles are not as straightforward as may be suggested above. In many cases, applied social psychologists combine different roles in their practice. For example, applied social psychologists may base their policy advice on an empirical study they conducted themselves.

Overview of the book

The first part of this volume provides a general overview of basic issues in applied social psychology. In this chapter, we have provided a brief introduction in applied social psychology. Chapter 2 discusses relevant social psychological concepts, principles and theories. In Chapter 3, intervention techniques are outlined that aim to improve social problems via behavioural change. Chapter 4 provides an overview of research designs that may be applied to study social problems. Together, the four chapters provide a conceptual, theoretical and methodological background for the second part of the book.

In the second part, the issues raised in the first four chapters are further elaborated on by demonstrating how social psychologists can help to understand and manage various social and practical problems. We will give many examples of how relevant theories, intervention techniques and research designs discussed in the first part of the volume are being applied to understand and solve social problems in various areas of application. In addition, specific theories and intervention techniques will be introduced for particular areas of applications. You will see that applied social psychologists tend to follow an inductive approach. A broad range of social problems is discussed, related to the following areas of application: economic behaviour (Chapter 5), issues of integration and immigration (Chapter 6), education (Chapter 7), environment (Chapter 8), gender issues (Chapter 9), physical health (Chapter 10), mental health (Chapter 11), organizational issues (Chapter 12) and political behaviour (Chapter 13). In each chapter, important problems in the particular area of application are outlined. We highlight to what extent these problems are rooted in human behaviour and cognitions. Furthermore, important research lines in the particular area of application are discussed. We focus our discussion on factors influencing behaviour, effective ways to change different types of behaviour, and research methods that may be fruitfully applied to understand and change relevant behaviour. We do not aim to be comprehensive in the coverage of each topic, but rather discuss important topics in some depth. For interested readers, references to relevant literature on specific areas of application are provided.

Conclusion

In this chapter, we first explained that many social problems are rooted in human cognition and behaviour. Solutions and prevention of such problems require changes in attitudes, values, behaviour and lifestyles. We illustrated that applied social psychology can play an important role in this respect, by studying antecedents of behaviour that significantly contributes to the particular problems. Using these antecedents, interventions can be designed and evaluated that target these social problems. We highlighted the correspondence between basic and applied social psychology: both are interested in developing and testing theories, both use scientific methods, both are motivated by the same goals of science and both include similar factors in their studies. The main difference between the two is that basic social psychologists are particularly interested in developing and testing theories and follow a deductive approach, while applied social psychologists focus on understanding and resolving practical problems and generally follow an inductive approach. Next, we discussed five other main features of applied social psychology: (1) it is not value free; (2) it typically uses multiple theories, interventions and research methods; (3) studies are often conducted in field settings as well as (4) in multidisciplinary settings; and (5) the social utility of results is of particular importance. Finally, we described three main roles that applied social psychologists fulfil in practice: (1) researcher, (2) consultant and (3) policy advisor.

Glossary

Accuracy: gathering and evaluating information that is as precise and error-free as possible.

Applied social psychology: the systematic application of social psychological constructs, principles, theories, intervention techniques, research methods and research findings to understand or solve social problems.

Causality: identifying causes of a phenomenon.

Construct: a clearly defined individual (psychological) characteristic that is generally latent and not directly observable.

Deductive approach: starting with a particular theory, and examining to what extent the theory is helpful in understanding various types of social behaviour.

Description: identifying and specifying the details and nature of a phenomenon.

Explanation: establishing why a phenomenon or relationship occurs.

Inductive approach: starting from a specific social problem, and examining to what extent various theories help to understand specific problems, and which theory provides the best explanation of the particular behaviour causing the problems.

Objectivity: minimizing bias in obtaining and evaluating data.

Open-mindedness: accepting evidence as valid, even if the evidence is not consistent with one's initial, and perhaps strongly held, beliefs and theories.

Prediction: knowing what factors are systematically related to the phenomenon of interests.

Principle: a statement of how a psychological process works.

Scepticism: accepting findings as accurate only to the extent that they have been verified over and over again by the data.

Scientific methods: methods that depend on empirical tests, that is, the use of systematic observations to evaluate propositions and ideas.

Social psychology: the scientific field that seeks to understand the nature and causes of individual behaviour and thought in social situations.

Theory: an integrated set of principles that describes, explains and predicts observed events.

Review questions

1. Give a definition of applied social psychology.
2. Discuss three correspondences between basic and applied social psychology.
3. In which respects do basic and applied social psychology differ?
4. Which are the most important features of applied social psychology?
5. Discuss three possible roles of applied social psychologists.

Further reading

Aronson, E., Wilson, T. D. & Akert, R. M. (2005). *Social psychology*. 5th edn. Upper Saddle River, NJ: Pearson Education.

Baron, R. A. & Byrne, D. (2004). *Social psychology*. 10th edn. Boston: Pearson Education.

Baumeister, R. F. & Bushman, B. J. (2008). *Social psychology and human nature*. Belmont, CA: Thomson Higher Education.

Oskamp, S. & Schultz, P. W. (1998). *Applied social psychology*. 2nd edn. Upper Saddle River, NJ: Prentice-Hall.

References

Ajzen, I. (1991). The theory of planned behavior. *Organizational Behavior and Human Decision Processes*, *50*, 179–211.

American Psychological Association (2003). Ethical principles of psychologists and code of conduct. Available on: www.apa.org/ethics/code2002.html.

Armitage, C. J. & Conner, M. (2001). Efficacy of the theory of planned behaviour: A meta-analytic review. *British Journal of Social Psychology*, *40*, 471–499.

Asch, S. E. (1955). Opinions and social pressure. *Scientific American*, *193* (5), 31–35.

Baron, R. A. & Byrne, D. (2004). *Social psychology*. 10th edn. Boston: Pearson Education.

Bell, P. A. (2005). Reanalysis and perspective in the heat–aggression debate. *Journal of Personality and Social Psychology, 89*, 71–73.

Buss, D. M. (1994). *The evolution of desire.* New York: Basic Books.

Buunk, B. P. & Gibbons, F. X. (eds.) (1997). *Health, coping and well-being: Perspectives from social comparison theory.* Hillsdale, NJ: Erlbaum.

Cialdini R. B., Kallgren C. A. & Reno, R. R. (1991). A focus theory of normative conduct: A theoretical refinement and reevaluation of the role of norms in human behavior. *Advances in Experimental Social Psychology, 24*, 201–234.

Gatersleben, B., Steg, L. & Vlek, C. (2002). Measurement and determinants of environmentally significant consumer behaviour. *Environment and Behavior, 34* (3), 335–362.

Gattig, A. & Hendrickx, L. (2007). Judgmental discounting and environmental risk perception: Dimensional similarities, domain differences, and implications for sustainability. *Journal of Social Issues, 63* (1), 21–39.

Geurts, S. A., Buunk, B. P. & Schaufeli, W. B. (1994). Health complaints, social comparisons and absenteeism. *Work and Stress, 8*, 220–234.

Hamermesh, D. S. & Parker, A. (2005). Beauty in the classroom: Instructors' pulchritude and putative pedagogical productivity. *Economics of Education Review, 24*, 369–376.

Kahneman, D. & Tversky, A. (1979). Prospect theory: An analysis of decision under risk. *Econometrica, 7*, 263–291.

Lewin, K. (1951). *Field theory in social science, selected theoretical papers* (D. Cartwright, ed.). New York: Harper & Row.

Milgram, S. (1970). The experience of living in cities. *Science, 167*, 1461–1468.

(1974). *Obedience and authority: An experimental approach.* New York: Harper & Row.

Oskamp, S., & Schultz, P. W. (1998). *Applied social psychology.* 2nd edn. Upper Saddle River, NJ: Prentice-Hall.

Rosenthal, R. & DiMatteo, M. R. (2001). Meta-analysis: Recent developments in quantitative methods for literature reviews. *Annual Review of Psychology, 52*, 59–82.

Smith, P. B. & Bond, M. H. (1993). *Social psychology across cultures.* Boston, MA: Allyn & Bacon.

Ulrich, R. (1983). Aesthetic and affective response to natural environment. In I. Altman & J. F. Wohlwill (eds.), *Behavior and the natural environment* (pp. 85–125). New York: Plenum.

West, S. G., Witney, G. & Schnedler, R. (1975). Helping a motorist in distress: The effects of sex, race and neighbourhood. *Journal of Personality and Social Psychology, 31*, 691–698.

Wood, J. V., Taylor, S. E. & Lichtman, R. R. (1985). Social comparison in adjustment to breast cancer. *Journal of Personality and Social Psychology, 49*, 1169–1183.

Yzer, M. C., Siero, F. W. & Buunk, B. P. (2000). Can public campaigns effectively change psychological determinants of safer sex? An evaluation of three Dutch safer sex campaigns. *Health Education Research, 15* (3), 339–352.

Zimbardo, P. G. (2002). Going forward with commitment. *Monitor on Psychology, 33* (1), 5.

2 The USE of theory in applied social psychology

P. WESLEY SCHULTZ AND MICA
ESTRADA-HOLLENBECK

Introduction

Jessica got to work on time today, but just barely. After driving down the freeway from the suburban community of Carlsbad to the city of San Diego at rush hour, she was personally aware of the congested roadways of this urban area. But unlike most of us who endure traffic delays, she gets to think about it all day at her job. Jessica works for the Metropolitan Transit System in San Diego, California. Her office oversees the bus, trolley and rail services throughout the city.[1] Her job is to work out ways to decrease road congestion and increase the public's use of the public transport systems. The problem is fairly clear – too many people (including Jessica!) take private cars to work. The existing streets and roadways cannot accommodate the 1.2 million residents that make use of them, and, especially during morning and evening hours when people are commuting to and from work, traffic is a major problem.

Like all of the social problems discussed throughout this book, human behaviour is the cause. Consequently, solving the problem will require a change in behaviour. But changing human behaviour can be challenging, and our chances of success can be greatly increased by incorporating a social-psychological perspective. We can begin with some basic psychological questions: What motivates a person to drive, rather than take the bus? Can we motivate and encourage residents to drive less by encouraging use of the existing public transport, a car-pool, or other alternative means of transport (like a bicycle)? And how do we know if our efforts to motivate behavioural change were successful? These questions reflect the primary functions of theory in applied social psychology – understanding (U), solution (S) and evaluation (E). See Figure 2.1.

For more than a hundred years, social psychologists have used the scientific method to understand the ways in which individuals think about, relate to and are influenced by others. The discipline has amassed a large volume of theories about human behaviour, and these theories provide a foundation for understanding and solving many social problems, such as the issue of traffic congestion we just described. In this chapter, we discuss the role of theory in the field of applied social psychology, provide a broad overview of the types of theories that are

---

[1] While the person described in this example is fictitious, the organization and problem are real. For more information, see www.sdcommute.com.

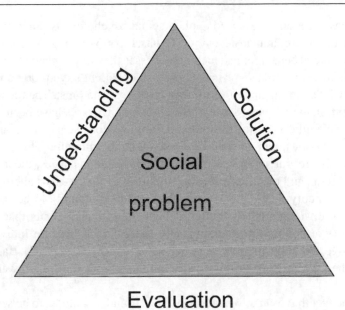

Figure 2.1 *Three functions of theories in applied social psychology (USE)*

discussed throughout this book, and conclude with some of the challenges that arise when using theory to solve social problems. This discussion complements the previous chapter on the discipline of applied social psychology, and sets the stage for the next chapters on interventions and the methods of applied social psychology.

The role of theory in the field of applied social psychology

For applied social psychologists, theories are the primary tool for understanding and solving social problems (Towson, 2005). And as pointed out in Chapter 1, theories are the starting point for creating an intervention. Without theories, we are left to 'guess' or intuitively understand the behaviour of interest. Often these guesses are based on our own individual experience, and we (falsely!) believe that through introspection and understanding of our own behaviour we can understand the behaviour of others. However, everyone is not the same and sometimes our intuition and introspection can misdirect well-intentioned efforts. While introspection can serve as a starting point, social-psychological theories provide both intuitive and counter-intuitive ideas that have been subjected to scientific scrutiny in a way that introspection has not been.

As previously mentioned, in applied work, theories are useful in three ways. By understanding the function of theories in applied work, we can better determine which theories are more relevant to applied social psychologists. First, theories provide explanations for human behaviour. That is, theories help us to organize and make sense of social behaviour and mental processes that may appear unrelated to the untrained observer. Just as a physician listens to a patient's symptoms and uses medical knowledge to diagnose the ailment, social psychologists use theories to analyse the problem and make sense of the situation. Theories have been tested, subjected to scientific scrutiny, examined for logical consistency, compared to other existing theories, and debated in the scientific community. This is not to say that theories are true in any absolute sense. In some instances, theories are found to be wrong, and new, more accurate theories are proposed as alternatives. Let's look at a theory that is known in the scientific community to be severely limited. The **knowledge-deficit model** of behaviour change posits that social programmes (like public transportation) are underutilized because individuals lack knowledge about the programme or the behaviour (Schultz, 2002). Based on this model, the solution to underutilized programmes is education or an awareness campaign.

Despite the fact that psychological science has found this model to be severely limited, it continues to emerge in policy and intervention programmes (see Box 2.1). For example, during the California energy crisis of 2000, energy experts attempted to motivate residents to conserve energy in their homes by distribut-ing media messages about how to do it (e.g., turn off lights, use fans instead of air conditioning on warm summer days). This approach was based on the faulty assumption that individuals were not conserving energy in their homes because they did not know what to do. As elaborated in Box 2.1, the existing research on this model is clear in showing that a lack of change in behaviour rarely results from a lack of knowledge. Thus, while intuition continues to lead policy makers to adopt the knowledge-deficit model, research reveals that knowing what to do, and how to do it, are pieces of the puzzle, but ultimately it is motivation that drives behaviour (Fisher & Fisher, 1992). While knowledge can be an important precursor to behaviour, by itself it is not sufficient to serve as a motivating force.

**Box 2.1   Knowledge is not enough: knowledge-deficit model
of behaviour change**

Across a variety of areas, policy makers and programme planners often assume that educating people about what to do, or how to do it, can produce behaviour change. The approach is often referred to as an *information campaign*, or *education campaign*. Unfortunately, social-psychological research suggests that while lack of knowledge might prevent people from acting, in most instances individuals already have sufficient information – what they lack is motivation. Here we highlight three examples where the approach has failed to produce behaviour change.

Energy conservation. In the summer of 2000, California experienced an energy crisis. The crisis entailed a greater demand for electricity than utility companies could supply. This resulted in skyrocketing prices and widespread power outages. In an attempt to intervene, our research team conducted a series of field experiments to test different approaches for motivating people to conserve electricity in their homes (Schultz *et al.*, 2007). Across several approaches, the *least* effective was providing residents with information about how to conserve (i.e., turn off lights, take shorter showers, use appliances more efficiently, use fans instead of air conditioning). Yet this was the approach most commonly used in radio, TV and print messages.

Cigarette smoking. For nearly fifty years, medical research has documented the health risks associated with cigarette smoking. Yet despite this evidence, people worldwide continue to smoke at alarming rates. At age 17, nearly one-in-four Americans are 'smokers' (defined as having 'smoked a cigarette in the past week'), and similar percentages have been reported in studies from many other countries. These high smoking rates have prompted a series of large-scale interventions, designed to educate people about the dangers of cigarettes and to provide them with information about how to quit. But despite these large budget interventions, the results have been disappointing, with very little behaviour change associated with these efforts.

Diabetes. Diabetes is a medical condition that results from improper levels of insulin in the body. The disease affects 7 per cent of the population worldwide, and can be treated through careful diet and exercise, or insulin injections. Without proper treatment and care, diabetes can cause heart disease and stroke, blindness, kidney failure, neurological damage and death (www.diabetes.org). To survive, diabetics must strictly follow medical treatment protocols. Yet many studies show that adherence among diabetics is low, and physicians have long wondered how to motivate their patients to take care of their disease. A recent series of studies by researchers at Duke University led to some startling conclusions. 'We spend so many resources on patient education with the assumption that it will make a difference, but what we seem to be finding is that while education may be a part of the puzzle, it is not adequate by itself' (Sanchez, 2005).

The findings from these studies summarized above are sobering. Despite large budgets and good intentions, these intervention efforts were unable to produce substantial, long-lasting changes in behaviour. But these failed examples can teach us as much as (if not more than) successful examples, and they illustrate the importance of connecting social psychological theory with intervention. Later chapters in this book highlight many of the successful examples of applied social-psychological research, but across the successes there is a common lesson – only providing people with information about what to do generally will not change their behaviour (Schultz, 2002).

While theories are quite useful for understanding the behavioural aspects of a social problem, they are useful in a second important manner. Good theories also suggest ways to change the problematic behaviour and thereby work towards solving some aspect of the problem. Returning to our analogy of the physician who had identified the symptoms and diagnosed the problem, she would then prescribe a treatment, such as some type of medication or surgery. A prescription in social psychology is often some form of intervention. Sometimes this involves training or education efforts targeting motivation. On other occasions, interventions involve structural changes, such as an incentive programme in which rewards are given for 'good' behaviour, a new programme or implementing a new technology. Theories provide a common language for discussing social problems and developing interventions. Terms such as attitude, reward, costs, attribution, social comparison and many others provide a starting point for articulating the logic of the intervention and the exact steps we can take to address the problem.

Finally, in an applied setting, theories can become 'practical'. Academic researchers develop most social psychological theories while working at universities. The theories are tested in controlled laboratory environments, often with university students as participants. The results are published in academic journals that are largely unavailable to individuals working in real-world settings. They are based on sound science, but will they apply to the real world? In some cases, applied research allows for broader tests of these theories. However, the application must be done carefully. Constructs and principles of the theory must be operationalized in ways that allow hypotheses to be tested. When this occurs, applied research provides important data to the experimental research community regarding how a theory succeeds or fails to explain 'real-world' behaviour. Concretely, this is done when an intervention, based upon a social psychological theory, is implemented and then data is systematically collected to see if the expected results occurred. If the social psychologist is following an **action research** model, the cycle would begin again with the researcher reanalysing the situation, refining the intervention, implementing it and then reassessing the situation and the relevance of the theories used.

Thus, theories have three major roles in applied social psychology: (1) they help make sense of social behaviour (*understand*), (2) they guide and inform the development of interventions intended to address a social problem (*solve*) and (3) they can be tested for practicality and usefulness in the real world (*evaluate*) (Figure 2.2). Keep these functions in mind as we clarify a few terms related to theories and then describe several types of social-psychological theories.

Theories, principles and constructs

As defined in the previous chapter, a theory is *an organized set of principles that describes, explains and predicts observed events*. In psychology, theories form the basis for our understanding of human behaviour, and *should* provide the

Figure 2.2 *Three roles of theory in applied social psychology*

foundation for our efforts to change behaviour. Theories are not facts; they are not observations; they are not laws. Theories are ideas, generated to explain observed events. Theories can be wrong, and science provides the methods for testing predictions derived from theories. For more information about the role of the scientific method in developing and testing theories, see Chapter 4.

As you read more about social psychology in this book, you will find a number of related terms: hypotheses, principles, models and constructs. As a starting point for understanding applied social psychology, it is useful to clarify and define these commonly used terms.

- A **theory** is an organized set of principles that describes, explains and predicts observed events. An example is cognitive dissonance theory, described later in this chapter.
- **Principles** describe a specific process, and they are often integrated into theories. An example is the **compatibility principle**, which is incorporated into the theory of planned behaviour discussed later in this chapter.
- A **hypothesis** is a testable prediction derived from a theory. Whereas theories provide broad explanations for behaviour, hypotheses are specific. By making empirical observations, we can test the accuracy of our hypotheses, and thereby test whether our theories about human behaviour are tenable (or wrong!). See Chapter 4.
- **Models** are frameworks that integrate theories and principles. Models typically describe multiple processes, each linked through some type of causal

sequence. An example is the elaboration likelihood model discussed later in this chapter.

- **Constructs** refer to the inferred affective, cognitive or motivational aspects of human behaviour. As a discipline, we have only the outward actions of individuals on which to base our theories. Everything else is inferred. To aid in our work, psychologists provide narrow definitions for psychological constructs, and then use these constructs to build their theories and principles. A good example of a psychological construct is an **attitude**. While there is general agreement among social psychologists that humans possess attitudes, they cannot be directly observed. Rather, they are inferred from people's stated preferences or actions. Constructs are the building blocks of psychological theories.

Let's return to our previous example to highlight each of these terms. The behaviour of interest is an individual's decision to drive their own car, rather than take public transport to work.[2] One theoretical perspective that might help to explain this behaviour is **rational choice theory**. Essentially, this theory maintains that individuals are motivated to act in ways that promote their self-interests (Scott, 2000). The theory contains a number of constructs – most notably *costs* and *rewards*. Rational choice theory also contains several principles, with each principle drawing on various psychological constructs. One principle incorporated into the theory is that perceived beneficial consequences of a behaviour are rewarding, and motivate the person to act. In the context of our example, getting to work faster is rewarding. Other rewards might include being able to control the time you arrive and leave work, listening to music you enjoy on the drive or being able to drive somewhere during your lunch hour. A second principle of rational choice theory is that perceived undesirable consequences of a behaviour are costs, and deter the behaviour. For example, travelling on the bus involves personal contact with strangers; perhaps it takes longer than driving by car; and there is less control over what time you leave your home in the morning. Note that it is the individual's subjective perceptions that define what is a cost and reward. As a result, costs and rewards can vary considerably from person to person.

Finally, the theory also leads to several testable hypotheses and ideas for interventions to change the behaviour. For example, you might hypothesize that those individuals who perceive that the rewards of driving a car to work exceed the costs will be less likely to take the bus. So, someone whose driving commute takes twenty minutes while the bus commute takes forty minutes should be more likely to drive a car, compared with another person whose travel times are twenty minutes by car and twenty-five minutes by bus. Similarly, we might hypothesize that increasing the efficiency of public transport (e.g., providing more express buses) will lead to an increase in people using the bus. Of course, people may

---

[2] To be more precise, the behaviour is driving. That it is 'decided' by the individual is inferred.

take into consideration other factors than commute time. In fact, in 2006 the price of petrol rose dramatically. At the same time, the use of car-pools and public transport also increased. Such a change in behaviour (increased use of public transport) is consistent with the rational choice theory. But what will happen when petrol prices drop?

From this brief example, you can see that Jessica is faced with a difficult task – changing the behaviour of motorists in San Diego is not simple. Fortunately, utilizing existing theories of human behaviour can help her to understand the psychology of this behaviour, and ultimately to create a programme to address this problem. In the next section, we summarize some prominent theories that social psychologists have used to understand, solve and evaluate social problems. As we review social psychological theories, keep in mind that in addition to social-psychological theories, the principles, hypotheses, models and constructs associated with each theory are also useful for understanding, solving and evaluating.

Social-psychological theories

Theories come in all shapes and sizes, ranging from grand theories of human behaviour to smaller theories that apply to very limited circumstances. In social psychology, there are literally hundreds of theories, and in many instances we can use a variety of theories to explain the same behaviour. In the following section, we provide a rough classification system for social psychological theories, with the goal of introducing some of the more prominent theories that appear in the subsequent chapters of this book.

As a framework for classifying relevant theories, we draw on the definition of social psychology provided earlier in this book. Social psychology is the basic science aimed at understanding human social behaviour and the motivations, cognitions and emotions related to such behaviour. As the definition indicates, the focus is on the individual and his or her thoughts, feelings and motivations related to social behaviour. In the section that follows, we review the major theoretical areas of social psychology, focusing on *thinking*, *influence* and *relationships* (see Table 2.1 for a summary of these areas).

Social thinking

Theories regarding social thinking typically describe how people appraise themselves and their social world. It includes the ways we gather, organize and interpret social information. From this area of study we have theories regarding attributions, attitudes, self-concept and **schemas**. In the social-psychological literature, researchers sometimes refer to this area of theory as *social cognition*. As the name implies, it draws heavily on the content and methods of cognitive psychology.

Table 2.1 *Summary of focus, examples and application of social-psychological theories*

	Social thinking	Social influence	Social relationships
Focus of theories	Describe how people appraise themselves and their social world.	Describe how the social environment changes an individual's thoughts, feelings and/or behaviours.	Describe what makes people relate to each other positively and negatively.
Types of theories	Attributions, cognitive dissonance theory, attitudes, theory of planned behaviour	Obedience, compliance, elaboration likelihood model	Ingroup/outgroup biases, stereotypes, prejudice, discrimination, contact theory, prosocial behaviour
Application of theories	To design tools or interventions that describe, predict, or change social appraisals	To design interventions that promote specific behaviours	To design interventions that improve social relationships

Below we will describe a few of the more prominent theories in this area of study.

One of the earliest social cognitive theories was **attribution theory**, which originated in the writings of Fritz Heider (1958). The basic principle that governs attribution theory is that people attempt to explain behaviour – both their own and that of other people. In this sense, Heider argued that people are naive psychologists, routinely trying to understand and explain their social worlds. In explaining behaviour, individuals typically make either internal (something about the person) or external (something about the situation) attributions. Attribution theory, as Heider outlined and as others subsequently elaborated, provides a system for understanding how, when and why people make the attributions they do. One of the early findings from attribution theory was that individuals typically attribute their own poor behaviour to external causes, and the poor behaviour of others to internal causes. The opposite attribution pattern occurs when explaining good behaviour. This basic tendency is known as the **fundamental attribution error**. To illustrate, consider our earlier example of Jessica driving her own car to work, instead of taking the train. When asked why she drives her car, she is likely to point out that the train is often late, or that she needs to use the car during her lunch break (both are external attributions). But when asked why other people don't take the train, she might note that they are lazy, self-indulgent or do not care about social issues (all of which are internal).

Generally speaking, attributions serve us well and help us to understand people and interpret situations rather rapidly. However, there are times when attributions result in bias and dysfunction between people or even groups of people. For this reason, attribution theory has been applied to a number of social problems, including marital counselling, depression, pessimism and physical health, happiness, interpersonal conflict and aggression, and road rage (see Schultz & Oskamp, 2000 for a summary). For example, consider the case of a couple that has been married for several years, but shows signs of deteriorating intimacy and increasing conflicts. One of the patterns of social thinking that is likely to emerge involves negative attributions – that is, internal attributions for bad events (e.g., 'it's my partner's fault') and external attributions for good events (e.g., 'she didn't mean it to happen'). A social psychologist might be involved in developing an intervention plan aimed at breaking these dysfunctional patterns of social thinking.

Another important area of study in social cognition is the study of attitudes. An **attitude** is a person's favourable or unfavourable evaluation of an object (or person, or idea) (Oskamp & Schultz, 2005). While initially there was an emphasis on how attitudes affect behaviour, subsequent research has shown that changing attitudes generally does not produce a corresponding change in behaviour. If you think about our initial question of how to get people to utilize public transport, one approach might be to educate people about the harmful effects on the environment of driving their own cars. As described earlier in this chapter, underlying this approach is the acceptance of the *knowledge deficit model* – if you give people information that will change their attitudes, their behaviours will change as well. But this approach generally fails. Current attitude theory suggests that changing attitudes typically does not produce a corresponding change in behaviour. In fact, a person might come to believe the message and develop a favourable attitude towards public transport, but still fail to take action. Indeed, such effects have been regularly observed in applied social psychological research across a variety of domains.

How is it that people can think one thing, but act differently? One of the earliest social cognitive theories proposed that people are motivated to maintain a basic level of consistency in their thoughts and actions. Festinger's (1957) **cognitive dissonance theory** suggests that it is psychologically uncomfortable when our actions and our attitudes are not congruent. The theory deals with the relationship between a person's attitudes, beliefs and behaviour about himself or his surroundings. Any two elements can be consonant with each other, dissonant or irrelevant. If any two elements are dissonant (for example, I hold a favourable attitude about public transport but continue to drive my own car) then we experience a psychologically uncomfortable state of dissonance and we are motivated to reduce it. When confronted with a dissonant situation, the individual can resolve the dissonance in one or more of the following ways:

- Change the attitude: 'Driving my car is not that bad.'
- Change the behaviour: 'I'm going to start taking the train to work.'
- Add new cognitions to bolster one of the dissonant elements: 'I don't really have a choice, since the train is so inefficient. Now if the train were to run more frequently, I would certainly use it.'

This third option – adding new cognitions – allows us to maintain apparently dissonant attitudes and behaviours. By justifying the behaviour, we can continue to drive our car to work and not switch to the train. Note that our example of new cognitions draws on the concept of choice. Indeed, subsequent research on dissonance theory has shown that if people feel that they have little or no choice in their actions, the amount of dissonance can be greatly reduced (Harmon-Jones, 2000). Given this basic summary of dissonance theory, how might an applied social psychologist use it to reduce the number of people driving their own cars to work? We'll leave this question for you to answer.

A final social psychological theory related to attitudes and social thinking is the theory of planned behaviour. The theory emerged in the early 1970s as an attempt to clarify the generally low relationship between attitudes and behaviours. As we noted above, it's quite common for a person's attitude towards a behaviour to be only weakly related (or sometimes even unrelated) to his or her actions. The **theory of planned behaviour** (TPB) emerged as a framework for understanding the relationship between attitudes and behaviours (Ajzen & Fishbein, 2005). According to this theory, the best predictor of an individual's behaviour is his/her *intention* to act, which in turn is caused by three constructs:

- **Attitude**: a person's favourable or unfavourable evaluation of the behaviour.
- **Subjective norms**: a person's beliefs about what others who are important to him think he should do.
- **Perceived behavioural control**: a person's beliefs about the extent to which the behaviour is achievable.

The theory has been used across a variety of applied domains with considerable success. One of the principles incorporated into the theory is the **compatibility principle**. Researchers have found that when attitudes, norms, behavioural control, intentions and behaviour are assessed using the same level of measurement, the outcome is more likely to predict the behavioural intention and behaviour. For example, asking motorists about their attitude towards traffic in general, and using that measure to predict whether a person intends to take the bus tomorrow, violates the principle (and as a result will likely show only a weak relationship). Rather, we need to ask questions that are as specific as the behaviour we want to predict. For example, attitudes towards taking the bus to work (rather than traffic in general) will be more strongly correlated with the probability that the person does indeed take the bus.

The TPB is one of the most widely utilized theoretical perspectives in applied social psychology. The theory provides a rather straightforward framework for studying a social problem, linking psychological constructs (i.e., attitudes, norms, behavioural control) and emphasizing the centrality of intentions in understanding behaviour. To illustrate how the theory might be applied, let's consider a series of studies conducted by Sebastian Bamberg and colleagues (Bamberg, Ajzen & Schmidt, 2003). Using surveys, the researchers began by examining the 'fit' of the TPB to students' decision to take the bus to university. The results showed that each of the TPB constructs was predictive of intention, and that intention was strongly linked with behaviour. The researchers used the survey results to 'diagnose' the source of the problem – students believed that the bus system was expensive and inefficient, and they misperceived that the bus system could meet their transportation needs. Subsequently, the researchers implemented an intervention in which university students could use public transport without charge (they just needed to show their student ID). The goal was to increase students' *perceived behavioural control* by giving them the knowledge and tools they needed to use bus transport. The results showed a doubling in the number of students who reported using the bus to get to university (from 15% before the intervention to 31% after), and also a substantial drop in the number of students using a private car (from 44% before to 30% afterwards).

Social influence

The theories in the area of social influence are all about change – changing people's thoughts, feelings and behaviours. Within this area of study we find theories regarding imitation, compliance, obedience, group decision making, and persuasion. Most applied social psychologists are well versed in theories of social influence because 'solving social problems' almost always involves influencing people to behave differently. And not surprisingly, those who do basic research in this area often also do applied work.

While the models of persuasion mentioned above require considerable amounts of mental processing on the part of the recipient, other forms of influence are more automatic. **Imitation** – the replicating of another's actions – appears to be an innate tendency for humans. Infants only several days old can mimic facial expressions. On occasion people imitate others intentionally because there are subtle social rewards, for instance, when you choose to smile at a passing stranger who smiles at you. More often, imitation occurs unintentionally. For instance, Chartrand and Bargh (1999) showed that people will unintentionally imitate the movements of other people, their speech patterns and their expressions during social interaction. Such studies show how subtle and prevalent social influence can be.

Unlike imitation, conformity is generally a conscious process. **Conformity** occurs when a person changes his or her behaviour to be consistent with real or imagined social expectations. Conformity theories seek to define the circumstances under which individuals are likely to change their behaviour to fit in with a group. Kelman (1961) suggests that we can predict when a person will conform depending upon a person's orientation towards the social expectation. For instance, if you are driving on a road late at night and see a red traffic light, the law is that you should stop. If you look around and there are no other cars in any direction, some people might go through the red light while others would wait. Kelman's social influence theory predicts that if a person is *rule oriented*, they will only follow the red light law when they know there are external consequences to breaking the law. In the absence of other cars or observers, they will break the law. People who are *role oriented* will follow the red light law to the extent that they feel it is their role to do so. Thus, if a person perceives himself in the role of 'a good citizen' who does not break laws, he will not go through the red light because doing so would violate his sense of who he is. Take this same person to a place where 'good citizens' commonly go through red lights, and they will start to do so as well. Finally, a person who is *value oriented* might choose to not go through the red light because they have a fundamental value that red lights should never (under any circumstances) be driven through. This later orientation occurs whenever a person complies because they feel it is the 'right' thing to do rather than because the action is consistent with social rules or their own role in society.

Whereas pressure to conform is generally subtle and unstated, **compliance** results from a plainly stated request. Robert Cialdini and Noah Goldstein (2004) offer a broad model in their research on compliance. They theorize that people are motivated to comply with a direct request when compliance results in individual goals being fulfilled. There are three possible goals:

- A person can reduce ambiguity in a situation and acquire a more accurate sense of reality (accuracy). Information about the correct course of action can come from other people in the situation (social norms), perceived authority figures or even one's mood.
- A person can develop or preserve meaningful social relationships (affiliation). A person is more likely to comply with a request that will lead to enhanced relationships (e.g., complying with a request from a friend) or preserve social harmony (e.g., reciprocating kindness from a stranger).
- A person can improve his or her self-concept, or maintain a favourable self-concept. A person is more likely to comply with a request that is consistent with his or her self-concept. For example, if a person perceives himself as studious, he is more likely to comply with a request to study on a Friday night than if he considers himself to be 'the life of every party'.

When behavioural change is in response to an explicit demand, we turn to theories of **obedience**. Obedience has received considerable research attention because of the controversial and disturbing findings of Stanley Milgram (1974). Milgram's obedience studies revealed that, given the proper circumstances, an ordinary person could be influenced to hurt another person. Particular to theories of obedience is the emphasis on legitimacy. Milgram, as well as others who have studied obedience in applied and basic research settings, have consistently found that obedience is more likely when a person perceives the order, the authority figure giving the order and the context as legitimate.

The original studies on conformity, compliance and obedience were quite dramatic and showed the basic human disposition for being influenced. Subsequent research has helped to refine the underlying principles of influence, and also linked these principles into larger theoretical models. One particularly influential theoretical perspective is the **elaboration likelihood model** (ELM). The theoretical model originated with Richard Petty and John Cacioppo's work in the 1970s, and quickly moved into applied projects in advertising, politics and marketing (Petty *et al.*, 2004). The basic tenet of the ELM is that there are different routes to persuasion. Some messages are processed with considerable scrutiny; the person attends to the specifics of the message, is motivated to process the arguments, carefully considers and elaborates on the merits of the message, and any subsequent change in attitude or behaviour occurs when the person agrees with the arguments. This type of processing of information is named the *central route*. On the other hand, some messages are processed more superficially. For any of a variety of reasons, the person does not attend to the specifics of the message, nor does he or she scrutinize the merits of the argument. Interestingly, persuasion can still happen through this route, but typically because the person likes the message (for example, it's funny, catchy, glamorous, attractive, provocative and so on). This type of processing of information is named the *peripheral route*.

While there are a number of constructs and principles incorporated into the ELM, the core revolves around these two routes: central-route processing and peripheral-route processing. The primary distinction between these two routes lies in the extent to which the individual cognitively elaborates on the arguments. The central route is characterized by high elaboration, the peripheral route by low elaboration. While persuasion can occur through the peripheral route, it tends to be weak, temporary and easily changeable. By contrast, persuasion generated through the central route is likely to be stronger, longer lasting and generally resistant to counter-attack. Central-route processing is more likely to occur among people who are involved in an issue, forewarned that they are about to be persuaded, or for whom the issue is more personally relevant. By contrast, peripheral-route processing is more likely to occur when the person is distracted, less interested in the topic or inattentive. For an example, see Box 2.2.

Box 2.2 Applying the elaboration likelihood model to reduce HIV-risky behaviours

Since it was initially discovered in the early 1980s, the AIDS epidemic has continued to grow worldwide. Unlike other viruses, the HIV virus that causes AIDS can only be transmitted through the exchange of body fluids, and the best way to prevent the spread of AIDS is by reducing HIV-risky behaviours (like unprotected sexual activity). This means that if people can be persuaded to avoid certain behaviours, they can greatly reduce the likelihood of contracting HIV.

Social-psychological theories, like the elaboration likelihood model, offer a promising pathway to reducing the spread of AIDS. Consider the case of messages created to promote condom use among sexually active adults. The topic has attracted considerable research attention and a number of theoretical and applied projects aimed at understanding and changing HIV-risky behaviour. To illustrate the use of the ELM in creating these types of persuasive messages, Igartua, Cheng and Lopes (2003) conducted an experiment assessing the impact of a persuasive short film that promoted condom use. The short films were taken from a larger series that had aired in France and several other European countries. In the experiment, half of the participants (university students) were told that 'young people ... 18–30 constitute a group of very high risk' while the other half were told that they were 'a group of very low risk'. The manipulation was intended to make the topic personally relevant, and thereby activate central or peripheral processing of the subsequent message. Two versions of the short films were created – one with dialogue and the other in musical format. As predicted by ELM, the musical format (peripheral route) was more effective at changing behavioural intentions (future condom use) for participants who were low in involvement, while the dialogue format (central route) was more effective for participants high in personal relevance.

In summary, applied social psychologists regularly use theories of social influence. These theories, like the elaboration likelihood model, offer insight into the ways in which individuals respond to persuasive messages, and provide an important foundation for creating interventions intended to change attitudes and behaviours.

Social relationships

Our third type of social-psychological theory pertains to relationships. Theories regarding social relationships typically describe what makes people 'get along' or conflict with each other. From this area of study we have a host of theories regarding prejudice, stereotypes, discrimination, aggression, conflict (and conflict resolution), attraction, romantic love, altruism, cooperation, helping and other forms of prosocial behaviours. For applied social psychologists, these theories typically suggest intervention techniques that will improve social relationships and reduce intergroup tensions.

Many of the theories regarding social relationships require that we know who we are and who we are not. Put into social psychological terminology, we have a basic tendency to distinguish between 'us' (the **ingroup**) and 'them' (the **outgroup**) whenever we encounter a person or social situation (Tajfel, 1982). In addition, social cognitive research shows that we have a basic ingroup bias that causes us to think better of our own group than of other groups. We particularly rely on these **biases** and **heuristics** when there is uncertainty, for instance when we are first introduced to a person or group of people. These social categorizations give rise to **stereotypes** – generalized beliefs about a person based on his or her membership in a group (see also Chapter 9).

Research on stereotypes and self-serving biases suggest that they are largely automatic. A self-serving bias refers to the tendency for individuals to interpret social information in a way that reflects positively on themselves. But can we perhaps control our biases so that we do not act in a discriminatory manner? Research suggests that even when people believe that a stereotype is false, they cannot avoid using it when they encounter a person from the stereotyped group (Devine, 1989). The perspective that stereotypes are activated automatically suggests that when you first encounter a person, your mind makes available that information associated with the salient groups to which the person belongs. For instance, you might quickly notice that the person is a woman, she has dark Hispanic features and she is not very tall. Automatically, without conscious control, stereotypic information related to gender, ethnicity and height will be activated. At this point a second information-processing stage follows, in which we either apply or do not apply the activated stereotype information. According to this theory, if we are willing and motivated to think carefully about what the person is like, we will not automatically apply the stereotype.

Stereotypes can (but not always) give way to **prejudice** – an unjustified negative attitude towards an individual based on his or her group membership. In fact, there is evidence that prejudiced persons can be taught to suppress or even ignore negative stereotypes when encountering a person from an outgroup. The key to understanding when stereotypes will result in prejudice appears to be **motivation**. An *intrinsically motivated* person values or believes it is personally important not to be a prejudiced person. In contrast, a person can be *extrinsically motivated* to avoid prejudice when they do not want to appear prejudiced to other people. A person can be motivated by both, neither or just one of these factors which results in the expression or non-expression of prejudice (Plant & Devine, 1998).

When people act upon their negative stereotypes and prejudiced beliefs, the result can be discrimination. **Discrimination** refers to unequal or unfair behaviour towards a person based on group membership. In essence, stereotypes are cognitive, prejudice is affective and discrimination is behavioural (see Fiske, 1998). While we have summarized some of the theories relevant to stereotyping, prejudice and discrimination, there has also been work on the response of the stigmatized individual. Surprisingly, even in the face of prejudice and discrimination, individuals often retain a positive self-esteem. The theory of identity maintenance contends that discriminated groups promote a positive collective identity that protects an individual's sense of worth and esteem. Groups achieve this by promoting ingroup pride in one's culture, gender, sexual orientation, religion or other identity factors. Instead of 'melting' into a homogenous pot, groups maintain and celebrate their own unique identity. This sense of group pride can serve to buffer the potentially harmful psychological effects of discrimination and prejudice.

Social psychologists studying social relations have devoted considerable attention to issues of intergroup relations. Many of the theories in this area seek to explain how groups can 'get along' better. One long-running line of work has focused on **contact hypothesis** (Pettigrew & Tropp, 2006; see Chapter 6). In an early set of studies by Sherif *et al.* (1961), two groups of boys were organized into summer camps – the 'Eagles' and the 'Rattlers'. Over time, the two groups learned of the existence of the other, and engaged in competitions against each other. Not surprisingly, when the groups of boys were brought together, there was considerable hostility and friction between the different groups. Even a series of cooperative activities (e.g., film night, fireworks together, or scavenger hunts) did not help to lessen the hostility. Indeed, several such events actually resulted in fights and confrontations. But through a series of activities designed to introduce a superordinate goal – working together towards a common good – Sherif's team was able to reduce the hostility and conflict between the groups.

The findings from this Robber's Cave study helped to identify the precursors to conflict, and highlighted a strategy of reconciliation. That is, when segregated groups are in competition with one another, this results in intergroup hostility and conflict. But what are the optimal conditions for decreasing hostility and improving social relations? Indeed, looking back at the Robber's Cave study, it seems clear that just bringing groups together can actually inflame the tensions. Contact theory maintains that contact between groups will only result in reduced prejudice if four features are present:

- The groups are of equal status.
- The groups share common goals.
- There is intergroup cooperation (and not competition).
- There is institutional support. That is, local laws, customs, and authorities support positive interactions.

Recent reviews of the fifty years of research on the topic of 'optimal conditions of contact', stress the positive effects of intergroup contact and also noted the 'facilitating' effects of these four optimal conditions (Pettigrew & Tropp, 2006).

In addition to contact theory, several theories have emerged that seek to predict what strategic choice a person or group will make when faced with a conflict of interest. One of the most widely used theories involves the **dual concern model** (Pruitt & Carnevale, 1993). For every conflict situation, the theory contends, a party (a person or a group) has two types of concern – concern for self and concern for other. The strength of the concern can be high or low. When a party has low concern for self and high concern for the other, he is likely to *yield* or 'give in'. When a person has low concern for self and low concern for the other, he is likely to do nothing (i.e., engage in *inaction*). When a person has high concern for self and low concern for the other, then he is likely to *contend*, or fight. Finally, when a person has high concern for self and the other, he is likely to problem solve. The implication is that if you can change the way a person or group appraises or thinks about the situation, then you can change the type of strategy they choose to use.

Given what we now know about stereotypes and ingroup/outgroup biases, let us return to the question of how to get people to use public transport. If your ingroup includes people who own nice cars and drive themselves to work, and your outgroup consists of people who are poor and must take the bus, then taking public transport may not feel comfortable. In fact, some people in the United States harbour strong socioeconomic and ethnic stereotypes regarding the types of people who do or do not use public transport. Using this theory that ingroup and outgroup biases exist regarding perceptions of public transport, what type of intervention might be useful for increasing its use?

Prosocial behaviour. In addition to describing under which circumstances groups will get along and how people make strategic decisions, there has also been a line of theories that describe under what circumstances individuals are likely to engage in **prosocial behaviour** – that is, acting in a manner that benefits others. The array of prosocial behaviours studied fall into one of two categories (Estrada-Hollenbeck & Heatherton, 1998). First, there are *relationship-mending* prosocial behaviours, which repair and restore relationships. For example, apologies, reparation, confession, expressing guilt and conceding would all be considered relationship-mending behaviours. On the other hand, *relationship-enhancing* prosocial behaviours promote, develop and sustain relationships. Examples of these behaviours include helping, politeness, volunteerism, and trustworthiness. Social-psychological theorists have given more attention to the relationship-enhancing behaviours – particularly helping and altruism. **Helping** occurs when one person intends to reduce another person's burden. **Altruism** occurs when the person is motivated to act in ways that benefit another person, while desiring little or no personal benefit in exchange. From the beginning, theories of helping have sought to explain why and under what circumstances people will help one another.

In 1964, there was a highly publicized case of Kitty Genovese, a New York City resident who was stabbed to death near her home in Queens. Newspaper articles sensationalized the lack of intervention by her neighbours, despite the fact that many of them heard her cries for help (an article in the *New York Times* estimated as many as thirty-eight people heard Kitty's cries for help!). The case served as inspiration for a pair of young social psychologists, John Darley and Bibb Latané, who set out on a multi-year series of studies on bystander intervention (1968). The cumulative result of this work was a decision-making model of prosocial behaviour, and later **social impact theory**. The bystander apathy observed in the Kitty Genovese case was relatively easy to replicate in more controlled settings, and several fundamental principles emerged. The first is **diffusion of responsibility**, which refers to the finding that as the size of the group increases, the probability of any single individual taking action decreases. For example, in one study participants completing a questionnaire overheard a woman in the next room fall, and then cry out for help. 'Oh my God, my foot . . . I . . . I . . . I can't move it. Oh my ankle. I . . . can't get this . . . thing off me' (Latané & Rodin, 1969). When the participant was alone, 70 per cent came to help. But when participants were working in pairs, only 20 per cent helped. When more people are present, there is general diffusion of responsibility, and no one individual feels compelled to act.

A second principle that emerged from this work is the concept of **pluralistic ignorance**. This is the tendency for people to look to others as a source of information when interpreting a situation. For example, Darley and Latané (1968) conducted an experiment in which participants were completing surveys either alone, or in three-person groups. During the session, the researchers piped smoke into the room through a wall vent. While all participants noticed the smoke almost immediately, those working in a group were substantially less likely to leave the room and report the smoke. In fact, after four minutes the room was filled with smoke, but only 10 per cent of participants working in a group left to report it. In comparison, more than 75 per cent of the participants working alone reported the smoke after four minutes.

The findings from this original research have led to applications in many different arenas. One area where the principle of pluralistic ignorance has been applied is to the issue of excessive alcohol consumption among university students. While many students hold personal beliefs about the importance of responsible drinking, they also believe that their peers consume much more alcohol than they really do. For example, Perkins, Haines and Rice (2005) found that 71 per cent of university students in a nationwide US sample overestimated the number of drinks students consumed on their campus. In addition, beliefs about alcohol consumption among peers are strongly (and positively) correlated with one's own drinking behaviour. In essence, just like the participants in Darley and Latané's smoke study, university students look to their peers as a guide for their behaviour. Unfortunately, this process results in incorrect overestimates of university student drinking rates. Subsequent studies have drawn on the basic principles of pluralistic ignorance to create interventions aimed at reducing this misperception. The results from these studies are encouraging, and suggest that normative feedback (providing information about what other students do, and approve of doing) can be an effective tool for lowering rates of binge drinking.

In summary. Social thinking, social influence and social relationships are three types of social-psychological theory. At the same time, theories from each area do not operate in isolation. Social influences can alter a person's social thinking, and social thinking can affect the manner in which a person is influenced. And both social thinking and influence affect social relationships. For this reason, many applied social psychologists are generalists, meaning that they know a lot about a wide range of theories. This enables them to analyse the situation, intervene and evaluate in a manner that best suits the problems they seek to address. As you read subsequent chapters in this book, note which theories the writers are using, how they use that theory to understand or diagnose the problem and how they use the theory to develop interventions. Finally, with the author, or on your own, see if the results of the research or intervention support or call into question the theory originally described. Doing so will take you from theory to practice and back again, a journey often taken by applied social psychologists.

Things to consider when using theory in applied work

As we have seen in this chapter, theories are the foundation of applied social psychological work. But despite the many advantages of utilizing theory in applied work, there are also a number of important considerations. First, not all social problems are identical. Some social problems are specific and relatively simple. For instance, if you have a small work team that needs to increase its production of packaging to meet a coming deadline, the behaviour, population and context are clearly defined and theory-based interventions will be relatively straightforward. More complex social problems are **multiply determined**, meaning that there are many variables that may need to be changed in order to solve the problem. For instance, if the problem is that an entire business needs to boost production and improve morale in the organization, it is unlikely that any single theory or principle will sufficiently explain how to achieve the desired behaviours and attitudes. In a laboratory, a research psychologist can isolate small pieces of a complex problem and control the outcome. When that same psychologist leaves the sterile laboratory of the university and begins doing research in real-world settings, the number of factors influencing an individual increases dramatically. Addressing social problems in the real world often means incorporating elements of several psychological theories, making it difficult to adhere strictly to the **boundary conditions** of any single theory – that is, conditions that distinguish when a theory does or does not apply. The result is that outcomes are less predictable.

Related to the issue of complexity of the problem is the complexity of the theory. Some theories are quite narrow in scope, focusing on a single process or small set of activating circumstances. For instance, David McClelland (1961) offers a theory that describes three needs (achievement, affiliation and power) that predict a person's level of motivation. According to this theory, individuals differ in the degree to which they are motivated to succeed (achievement), maintain harmonious relationships with other people (affiliation) or have influence over other people (power). Individuals acquire these needs over time and, based upon life experiences, determine which are most important. Because of the relative simplicity of this theory, it has been applied quite frequently, particularly in the applied domains of business and management. Other more complex theories of motivation take into account many more variables, such as the impact of the environment, opportunity, goals, satisfaction, effort and ability. Although these complex theories are more likely to predict outcomes in a laboratory, they are also more difficult to apply in the real world because they have so many parts. As theories get larger and broader, they reach a point where they seem to fit almost any situation. In fact, some very famous theorists did at times use their broad theories to explain results that contradicted their expectations. Examples of such large theories include the psychodynamic theory of Sigmund Freud (now largely discredited), learning theory (still widely utilized) and more recent sociobiological theories. While the level of generality makes these broad theories useful for explaining behaviour, applying them to change behaviour is often challenging. Because there are so many constructs and principles, creating an intervention to address each part of the theory is extremely difficult.

A third challenge of using theories in applied work is that prediction and explanation are not equally attainable. Prediction means forecasting (prognosticating): making statements about what *will* happen given a set of theoretical principles. Such forecasts are difficult to make, and social psychologists are very reluctant to make brash predictions. Part of the problem is that in many real-world situations, different theories lead to different predictions because it is unclear exactly which set of boundary conditions is present. Thus, it is likely that several different outcomes can be predicted, depending on which theoretical perspective one adopts. In addition, even if you know which theory to apply, there are challenges to predicting an outcome. As you may have noticed while reading this chapter, many of the theories we have described are at least partially based on an individual's perceptions, which are generally not known. This was the case with rational choice theory, which is based on *perceived* costs and rewards. Different people can perceive the same outcome differently. This poses a serious challenge to applied social psychologists, who need to make predictions about the outcomes of interventions. Indeed, designing an intervention always requires making predictions – if we do X, behaviour Y will change. For example, if we add more routes and times to the bus schedule, bus use will increase. Such a prediction is reasonable, but only if the rational choice theory is an accurate explanation for an individual's decision to take the bus.

Explanation, on the other hand, is much more straightforward. Once a behaviour happens, it is relatively easy to generate theoretical explanations for *why*. As a case in point, consider Stanley Milgram's (1974) obedience studies. In his initial experiment, 68 per cent of participants obeyed fully the directions of the researcher and administered the highest level of shock (300 volts) – potentially harming another participant in the study. Looking back at these results, they seem to make sense (or at least we can create a theory that would explain them). But before conducting the experiments, Milgram described the situation to 110 psychiatrists, students and middle-class adults, all of whom predicted that participants in the experiment would defy the authority by about 135 volts. Indeed, the psychiatrists estimated that only one-in-a-thousand participants would administer the highest level of shock. Clearly, theories are better at explaining behaviour than predicting behaviour – and this is particularly true in an applied setting.

A fourth challenge in using theory in applied work is connecting the principles and constructs defined in the theory to the situation in the real world. That is, if our goal is to change behaviour, and we have identified a theoretical model that we believe applies to the situation, the next step is to utilize the elements of the theory to craft an intervention. But identifying the boundary conditions in the real world can be challenging, and it requires some stretching. For example, consider a case of verbal harassment at work. If the harassment is coming by means of an anonymous e-mail, we might speculate that the Internet has created a sense of **deindividuation**, thereby loosening the everyday constraints on behaviour. We know how the theory's constructs have been defined in laboratory research, but how do we stretch these precise definitions to the problem on hand? And do they match? In the laboratory, deindividuation is often induced by placing participants in groups, creating a sense of anonymity or taking steps to decrease participants' sense of self-awareness (Postmes & Spears, 1998). Does the anonymity afforded by the Internet in the harassment case above create the same sense of deindividuation? Often it is unclear whether the behaviours causing the problem match the constructs used to build theories. Fitting a theory to a real situation is particularly challenging when the theories describe a static state (meaning nothing in the situation is moving or changing) while the situation is very dynamic.

Similarly, how does the theory connect to our intervention? Whereas matching the theory to the problem required stretching, this will require a leap – taking what is known in the laboratory and using it to design an intervention. That is, using the theory to identify a point of intervention, and then doing something to change the behaviour. For researchers trained in the narrow confines of university laboratories (as most of us are), this can be a harrowing step. For example, consider the intervention described earlier in which Bamberg and colleagues (2003) gave students free use of the local bus system (students needed only to show their ID). Such an intervention was intended to target perceived behavioural control – one of the elements in the theory of planned behaviour. But this was a leap. Would free bus travel actually alter students' sense of efficacy and control? Fortunately, the scientific method can provide a safety net, and with careful evaluation we can generate results that will inform us how our applied work succeeded.

How basic, applied and use-inspired researchers develop theory

Throughout this chapter we have discussed how theories are the foundation of applied social-psychological work. What we have not discussed is the importance of applied work in theory development. Historically, there has been a long-standing tension in science between **basic** and **applied research**. While basic research focuses primarily on the process of discovery and the development of theoretical models, applied research has focused on using existing theories to solve social problems. But the distinction between basic and applied research does not capture much of the work of applied social psychologists. Indeed, as pointed out in Chapter 1, applied social psychologists often move back and forth between an interest in theoretical advancement and in solving real-world problems. In this sense, it is neither purely basic nor applied. Indeed, the work of applied social psychologists is better characterized as **use inspired**.

In his book *Pasteur's Quadrant*, Donald Stokes (1997) argues that any line of inquiry can be classified along two dimensions: quest for fundamental

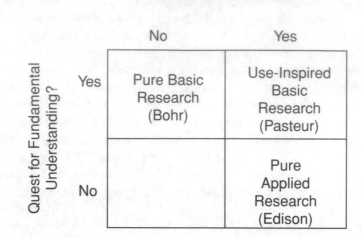

Figure 2.3 *Quadrant model of scientific research (Stokes, D. (1997).* Pasteur's quadrant: Basic science and technological innovation. *Washington, DC: Brookings. Redrawn from p. 73.)*

understanding, and consideration of the usefulness of the research findings. The resulting 2 × 2 classification system is shown in Figure 2.3. What we refer to as 'basic' research falls into the top left quadrant. It is research for the sake of knowing, with no consideration of its ultimate use. Stokes illustrates this type of research with the example of Niels Bohr's research in the early 1900s into the structure of the atom. In social psychology, we might classify some of the research in social cognition in this tradition, along with social neuroscience, and studies of personality. The primary goal is to develop knowledge, and whether or not it can be useful is irrelevant.

On the other hand, purely applied research has its genesis in solving a problem. In the physical sciences, this often takes the form of technology or invention. Stokes (1997) argues that such applied research is exemplified by the work of Thomas Edison, the famous American inventor whose many patents in the areas of electric lighting, film cameras and phonography continue to be used today. But Edison's interests were solely in the application of science to create new technologies, and any scientific discoveries along the way were simply required to overcome obstacles in the innovation process. In social psychology, we might classify some of the research in advertising and marketing in this quadrant, along with military studies, research on violence-prevention programmes for adolescents and some of the many applications to health or environmental problems. The emphasis in these areas is on solving the problem (e.g., reducing cigarette smoking rates, reducing HIV-risky behaviours, or increasing rates of recycling).

Academic researchers do not typically conduct applied projects like those mentioned above. Rather, government entities, private corporations and activist organizations conduct them. We would argue that while important, these types of applied projects generally do not contribute to the theoretical knowledge base of the discipline. But there is another quadrant in this framework that more fully captures the work of applied social psychologists: **use-inspired research**. This quadrant is illustrated by the French microbiologist Louis Pasteur, who on the one hand wanted to solve practical problems related to the treatment of disease, but who set about this applied work by conducting basic research into germ theory and bacteriology (Stokes, 1997). His theoretical research was use inspired, and it ultimately resulted in a number of new technologies, including pasteurization and a vaccine for rabies. It is in this quadrant that we find many applied social psychologists. Although a specific event or problem often inspires the research process, the work ultimately leads to important theoretical developments as well. To illustrate, let's revisit an example of social psychological research inspired by a real-world problem.

Our earlier discussion of Latané and Darley's research and theory of prosocial behaviour nicely illustrates use-inspired work. It began with a real-world problem (bystander apathy) and proceeded to develop theoretical models that could explain this behaviour. The resulting decision-making model (and later social impact theory) spawned basic research to test the principles and linkages of the theory, and helped to refine the concepts of pluralistic ignorance and diffusion of responsibility. Finally, we saw examples of applied projects, with university staff and administrators implementing the theories and principles to reduce alcohol consumption among university students. Note that this applied work can also spawn new use-inspired research, along with new lines of basic research and theory.

Conclusion

In this chapter, we have outlined the important role of theory in applied social psychology. A theory is an integrated set of principles that explains and predicts observed events. Theories have three main roles in applied work. They are essential for understanding the behaviours associated with a social problem; they can inform efforts to solve social problems; and they can be tested for usefulness through evaluation. Social-psychological theories fall into three major areas – social thinking, social influence and social relationships. These areas of research cover a wide range of human behaviour, and within each resides a number of potentially useful theories. We described several challenges of using theory in applied work. Theories tend to work best when applied to simple problems, and some theories are so broad that they seem to apply to every behaviour. Yet despite the challenges, theories remain an essential and important element in applied research. Finally, we concluded with a brief description of how use-inspired research enables us to develop theory that is both scientifically sound and useful to applied social psychologists.

Glossary

Action research: an approach to solving social problems that draws on social-psychological theory.

Altruism: a motivation to act in a way that benefits another person.

Applied research: scientific inquiry aimed at solving a specific problem.

Attitude: an individual's favourable or unfavourable evaluations of a person, object or idea.

Attribution theory: the tendency to give causal explanations for the behaviour of ourselves and others.

Basic research: scientific inquiry aimed at developing new knowledge.

Biases: errors in judgement that result from the use of mental short cuts.

Boundary conditions: conditions that distinguish when a theory does or does not apply.

Cognitive dissonance theory: theory that emphasizes the importance of consistency in a person's attitudes, beliefs and behaviours.

Compatibility principle: prescription from the theory of planned behaviour that attitudes, subjective norms and perceived behavioural control should be measured at the same level of specificity.

Compliance: the act of changing behaviour following a direct request.

Conformity: the act of changing behaviour to be consistent with a real or imagined social expectation.

Construct: a clearly defined individual (psychological) characteristic that is generally latent and not directly observable.

Contact hypothesis: the theory that bringing members of conflicting groups together will reduce prejudice and improve intergroup relations.

Deindividuation: the loss of self-awareness and loosening of everyday moral constraints on behaviour, often brought about by anonymity.

Diffusion of responsibility: principle of helping behaviour that states that as the size of a group increases, the probability that any single individual will take action to help decreases.

Discrimination: unequal or unfair behaviour towards a person based on group membership.

Dual concern model: a strategic choice model that predicts when a person will yield, choose inaction, contend or problem solve in response to a conflict of interest.

Elaboration likelihood model: a framework that distinguishes between the central and peripheral routes to persuasion.

Fundamental attribution error: the tendency to overestimate the influence of personality (i.e., dispositional) variables and underestimate the influence of the situational variables when explaining other people's behaviours.

Helping: behaviour that is intended to benefit another person.

Heuristic: mental short cuts used to solve problems or make judgements.

Hypothesis: a testable prediction derived from a theory.

Imitation: the replicating of another's action.

Ingroup: any group of which you are a member.

Knowledge-deficit model: a theoretical model of behaviour change which posits that social programmes are underutilized because individuals lack knowledge about the programme or the behaviour. Psychological research has shown that this model is generally inadequate at explaining why individuals don't make use of programmes.

Model: a framework that integrates theory and principles. Models typically describe multiple processes, each linked through some type of causal sequence.

Motivation: a person's desire and willingness to act in a certain way.

Multiply determined: the notion that an individual's behaviour is determined by many psychological and contextual variables, and cannot be completely explained by any single theory.

Obedience: the act of changing behaviour following an order.

Outgroup: any group of which you are not a member.

Perceived behavioural control: a person's beliefs about the extent to which the behaviour is achievable by him or herself

Pluralistic ignorance: the tendency to believe the private attitudes and beliefs of others are different from one's own despite identical public behaviour.

Prejudice: unjustified negative attitude towards an individual based on his or her group membership.

Principle: a statement of how a psychological process works.

Prosocial behaviour: behaving in a manner that benefits another.

Rational choice theory: a broad social science theory for human behaviour that focuses on the perceived costs and benefits of an action.

Schemas: the cognitive organization of a person's past experiences, beliefs and knowledge.

Social impact theory: the amount of influence others have in a given situation is a function of the *number* of people present, the *strength* or importance of the people and the *immediacy* (or closeness) of the target person to the influencing agent(s).

Stereotypes: generalized beliefs about a person based on his or her membership of a group.

Subjective norms: construct in the theory of planned behaviour that refers to a person's beliefs about what other people who are important to him think he should do.

Theory: an integrated set of principles that describe, explain and predict observed events.

Theory of planned behaviour: a model for explaining behaviour, using intention, attitudes, subjective norms and perceived behavioural control.

Use-inspired research: scientific inquiry aimed at developing new knowledge that is needed to understand or solve a social problem.

Review questions

1. Define the following terms: theory, principle, hypothesis, model and construct.
2. In the chapter, we stated that 'Without theories, we are left to intuitively understand the behaviour of interest.' Why is intuition limited? Discuss three ways in which theories provide a better approach for understanding behaviour.
3. Describe three challenges of using theory in applied research.
4. In what three ways is a physician fixing a broken arm similar to an applied social psychologist working to solve a social problem?
5. What are the three categories of theories described in this chapter and what do each of those theories typically describe or explain regarding human behaviour?
6. What are some of the challenges of using theories to solve real-world problems? Describe four issues to consider when using theory in applied work.
7. How does use-inspired research contribute to the development and refinement of social-psychological theory?

Further reading

Donaldson, S., Berger, D. & Pezdeck, K. (2006). *Applied psychology: New frontiers and rewarding careers.* Mahwah, NJ: Erlbaum.

Schultz, P. W. & Oskamp, S. (2000). *Social psychology: An applied perspective.* Upper Saddle River, NJ: Prentice-Hall.

References

Ajzen, I. & Fishbein, M. (2005). The influence of attitudes on behavior. In D. Albarracin, B. T. Johnson & M. Zanna (eds.), *The handbook of attitudes* (pp. 173–221). Mahwah, NJ: Erlbaum.

Bamberg, S., Ajzen, I. & Schmidt, P. (2003). Choice of travel mode in the Theory of Planned Behavior: The roles of past behavior, habit, and reasoned action. *Basic and Applied Social Psychology*, 25 (3), 175–187.

Chartrand, T. L. & Bargh, J. A. (1999). The chameleon effect: The perception–behavior link and social interaction. *Journal of Personality and Social Psychology*, 76, 893–910.

Cialdini, R. B. & Goldstein, N. J. (2004). Social influence: Compliance and conformity. *Annual Review of Psychology, 55*, 591–621.

Darley, J. D. & Latané, B. (1968). Bystander intervention in emergencies: Diffusion of responsibility. *Journal of Personality and Social Psychology, 8*, 377–383.

Devine, P. G. (1989). Stereotypes and prejudice. *Journal of Personality and Social Psychology, 56*, 5–18.

Estrada-Hollenbeck, M. & Heatherton, T. F. (1998). Avoiding and alleviating guilt through prosocial behavior. In J. Bybee (ed.), *Guilt and children*. San Diego, CA: Academic Press.

Festinger, L. (1957). *A theory of cognitive dissonance*. Evanston, IL: Row-Peterson.

Fisher, J. D. & Fisher, W. A. (1992). Changing AIDS-risk behavior. *Psychological Bulletin, 111*, 455–474.

Fiske, S. (1998). Stereotyping, prejudice, and discrimination. In D. T. Gilbert, S. T. Fiske & G. Lindzey (eds.), *Handbook of social psychology*. 4th edn (Vol. 2, pp. 357–411). Boston: McGraw-Hill.

Harmon-Jones, E. (2000). A cognitive dissonance theory perspective on the role of emotion in the maintenance and change of beliefs and attitudes. In N. Frijda, A. Manstead & S. Bem (eds.), *Emotions and beliefs: How feelings influence thoughts* (pp. 185–211). Paris, France: Cambridge University Press.

Heider, F. (1958). *The psychology of interpersonal relations*. New York: Wiley.

Igartua, J. J., Cheng, L. & Lopes, O. (2003). To think or not to think: Two pathways towards persuasion by short films on AIDS prevention. *Journal of Health Communication, 8*, 513–528.

Kelman, H. C. (1961). Processes of opinion change. *Public Opinion Quarterly, 25*, 57–78.

Latané, B. & Rodin, J. (1969). A lady in distress: Inhibiting effects of friends and strangers on bystander intervention. *Journal of Experimental Social Psychology, 5*, 189–202.

McClelland, D. (1961). *The achieving society*. New York: Van Nostrand.

Milgram, S. (1974). *Obedience to authority: An experimental view*. New York: Harper-Collins.

Oskamp, S. & Schultz, P. W. (2005). *Attitudes and opinions*. 3rd edn. Mahwah, NJ: Erlbaum.

Perkins, H. W., Haines, M. P. & Rice, R. (2005). Misperceiving the college drinking norm and related problems: A nationwide study of exposure to prevention information, perceived norms and student alcohol misuse. *Journal of Studies on Alcohol, 66* (4), 470–478.

Pettigrew, T. & Tropp. L. (2006). A meta-analytic test of intergroup contact theory. *Journal of Personality and Social Psychology, 90*, 751–783.

Petty, R. E., Rucker, D., Bizer, G. & Cacioppo, J. T. (2004). The elaboration likelihood model. In J. S. Seiter & G. H. Gass (eds.), *Perspectives on persuasion, influence, and compliance gaining* (pp. 65–89). Boston: Allyn & Bacon.

Plant, E. A. & Devine, P. G. (1998). Internal and external motivation to respond without prejudice. *Journal of Personality and Social Psychology, 75*, 811–832.

Postmes, T. & Spears, R. (1998). Deindividuation and antinormative behavior: A meta-analysis. *Psychological Bulletin, 123*, 238–259.

Pruitt, D. G. & Carnevale, P. J. (1993). *Negotiation in social conflict*. Pacific Grove, CA: Brooks/Cole.

Sanchez, C. (2005, June 2). *Diabetes knowledge has little effect on improving outcomes*. Duke University Medical Center. Available online at: www.diabetesincontrol. com/modules.php?name=News&file=article&sid=2822

Schultz, P. W. (2002). Knowledge, education, and household recycling: Examining the knowledge-deficit model of behavior change. In T. Dietz & P. Stern (eds.), *New tools for environmental protection* (pp. 61–82). Washington, DC: National Academy of Sciences.

Schultz, P. W. & Oskamp, S. (2000). *Social psychology: An applied perspective*. Upper Saddle River, NJ: Prentice-Hall.

Schultz, P. W., Nolan, J., Cialdini, R., Goldstein, N. & Griskevicius, V. (2007). The constructive, destructive, and reconstructive power of social norms. *Psychological Science, 18*, 429–434.

Scott, J. (2000). Rational choice theory. In G. Browning, A. Halcli & F. Webster (eds.), *Understanding contemporary society: Theories of the present*. Thousand Oaks, CA: Sage.

Sherif, M., Harvey, O., White, J., Hood, W. & Sherif, C. (1961). *Intergroup conflict and cooperation: The Robber's Cave experiment*. Norman, OK: University Book Exchange.

Stokes, D. (1997). *Pasteur's quadrant: Basic science and technological innovation*. Washington, DC: Brookings.

Tajfel, H. (1982). *Social identity and intergroup relations*. Cambridge University Press.

Towson, S. (2005). Social psychological theory. In F. Schneider, J. Gruman & L. Coutts (eds.), *Applied social psychology: Understanding and addressing social and practical problems* (pp. 19–34). Thousand Oaks, CA: Sage.

3 Applications of social psychology to increase the impact of behaviour-focused intervention

PHILIP K. LEHMAN AND E. SCOTT GELLER

Introduction

Watching the evening news on any given night should assure you applied social psychologists have plenty of work to do. Societal problems abound. Epidemics such as HIV and obesity, violence and drugs in schools, wars, traffic fatalities and environmental degradation pose significant economic consequences, as well as devastating costs in terms of human suffering and loss of life. Although human behaviour contributes to each of these societal problems, human behaviour can also be a critical part of the solution. As experts in the development and evaluation of behaviour-focused interventions, behaviour analysts and social psychologists are uniquely equipped to tackle these problems and make a difference in improving the quality of life on our planet.

The aim of this chapter is to provide you with an overview of techniques used for large-scale behaviour-based intervention. When it comes to applying psychological principles to change behaviour on a large scale, behaviour analysts have been at the forefront. We therefore begin by describing some of the fundamental assumptions of a behaviour-analysis approach to intervention design and evaluation. Next, we outline six intervention techniques which have been successfully used by behaviour analysts to change behaviours in beneficial ways. Finally, we outline six social-psychological principles which can serve to enhance the impact of these interventions. When you finish reading this chapter, you will understand the principles and procedures of a variety of interventions which can be used to improve relevant human behaviour.

A behaviour-analysis approach to intervention

The **applied behaviour-analysis** approach to intervention is based on the scientific philosophy of B.F. Skinner. Instead of targeting internal events such as thoughts and attitudes, Skinner believed psychologists should focus their attention on observable behaviour. Thus, the behaviour-analysis approach to interventions measures an observable behaviour or behavioural outcome as the dependent variable.

A second tenet of Skinner's approach is 'selection by consequences'. In other words, we do what we do because of the consequences that follow our behaviour. More specifically, we do what we do in order to gain positive consequences and avoid or escape negative consequences.

Interestingly, not all consequences are created equal. The most motivating consequences are those which are 'soon' and 'certain' (Geller, 2001). For example, smokers find the soon and certain consequences of relief from cravings and the pleasurable feeling of inhaling and exhaling smoke much more motivating than the distant and uncertain prospect of dying a horrible death of lung cancer or emphysema. In this case, the sizeable negative consequence of death is remote and uncertain. If the smoker believed the next drag on his cigarette would cause soon and certain illness and death, he would be likely to avoid that behaviour.

The soon and certain factors are also relevant for environmental degradation. For example, soon and certain consequences of convenience and comfort motivate many of us to drive our own vehicle. But if you believed driving your vehicle to work or university for the week would certainly cause global temperatures to rise to the point where we all cooked the following week, you might consider walking or riding your bicycle – or at least joining a car-pool.

This discussion of consequences has perhaps given you ideas for an intervention technique. One effective way to increase the frequency of desirable behaviour or decrease the occurrence of undesirable behaviour is to change the consequences (or the salience of the consequences) which *follow* the behaviour. An alternative approach is to alter the environmental stimuli that occur *before* a target behaviour.

While consequences *control* behaviour, antecedent stimuli *direct* behaviour. Stimuli in the environment often announce the availability of consequences. These stimuli are termed **antecedents** or activators, because they precede and direct behaviours necessary to obtain a desired consequence. For example, people who are overweight and dieting may fall victim to the antecedent stimulus of the sign in front of a fast-food restaurant, directing them to drive into the car park, walk into the restaurant, and open their wallets in order to get the immediately reinforcing consequence of a large burger and supersized fries.

So far, we have discussed the importance of focusing on observable behaviours, and a rationale for the importance of the events immediately preceding a behaviour (antecedents) and those which follow (consequences). The sequence of antecedent→ behaviour→ consequence has been termed the **three-term contingency**. It provides the theoretical foundation for the behaviour-change interventions developed and evaluated by applied behaviour analysts.

In order to change behaviour in a desired direction, behaviour analysts carefully define a problem behaviour and identify the antecedents that precede it and the consequences that follow. Ideally, this analysis of behaviour is accomplished through direct observation but, in some cases, surveys or interviews can be used to define the relevant antecedents and consequences of a behaviour. When the antecedents and consequences are defined, behaviour analysts attempt to change the behaviour by altering existing contingencies (e.g., by adding new antecedents or consequences).

Behavioural intervention strategies

Most large-scale interventions designed to improve behaviour can be classified as either antecedent or consequence strategies. We outline below four antecedent strategies and three consequence strategies behaviour analysts have applied successfully to change socially important behaviours.

Antecedent strategies

Antecedent interventions include (1) education, (2) verbal and written prompts, (3) modelling and demonstrations and (4) commitment procedures.

Education and training

Before attempting to change a behaviour, it is often important to provide a strong rationale for the requested change (i.e., education). In some cases this involves making remote, uncertain or unknown consequences more salient to the target audience. For example, an intervention designed to increase recycling could provide information about (1) the negative consequences of throwing cans in the rubbish bin (e.g., wasted resources, energy consumption and overflowing landfills), and (2) the positive consequences (e.g., energy savings, decreased pollution, reduced use of landfill space) associated with recycling behaviour.

Training is different from education in that training usually involves adding a role-playing and feedback component to verify participants can perform the target behaviour.

Educational and training information can be delivered through print or electronic media, or personally in individual or group settings. Research has demonstrated that information delivered interpersonally is more effective when it is done in small, rather than large, groups and when it actively involves participants in relevant activities and demonstrations. In addition, the effectiveness of educational and training interventions can be enhanced by tailoring the information to the target audience. For example, Daamen, Staats, Wilke and Engelen (2001) demonstrated tailored messages containing specifics about how oil pollution in a specific garage could be minimized led to more behaviour change than general messages sent to a group of comparable garages. For a detailed description of tailored interventions see Chapter 10.

Although providing information and promoting awareness of a problem are often important components of a behaviour-change intervention, information alone is seldom sufficient to change behaviour. This is especially true when the desired behaviour is inconvenient (see also Chapter 2). Information presentations

Figure 3.1 *Polite prompts are usually more effective*

have often been combined with other intervention components, as we discuss below.

Prompts

Prompts are verbal or written messages strategically delivered in the place where the target behaviour occurs. These messages serve as antecedent reminders to perform the target behaviours. Geller, Winett and Everett (1982) identified several conditions under which prompting strategies are most effective. Specifically, prompts work best when (1) the target behaviour is clearly defined by the prompt, (2) they are relatively easy to perform, (3) the message is displayed where the target behaviour can be performed and (4) the message is stated politely. Figure 3.1 illustrates two types of activators to prompt safety-belt use. Which one do you think will be most effective? Of course, the crash-test dummy would get more attention.

As you might imagine, rude or overly demanding messages often backfire and result in individuals doing the opposite of what the prompt demands. This tendency to rebel against a top-down request was termed **countercontrol** by Skinner (1971) and psychological reactance by social psychologist Jack Brehm (1966). We return to these concepts later in the chapter.

Prompts are popular because they are (1) simple to implement, (2) relatively low cost, and (3) can have considerable impact if applied properly on a large scale. For example, Werner, Rhodes and Partain (1998) dramatically increased the rate of polystyrene recycling in a university cafeteria by increasing the size of signs designed to prompt recycling, and placing them next to the recycling bins. In a large-scale intervention that significantly increased safety-belt use on a university campus, Geller, Kalsher, Rudd and Lehman (1989) designed prompts to be hung from the rear-view mirrors of people's vehicles. Note that in both of these cases the prompts were displayed in close proximity to where the target behaviour could be performed, and the behaviour requested was relatively convenient to perform.

Modelling

While prompts are appropriate for simple behaviours, modelling may be a more appropriate approach when the desired behaviour is complex. **Modelling** involves demonstrating specific behaviours to a target audience. Research suggests modelling may be more effective when the models are presented with rewarding consequence immediately after the desired behaviour is performed. Modelling can involve in vivo demonstrations, but reaches a broader audience through electronic media.

The research by Winett, Leckliter, Chinn, Stahl and Love (1985) exemplifies a large-scale intervention to increase energy conservation behaviours. Participants who viewed a twenty-minute videotaped presentation of conservation behaviours significantly decreased their residential energy use over a nine-week period compared to controls. Importantly, the video also specified the positive financial consequences of performing the conservation behaviours.

Behavioural commitment

This intervention approach is simple and often very effective. In a sense, all behavioural interventions request individuals to change their behaviour. **Behavioural commitments** take this process a step further by asking individuals to formally agree to change their behaviour, thereby making a behavioural commitment. Intervention research has repeatedly demonstrated that asking individuals to make a written or verbal commitment to perform a target behaviour increases the likelihood that behaviour will be performed (Geller, 2001, 2002).

When individuals sign a pledge or promise card to increase a desirable behaviour (e.g., recycle, exercise, buckle up) or cease an undesirable behaviour (e.g., smoke cigarettes, drop litter, drive while impaired) they feel obligated to honour their commitment, and often do. Figure 3.2 depicts a generic promise card which can be used to obtain a behavioural commitment for a variety of target behaviours.

Behaviour analysts explain the tendency to follow through on commitments with the notion of rule-governed behaviour. Individuals learn rules for behaviour and through experience learn that following the rule is associated with positive social and personal consequences, and breaking the rule is usually followed by negative consequences. Social psychologists attribute this tendency to follow through on a behavioural commitment to the powerful social norm of consistency, which creates pressure to be internally and externally consistent (Cialdini, 2001).

Figure 3.2 *A promise card can be used to encourage a number of behaviours*

We discuss the consistency principle in greater detail later in this chapter, along with some techniques for increasing the effectiveness of commitment strategies.

Obtaining a behavioural commitment has been an effective component of many behaviour-based interventions. Geller *et al.* (1989) combined commitment and prompting strategies by asking individuals to sign a card promising to use their safety belts. Participants also agreed to hang the 'promise card' on the rear-view mirror of their vehicles, which served as a proximal prompt to buckle up. Results indicated students who made the commitment and displayed the prompt increased their safety-belt use by 40 per cent over baseline while non-signing controls showed no change.

Consequence strategies

Now let's consider intervention techniques that employ consequence strategies. As explained above, behaviour analysts consider consequences to be the primary determinant of voluntary behaviour. In fact, many of the antecedent strategies reviewed above are presumed to work because they announce the availability of consequences associated with the desired behaviour. Let's consider three basic consequence strategies: penalties, rewards and feedback.

Penalties

Interventions employing **penalty** techniques identify undesirable behaviours and administer negative consequences to those who perform them. Although this approach seems to be favoured by governments, behavioural psychologists have typically avoided this approach in community interventions for a variety of reasons. One practical reason is penalty interventions usually require extensive enforcement in order to be effective, and enforcement requires backing by the proper authority. For example, if you tried to reduce the wasteful disposal of cans in your community by fining people who threw their cans in the rubbish bin, you would probably have a hard time catching them, and even more difficulty getting them to pay up when you knock at their door. Although these are significant obstacles, it could be overcome by psychologists working with local governments to pass laws and hire individuals to enforce them.

The main reason behavioural psychologists have opposed the use of negative consequences is the effect it has on the attitudes and long-term behaviours of those who receive it. How do you think attitudes towards recycling would be affected by an intervention that punished people for not recycling? Would community members be more likely to focus on the positive environmental consequences of recycling, or be resentful of a programme that punishes them for throwing litter in the rubbish bin where it belongs? When the 'can enforcer' is not watching would they be likely to recycle? As you probably guessed, most individuals react to penalties with negative emotions and attitudes. Instead of performing a behaviour because of its positive consequences, they simply do it to avoid negative consequences. And, when enforcement is not consistent, behaviours are likely to return to their previous state. For example, do you think the runner in the cartoon in Figure 3.3 is likely to be highly motivated to run quickly when his coach is not available to hold him accountable?

Rewards

Because of the negative side-effects associated with penalties, behavioural psychologists have typically favoured the strategy of following a desirable behaviour with a positive consequence, or **reward**. Rewards can come in the form of a variety of positive consequences, including money, merchandise, verbal praise or special privileges. Although reward strategies have some problems of their own, many community-based reward interventions have produced dramatic increases in targeted behaviours.

Before going further in our discussion of rewards, let's be clear on relevant terminology. Since rewards follow behaviours, we include them in the consequence section of this chapter. However, rewards are often preceded by antecedent messages announcing the availability of the reward upon completion of a specified behaviour. This antecedent message is termed an **incentive**. Similarly, an antecedent message announcing a punitive consequence or penalty for undesirable behaviours is considered a **disincentive**. In some cases rewards can be used without incentives. In these cases you would simply provide the reward immediately following the behaviour – without announcing its availability in advance.

Note also that some would refer to rewards as 'positive reinforcement' and penalties as 'punishment', but this is technically incorrect. Why? Because positive

Figure 3.3 *Negative consequences motivate, but don't make us happy*

reinforcement and punishment always influence the behaviour they follow. **Positive reinforcement** increases future occurrences of a behaviour, while **punishment** decreases behaviour through the delivery of a consequence. In both cases, the correct terminology is dependent on subsequent behaviour. If a consequence does not increase or decrease the prior behaviour, positive reinforcement or punishment was technically not implemented. Thus, we avoid this technical issue by using the more popular real-world terms of rewards and penalties.

A wide range of behaviours have been targeted with incentive/reward programmes. For example, studies have shown significant beneficial impact of incentive/reward programmes to increase safety-belt use, medication compliance, commitment to organ donation, and to decrease drug use and environmental degradation.

In addition, incentives and rewards are used frequently and effectively by employers to increase the productivity of their workers. Jenkins, Mitra, Gupta and Shaw (1998) used a statistical technique called meta-analysis to evaluate the effects of financial incentives on performance quantity in 39 studies. In a meta-analysis, results from various studies are combined and analysed statistically, thus providing insight into the consistency of effects across studies. Averaged across all studies, workers offered financial compensation for increased production increased their productivity by 34 per cent over those who were not offered behaviour-based rewards (Jenkins *et al.*, 1998).

Given the consistent effectiveness of incentive/reward strategies, you might be asking, 'Why use anything else?' Unfortunately, there are a few disadvantages to incentive/reward strategies. An obvious practical disadvantage of using rewards is they can be expensive to implement. This shortcoming can be addressed in part by providing rewards only after a behaviour has been completed a set number of times, or by varying the number of times a behaviour needs to be completed before a reward is offered. The technical terms for these practices are known respectively as fixed and variable-ratio reinforcement, while continuous rein- forcement refers to a process in which an individual receives a reward each time he or she completes a behaviour. Although fixed and variable-ratio reinforcement schedules both produce high rates of responding, individuals who are on a fixed- ratio schedule are more likely to stop performing a behaviour immediately after receiving their reward, because they know the next reward is distant. Variable- ratio schedules are favoured by many (including the makers of slot machines for gamblers), because the unpredictability of the reward leads to the most consistent behaviour pattern.

A second limitation of rewards is that the target behaviours on which they are contingent tend to decrease when the rewards are removed almost as dramatically as they increased when the rewards were implemented. In fact, this effect is so reliable behaviour analysts often use it as their research–design strategy. They first measure the pre-intervention level (baseline) of a target behaviour, then assess the increase in the frequency of the behaviour while rewards are in place and finally, document a decrease in behavioural occurrence when the rewards are removed. When behaviour analysts show a target behaviour occurs more often while an intervention is in place and returns to near baseline levels when the intervention is withdrawn, they demonstrate *functional control* of the target behaviour. The intervention is shown to be effective. Of course, an obvious solution to this reversal problem is to keep a reward strategy in place indefinitely. For example, in the United States, bottle bills, which provide a refund of 5–10 cents when bottles and cans are returned, illustrate an effective long-term incentive/reward strategy.

Finally, reward interventions have been criticized by some who contend rewards diminish **intrinsic motivation**. The contention is that instead of focus- ing on the positive aspects of completing a task for its own sake, individuals become *extrinsically* motivated to perform the behaviour. In essence they rea- son that if someone is paying or rewarding me to perform a behaviour, it must be unpleasant and not worth performing when the opportunity for reward is removed (Figure 3.4).

Feedback

Feedback strategies involve providing information to participants about the rate or consequences of their behaviours. Such data make the consequences of desir- able behaviours more salient (e.g., money saved from carpooling, or weight lost from an exercise programme), and increase the likelihood of behaviour change corresponding with the consequences. Feedback strategies were used in many

Figure 3.4 *Extrinsic rewards can stifle intrinsic motivation*

early environmental-protection interventions targeting home-energy consumption, and most of these interventions showed modest, but consistent energy savings (Geller, Winett & Everett, 1982). Other research has demonstrated feedback to be an effective strategy for addressing a variety of problems, including unsafe driving, smoking and depression. For further discussion of feedback strategies in environmental interventions, see Chapter 8.

You now have an overview of seven intervention techniques (education, prompts, modelling, commitment, penalties, rewards and feedback) that behaviour analysts have used successfully to change behaviours on a large scale. Although we reviewed them separately, in practice several are often combined in a single intervention. For example, most interventions have some sort of education or information, which is combined with other behaviour-change strategies such as prompts, feedback or commitment strategies.

We have devoted substantial space to applied behaviour analysis in a book focused on applied *social* psychology. Why? Because applied behaviour analysts have conducted the most intervention-based research on societal problems. Now we turn to a discussion of how social influence principles can be used to enhance the intervention strategies implemented and evaluated by behaviour analysts. The synergy from combining the practical behaviour-change strategies of behaviour analysis with the tools of social influence can enable greater and longer-term intervention impact.

Enhancing interventions through social influence

In his popular book *Influence*, Robert Cialdini outlines six social-influence principles used frequently by marketing professionals to increase sales of their products: (1) consistency, (2) social proof, (3) authority, (4) liking, (5) reciprocity and (6) scarcity. Cialdini describes the principles as compliance techniques, because they are frequently used to increase the odds a target indi vidual will comply with a request.

These principles are relevant for intervention design because most behaviour-change interventions involve an intervention agent asking a target individual to comply with a request (e.g., increase recycling behaviour, practise safe sex, buckle up, or wear a bicycle helmet). It is logical that the same techniques that have proved successful in evoking purchasing behaviour should be effective in encouraging individuals to change other behaviours, or at least to make a commitment to attempt change. Once the behaviour has been initiated, further applications of the principles may activate social consequences with potential to maintain the behaviours for longer periods of time. The remainder of this chapter addresses ways to integrate these six principles with the intervention techniques discussed so far in order to make them more influential.

Consistency

The idea that a desire to be consistent is a fundamental human motive has served as the basis for some of the most influential theories in social psychology, including cognitive dissonance and balance theory. In addition to the desire for internal **consistency**, as outlined in dissonance and balance theory, other research has demonstrated that individuals also have a strong desire to show others they are consistent (Cialdini, 2001).

In the United States, the public demand for consistency was reflected by the 2004 presidential campaign strategy of George W. Bush. Because his Democratic opponent, John Kerry, had first supported and subsequently opposed the war in Iraq, he was labelled a 'flip-flopper'. Although one might not consider a change of heart such a negative thing, in a society that demands consistency, a label implying inconsistency can have powerfully negative connotations. Given that consistency is a valued attribute, let's explore some ways in which the consistency principle can enhance the impact of behaviour-change interventions.

Foot in the door

You may wish to consider beginning your intervention with a **foot in the door**. No, we don't mean knocking on doors of community members and quickly inserting your foot before they can be slammed in your face. As introduced in Chapter 1, the foot-in-the-door (FITD) principle refers to the observation that individuals who comply with a small request are more likely to comply with a subsequent larger request. The FITD technique is thought to function through internal consistency motives and the desire to appear consistent to others (Cialdini, 2001). In other words, once you start along a behavioural course, you are likely to stay on it in order to appear consistent to yourself and others.

Freedman and Fraser (1966) demonstrated the FITD technique in a classic study in which they increased compliance with a request to place a large sign promoting driving safety on private property by first asking them to display a small sticker in their window. Katzev and Johnson (1984) demonstrated the utility of the FITD technique for reducing residential energy consumption by preceding a request to conserve energy with a request to complete a short survey. During a twelve-week follow-up period, 71% of the households in the FITD condition conserved energy compared to only 37% of a group asked simply to conserve energy without first completing the survey.

Cognitive dissonance

Cognitive dissonance is the state of uncomfortable psychological tension that occurs when individuals become aware of inconsistencies among their behaviours and attitudes (Festinger, 1957). Dissonance is most pronounced when a behaviour or decision that conflicts with an attitude or value is seen as freely chosen and produces foreseeable negative consequences. According to cognitive dissonance theory, individuals are motivated to reduce the negative tension by changing their behaviour, or adjusting their attitudes to match the behaviour.

Because the desire to reduce attitude/behavioural inconsistencies can be a powerful motivator of behaviour, interventions should attempt to 'clang the dissonance gong' whenever possible in educational materials and when trying to obtain a behavioural commitment. And there are usually plenty of opportunities to do this. Because psychologists tend to intervene in behaviours with problematic outcomes (e.g., substance abuse, environmentally harmful behaviour, unsafe sex) arousing dissonance may be as simple as getting people to reflect on the potential negative outcomes of their undesirable behaviour.

For example, individuals who may have a problem with drinking too much alcohol may be asked to list the 'good' and 'not so good' things about consuming alcohol. If the individual has a problem with alcohol, the list of good things (e.g., taste, social lubrication, relaxation) is likely to be quite small compared to the not-so-good list (e.g., expense, hangovers, missed work, lost jobs, legal problems, fights with spouse, medical problems, etc.). In a case like this, the dissonance gong is likely to be sounding quite loudly when the individual is confronted with the list of negative consequences of excessive alcohol consumption, and motivation for change should be increased. Indeed, arousing cognitive dissonance to motivate change is a basic component of motivational interviewing, a promising therapeutic technique that has been applied to a number of clinical problems (Miller & Rollnick, 2002).

Dissonance strategies have been effective when applied on a large scale to problems like environmentally harmful behaviours. For example, Aitken, McMahon, Wearing and Finlayson (1994) used a dissonance strategy to reduce water consumption in Australia. An initial survey of area residents revealed (1) many residents had very positive attitudes towards conserving water, and (2) positive attitudes towards water conservation were poor predictors of actual water conservation as measured on water meters. Aitken *et al.* applied dissonance by delivering postcards to residents (1) reminding them they had strongly agreed on the survey it was their duty to conserve water, and (2) providing feedback about how their household water consumption compared to similar-sized households in the region. Results indicated households that received the dissonance manipulation significantly reduced their water use, while a comparison group who simply received the feedback without the dissonance manipulation did not.

Although these studies and others demonstrate the promise of dissonance-based interventions, the bad news is that it is also possible that individuals may reduce dissonance by changing their *attitudes* instead of their behaviours. When behaviours are difficult or inconvenient to perform, changing one's attitude may be far easier. For example, in a study conducted in the Netherlands, Tertoolen, Van Kreveld and Verstraten (1998) found individuals who scored high on an initial measure of environmental awareness scored lower on the same measure after they were given feedback about the environmental consequences of frequent use of their own cars.

Public commitment

Behavioural commitment (as discussed in the section on antecedent interventions) may be the most practical and frequently used application of the consistency principle. Viewed through the lens of the consistency principle, it is easy to see that fulfilling a behaviour-change promise follows the consistency principle and failing to change violates it.

Social psychologists have found that commitment strategies work best when the commitment is active, public and perceived as voluntary (Cialdini, 2001). The requirement that commitment be voluntary makes sense, because breaking a promise you were forced to make is unlikely to arouse much dissonance. In fact, it is reasonable to question if a coerced commitment amounts to a commitment at all.

Individuals who actively voice a commitment or sign a promise card are more likely to fulfil their promise than those who passively nod their heads in agreement. Active commitments are more concrete, and make future violations more likely to cause dissonance. Because individuals are motivated to appear consistent to themselves and to others, commitments should also be made publicly whenever possible.

Interestingly, there is some evidence suggesting that commitments may become more effective when followed by reminders of past failures to live up to the values espoused in the commitment. Social psychologist Elliot Aronson has termed this phenomenon the 'hypocrisy effect' and speculates it functions through cognitive dissonance. Box 3.1 describes two research studies conducted by Aronson which illustrate this intervention.

Pallak and Cummings (1976) demonstrated the effectiveness of a public commitment in an intervention targeting energy consumption. The investigators began by meeting with homeowners to discuss strategies for conserving natural gas and electricity (foot-in-the-door). After presenting the information, the researchers either (1) simply asked the participants to sign a form consenting to their participation, or (2) asked the individuals to sign a form giving their consent to participate in the research *and* have their names published in the local newspaper in order to publicize the project. As predicted, during the month following the intervention, participants in the public-commitment condition had significantly lower percentages of energy use than those in the private-commitment condition.

Perhaps the most interesting aspect of the Pallak and Cummings study was that participants in the public-commitment condition continued to show significantly lower energy usage in a follow-up study conducted a year later, after being informed the study had concluded and their names would *not* be published in the paper. Subsequent research has also indicated commitment strategies may be among the best for maintaining long-term behaviour change (Geller, 2002).

Although there are internal and social consequences associated with being consistent and honouring a commitment, what might account for continuing the behaviour after the commitment period is over? Cialdini (2001) notes individuals who become strongly committed to performing a behaviour often adjust their identities to become consistent with that behaviour. When individuals repeatedly perform a behaviour they are more likely to adopt an identity consistent with that behaviour, and thus be more likely to perform it in the future.

The maintenance of post-commitment behaviour can also be explained by the process of **behavioural self-perception** (Bem, 1972). According to Bem, individuals infer their attitudes and other internal states from their overt behaviours. Bem's theory could also account for the failures of reward interventions to maintain behaviours when the rewards are removed. Individuals who are receiving rewards are likely to attribute their behaviour to the reward and changes in self-perception are unlikely to occur. Because of this, interventions using reward strategies should consider presenting rewards as tokens of appreciation, and consider offering rewards that are just large enough to encourage behaviour in order to allow for behavioural self-perception to occur (Geller, 2002).

Box 3.1 The hypocrisy effect: facilitating behaviour change with reminders of past failures

American social psychologist Elliot Aronson developed an innovative method for enlisting the power of cognitive dissonance. The first step of the *hypocrisy effect* involves obtaining a commitment to a certain course of action. Next, individuals complete an exercise in which they are reminded of past failures to perform according to their commitment. Aronson hypothesized this process of making hypocrisy salient should enhance dissonance and increase the likelihood future behaviours will align with the commitment.

Aronson and colleagues demonstrated the utility of the hypocrisy effect in interventions to increase condom use and water conservation (Aronson, 1999). In the condom experiment, individuals were asked to give a persuasive speech about the importance of using condoms in order to prevent the spread of AIDS. The speech was videotaped, and participants were told their speech would be shown to high-school students as a part of their sex-education classes. Participants in the hypocrisy condition were then asked to write about times when they had found it difficult, or impossible, to use condoms. When given an opportunity to buy condoms immediately after the manipulation, significantly more individuals in the hypocrisy condition (83%) bought condoms than participants in two control conditions which included only the persuasive speech (33%) or reminders of past failures to use condoms alone (50%). In addition, in a follow-up survey conducted three months later, individuals in the hypocrisy condition reported using condoms more frequently than those in the control conditions.

In the water conservation experiment, university students were asked to sign a poster declaring the importance of conserving water by taking shorter showers. Next, participants in the hypocrisy condition were asked to complete a short survey designed to remind them of past failures to conserve. A discreetly planted research assistant observed the hypocrisy manipulation had the desired effect on behaviour — immediately after the intervention, those in the hypocrisy condition took significantly shorter showers than those who simply signed the commitment.

The results of these studies suggest combining commitment and cognitive dissonance strategies may be an effective application of the consistency principle. Geller (2005) has advocated using the hypocrisy effect to promote occupational safety by asking individuals who espouse safety as a core value to recall times when their behaviour was inconsistent with this value. This is presumed to motivate participants to perform safe behaviour in order to reduce the tension caused by the noted inconsistency.

Figure 3.5 *When peers perform, there's pressure to conform*

Social proof

Although most people like to be considered consistent, many would cringe if called conformist. Despite negative connotations, there is no denying the fact our behaviour is profoundly influenced by those around us. In unfamiliar situations we follow the crowd in order to act effectively (if most people are doing it, it must be the right thing to do); and in other situations, we conform in order to gain social approval (Cialdini, 2001). Cialdini uses the term '**social proof**' to describe the compliance technique in which evidence about the behaviour of others is provided in order to evoke a conforming response. For example, salespeople and advertisers frequently cite the popularity of an item to increase sales. Although the gentleman in Figure 3.5 is probably neither a salesperson nor a psychologist, he seems to understand how to apply the principle of social proof.

Social norms can be defined as codes of conduct which inform members of a social group how to act in various situations. Unlike laws, which are explicitly outlined, norms are implicit and spread through interactions within groups. Social psychologists have distinguished two distinct types of social norms, and believe individuals' perceptions of both can have considerable impact on behaviour.

Descriptive norms are what members of the social group typically do, while **injunctive norms** describe what the group approves or disapproves (Cialdini, 2001). Sometimes descriptive and injunctive norms are aligned, and other times they are not. For example, although most people probably believe littering is inappropriate (i.e., an injunctive norm against littering exists), littered environments provide a salient descriptive norm, making littering appropriate here.

Normative prompts

According to Cialdini (2003), those creating messages to encourage behaviour change should consider both injunctive and descriptive norms when designing their messages. Cialdini notes that pro-environmental messages frequently emphasize descriptive norms by describing the high prevalence of the problematic behaviour. He cites the wording of an ineffective sign at the Petrified Forest National Park as an example: 'Your heritage is being vandalized every day by theft losses of petrified wood of 14 tons a year, mostly one small piece at a time' (p. 107). Although this message draws attention to the scope of the problem, it also powerfully communicates the fact that many people take fossils from the forest. According to the principle of social proof, the knowledge that many people engage in theft is more likely to increase the behaviour than prevent it.

Correcting misperceived norms

In some cases, individuals' perceptions of norms are inaccurate. For example, students in US colleges and universities tend to overestimate the extent to which their peers approve of and engage in alcohol consumption (Borsari & Carey, 2003). In addition, college students' drinking behaviours are associated with their estimates of the drinking behaviour and attitudes of others. Specifically, those who estimate a large percentage of college students drink heavily are more likely to be heavy drinkers themselves (Perkins, 2003; see also Chapter 2). Based on the logic that college students are likely to conform to inflated drinking norms, researchers have designed numerous large-scale interventions to provide college students with accurate information about drinking norms on campus (e.g., Haines & Spear, 1996). Box 3.2 reviews potential causes of inflated drinking norms and provides an overview of norm-based marketing campaigns to reduce harmful levels of alcohol consumption among college students.

Personalized normative feedback

In addition to their relevance for prompting and education, social norms can be integrated with feedback interventions. **Normative feedback** compares an individual's behaviour to typical or average group behaviour.

Neighbors, Larimer and Lewis (2004) conducted an experiment with 252 college students who had been screened as heavy drinkers. After completing a computer-based questionnaire about their own drinking behaviour and perceptions about drinking norms on campus, participants received a graph contrasting their drinking behaviour with the actual drinking rates on campus. Follow-up analyses revealed the intervention significantly reduced participants' perceptions of student drinking and more importantly, significantly reduced their self-reported drinking in three- and six-month follow-up surveys.

Box 3.2   The social-norms approach to reducing college student drinking

As noted above, several studies that have documented college students in the United States consistently overestimate descriptive and injunctive drinking norms among their peers (see meta-analysis by Bosari & Carey, 2003).

The widespread existence of inflated alcohol-use norms begs the question of their origin. According to Perkins (2003) inflated injunctive norms may be due to pluralistic ignorance and attribution biases. **Pluralistic ignorance** (see also Chapter 2) is the belief others' private attitudes and beliefs are different from one's own despite the fact that their public behaviour is identical. Although many students may share the private belief moderate use or abstinence is best, they may feel pressured to drink heavily by the behaviour of others, who share similar beliefs but are feeling the same social pressure. Attribution theory predicts individuals are likely to dismiss their own behaviour as socially pressured, while attributing the behaviour of their fellow students to stable internal attitudes. This tendency to underestimate the situational influences for others is known as correspondence bias or the **fundamental attribution error**.

A contributor to inflated descriptive norms may be the **availability heuristic**, which states we calculate the probability of an event's occurrence based on the ease with which we can bring that event to mind. At university parties the behaviour of students who are drinking heavily may be amusing, disturbing or revolting, any of which would likely make it more salient at the party and more memorable long afterwards. In addition, dramatic events at parties are likely to be the subject of conversation and dissemination long after the party, further exacerbating the perception that heavy drinking is the norm (Perkins, 2003).

Regardless of the source of the inflated norms, their existence combined with the consistent finding that perceived drinking norms are predictive of individual use have made social-norms interventions a popular prevention approach on college campuses. The popularity of norms-based approaches to prevention has been fuelled in part by a handful of colleges that implemented comprehensive campus-wide social-norms marketing campaigns and subsequently reported significant decreases in alcohol abuse in the following years (e.g., Haines & Spear, 1996).

Perkins (2003) outlines a model for primary prevention programmes on college campuses. It begins with a baseline measurement period in which data are collected to document real and misperceived norms. Next, publicity campaigns are enacted to educate students about the actual norms on campus. It is important these messages are positively stated, with the emphasis on the healthy choices of the majority of students who choose to drink responsibly. According to the theory behind this approach, placing the emphasis on negative outcomes or trying to scare students with high drinking rates could serve to increase use.

Ideally the campaign should be multimedia and be extensively repeated to ensure wide dissemination of the facts. Focus groups are often used to test the clarity and impact of the message. According to Perkins (2003), a well-planned and well-executed publicity campaign will result in more accurate (i.e., lower) perceptions of the amount of alcohol consumed on campus, and over time students will engage in less risky alcohol consumption.

Despite the popularity of social-norms interventions to prevent excessive drinking among college students, the studies conducted to date only provide partial support for the efficacy of the approach. Critics of the approach assert many of the campaigns do not seem to have an impact and the best large-scale 'success stories' have occurred in uncontrolled case studies.

Make participation salient

A final practical implication of the principle of social proof is that intervention agents should take steps to make their interventions as salient as possible. This could involve brightly-coloured recycling bins, stickers, T-shirts and publicity establishing many individuals are both concerned about the problem addressed by the intervention and involved.

Authority

The principle of **authority** states that people are more likely to comply with a request from an authority figure than someone who lacks status (Cialdini, 2001). Milgram's (1963) experiment provides a chilling example of the tendency to obey authority blindly. Although it is unlikely you will find yourself in a situation where you are ordered to shock a helpless learner, most of us comply, to some extent, with social norms stating we should obey rules and those in charge. Uniforms and titles can enhance these effects (Cialdini, 2001), as does the power of authority figures to control positive and negative consequences.

The influence of authority, however, is not limited to cases where there is a power differential. The opinions of experts are often used as heuristics for making correct choices. When the opinions of professionals or authority figures appear prominently in newspapers and on television, public opinion tends to move towards agreement with the designated experts (Cialdini, 2001). In addition, advertisers frequently employ real or purported experts to endorse their products.

Craig and McCann (1978) demonstrated the relevance of the authority principle for interventions to reduce energy consumption. They sent a letter to residents of New York City, listing a variety of conservation tips and specifically asking recipients to conserve energy by reducing their use of air conditioning. The independent variable for the study was the source of the letter. One group received a letter from the chair of the New York Public Service Commission on official letterhead, while the other received a letter identical in content, but from the local power company and on company letterhead. Comparisons of kilowatt hours of electricity use for the two groups demonstrated that those receiving the plea from the public service commission used significantly less electricity. Craig and McCann attributed the observed differences to the credibility of the source, speculating a government authority represented a more credible authority than the power company.

Other researchers have attempted to enhance their interventions by communicating the association with or endorsement by authority figures without testing for effects. For example, Burn (1991) emphasized his recycling programme was endorsed by the local government. In their effort to encourage residents of military bases to conserve energy, McMakin, Malone and Lundgren (2002) made it clear that although participation in the programme was voluntary, participation was encouraged and endorsed by high-ranking military officials.

Liking

Simply stated, the social influence principle of **liking** is based on the fact we are more likely to do things for people we *know* and *like* (Cialdini, 2001). Research has shown people tend to like those similar to them and those who compliment them. Sales professionals are well aware of these effects, and use compliments frequently and point out similarities between them and potential customers (Cialdini, 2001). In a social influence experiment, Burger, Messian, Patel, del Prado and Anderson (2003) demonstrated that bogus superficial similarities in names, birthdays and fingerprint types resulted in increased compliance with a request. Figure 3.6 illustrates a consultant who successfully applied the similarity component of the liking principle.

Identify with the target audience

The liking principle suggests similarities between intervention agents requesting behaviour change and targets should be emphasized whenever possible. In addition, interventions which make use of observational learning should pick models who closely match the target audience. In a study that used television modelling successfully to increase energy conservation, Winett *et al.* (1985) noted they intentionally selected the actors, homes and scenes depicted in the programme to match specific characteristics of the target audience.

Block-leader approach

A second implication of the liking principle is the opinions and advice of those we know and like carry more weight than the advice of strangers. The **block-leader approach** is an application of the liking principle for behaviour-change

Figure 3.6 *Similarity increases liking*

intervention. Block leaders are members of a community recruited to serve as intervention agents and encourage programme participation in their neighbourhoods. Although there is no way of knowing if block leaders are 'liked' by their fellow community members, the fact they are members of the same neighbourhood demonstrates a degree of similarity; and in close-knit communities, block leaders are likely to know their neighbours. For examples of block-leader approaches to behaviour-change intervention, see Burn (1991). In this study and others, recycling pleas delivered by block leaders were significantly more effective than similar pleas delivered by experimenters.

Reciprocity

Reciprocity reflects the norm that people should repay others for benefits received from them. The reciprocity norm has been shown to exist in all cultures, and is thought to facilitate social exchange and create a sense of interdependence (Cialdini, 2001). Cialdini notes reciprocity-based strategies have been used to (1) fund the Hare Krishna movement (e.g., a gift of a carnation preceded donation request), (2) increase donations to charitable organizations (e.g., free address labels included with donation requests), and (3) sell products (e.g., free samples

Figure 3.7 *The reciprocity norm involves payback*

distributed to potential customers). Figure 3.7 depicts an amateur psychologist's attempt to apply the reciprocity principle.

Reciprocity-based strategies have also been shown to be useful in increasing the return rates for mailed surveys. Including a cash or cheque payment in advance often outperforms offers of payment upon receipt of the survey (e.g., James & Bolstein, 1992). Recent applied work has demonstrated restaurant staff can enhance their tips by giving their customers sweets or writing a pleasant message on the back of their cheque (e.g., Strohmetz, Rind, Fisher & Lynn, 2002).

Pre-behaviour rewards

The reciprocity norm suggests offering a pre-behaviour reward (antecedent) may be a useful alternative to conventional incentive/rewards. An experiment by Boyce and Geller (2001) compared the effectiveness of a reciprocity-based strategy with conventional rewards. The rewards were given to encourage participants to deliver thank-you cards to people who helped others or performed environmentally friendly behaviours. Participants were given 30 cards and asked to sign a commitment to distribute at least five cards weekly over a five-week period. Participants who received a gift of an insulated travel mug and T-shirt upon signing the commitment delivered significantly more cards over the five weeks (mean = 28 cards) than those who signed a commitment and were promised the same gifts upon delivery of five cards (mean = 16 cards).

Reciprocity prompts

An experiment by Cialdini (2005) provides an example of the application of the reciprocity principle to behavioural prompts. The target behaviour was reusing hotel room towels rather than discarding them on the floor to be exchanged for clean ones. Instead of a message stating the hotel would donate a portion of the money saved from guests reusing their towels to environmental causes, the message was changed to indicate donations to environmental causes had already been made on behalf of the guests. The message invoked reciprocity by inviting guests to help recover the expense and help the environment by reusing their towels. The reciprocity-based message resulted in a 47% towel-reuse rate, compared to a 36% reuse rate for the message that promised a future donation.

Scarcity

The principle of **scarcity** can be conceptually linked to the economic principle of supply and demand. The extent to which something is rare or difficult to obtain serves as a heuristic to determine its perceived value. According to Cialdini (2001), scarcity-based influence techniques gain part of their power through our desire to have freedom of choice and avoid loss. Cialdini describes numerous scarcity techniques used by advertisers and salespeople, including one-day-only sales, limited supplies and high-pressure sales techniques requiring customers to make an immediate decision to buy before a special price is withdrawn forever.

Avoid reactance

Cialdini (2001) also relates reactance (Brehm, 1966) to the scarcity principle. **Reactance** is the tendency of individuals to act in ways to re-establish freedom when it becomes limited or threatened. In addition to desiring items that are scarce, freedom becomes more desirable when it is limited or threatened. Note that reactance is virtually identical to the concept of countercontrol discussed earlier. Geller (2002) points out the relevance of the scarcity principle for professionals working in occupational safety, cautioning safety professionals to avoid top-down, rule-based approaches that might elicit reactance. Avoiding reactance is important for behaviour-change interventions, because a message or manipulation that results in perceptions of authoritarian control or lost freedom may backfire and result in behaviour opposite to that desired (Skinner, 1971).

The negative impact of reactance is exemplified by Aronson and O'Leary's (1982) observation that an obtrusive sign promoting water conservation in a university shower was knocked over by some subjects, and those subjects subsequently took inordinately long showers. Another example is provided by the personal experience of the second author of this chapter. In the midst of an intervention designed to increase safety-belt use, the 70-pound sign that gave feedback about community safety-belt use was carried approximately 100 yards and deposited in his fish pond (Geller, 2001). It is possible this one-person decision to put up a community sign irritated some residents, and they reacted in this way to reassert their freedom.

Make potential losses salient

Another implication of the scarcity principle is that the threat of loss may be more motivationally powerful than the promise of gaining something of similar value (Cialdini, 2001). In other words, messages framing consequences in terms of what will be lost if behaviour is not changed may be more effective than those emphasizing what will be gained if a change is made (see also Chapters 1 and 10).

Capitalizing on this idea, Aronson and colleagues trained a group of home-energy auditors to emphasize the amount of energy and money that would be lost (as opposed to gained or saved) if homeowners failed to make the efficiency improvements they recommended. Auditors were trained to use vivid language, such as 'it's like having a hole in your pocket', or 'your hard earned cash is flying up the chimney' (Aronson & Gonzales, 1992, p. 321). The researchers showed that auditors who received the training programme were more effective at influencing homeowners to invest in energy-conserving improvements than those who had not. More specifically, homeowners who received a visit from one of the trained energy auditors were 64 per cent more likely to invest in energy-conserving improvements.

Fear appeals

The ultimate scarcity message is one in which an individual is reminded that he or she may be seriously injured or die if behaviour does not change. **Fear appeals** are motivational messages which attempt to change behaviour by highlighting negative consequences. This technique has been widely used in health-information campaigns with varying results. In a meta-analysis of over 100 fear-appeal interventions, Witte and Allen (2000) found fear appeals are effective when they persuade the target audience (1) they are susceptible to the negative consequence, (2) the consequence is severe and (3) the target audience receives a prevention strategy they can apply successfully to avoid the negative consequence.

In other words, successful fear appeals convincingly present a scary problem and an efficacious solution. Messages that arouse fear without convincing the target audience they can successfully perform the behavior required to avoid the undesirable consequence often result in reactance or denial of the threat (Witte & Allen, 2000). For further discussion on the use of fear appeals, see Chapter 10.

Along these lines, Geller (2005) proposes industrial safety programmes motivate use of personal protective equipment (PPE), for example, safety glasses, or steel-toed boots, by having employees talk about their personal injuries and close calls. This testimonial approach can become a wake-up call by calling people's attention to the potential loss of something they take for granted (i.e., a body part). In this case, the behaviours required to avoid injury (wearing appropriate PPE) are relatively simple to accomplish.

Conclusion

In this chapter we have reviewed a variety of intervention techniques that have been used successfully by behaviour analysts and social psychologists. We believe integrating the strengths of applied behaviour analysis (i.e., a focus on environmental determinants of behaviour) and social psychology (i.e., understanding the interpersonal and social dynamics of behaviour) results in a powerful set of tools for large-scale behaviour-change intervention. Table 3.1 outlines the six social influence principles and their potential application to intervention design.

Table 3.1 *Applications of social influence principles for behaviour-focused intervention*

Social influence principle	Intervention application
Consistency	• Begin with a small request and build (foot-in-the-door technique) • Make behavioural commitments active, public and voluntary • Activate cognitive dissonance with prompts and education by making inconsistencies in attitudes and behaviours salient • Use small 'token of appreciation' rewards to prevent de-motivation and allow for changes in self-perception
Social proof	• Add injunctive and descriptive norms to support the prompting and educational intervention • Provide corrective information when norms are inaccurately perceived to conflict with target behaviour • When desired behaviour is below the norm, provide personalized normative feedback • Make intervention participation salient
Authority	• Use authoritative sources in information about behavioural consequences • Emphasize affiliation and endorsement of interventions by local governments or universities
Liking	• Match models to relevant characteristics of the target audience • Recruit community members to serve as intervention leaders
Reciprocity	• Use pre-behaviour rewards to encourage participation • Give a gift that also serves as a prompt
Scarcity	• Avoid reactance by politely wording requests for behaviour change • Make the threat of loss salient • Activate fear, but teach a preventive strategy

Glossary

Antecedents: environmental stimuli which attempt to direct a target behaviour through persuasion and/or announcing a consequence.

Applied behaviour analysis: an intervention approach that targets observable behaviours, and alters behavioural antecedents and consequences to influence beneficial change.

Authority: the social influence principle describing the tendency of individuals to (1) comply with the requests of high-status/power individuals, and (2) follow the advice of experts.

Availability heuristic: the tendency to calculate the probability of an event's occurrence based on the ease with which we can bring that event to mind.

Behavioural commitment: a written or verbal promise to perform a target behaviour.

Behavioural self-perception: the tendency to infer one's own attitudes and traits based on self-observations of one's behaviour.

Block-leader approach: an intervention technique in which members of a community neighbourhood are recruited to serve as intervention agents and encourage participation in a particular programme.

Cognitive dissonance: the uncomfortable tension that arises when individuals become aware of inconsistencies in their attitudes and behaviours.

Consistency: a fundamental human motive which drives us to be internally and externally consistent.

Countercontrol: an attempt to regain perceived freedom by performing behaviour contrary to that advocated by a behaviour-change intervention.

Descriptive norms: an individual's perceptions about what members of the social group typically do.

Disincentive: an antecedent message or activator announcing negative consequences for a specific undesirable behaviour.

Fear appeals: motivational messages which attempt to change a behaviour by explaining negative consequences which will occur in the absence of behaviour change.

Feedback: providing individuals with data about the frequency of a target behaviour and/or the consequences of that behaviour.

Foot-in-the-door technique: a consistency-based social influence technique in which compliance with a small request precedes a larger subsequent request.

Fundamental attribution error: the tendency to overestimate the influence of personality on the behaviour of others while underestimating the influence of the situation.

Incentive: an antecedent message announcing the availability of a particular reward upon completion of a specified behaviour.

Injunctive norms: an individual's perception about what behaviours members of a social group approve or disapprove.

Intrinsic motivation: motivation to complete a task for the sake of the task itself rather than the availability of external rewards.

Liking: the social influence principle describing the tendency of individuals to comply with the requests of attractive, similar and familiar others.

Modelling: intervention technique which involves the demonstration of a desired target behaviour.

Normative feedback: an intervention technique which provides data comparing an individual's behaviour to typical or average group behaviour.

Penalty: a negative consequence delivered after an undesirable behaviour designed to decrease its future occurrence.

Pluralistic ignorance: the tendency to believe the private attitudes and beliefs of others are different from one's own despite identical public behaviour.

Positive reinforcement: the delivery of a consequence that increases the probability the behaviour it follows will recur.

Prompts: verbal or written messages designed to remind people to perform a target behaviour.

Punishment: the delivery of a consequence that reduces the probability the behaviour it follows will reoccur.

Reactance: the tendency of individuals to act in ways to re-establish freedom when it becomes limited or threatened.

Reciprocity: the social norm that pressures people to repay benefits received from others.

Reward: a positive consequence delivered after a desirable behaviour which is intended to increase future occurrences of the behaviour.

Scarcity: the human tendency to value scarce resources and opportunities.

Social norms: codes of conduct which inform members of a social group how to act in various situations.

Social proof: technique in which the behaviour of others is presented as validation for a course of action.

Three-term contingency: the sequence of antecedent→ behaviour→ consequence which provides the theoretical foundation for the behaviour-change interventions developed by applied behaviour analysts.

Review questions

1. In an effort to decrease littering on a university campus you post signs stating: 'Individuals who litter will be fined £100.' Unfortunately, your data indicate littering rates *increase* after the signs are posted.
   a. Which psychological theory might account for the increased littering?
   b. Design an alternative sign based on the material in this chapter.

2. Despite the presence of recycling bins throughout a university building, large numbers of cans are being thrown away. Describe one antecedent and one consequence strategy you could use to increase can recycling.
3. To promote safety-belt use on a university campus, students and faculty were asked to sign buckle-up promise cards. A portion of each card was entered in a weekly raffle for prizes, while another portion could be hung from a vehicle's rear-view mirror. What behavioural and social psychology principles were used in this intervention?
4. Why is the disincentive/penalty approach most popular among government agencies?
5. Why do behaviour analysts prefer incentive/reward strategies to disincentive/penalty techniques?
6. Explain the role of cognitive dissonance in affecting the impact of behaviour-change interventions.
7. Describe a situation in which one or more social influence principles were used to influence your behaviour. List each social influence technique used and its impact.

Further reading

Aronson, E. (1999). The power of self-persuasion. *American Psychologist*, *54*, 875–884.
Cialdini, R. B. (2001). *Influence: Science and practice*. 4th edn. Boston: Allyn and Bacon.
Geller, E. S. (2002). *The participation factor: How to increase involvement in occupational safety*. Des Plaines, IL: American Society of Safety Engineers.
Lehman, P. K. & Geller, E. S. (2004). Behavior analysis and environmental protection: Accomplishments and potential for more. *Behavior and Social Issues*, *13*, 13–32.

References

Aitken, C. K., McMahon, T. A., Wearing, A. J. & Finlayson, B. L. (1994). Residential water use: Predicting and reducing consumption. *Journal of Applied Social Psychology*, *24*, 136–158.
Aronson, E. (1999). The power of self-persuasion. *American Psychologist*, *54*, 875–884.
Aronson, E. & Gonzales, M. H. (1992). Alternative social influence processes applied to energy conservation. In J. Edwards, R. S. Tindale, L. Heath & E. J. Prosavac (eds.), *Social influence processes and prevention* (pp. 301–325). New York: Plenum Press.
Aronson, E. & O'Leary, M. (1982). The relative effectiveness of models and prompts on energy conservation: A field experiment in a shower room. *Journal of Environmental Systems*, *12*, 219–224.
Bem, D. J. (1972). Self-perception theory. In L. Berkowitz (ed.), *Advances in experimental social psychology* (Vol. 6, pp. 1–60). New York: Academic Press.

Borsari B. & Carey, K. B. (2003). Descriptive and injunctive norms in college drinking: A meta-analytic integration. *Journal of Studies on Alcohol*, *64*, 331–341.

Boyce, T. E. & Geller, E. S. (2001). Encouraging college students to support pro-environment behavior: Effects of direct versus indirect rewards. *Environment and Behavior*, *33*, 107–125.

Brehm, J. (1966). *A theory of psychological reactance*. New York: Academic Press.

Burger, J. M., Messian, N., Patel, S., del Prado, A. & Anderson, C. (2003). What a coincidence! The effects of incidental similarity on compliance. *Personality and Social Psychology Bulletin*, *30*, 35–43.

Burn, S. M. (1991). Social psychology and the stimulation of recycling behaviors: The block leader approach. *Journal of Applied Social Psychology*, *21*, 611–629.

Cialdini, R. B. (2001). *Influence: Science and practice*. 4th edn. Boston: Allyn and Bacon.

(2003). Crafting normative messages to protect the environment. *Current Directions in Psychological Science*, *12*, 105–109.

(2005). Don't throw in the towel: Use social influence research. *APS Observer*, *18*, 33–34.

Craig, C. S. & McCann, J. M. (1978). Assessing communication effects on energy conservation. *Journal of Consumer Research*, *5*, 82–88.

Daamen, D. D. L., Staats, H., Wilke, H. A. M. & Engelen, M. (2001). Improving environmental behavior in companies: The effectiveness of tailored versus nontailored interventions. *Environment and Behavior*, *33*, 229–248.

Festinger, L. (1957) *A theory of cognitive dissonance*. Stanford University Press.

Freedman, J. L. & Fraser, S. C. (1966). Compliance without pressure: The foot-in-the-door technique. *Journal of Personality and Social Psychology*, *4*, 195–203.

Geller, E. S. (2001). *The psychology of safety handbook*. Boca Raton, FL: CRC Press.

(2002). *The participation factor: How to increase involvement in occupational safety*. Des Plaines, IL: American Society of Safety Engineers.

(2005). *People-based safety: The source*. Virginia Beach, VA: Coastal Training Technologies.

Geller, E. S., Winett, R. A. & Everett, P. B. (1982). *Environmental preservation: New strategies for behavior change*. New York: Pergamon Press.

Geller, E. S., Kalsher, M. J., Rudd, J. R. & Lehman, G. R. (1989). Promoting safety-belt use on a university campus: An integration of commitment and incentive strategies. *Journal of Applied Social Psychology*, *19*, 3–19.

Haines, M. P. & Spear, S. F. (1996). Changing the perception of the norm: A strategy to decrease binge drinking among college students. *Journal of American College Health*, *45*, 134–140.

James, J. M. & Bolstein, R. (1992). Large monetary incentives and their effect on mail survey response rates. *Public Opinion Quarterly*, *56*, 442–453.

Jenkins, G. D., Mitra, A., Gupta, N. & Shaw, J. D. (1998). Are financial incentives related to performance? A meta-analytic review of empirical research. *Journal of Applied Psychology*, *83*, 777–787.

Katzev, R. D. & Johnson, T. R. (1984). Comparing the effects of monetary incentives and foot-in-the-door strategies in promoting residential electricity conservation. *Journal of Applied Social Psychology*, *14*, 12–27.

McMakin, A. H., Malone, E. L. & Lundgren, R. E. (2002). Motivating residents to conserve energy without financial incentives. *Environment and Behavior, 34,* 848–863.

Milgram, S. (1963). Behavioral study of obedience. *Journal of Abnormal and Social Psychology, 67,* 371–378.

Miller, W. R. & Rollnick, S. (2002). *Motivational interviewing: Helping people change.* 2nd edn. New York: Guilford Press.

Neighbors, C., Larimer, M. E. & Lewis, M. A. (2004). Targeting misperceptions of descriptive drinking norms: Efficacy of a computer delivered personalized normative feedback intervention. *Journal of Consulting and Clinical Psychology, 72,* 434–447.

Pallak, M. S. & Cummings, N. (1976). Commitment and voluntary energy conservation. *Personality and Social Psychology Bulletin, 2,* 27–31.

Perkins, H. W. (2003). The emergence and evolution of the social norms approach to substance abuse prevention. In H. W. Perkins (ed.), *The social norms approach to preventing school and college age substance abuse: A handbook for educators, counselors, and clinicians* (pp. 3–17). San Francisco: Jossey-Bass.

Skinner, B. F. (1971). *Beyond freedom and dignity.* New York: Knopf.

Strohmetz, D. B., Rind, B., Fisher, R. & Lynn, M. (2002). Sweetening the till: The use of candy to increase restaurant tipping. *Journal of Applied Social Psychology, 32,* 300–309.

Tertoolen, G., Van Kreveld, D. & Verstraten, E. C. H. (1998). Psychological resistance against attempts to reduce private car use. *Transportation Research A, 32,* 171–181.

Werner, C. M., Rhodes, M. U. & Partain, K. K. (1998). Designing effective instructional signs with schema theory: Case studies of polystyrene recycling. *Environment and Behavior, 30,* 709–735.

Winett, R. A., Leckliter, I. N., Chinn, D. E., Stahl, B. & Love, S. Q. (1985). Effects of television modeling on residential energy conservation. *Journal of Applied Behavior Analysis, 18,* 33–44.

Witte, K. & Allen, M. (2000). A meta-analysis of fear appeals: Implications for effective public health campaigns. *Health Education and Behavior, 27,* 591–615.

4 Research designs in applied social psychology

MELISSA BURKLEY AND HART BLANTON

Research designs in applied social psychology

In 1999, Eric Harris and Dylan Klebold launched an assault on Columbine High School in Littleton, Colorado, murdering 13 people and wounding 23 before killing themselves. Similar school shootings have occurred in other communities, such as Paducah, Kentucky, Jonesboro, Arkansas, and, most recently, Blacksburg, Virginia. Although the exact causes for these attacks may never be known, one characteristic that these events share is that all the shooters were young adults who habitually played violent video games.

Since their introduction thirty years ago, video games have become increasingly violent. A review conducted in 1998 indicated that 80 per cent of video games on the market were violent in nature (Dietz, 1998). Unfortunately, little is known about the consequences of such exposure. Craig Anderson, along with his colleagues, has attempted to address this important social issue by designing a programme of research that investigates the relation between violent video game use and aggression. In our opinion, this line of research represents an ideal for the applied social scientist. Anderson and his colleagues created a research programme that uses multiple studies with multiple designs in order to investigate a socially relevant topic. As a result, our chapter will use this work as a springboard for discussing research design in applied social psychology.

Selecting a research method

Once a researcher decides upon the applied topic to be studied, the most important issue to address in designing a given study is determining which type of method to use. The researcher might choose to run an experiment in an artificial laboratory environment or to study behaviour *in situ* using a cross-sectional design, or the researcher might study a large representative sample using a random digital dialling technique. Myriad approaches to the study of applied social behaviours exist. Unfortunately, there rarely is a single 'right' decision that will help a researcher gain a complete grasp of any given applied problem and therefore deciding on a research method becomes a complex process. In short, all approaches to research designs have their unique advantages and disadvantages and so most research choices involve trade-offs. Joseph McGrath (1982)

Table 4.1 *Summary of the four research designs*

| | McGrath's properties | | |
Design	Precision	Generalizability to situations	Generalizability to people
True experiment	High	–	–
Correlational	–	High	–
Quasi-experimental	Moderate	Moderate	–
Survey	–	Sometimes	High

Figure 4.1 *Three-horned dilemma: most research choices involve trade-offs*

described the most common trade-offs researchers must consider as a 'three-horned dilemma'. He noted that the most common approaches to research vary in three desirable qualities: precision, generalizability to situations and generalizability to people. The researcher's dilemma lies in the fact that any attempt to maximize one of these qualities through a particular design will result in the reduction of the other two. Consequently, McGrath argues that in principle it is impossible to create an unflawed study. In order to address this problem, the good researcher must create a research programme that includes multiple studies that employ different designs, each of which maximizes one of the desirable qualities (Figure 4.1).

In this chapter, we adopt a similar approach to McGrath. We believe that there is no single perfect method – all research designs have flaws. Therefore, a good researcher must (1) know the unique advantages and disadvantages for each research design, (2) conduct studies that make the best use of each design's advantages while minimizing disadvantages and (3) carefully construct a research programme using multiple designs that compensate for each method's weaknesses. This chapter focuses on the four designs most commonly used by applied social psychologists: true experimental, correlational, quasi-experimental and survey. For each design, we will identify its defining attributes and provide an illustrative study from the literature on violent video games and aggression. Furthermore, we will describe each design's ability to capitalize on one of McGrath's three desired qualities and the limitations it possesses in respect to the other two. As a way of introduction, the key features we will outline are presented in Table 4.1.

True experiments: maximizing precision

As social psychologists, we are often concerned with uncovering the reasons behind social behaviours. For example, we may ask: What factors lead to binge drinking by students? Why do people litter? How can we reduce racism? All of these questions seek to discover the *cause* of a particular behaviour. When a researcher is most interested in isolating a causal factor, a true experiment typically will be the most informative. Although true experiments are often used in 'basic' research to test general theories, their ability to locate cause-and-effect relations makes them an ideal tool for the applied scientist as well. In fact, some have advocated an 'experimenting society', one in which experimental methods would be used to make informed decisions about all public policies (Campbell, 1969; Popper, 1966).

Defining features of true experiments

A **true experiment** has two components that allow it to test a causal relationship between two (or more) variables: manipulation and random assignment. **Manipulation** occurs when the experimenter systematically varies the level of one (or more) variables while holding constant other variables that may have an effect. The manipulated variable (potential cause) is referred to as an **independent variable** and the outcome variable (effect) is referred to as the **dependent variable**. Manipulation is employed to determine if changes in the independent variable lead to corresponding changes in the dependent variable. **Random assignment** occurs when the experimenter assigns participants to groups on an arbitrary basis. The use of random assignment therefore ensures that *every participant has an equal chance of being assigned to any condition in the experiment*. For an example of a true experiment, see Box 4.1.

Random assignment is essential to an experiment because it separates participants into groups that should be equal on every imaginable dimension. For example, an experimenter investigating the effect of violent video games may flip a coin to determine which participants are exposed to the violent game and which are exposed to the non-violent game. In doing so, the experimenter has every expectation that the participants in these two groups resemble one another in terms of age, intelligence, natural hostility and all other variables that might influence aggressive tendencies. If a study using random assignment does show that those in the violent video game condition display more aggressive behaviours on a subsequent task when compared to a control group, then the experimenter can be fairly confident that this difference in aggression was caused by exposure to the game's violence, and not by some other extraneous individual difference variable.

Box 4.1   Example of experimental research

Anderson and Dill (2000, study 2) designed an experiment to test the theory that violent video game play increases aggressive behaviour. A total of 210 undergraduate students were brought into a laboratory where they were randomly assigned to play several 15-minute sessions of a violent (*Wolfenstein 3D*) or non-violent (*Myst*) video game. Next, participants' aggressive behaviour was assessed through the competitive reaction time task, a common procedure used to measure aggressive behavior in a laboratory setting. Participants were led to believe they were competing against another student on a racing task in which they had to push a button faster than their opponent. When participants lost a trial, they received a noise blast at a level supposedly set by their opponent, but which the computer in fact set. When participants won a trial, they delivered a noise blast to their opponent. A total of 25 trials were administered and the participant always won 13 trials and lost 12. Aggressive behaviour was measured by the intensity and duration of the noise blasts participants selected to deliver to their opponent. Thus, in this study, the type of video game (violent vs non-violent) was manipulated and therefore was the independent variable, whereas aggressive behaviour (intensity and duration of noise blasts) was measured and therefore was the dependent variable.

The results of the study provided evidence that short-term exposure to violent video games causes an increase in aggressive behaviour (Figure 4.2). As predicted, participants who played the violent game delivered longer noise blasts after losing a trial ($M = 6.81$ seconds) compared to those who played the non-violent game ($M = 6.65$ seconds), $F(1, 87) = 4.82, p < .05$.

Advantages of true experiments

As already noted, true experiments are superior to other research designs in terms of their precision and this is the primary reason for studying an applied problem with this method. True experiments are able to maximize precision in several ways. First and foremost, true experiments eliminate the influence of confounds. A **confound** is an additional variable that systematically varies with the independent

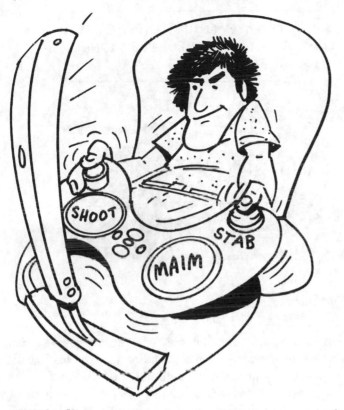

Figure 4.2 *Violent video games cause an increase in aggressive behaviour*

variable and influences the dependent variable. Confounds are particularly problematic because when one is present in a study, the experimenter is unable to determine if changes in the dependent variable are due to the independent variable or the confound (Figure 4.3).

Confounds can be broken into person confounds and procedural confounds (Pelham & Blanton, 2003) and both can be best addressed with true experiments. A **person confound** occurs when the presence of an individual difference influences the outcome variable. Because true experiments use random assignment, they are strongly protected against this type of confound. For example, one reason that violent video games may relate to aggression is simply that aggressive people prefer to play violent games. If this were the case, then aggression would not be caused by the type of video game, but rather by an individual difference. Now imagine if, instead of randomly assigning participants to play the *Myst* or *Wolfenstein 3D* game, Anderson and Dill had asked participants which game they would prefer to play and then measured subsequent aggression (described in Box 4.1). In this case, game preference would be a person confound and, as a result, the researchers would be unable to decipher if changes in aggressive

Figure 4.3 *Confounds*

behaviour were due to actual violent game use or to the individual's preference for violent games. By using random assignment, the influence of this potential person confound is eliminated. A **procedural confound** occurs when the experimenter unwittingly varies two or more variables at once. For example, in the Anderson and Dill experiment, all participants received identical recorded instructions over an intercom system. This was done to ensure the instructions were read to all participants in the same manner. Imagine instead that the researchers had hired two research assistants, one to administer instructions to those in the *Myst* condition and one for those in the *Wolfenstein 3D* condition. If this were the case, the different research assistants would be a procedural confound, because they covary with the type of game played. Such a confound would reduce our confidence in the causal interpretation of the results, because it is possible that the assistant in the *Myst* condition happened to be nicer, and that could be why the researchers found a difference in aggressive behaviour. Although there is nothing inherent in a true experiment that guards against confounds, the environment of the typical experiment does provide this protection. Most true experiments occur in a research laboratory, where researchers can orchestrate all of the experiences participants encounter. By carefully constructing experimental procedures that are free of confounds, laboratory researchers are able to avoid interpretational ambiguities regarding causality.

When true experiments are conducted in a laboratory, they not only reduce confounds but they can also minimize noise within a study. **Noise** refers to variables that influence the dependent variable, but, unlike confounds, they are evenly distributed across conditions (Pelham & Blanton, 2003). The presence of noise is problematic because it increases the variability in the dependent variable, thereby making it more difficult to detect the true influence of the independent variable. For example, factors such as time of day, temperature, mood and hunger could all influence how aggressively a participant may respond in a study. Each of these features can be held at a constant in a laboratory setting, greatly increasing the researcher's ability to observe causal relations that are of interest.

By increasing the experimenter's precision, true experiments offer the additional advantage of allowing researchers to test more complex predictions. In particular, they allow researchers to study statistical interactions. **Interactions** indicate that the *effect that one or more independent variables has on the dependent variable depends on an additional independent variable*. It often is important for applied researchers to test for statistical interactions in their data because, in the real world, causal factors commonly do combine in complex ways to influence behaviour.

It is out of an appreciation for statistical interactions that the **2 × 2 factorial design** has become the most common laboratory method for studying social behaviour. In this design, the investigator is interested in studying the independent and combined effects of two independent variables, each with two levels. For instance, a researcher may believe that violent video games increase aggression, but only when the participant identifies with the game's aggressor. The researcher would therefore be predicting an interaction between violent video games and aggressor identification. Unfortunately, such a design can only test the simplest of interaction patterns and it is unlikely that this single interaction fully captures the complex causal dynamics surrounding violent video games and aggression. However, a series of 2 × 2 factorial studies that investigate conceptually related interactions could break down a complex causal story into its simple parts. A programme of research that involves a series of simple 2 × 2 factorial studies might reveal, for instance, that violent game effects depend not only on aggressor identification but also on aggressor likeability, the degree of similarity between the actor and aggressor, and the level of realism of the video game. Combined, the distinct and simple interaction patterns that are uncovered in separate studies would support a single theory of aggression, one in which individuals internalize the behaviour of aggressive role models.

Statistical interactions are also useful because they identify the **boundary conditions** of a theory: conditions that demarcate when a theory does or does not apply. Boundary conditions are important to study because no theory that is of applied use will be correct under all circumstances (see McGuire, 1973). It is thus important for researchers to identify the limiting conditions of their theory. Not only does this improve the applicability of a theory by helping a researcher know the conditions under which it applies and the conditions under which it does not, but it also provides useful information regarding the nature and limits of the topic being studied. In the example just described, the presence of an interaction between violent games and aggressor identification would not only show that there are limits to the effects that violent video games can have on behaviour, but it also would provide a clue as to why such games increase aggression.

Disadvantages of true experiments

The true experiment's increased precision unfortunately comes at the cost of generalizability. Compared to other research designs, experiments are typically low in their ability to (1) generalize to other people and (2) generalize to other situations.

True experiments lack the ability to generalize to other people because they typically use convenience samples drawn from homogeneous populations. The best example of this is the common use of university students as research participants. True experiments rely on such narrow samples for both incidental and purposeful reasons. The incidental reason is that research laboratories are often situated on university campuses, and it is very easy and cost effective to utilize this resource. The purposeful reason is that using homogeneous samples reduces noise. Consider all of the potential factors that influence aggression that are held constant by using a student sample (e.g., age, education level, socioeconomic background). By limiting such 'noisy' factors, researchers are able to maximize precision in the ways we suggested earlier. But, by definition, this limits the ability to generalize the results to different populations.

Because homogeneous samples limit generalizability, many have argued that laboratory studies that rely on such samples are of limited value to applied researchers. It does seem compelling that a method that orients researchers towards convenience samples will also cause them to document results that will not generalize. Consider Anderson and Dill's experiment. If the students they studied were mostly white, affluent and well educated, then their results might not generalize to the many video game players who differ on these dimensions. Thus, a concern with Anderson and Dill's study is that it might reveal causal relations that only apply to a small subset of people who play video games.

Experiments are also quite low in their ability to generalize to different situations. This is in part because researchers' efforts to remove noise leaves them studying causal dynamics that occur in a setting that is more 'sterile' than those found in everyday life. It is also problematic that researchers often create situations in the laboratory that are contrived or patently artificial. To wit, Anderson and Dill's experiment used a measure of aggression that would not occur in everyday situations (giving noise blasts in a competitive game). This choice of behaviour is justifiable for much the same reasons as one justifies homogeneous samples. By having participants 'aggress' in a way that is unfamiliar to them, it is not likely that there will be variability in the sample's past experiences with this behaviour, thereby reducing noise. Although the use of a contrived form of aggression does aid in the pursuit of prediction, it might create concerns with generalizability. It may be that the form of aggression that Anderson and Dill studied would not generalize to more traditional forms of aggression (e.g., physical or emotional attacks).

Minimizing the disadvantages of true experiments

Although the reliance on convenience samples and contrived situations limits the ability of many true experiments to generalize, various strategies can be pursued to minimize these concerns. With regard to generalizing to situations, researchers can conduct experiments in applied settings that are of interest. With regards to generalizing to people, researchers can expand the list of samples in a series of steps. Although it is desirable for researchers to use a homogeneous sample for their study in order to maximize precision, they can pursue a programme of related studies that utilize a wide range of homogeneous samples. For instance, Anderson and Dill could conduct follow-up studies that use samples of adolescents from low socioeconomic families, samples of minority students and so forth. By expanding the range of samples in calculated steps, researchers can gain a sense of how their findings would apply to ever-expanding groups of interest.

The difficulty with these approaches, however, is that researchers can rarely, if ever, find the one 'perfect' situation that captures the range of situations of interest or the ideal complement of samples that will define the degree to which an effect generalizes to different people. Moreover, each new setting and each new sample will build in new constraints that might make it more difficult to carry out a study. For instance, although it is easy to manufacture situations where college students send 'noise blasts' at one another, it is a challenge (and ethically questionable) to set up situations where young children might come to blows in a school playground. It seems only natural that researchers who begin to confront the difficulties of studying exotic samples in real-world settings will feel a natural pull to return to the manufactured settings and convenience samples that give them the control they desire.

It would be a mistake, however, to assume that applied laboratory researchers have simply given up on the generalizability issue. More often than not, they have found ways of addressing this concern logically rather than empirically. To understand how this is done, it is useful to consider why researchers try to generalize their results. Aronson and Carlsmith (1968) noted that concerns for generalizability arise out of a more general desire for studies to be 'realistic'. Researchers who choose to study media influences on aggression will only have licence to comment on real-world phenomena if they have found ways of creating realistic video games that lead real groups of individuals to engage in realistic forms of aggression.

The concern for realism in research seems straightforward enough, but as Aronson and Carlsmith (1968) note, there are multiple ways of interpreting the realism of a laboratory experiment. Studies can be high in **mundane realism**, in the sense that the physical setting of the study is similar to the real-world setting in which the phenomenon of interest typically occurs. Consider as an example a researcher who wishes to determine if video games increase physical aggression among primary school children when they play together in the school playground. The researcher could randomly assign children to either play violent video games or not and measure the resulting rates of physical aggression that occur in a school playground. By having a 'realistic' sample and a real-world dependent variable, there is good reason to think that the results from such a study would generalize. But we do not think this researcher addressed the generalizability question in an optimal fashion. Although this hypothetical study would satisfy the researcher's goals, it would be done at great cost. Rather than tackling a broad research question, such as, 'Is there evidence that video game violence influences aggression?' this researcher focused on a very narrow applied issue in a specific population in a specific setting. It was only by defining the question in this way that the researcher was able to pursue mundane realism. However, as Aronson and Carlsmith (1968) note, this researcher might have been better off pursuing a different type of realism. Aronson and Carlsmith termed this second type *experimental realism*, although we prefer the term **psychological realism** (Pelham & Blanton, 2003).

Laboratory researchers maximize psychological realism not by asking if a given study 'looks' realistic on observable dimensions but rather by asking if it 'feels' realistic on psychological dimensions. The move to psychological realism reflects an appreciation of the obstacles that prevent researchers from replicating the mundane qualities of everyday life in the laboratory. Try as one might, the laboratory will rarely look like the real world. Even the act of studying people in the laboratory alters how they might feel and act. Nevertheless, one can pursue broad theoretical questions using the laboratory setting to recreate psychological dynamics of interest. As an example, it is telling that Anderson and Dill chose not to narrow their research question in such a way that it would allow them to focus attention on a specific group, a specific act or a specific social context where aggression might occur. By asking their question more broadly, Anderson and Dill were free to create a form of aggression in the laboratory that was probably 'realistic' in the psychological sense (in that participants felt aggressive when they used noise blasts), even if it was not realistic in the mundane sense (in that the noise blasts do not resemble more common forms of aggression). In fact, most of the research on violent video games and aggression are high in psychological realism, and, as a result, they are often shown to be high in external validity and are highly correlated with the effects from non-laboratory studies (see Anderson & Bushman, 1997, for review).

Although we believe that Anderson and Dill followed a strategy that laboratory researchers should frequently pursue, we acknowledge that psychologists will often feel they need to pursue mundane realism in order to show their research has applied implications. Applied psychologists are often called upon to reveal how specific factors (e.g., alcohol use) cause specific individuals (e.g., HIV-positive gay men) to engage in specific behaviours (e.g., unprotected sexual intercourse).

The research laboratory will rarely be able to accommodate these specifics. However, if a researcher is willing to step back and think about the more general psychological processes that influence specific phenomena (e.g., the way in which intoxication raises feelings of invulnerability and thereby promotes a risky decision), then the research laboratory will again become useful. By defining research questions in the broadest possible terms, applied laboratory researchers can find realism in even the most contrived of laboratory studies and thereby gain precision and control.

Correlational research: generalizing to situations

Sometimes, however, researchers do have specific questions in mind and do worry about the mundane. Consider again the researcher interested in studying the risky sexual practices of gay men. This person might learn a fair amount about the psychological processes that increase risk in this group by studying tendencies in the laboratory, but the studies that result will be far removed from the actual topic that was originally of interest. Dissatisfaction with the ability of true experiments to invoke mundane reality has led many researchers to focus on correlational methods. We now turn to this method and describe how researchers can use correlational methods to generalize to situations (we explain how researchers generalize to people in a later section on survey methodology).

Correlational research investigates the relationship between different measured variables, typically with an interest in determining how these variables interrelate in naturally occurring situations. For example, the applied social scientist may ask: Do illusions of invulnerability predict riskier sexual practices among adolescents, are wealthy people happier or do men and women differ in their spending habits? Notice that all these questions ask if a relationship exists between two variables without a strong statement about a causal link, as would be more common in a true experiment. Notice also that each question brings to mind both a phenomenon and a situation that are intrinsically meaningful. It is this concern for specific situations that cause many researchers to pursue correlational research.

Defining features of correlational research

When conducting a correlational study, the researcher must generate a fixed set of observations about a group of people. For example, one could decide to investigate whether or not increased exposure to violent video games is related to the number of fights an adolescent engages in at school. Once a research question of this sort is seized upon, the correlational researcher must tackle the thorny issue of measurement. Unlike in true experiments, where some variables are manipulated, correlational research takes a more passive approach to studying variability. All variables in a correlational study are allowed to vary naturally and the applied researcher merely assesses the variables of interest. To assess video game exposure in an adolescent sample, for instance, one could ask adolescents to report on the type of games played and the amount of time devoted to them. To assess fighting behaviour, one could interview teachers, search school records or observe adolescents' behaviour in and outside the classroom. For an example of a correlational study, see Box 4.2.

Once measures are developed and data are collected, the correlational researcher must statistically analyse the relationships between these measured variables to determine if they are largely consistent or inconsistent with the predicted hypotheses. The simplest way of doing this in a correlational study is to compute a correlation coefficient. The **correlation coefficient** ranges from −1 to +1. The absolute numerical value indicates the magnitude of the relation, with higher numbers showing a stronger connection between the variables. The sign indicates the direction of the relationship. A **positive correlation** indicates that as the value of one variable increases, so does the other variable. A **negative correlation** indicates that as the value of one variable increases, the other variable decreases. It is important to note that a common misconception is that 'correlational research' occurs any time a researcher reports a correlation coefficient. This is not true and it is important not to confuse correlational *statistics* with correlational *research*.

Box 4.2   Example of correlational research

Anderson and Dill (2000, study 1) conducted a correlational study to investigate the long-term effects of violent video game play. A total of 227 university students responded to questions regarding their use of video games (e.g., type of games played, time spent playing), self-reported aggressive behaviour, delinquency behaviour and academic achievement. Consistent with the researchers' predictions, long-term exposure to violent video games was positively related to aggressive behaviour ($r = .46, p < .05$) and delinquency behaviour ($r = .31, p < .05$), but not academic achievement ($r = .08, p > .05$). Importantly, these relationships remained significant even after statistically removing the influence of participants' aggressive personality, gender and time spent playing video games in general, $B = .24, p < .05$. The percentage of variance accounted for dropped from 21 per cent to 13 per cent when these variables were included. Thus, this study provides strong correlational evidence that long-term exposure to violent video games can lead to increases in aggressive and delinquent behaviours.

Advantages of correlational research

As previously noted, the primary advantage of correlational research is that it maximizes generalizability to situations. Behaviours of interest can be measured within natural settings, thereby increasing the chances that the research findings are representative of what occurs naturally in the 'real world'. Well-implemented correlational studies can be very adept at uncovering normal relations among variables, and as a result they are often conducted as the initial stage of a research programme. Correlational research can also provide a follow-up to a true experiment by testing if an effect that was established in the lab actually occurs in the real world.

Because correlational research focuses on naturally occurring variables, this method is particularly useful when circumstances prevent the use of manipulations. Some variables, such as gender or personality, are impossible to manipulate experimentally. Similarly, some variables, such as inflicting participants with extreme stress or physical danger cannot be ethically manipulated. Nor would it be ethical (or practical) to expose adolescents to sustained violent video games to see if they do in fact grow up with violence problems. However, these circumstances do occur 'in nature' and most psychologists feel it is morally responsible to study people who are placed in such situations by naturally occurring circumstances.

Disadvantages of correlational research

In order to increase generalizability to situations, correlational research forfeits measurement precision. This lack of control results in the design's primary limitation: *inability to infer causality*. As the old adage goes, 'correlation does not equal causation'. The reason for this is that there are multiple ways to interpret a significant correlation between two variables. For example, if a correlational study demonstrates a positive relationship between hours spent playing violent video games and aggressive behaviour, we cannot interpret this as evidence that game playing causes aggression. First, the true direction of this relationship may be reversed. It is just as plausible to assert that aggressive adolescents are more interested in playing violent video games than non-aggressive individuals. This is referred to as an issue of **reverse causality**. Additionally, there may be a **third variable problem**, such that an additional variable is responsible for the observed relation between these two variables. It may be that children who are raised in families with poor parenting skills are more likely to be aggressive and more likely to be allowed to play violent video games. In this case, the relationship between game play and aggression is *spurious*; it only exists because these two variables share a similar cause. Therefore, for every correlational relationship there exist three potential explanations: causality, reverse causality and a third variable. Because this method does not allow us to disentangle these various interpretations, we can conclude that a relationship exists but we cannot state the nature or direction of this relationship.

Although correlational studies are high in generalizability to situations, they tend not to be high in generalizability to other people. Correlational studies are less likely than experiments to only include university students, yet many studies do rely on this convenience sample (e.g., the Anderson and Dill study described above). Sometimes researchers will leave the comfortable confines of the university campus to study special samples that are pertinent to a particular study and the 'portability' of questionnaires is often an improvement over true experiments. A researcher studying correlates of academic striving in a Latino population will probably go to a town or district with a large Latino population and a researcher interested in studying the correlates of aggression in incarcerated populations will probably seek permission to bring paper and sharp pencils into local prisons. It is important to realize, however, that even these samples are restricted in their scope. One has no assurance that a sample of nearby Latino students or a group of neighbouring prisoners are representative of the entire population of Latino students or prisoners that might be relevant to one's theory. Moreover, just as there is pressure in experimental studies to limit the heterogeneity of samples in order to reduce noise, so too is the case for correlational studies. It might be feasible to study the sexual habits of commercial sex workers to get some sense of the health beliefs of 'high HIV risk' individuals, but it seems unlikely that any one study can target all the groups that comprise the high-risk category (intravenous drug users, individuals with other venereal diseases, etc.). Consequently, this limits one's confidence in generalizing the results of correlational studies to other populations of interest.

Minimizing the disadvantages of correlational studies

Although correlational methods are inherently limited in their ability to determine causality, good researchers do not accept these shortcomings without a fight. As you will see, the primary strategies that researchers pursue are statistical in nature.

With regard to third-variable problems, the most common method for addressing this concern is through the use of **covariates**. Recall that Anderson and Dill found effects of violent video games on aggression, even after controlling for aggressive personality, gender and time spent playing video games overall. Their use of these statistical controls reflected their deliberate attempt to address a plausible set of third-variable confounds. If covariates were not included in this study, Anderson and Dill would know only that long-term exposure to violent video games was positively related to aggressive behaviour and their findings would be less compelling. For example, consider the role that aggressive personality might play. It could be that an aggressive personality (1) causes people to engage in more aggressive behaviours and also (2) causes people to like violent video games. These two causal effects could result in a spurious correlation between violent game use and aggressive behaviour. However, by measuring aggressive personality as a covariate and statistically removing its effects on aggressive behaviour, Anderson and Dill provided strong evidence that the relationship between violent game use and aggression was not due to this particular variable.

Is the result of this (or any other) statistical control conclusive? Certainly not. It is entirely possible that Anderson and Dill did not use a very good measure of aggressive personality and so they did a poor job of covarying out this variable's effect on aggression. It is also important to be mindful that, although the measure of aggressive personality did not eliminate the effect of interest, this does not mean that some other personality variable is not acting as a third variable. It could be that variables such as self-esteem or sensation seeking are leading to spurious correlations between video game exposure and aggressive behaviour. Therefore, correlational researchers must have strong theories that guide their efforts to identify relevant covariates.

When researchers do have strong theories that suggest a plausible third variable, they should seek valid measures of these constructs and include them in their studies. It is important to note, however, that it will never be possible to think of every third variable that might be increasing correlations. No matter how diligent a researcher may be, no study can ever offer definitive proof that some third variable or another is not operating, and this is one reason that a correlational result can never establish causation. Nevertheless, a researcher who gives careful thought to the third-variable problem and who accurately measures and statistically controls for such variables can address many of the most obvious concerns.

But third variables are only part of the problem. Correlational studies are also open to alternative interpretations due to reverse causality. Researchers who address this issue rely on covariates as well, but they also pair these with a design change. As previously mentioned, researchers may incorporate **longitudinal designs** into their correlational studies whenever reverse causality offers a plausible alternative explanation. In a longitudinal design, the variables of interest are measured at two (or more) time periods and then the correlations between these variables are analysed between and across time points. Such a design allows researchers to track individuals over time in order to determine if changes in the predictor variables at one point in time lead to changes in the outcome variable at subsequent points in time. For example, Eron, Lefkowitz, Husemann and Walder (1972) assessed violent media exposure and aggressive behaviour in over two hundred boys during grade 3 (ages 8–9) and again at grade 13 (ages 18–19). At grade 3, there was a significant correlation between preference for violent media and aggression. Although this could be due to the fact that violent media exposure causes aggression, it is also possible that aggressive temperament causes a preference for violent media. To rule out this second possibility, the grade 3 measures were correlated with the grade 13 measures (see Figure 4.4). The results showed that there was a significant correlation between violent media preference at grade 3 and aggression at grade 13 ($r = .31$). Conversely, there was no significant correlation between aggression at grade 3 and violent media preference at grade 13

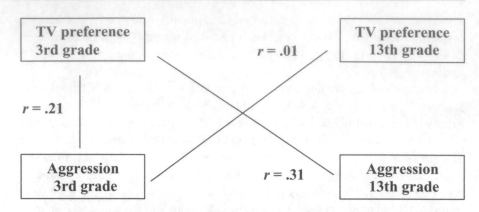

Figure 4.4 *Effects of violent media preference and aggression during grade 3 and grade 13 (Eron et al., 1972)*

($r = .01$). These data provide support for the idea that violent media exposure causes aggression, and not the other way around, even though the researchers did not use an experimental design.

Although longitudinal designs are quite useful, we believe it is important that researchers using such designs also include relevant covariates. This is because measures at time-1 can serve as indirect indicators of reverse causality. For example, imagine a researcher discovers that video game use at time-1 is correlated with aggression six months later at time-2. The reverse causality explanation cannot be completely discarded because it is possible that game use at time-1 served as an indicator of aggression at time-1. Thus, violent game use at time-1 might correlate with aggression at time-2, simply because an indirect indicator of aggression at time-1 can predict aggression at time-2. This is why longitudinal designs typically include covariates.

In most instances, researchers can address this issue by measuring the outcome variable at time-1 and covarying out this estimate when predicting time-2 levels from the time-1 predictor variable. For example, the researcher could measure both the predictor variable (violent video game play) and a premeasure of the outcome variable (aggressive behaviour) at time-1. At time-2, the researcher would then measure the outcome variable a second time. If violent game use predicts aggression at time-2, controlling for aggression at time-1, then this result offers highly suggestive evidence that reverse causality is not a concern.

Although a longitudinal study that controls for prior levels of the outcome can offer some assurance against reverse causality, there are limitations to this procedure as well. As with standard third variables, the strategy of covarying out prior measures of the outcome will fail if one uses bad measures. It is also important to find a meaningful time period to build into a longitudinal study when setting it up. In the hypothetical study above, the researcher assumed that violent video games would predict aggression six months later. But what if the effect is more immediate and then dissipates before six months have passed? In this case, a researcher using a six-month follow-up will have difficulty detecting the true effects of violent video games on aggression. It is informative in this regard to look again at the methods in Anderson and Dill.

Anderson and Dill did not use a longitudinal design but instead had participants list their video game use at various times in the past (e.g., 'in recent months', 'during the ninth and tenth grades'). We suspect that the range of time periods they used reflected their appreciation of the many different time courses that might be plausible. Rather than tracking a group of individuals for six months (or more or less) and then finding out the chosen time period was inappropriate, these researchers began by conducting a study that relied on retrospective self-report. A good follow-up to their study would be to track behaviour over time to determine if the self-report results would replicate in a longitudinal design.

In summary, correlational studies can address problems of third variables and reverse causality by (1) controlling for known third variables, (2) incorporating longitudinal designs and (3) controlling for past levels of the outcome variable. When good measures of covariates are employed and when analyses are guided by a strong theory, these strategies can provide strong evidence in support of a specific causal interpretation.

That said, neither of these strategies is definitive and so the experimenter who wishes to assert causality must return to the research laboratory, where the concern for generalizability will again rear its head. It is also important to realize that these statistical techniques do not address the shortcoming that correlational research shares with true experiments: inability to generalize to people. Before turning to ways of maximizing generalizability to people, we first consider an experimental design that tries to balance the desire for precision against the desire to generalize to situations, namely the quasi-experimental design.

Quasi-experiments: compromising between precision and generalizability to situations

In many circumstances, a researcher may want to combine the benefits of an experiment with the benefits of correlational research. This is often the case when we want to keep a great deal of control in our study but for some reason it is impossible to assign participants randomly to conditions. For example, we may want to investigate the relationship between a poor parenting environment and aggression, but we cannot randomly assign participants to live with good or bad parents. In such a case, the researcher can employ a quasi-experimental design.

Defining features of quasi-experimental research

In a **quasi-experimental design**, the researcher has only partial control over the independent variables. Because random assignment is impossible, participants are assigned to groups based on some other, usually naturally occurring, crite-rion. These designs, however, are still particularly high in the level of control over dependent and extraneous variables. For example, rather than assigning participants to violent or non-violent video game conditions, we could select par-ticipants based on their previous game-playing behaviour. To do so, we would identify students who often play with violent video games (experimental group) and students who never play such games (control group). We could then bring them into the lab and have them participate in the noise-blast task. For an example of a quasi-experiment, see Box 4.3.

Although there are many types of quasi-experimental designs (see Campbell & Stanley, 1963), one of the most commonly used designs in social psychol-ogy is the **person-by-treatment quasi-experiment**. In this design, one of the independent variables is *manipulated* (treatment variable) and one is *measured* (person variable). This design is structured just like a true experiment but with the addition of a second naturally occurring independent variable. This design is popular among applied psychologists because it allows the researcher to examine if different people (people with different attitudes, personalities, demographic characteristics) respond differently to different treatments (or situations) and this can help them get a better understanding of both individual and situational influ-ences of interest. Consider, for example, a researcher who believes that exposure to violent video games causes adolescents to become desensitized to violence. This hypothesis could be tested using a person-by-treatment quasi-experimental design, whereby adolescents with or without a history of violent game use (person variable) are randomly assigned to view either violent or non-violent television shows (treatment variable) while measuring their physiological reactivity (e.g., heart rate, pupil dilation, etc.). If the high game use adolescents showed less phys-iological reactivity while watching violent shows compared with the other groups, this would provide evidence that game exposure leads to violence desensitization.

Even though quasi-experiments have less control than true experiments, there are particular measurement procedures that increase precision in these designs. One way in which a researcher can do this is through the use of statistical controls such as covariates. In a true experiment, random assignment would offer strong assurance that the experimental groups are equivalent on variables other than our independent variable and would reduce the influence of potential confounds. Because a quasi-experiment does not utilize random assignment for all variables, such assurances are no longer present. Some confidence in interpretation can be recovered, however, with the thoughtful use of statistical covariates.

As mentioned previously, covariates allow experimenters statistically to remove the influence of variables. When potential confounds are known, they can be mea-sured and their influence covaried out of the dependent variable, thereby equating the groups along these dimensions. Recall the hypothetical study examining phys-iological reactivity to violent television. Although the expected results would be highly suggestive, various person confounds would not be eliminated (due to the lack of random assignment to high and low exposure groups) and this can introduce ambiguities. In short, the adolescents with a history of violent game use might differ in a variety of ways from their counterparts who do not play video games, and these differences might be driving the effects observed in the laboratory. A wide range of factors, from physical health to social maturity, could be causing the appearance of a spurious effect. However, by measuring these constructs before the study and statistically removing their influence, the researcher can increase confidence that these particular person confounds are not creating the differences observed. Of course, one can never be sure that all relevant person confounds were measured. As a result, covariates are not as powerful as random assignment in creating confidence about causal interpretations. Still, a qualified assurance that person confounds are not driving an effect is better than no assurance. For this reason, statistical covariates are built into quasi-experimental studies to a greater degree than true experiments (for further discussion of covariates, see Jaccard, 2007).

Box 4.3   Example of quasi-experimental research

Bartholow and Anderson (2002) conducted a person-by-treatment quasi-experimental study to investigate gender differences in the relationship between video game violence and aggression. Previous research on the effects of video game violence among women and men is mixed, with some studies showing sex differences and others showing no differences. However, most of these studies had been conducted with young children, so it was unclear if such gender effects would be present in young adults. Bartholow and Anderson therefore conducted a study comparing the effects of video game violence in female and male university students.

The structure of the study was similar to the Anderson and Dill experiment described in Box 4.1, with the addition of a second, non-manipulated variable: gender. Forty-three undergraduate students (twenty-two men and twenty-one women) were brought into the lab and randomly assigned to play *Mortal Kombat* (violent) or *PGA Tournament Golf* (non-violent) for ten minutes. Next, participants completed the competitive reaction time task. Intensity of the noise blasts given to one's opponent were recorded on a scale ranging from one (60 decibels) to ten (105 decibels) and served as the measure of aggression.

To analyse the data, Bartholow and Anderson used a 2 (violent vs non-violent game) × 2 (men vs women) analysis of variance. First, there was a significant main effect of video game violence, $F(1, 35) = 11.06, p < .01$. Those who played *Mortal Kombat* delivered higher-level noise punishments ($M = 5.97$) than those who played *PGA Tournament Golf* ($M = 4.60$). Second, there was a significant main effect of gender, $F(1, 35) = 5.01$, $p < .05$. Men delivered more intense noise punishments ($M = 5.61$) than women ($M = 4.80$). Importantly, there was also a significant interaction

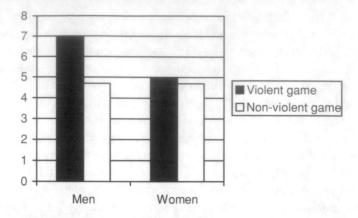

Figure 4.5 *Effects of video game violence and gender on noise blast intensity (Bartholow & Anderson, 2002)*

between these two variables, $F(1, 35) = 5.13, p < .05$. As can be seen in Figure 4.5, men in the violent condition delivered greater intensity noise blasts than men in the non-violent condition, $t(18) = 3.09, p < .01$; however, this was not the case for women, $t(19) = 1.12, p > .25$. This study also included a second measure of aggression: the number of times high-intensity settings were used. The results showed that the violent game increased the number of high-intensity trials to a greater degree for men than for women, once again resulting in a significant interaction, $F(1, 35) = 6.69, p < .05$.

This study was an important addition to the video game literature because it demonstrated that the relationship between video game violence and aggression is more complex than previously thought. It appears that men are more sensitive than women to the deleterious effects of violent games and it is likely that other individual differences, such as trait hostility or violence desensitization, may also be influential factors. By including non-manipulated variables such as these, quasi-experimental studies provide a more realistic picture of the complex relationship between video game violence and real-world aggression. In future studies, plausible third-variable accounts of this gender difference might be explored by including covariates that are statistically controlled.

Advantages of quasi-experimental research

Quasi-experiments are advantageous because they offer a compromise between the 'strict' true experiment and the 'loose' correlational study. Unlike correlational studies, this design preserves much of the control over confounds and extraneous variables that occur with true experiments. Unlike true experiments, this design lends itself to natural measures of behaviour and it can be used to study independent variables that would be impossible or unethical to manipulate in the lab. This design therefore differs from the ones discussed earlier in that it does not seek to maximize one of McGrath's desired qualities at the expense of the other two. Instead, it takes the middle-of-the-road approach by seeking a moderate level of precision while providing some assurances that the results will generalize to meaningful situations.

Disadvantages of quasi-experimental research

Because quasi-experiments combine aspects of true experiments with correlational studies, any particular quasi-experiment can fall short on one or more of the problems associated with its parts. Thus, a bad quasi-experimental design can be imprecise and fail to generalize to situations. The extent to which these disadvantages are present depends upon where the quasi-experiment falls on the 'experiment-to-correlational' continuum. Quasi-experiments that closely resemble true experiments (by using laboratory methods) are more likely to suffer from artificiality. Quasi-experiments that resemble correlational studies (by going into the field) are more likely to suffer from the influence of confounds and noise. Finally, generalizability to people is typically limited in the ways described for true experiments and correlational studies. The limitations of the quasi-experiment can be addressed in many of the ways discussed above, but none of these address the issue of generalizing to people. This concern is addressed by an entirely distinct design.

Survey research: generalizing to people

All research questions are aimed at generalizing to a particular population of individuals. The population of interest may be broad (citizens of the United States), or narrow (entry-level employees at IBM). Unless the population is quite small, such that every individual within it can be studied, researchers typically select a sample (or subset) from this population. The driving assumption behind samples is that the data collected from this smaller group will yield insights that generalize to the larger population of interest. However, the generalizability of the data depends on how representative the sample is of the population. For example, a sample of students from a wealthy university in Italy probably does not adequately represent the majority of Italian citizens. This lack of representativeness may not be a problem if one is studying psychological phenomena that do not vary across educational or socioeconomic levels, but it would be a serious problem if one were studying phenomena that do (e.g., political attitudes, body image concerns). If the effect of interest in a study varies in systematic ways across subgroups within a population, then a study can be misleading if these subgroups are not represented in the sample to the same degree as in the population. Thus, to generalize from a sample to a population, one must have a *representative sample*.

Defining features of survey research

Survey research is broadly defined as *the process of collecting information from a sample of people who have been systematically selected to represent a larger population*. By engaging in procedures to ensure that the sample is representative of the population of interest, the researcher gains a degree of confidence that the results will generalize to the population. Researchers often incorrectly use the term 'survey' to refer to any study that uses a questionnaire; the term survey should be restricted in use to refer only to studies that have some form of systematic sampling. For an example of a survey, see Box 4.4.

The primary challenge in designing a survey is in regard to the selection of a sample. Fortunately, there are several procedures that a researcher can use to ensure a representative sample. A common method is random sampling. **Random sampling** selects participants from the larger population in a random fashion. In essence, this procedure places everyone from the population into a 'lottery' where they have an equally likely chance of being selected to participate in the study. In practice, however, it is rarely this simple. Researchers often have incomplete lists of potential respondents and have to draw on imperfect sources. For instance, a common way of generating a participant list is to use random digit dialling, in which a computer randomly generates telephone numbers. This method will ensure that even respondents with unlisted numbers are equally likely to be chosen. When a sample is drawn using this procedure, there is good reason to assume that the sample chosen closely resembles the population of people who have phone numbers. But this population may or may not resemble the population of interest. If one wishes to assess the life satisfaction of Americans in general, then random digit dialling will, at best, provide only an estimate of the life satisfaction of people who have phone numbers. These individuals might be happier than people who do not have phone numbers.

Another challenge to conducting a population survey is that one will often want to administer surveys in person, though it can be prohibitively expensive to contact all the individuals that would be chosen for a completely random sample. Imagine how many places one might have to travel to if random digit dialling was used to identify a random sample of participants. One method for minimizing the logistical problems involved in conducting surveys is cluster sampling. **Cluster sampling** is an alternative to random sampling. Researchers who use this technique begin by creating a population list of locations rather than people. Instead of selecting from a list of all US high school students, a researcher who is conducting a cluster sample might begin with a list of all US high schools and then randomly sample a subset of schools to study in more detail. If this procedure yielded 20 different schools, the researcher could then travel to each of these schools and obtain a list of students. From these lists, it would be possible randomly to sample students for further study. Although a study such as this would be difficult, it would be considerably easier than trying to work with a completely random sample.

Whether a researcher uses random sampling, cluster sampling or one of the many other sampling techniques available to survey researchers, a population survey can reveal fairly accurate information about trends occurring within a population of interest. Of course, these estimates will never be entirely accurate. Although 80 per cent of the high school students in a cluster sample might have played a particular video game, this does not mean that exactly 80 per cent of all US high school students have done similarly. One advantage of drawing a random sample, however, is that this procedure makes it possible to estimate how much error is likely to exist in a sample estimate. The error associated with a sample estimate is called sampling error (i.e., *margin of error*).

Sampling error is the likely discrepancy between the results obtained in a representative sample and the results one would have obtained if everyone in the population of interest had been studied. Suppose, for instance, that 80 per cent of all of the students in a random sample state that they have played *Doom*. Using conventional probability values of 5%, a 3% margin of error in this study would indicate that there is a 95% likelihood that the actual percentage for the population is 80%, plus or minus 3% (i.e. between 77% and 83%). One of the interesting things about population surveys is that one can obtain a very high degree of certainty (i.e., small margin of error) using reasonably small samples to estimate quite large populations. To estimate the video game use of all US high school students, for instance, one might only need to work with a sample of 1,000 students.

Box 4.4   Example of survey research

To our knowledge, there are no survey studies specifically designed to assess the use of violent video games and their relation to aggressive behaviour. This is likely because video games are a fairly new societal influence. In fact, violent video games only emerged in the 1980s and the level of realism only became a concern for most in the 1990s. However, a few national surveys have looked at the overall influence of media use in children, including that of video games. For example, the Kaiser Family Foundation worked with Stanford University professor Donald Roberts to design a national survey of media use in US children aged 2–18 (Roberts, Foehr, Rideout & Brodie, 1999).

The study reported results from two nationally representative samples, which when combined totalled 3,155 children. The first sample consisted of 1,090 children ages 2–7. This sample was obtained by randomly selecting from a US Census list of 225,000 neighbourhood groups in the continental United States. The second sample consisted of 2,065 students in grades 3–12 (ages 8–18). To obtain this sample, schools were first randomly selected from a list of 80,000 state, independent and faith schools in the United States. Next, grades and classes within these grades were randomly selected to participate in the survey.

A wealth of data was collected in this survey, but of particular interest was the reported use of video games among children. Although the survey did differentiate by types of media, it did not make a distinction between violent and non-violent video game use. Nonetheless, previous research has shown that the majority of young children who play video games prefer ones that are violent in nature (73% of boys and 59% of girls; Buchman & Funk, 1996). The Kaiser Family Foundation survey showed that television is the most frequently used media, comprising over 50% of the children's media use. However, video games seemed to be increasing in popularity, with 30% of the sample playing video games. For children aged 8 to 13 years, game use was more pronounced, with a daily average of 32 minutes of game play and 13% of this age group reported spending over an hour per day on video games. Among older children (14–18 yrs), game play dropped to 20 minutes daily. In addition to these age differences in game use, gender differences were also found, with 44% of boys versus 17% of girls playing video games. Boys were also found to play the games longer (average of 31 minutes daily) than girls (average 8 minutes daily). Thus, the overall results suggest that video games are most popular among children in the middle age range (8–13) and particularly with boys, who play them more often and longer than girls. Moreover, because this study had a margin of error of just 3%, one can feel fairly confident that the results from this study are representative of national trends. These descriptive results have important implications for video game researchers, particularly in identifying which populations are at greatest risk for the deleterious influences already uncovered in experimental and correlational research.

Advantages of survey research

When researchers adhere to systematic sampling procedures, surveys are the most capable method for describing and representing information about a large population. This is why surveys and polls are commonly used by the government and media, as well as by applied social scientists. Surveys have been used to make informed decisions regarding public policies, to predict voting behaviours, to market new products, to test psychological theories and to provide assistance in addressing important societal problems. Clearly, the survey is an efficient and flexible method that can be employed for a wide range of uses.

Disadvantages of survey research

Unfortunately, there are several disadvantages associated with survey research. As would be expected, the increased ability to generalize results to people typically comes at the cost of the other two 'horns' of research, precision and generalizability to situations. In addition, survey research is costly, in terms of time and

Figure 4.6 *Context of survey research can impact the quality of the data*

money, and the sampling process used typically involves complex and technical procedures that require the use of paid consultants. Moreover, researchers must pay especially careful attention to many aspects of the design process in order to ensure the quality of the survey. Question wording, format, order and context can all dramatically impact the quality of the data and the accuracy of the conclusions (see Schwarz, 1996) (Figure 4.6). Finally, survey questionnaires must often be short because of limited time for interviews or limited space for mailings. As a result, the researcher is restricted in the types of questions that can be asked and the amount of detail that can be assessed. For this reason, surveys are generally used for descriptive purposes. Although relationships between variables can be assessed, doing so is more difficult given the heterogeneity of the samples studied.

Minimizing disadvantages of survey research

The best way to minimize the disadvantages of survey research is to pair a sampling procedure with either a true experimental or a correlational design. For instance, one could randomly assign a randomly selected sample to one of two experimental conditions to determine if video game violence influences aggression in a population of interest. Suppose, for instance, that Anderson and Dill had used a random sample in their laboratory study on violent video games and aggression (described in Box 4.1). They might randomly select a group of high school students for their study so that they could assert with confidence that their influences generalize to US high school students. Although such a study would be a powerful addition to their research programme, it is not at all practical. The financial and practical constraints that would stand in the way of bringing a representative sample into the laboratory are great. Imagine how expensive it would be to cover the travelling expenses of 50 participants coming from all corners of the country! By considering the difficulty of bringing representative samples to the lab, one begins to appreciate why laboratory researchers finesse this issue by defining their questions more broadly. Similar concerns arise when one considers the challenges of tracking large and representative samples over time in a longitudinal design. Although there are some remarkable examples of longitudinal studies that use large and representative samples (see Bearman, Jones & Udry, 1997), the costs and challenges are prohibitive. For this reason, survey research tends to stand on its own. It is the only method designed to address McGrath's (1982) concern for generalizing to people, but the pursuit of this method typically forces the researcher to sit squarely on the other two horns.

Conclusion

Summary

The various methods available to the applied social scientist have distinct advantages and disadvantages. A true experiment offers superior precision and control, but is generally lacking in the ability to generalize its findings to other situations and people. The ways of minimizing these disadvantages rely on the pursuit of psychological realism, leading researchers to test broad theories about human nature rather than narrow theories regarding specific phenomena. Correlational research measures behaviours in their natural setting, thus maximizing generalizability to other situations; however, the design is low in precision and generalizability to other people. The ways of minimizing these disadvantages rely on the use of statistical controls and longitudinal designs. Quasi-experiments offer a compromise between experimental and correlational research. This particular design preserves some of the control found in true experiments, but also includes naturally occurring groups. As a result, the design has moderate levels of precision and generalizability to situations. Finally, survey research maximizes generalizability to people by employing complex sampling procedures. However, this is often at the cost of precision and ability to infer causality.

Programmatic research

Because each method has its own advantages and disadvantages, and because the methods of minimizing the disadvantages typically are suboptimal, researchers interested in understanding the full nature of an applied problem will typically want to engage in multi-method research. Although no single study can maximize precision and the two forms of generalizability, a programme of multiple studies that uses several methods can offer multiple assurances. Multi-method research is particularly powerful when a researcher is mindful of the shortcomings of each method and works carefully to address these problems in each of the individual studies. Attention to psychological realism in experimental studies, statistical controls in correlational and quasi-experimental research and the combination of surveys with other methods can offer assurances that the conclusions drawn are valid. We illustrated this point by examining the research on aggression, particularly the research by Craig Anderson and his colleagues. Although each study conducted by these researchers informed us about the relationship between violent video games and aggression, it is the entire research programme as a whole that provides the most valuable information. Because these researchers used varying methods and designs, we can be quite confident that media violence causes aggression in a number of ways and through a number of mechanisms, and that this effect occurs in the laboratory and real-world settings.

From our analysis of these studies, we hope it is clear to the reader that the applied research process involves a series of interrelated choices. One should not view the research process as an attempt to find the 'right' design for studying a particular behaviour – no single design can answer all questions. Rather, the researcher should view this process as a set of negotiations. Instead of trying to avoid design disadvantages altogether, a good researcher addresses them head-on by understanding each study's limitations and then developing a strong research programme in which each study compensates for the others' weaknesses.

Glossary

Boundary conditions: conditions that distinguish when a theory does or does not apply.

Cluster sampling: a sampling technique in which the investigator first selects several subgroups of potential participants and then randomly samples from these subsets.

Confound: some additional variable that affects the dependent variable and varies systematically with the independent variable(s).

Correlation coefficient: a statistic used to represent the association between two variables (ranges from -1 to $+1$).

Correlational research: a study in which the investigator measures several variables and assesses the relationship between these variables.

Covariates: nuisance variables whose influences are statistically controlled.

Dependent variable: the variable in an experiment that is measured (expected effect).

Independent variable: the variable in an experiment that is manipulated by the experimenter (expected cause).

Interaction: occurs when the effect of an independent variable on the dependent variable varies as a function of the level of another independent variable.

Longitudinal design: a correlational research design in which the investigator measures the variables of interest at several time points.

Manipulation: systematically exposing different groups to different levels of a variable.

Mundane realism: the degree that a physical setting in an experiment is similar to the real world setting in which the independent and dependent variables are most likely to operate.

Negative correlation: indicates that as the value of one variable increases, the value of the other variable decreases.

Noise: nuisance variables that influence the dependent variable.

Person confound: a confound caused by an individual difference variable.

Person-by-treatment quasi-experimental design: a design in which one of the independent variables is manipulated (treatment) and one is measured (person).

Positive correlation: indicates that as the value of one variable increases, the value of the other variable also increases.

Procedural confound: a confound caused by a methodological problem.

Psychological realism: the degree that the subjective experiences of research participants are realistic and psychologically meaningful.

Quasi-experimental design: a design in which the researcher has only partial control over the independent variables.

Random assignment: technique used to assign participants to different conditions in the experiment. It ensures that every person in the study has an equal chance of being assigned to any of the conditions.

Random sampling: a sampling technique that ensures every person in the population has an equal chance of being selected into the study.

Reverse causality: when two variables are related, it is not possible to tell which variable caused the other.

Sampling error: the discrepancy between the results based on a selected sample and the results one would have obtained if everyone in the population had been studied.

Survey research: research that employs complex sampling procedures.

Third variable problem: when two variables are related, it may be because a third variable causes the other two.

True experiment: a study in which the investigator exposes two or more seemingly identical groups of participants to different levels of a manipulated variable(s).

2 × 2 factorial design: a design consisting of 2 independent variables, with each independent variable having 2 levels.

Review questions

1. According to McGrath, what are the three desirable qualities in a research study? How can a researcher design a research programme that maximizes all three qualities?
2. What are the defining features of a true experiment? What are the advantages and disadvantages associated with a true experiment?
3. When would a researcher prefer a quasi-experimental design over an experimental design? When would a correlational design be preferred over an experimental design? How can correlational designs be used to rule out alternative explanations?
4. What are the defining features of a survey? What are the advantages and disadvantages associated with survey research?
5. What is the difference between mundane and psychological realism? Which one should a researcher be most concerned about?
6. What is the difference between noise and a confound?

Further reading

Anderson, C. A. & Bushman, B. J. (1997). The external validity of 'trivial' experiments: The case of laboratory aggression. *Review of General Psychology*, *1*, 19–41.
McGrath, J. E. (1982). Dilemmatics: The study of research choices and dilemmas. In J. E. McGrath & R. A. Kulka (eds.), *Judgment calls in research* (pp. 69–102). Beverly Hills, CA: Sage.
Pelham, B. W. & Blanton, T. (2007). Conducting research in psychology: Measuring the weight of smoke. 3rd edn. Belmont, CA: Wadsworth/Thomson Learning.

References

Anderson, C. A. & Bushman, B. J. (1997). The external validity of 'trivial' experiments: The case of laboratory aggression. *Review of General Psychology, 1*, 19–41.
Anderson, C. A. & Dill, K. E. (2000). Video games and aggressive thoughts, feelings, and behavior in the laboratory and in life. *Journal of Personality and Social Psychology, 78*, 772–790.
Aronson, E. & Carlsmith, J. M. (1968). Experimentation in social psychology. In G. Lindzey & E. Aronson (eds.), *The handbook of social psychology*. 2nd edn (Vol. 2, pp. 1–79). Reading, MA: Addison-Wesley.
Bartholow, B. D. & Anderson, C. A. (2002). Effects of violent video games on aggressive behavior: Potential sex differences. *Journal of Experimental Social Psychology, 38*, 283–290.
Bearman, P. S., Jones, J. & Udry, J. R. (1997). *The National Longitudinal Study of Adolescent Health*. Located at www.cpc.unc.edu/projects/addhealth.

Buchman, D. D. & Funk, J. B. (1996). Video and computer games in the '90s: Children's time commitment and game preference. *Children Today*, *24*, 12–16.

Campbell, D. T. (1969). Reforms as experiments. *American Psychologist*, *24*, 409–429.

Campbell, D. T. & Stanley, J. C. (1963). *Experimental and quasi-experimental designs for research*. Dallas, TX: Houghton Mifflin.

Dietz, T. L. (1998). An examination of violence and gender role portrayals in video games: Implications for gender socialization and aggressive behavior. *Sex Roles*, *38*, 425–442.

Eron, L. D., Lefkowitz, M. M., Huesmann, L. R. & Walder, L. Q. (1972). Does television violence cause aggression? *American Psychologist*, *27*, 253–263.

Jaccard, J. (2007). A theoretical partialling: Pitfalls in the use of covariates in multiple regression analysis. Unpublished manuscript.

McGrath, J. E. (1982). Dilemmatics: The study of research choices and dilemmas. In J. E. McGrath & R. A. Kulka (eds.), *Judgment calls in research* (pp. 69–102). Beverly Hills: Sage.

McGuire, W. J. (1973). The yin and yang of progress in social psychology. *Journal of Personality and Social Psychology*, *26*, 446–56.

Pelham, B. W. & Blanton, T. (2003). Conducting research in psychology: Measuring the weight of smoke. 2nd edn. Belmont, CA: Wadsworth/Thomson Learning.

Popper, K. (1966). *The open society and its enemies*. 5th edn. Mahwah, NJ: Princeton University Press.

Roberts, D. F., Foehr, U. G., Rideout, V. G. & Brodie, M. (1999). *Kids & media @ the new millennium*. Menlo Park, CA: Kaiser Family Foundation.

Schwarz, N. (1996). Survey research: Collecting data by asking questions. In G. R. Semin & K. Fiedler, *Applied social psychology* (pp. 65–90). Thousand Oaks, CA: Sage.

5 Social psychology and economic behaviour: heuristics and biases in decision making and judgement

W. FRED VAN RAAIJ

Introduction

Economic theory of utility maximization

The British philosopher Jeremy Bentham postulates in his book *The principles of morals and legislation* (1789/2000) that the pursuit of pleasure and the avoidance of pain explain all human behaviour. Later this principle was called '**hedonic utility**'. **Utility** was then considered to be a cardinal measure of pleasure. Cardinal means that utility should be measured in absolute numbers. Disutility referred to negative emotions that people avoid, such as pain. People select the maximum utility: the net balance of the pursuit of pleasure and the avoidance of pain. People act rationally if they maximize their utility. The notions of maximizing utility, and thus acting rationally, were extremely relevant for nineteenth-century economists. Economists (Jevons, 1871/1970) saw the principle of **hedonic calculus**, the computation of utility as the net balance of pleasure and pain, as a universal law of human behaviour from which economic relations and market exchange behaviours could be derived.

Economists did not get the support of psychologists of that time for their principle of hedonic calculus. William James (1890) criticized this approach, arguing that the determinants of behaviour cannot be reduced to a simple hedonic calculus.

This instigated the idea of freeing economic theory from psychological influences, either by accepting hedonic calculus as a simple starting point for economic theorizing or by excluding psychology completely by measuring utility from expenditure or preference. It also implied that economists gradually shifted from measuring cardinal (metric) to ordinal (non-metric) utility. **Ordinal utility** is easier to measure, because it is based on ranking options. If a person prefers object A over object B, object A has a higher utility than object B, not quantifying how much higher. **Cardinal utility** is based on rating options on a utility scale. A person gives a utility score for each option. Economics started to build a theory of economic behaviour in terms of ordinal utility, free of any explicit psychological basis.

The road taken in economics to exclude psychological assumptions is comparable to the behaviouristic approach in psychology. In a behaviouristic approach unobservable mental constructs are avoided as an explanation of behaviour. Only behavioural observations and causations are allowed in the explanation of behaviour. In economics, in a similar way, the actual choices of options and being indifferent between options, thus behaviour, became the basis for ordinal utility as a preference ranking.

Anomalies

On the same day that you win €50 in a lottery you also have to pay a €50 fine for speeding on the motorway. Your friend did not win a prize in a lottery and did not get a fine either. You are just as happy as your friend on that particular day because the gain and the loss cancel each other. True or not?

The theory of **subjective expected utility** (SEU) (Edwards, 1954) was the dominant theory of decision making. SEU posits that costs and benefits of options are multiplied by the perceived likelihood they occur and that the option with the best net balance of costs and benefits (highest SEU) will be chosen. An **anomaly** is an example that is in conflict with SEU theory. Prospect theory (Kahneman & Tversky, 1979) assumes an asymmetric relationship between gains and losses, and can thus explain some anomalies. **Gains** and **losses** are relative concepts and are evaluated from a reference point. Receiving an unexpected inheritance (windfall income) will be regarded as a gain. Not receiving an end-of-the-year bonus may be considered a loss, if the bonus has been received during a number of years. See Box 5.1 for an example of choice prospects.

Box 5.1   Applying research methods: choice prospects (Kahneman and Tversky, 1979)

Suppose you have the choice between: (A) a 50% chance of winning a three-week tour to Canada and (B) a 100% certainty of a one-week tour to Canada. Which would you take?

Suppose you have the choice between: (C) a 5% chance of winning a three-week tour to Canada and (D) a 10% chance of winning a one-week tour to Canada. Which would you take?

In this experimental study, 22% of the respondents took A and 78% took B, while 67% of the respondents took C and 33% took D.

What do we learn from this? When choosing between A and B, most respondents go for the certainty of a short tour rather than the chance of getting a long tour. They seem to avoid the possibility of getting nothing. This can be explained by loss aversion. When choosing between C and D, both small chances, most respondents go for the chance of getting the long tour. They seem to think that 5% and 10% chance are both small probabilities, and thus take the long tour.

According to **prospect theory**, losses are more painful than gains are pleasurable. People give a higher negative value to a loss than they give a positive value to an equivalent gain. People are more upset by a loss of €100 than they are happy with a gain of €100. This means that you are not just as happy as your friend in the above example. For economists, this is an anomaly, because a gain of €100 and a loss of €100 on the same day should cancel out and result in a neutral state of 'no change'. Note that we included 'on the same day', assuming that within a short period people do not adapt to their changed wealth. If the gain and loss occur with a longer time interval, people adapt to the changed wealth and take the new situation as their reference point.

Anomalies pose a problem for the defenders of a dominant theory or **paradigm** (Kuhn, 1962). Either the theory has to be adapted to incorporate the anomalous situations, or the theory has to be abolished and be replaced by a more accurate theory that is able to explain the anomalies. Behavioural economics and economic psychology comprise a new paradigm combining psychological and economic concepts into a new set of theories of economic behaviour of consumers, investors and entrepreneurs.

Social-psychological factors

In this chapter we focus on a few basic determinants of decision making and judgement. Personal, social and situational reference and comparison factors will be discussed. Loss aversion and time preference will be central concepts in this chapter to explain economic behaviour.

Personal, social and situational reference

Personal reference

You have been working for a firm for more than five years and each year in December you have received a Christmas bonus. This year the Christmas bonus will not be given because of adverse economic conditions. You were happy with the bonus, but you are not unhappy that the bonus will not be given this year. True or not?

In utility theory, the attractiveness of an alternative depends on the final outcome. In gambles over money outcomes, utilities are usually defined as the final state of wealth, combining several sources of gain and loss into a final state. However, prospect theory and other psychological theories such as adaptation theory (Helson, 1964) assume that the evaluation is sensitive to points of reference. Decision makers care about changes in outcomes and about the final outcomes themselves. Depending on the point of reference, a change is perceived as a gain or a loss. Tversky and Kahneman (1981) show that a negative **framing** of a problem (in terms of losses and victims) gives other reactions than a positive framing (in terms of gains and lives saved). In negative framing, people are more willing to accept a risk to avoid a loss than (in positive framing) to get an equivalent gain.

Personal reference is the comparison of one's present welfare with welfare in the past. People enjoy a salary increase, even if the increase is smaller than the inflation rate. They evaluate the salary increase with their former salary as the reference point, and thus consider it a gain. If they were to realize that the salary increase is lower than the inflation rate, they would consider it a loss. In addition, they may attribute the salary increase to their good performance, and this contributes to their enjoyment. Thus, a nominal wage raise that does not compensate for inflation seems to be acceptable, because it is perceived as a gain for the employee relative to the reference wage. But if coded as a loss, it will be judged as unfair. Whether people judge it a gain or a loss may thus be a matter of framing, and consequently as fair or unfair.

Van Praag (1971) developed the **welfare function of income**. In this research, people answer questions such as 'Which income level do you consider to be sufficient for yourself?' They assign income levels to evaluations such as 'excellent', 'sufficient', 'insufficient' and 'poor'. They usually assign a higher income level than they actually earn to the evaluation 'sufficient'. After an income increase people get adapted to the higher income and take the higher income as their new reference point. They may also adapt their consumption level to the new reference point. Van Praag calls this a **preference shift**. As a result they are less satisfied after the change than they expected before, and they are even looking forward to the next salary increase, which will bring them the ultimate satisfaction. In a similar way, people expect to be happy with their new car. But they are happy with the new car only for a few weeks. Then they adapt to the new situation and become less happy than they were before. They might even start looking forward to the next car. People are victims of a 'hedonic treadmill' of continuously changing preferences and satisfactions.

Social reference

You booked a ticket for a flight from Amsterdam to Chicago some time ago. During the flight you talk to your neighbour and you discover she paid considerably less for her ticket than you did and she receives the same service. Are you dissatisfied about the price you paid or not?

Satisfaction with income and consumption is not only dependent on the former income and consumption level, but also on the income and consumption of other persons. **Social reference** is the comparison of one's personal welfare with the welfare of relevant others. People compare their job and their income with the jobs and incomes of other people. If their friends or colleagues earn more with similar jobs, people get dissatisfied with their income. Van Praag, Kapteijn and Van Herwaarden (1979) call this a **reference shift**. A person making a jump in their career will often move to a more expensive house in a better neighbourhood, get other neighbours and colleagues and thus another reference point. Thus, their references shift to a higher level. As a result they are less satisfied after the change than they expected before. What makes it even worse is that preference shift and reference shift often come together.

Another case of social reference is **altruism**, a selfless concern and behaviour to improve the welfare of others. According to traditional economic theory, if economic actors pursue their self-interest in their transactions with other economic actors, an equilibrium will be formed by the 'invisible hand' (Adam Smith). The baker bakes bread not for altruistic reasons but to earn money. This means that self-interest at the individual level may lead to an efficient market distribution at the aggregate level. We observe that people show altruistic behaviour in their donations to charities and their allocation of money, for instance, in an **ultimatum game** (Güth, Schmittberger & Schwarze, 1982). In an ultimatum game, a person (allocator) has to divide a sum of money, say €10, between himself and another person (recipient). If he offers €1 to the recipient, he receives €9 for himself. But the recipient may reject the offer, and then neither of them will receive anything. According to economic theory (Rubinstein, 1982), the allocator should offer a small amount to the recipient and keep most for himself. The recipient should accept this offer, because receiving one cent is better than nothing. However, most people do not behave according to economic theory. Many allocators decide on a 50 per cent split. And many recipients reject small offers. The mean offer of allocators is 37 per cent, keeping 63 per cent for themselves. People are obviously not as selfish as economic theory assumes.

Altruism depends on the situation. Allocators behave in a more altruistic way if it is not a one-time transaction and allocator and recipient are expected to have more transactions in the future, if allocator and recipient are not anonymous and know each other, and if allocator and recipient will change roles in future transactions. This means that altruism is not 'pure', but motivated by a good relationship with people in future transactions. It thus serves egoistic interests. Even donating money to a charity may not be purely altruistic. Giving money to the Cancer Foundation helps funding research to find preventions and cures for this disease. Donators may benefit themselves from this in the future, if they get cancer. And they may feel good because they help others.

Situational reference

A shortage has developed for the popular Kia Sorento. Customers must now wait more than six months for the delivery of this car. Dealer A has been selling this car for the list price. When dealer A hears of the shortage, he sets the price of this car €500 above the list price. Dealer B has been selling this car €500 below the list price. When dealer B hears of the shortage, he sets the price of this car at the list price. Are the behaviours of dealers A and B fair or unfair?

Both dealers take advantage of the situation. More people judge the behaviour of dealer A as unfair (71 per cent) than the behaviour of dealer B as unfair (42 per cent). The behaviour of dealer A is perceived as the creation of a loss:

paying more than the list price. The behaviour of dealer B is perceived as the removal of a gain: not getting the discount any more. People react more negatively to incurring a loss than to losing a gain.

In **situational reference** people compare cases in the market of setting prices and wages, and evaluate these cases on their **fairness**. In the above example, most people will judge it as unfair that a store takes advantage of the situation to raise the price above the list price. Kahneman, Knetsch and Thaler (1986) summarize these fairness judgements by the principle of dual entitlement.

Consumers have the **entitlement** (right) to the terms of reference transactions using historical market prices and posted prices. Consumers use past prices to judge the present transaction. And they use prices in catalogues and price tags on products. The most recent price, wage or rent will then be used as a reference, unless the previous transaction was explicitly temporary, for instance a temporary price discount. Consumers think it is unfair if sellers take advantage of external situations outside their control to raise their prices.

Most people accept that sellers are entitled to their reference fair profit. When the reference profit of a firm is threatened, the firm may set new terms that protect its profit and continuity at the expense of consumers. A firm may not increase its prices by arbitrarily violating the entitlement of consumers. People also accept that firms maintain prices when costs diminish. People do not accept that firms reduce the wages of their employees in periods of high unemployment. These standards of fairness deviate from economic theory and the operation of markets. Economic theory would predict and advise changing prices and wages according to market demand. These standards thus explain market anomalies with regard to price and wage competition.

Loss aversion

Introduction

This evening in the casino you are not lucky and you have already lost a large sum of money at the roulette table. You don't like to accept this loss, and you start betting a large number of tokens on a specific roulette number (Figure 5.1). If you win this bet, you will recoup your loss. But if you lose this bet, which is more likely, your final loss will be doubled. Why do you take this risk?

People don't like losses. They even dislike losses more than they like gains of the same size. **Loss aversion** seems to be a basic motivation of people. Neurologists claim that a potential loss activates the amygdala part of the brain. This part of the brain is the activation centre for danger (Trepel, Fox & Poldrack, 2005). Thus, potential loss seems to be associated with danger.

Loss aversion is the basic characteristic of prospect theory (Kahneman & Tversky, 1979). The asymmetric value function of prospect theory is steeper for losses than for gains (Figure 5.2). A gain of €20 brings a positive value of 100 (distance

Figure 5.1 *Risk taking to avoid loss*

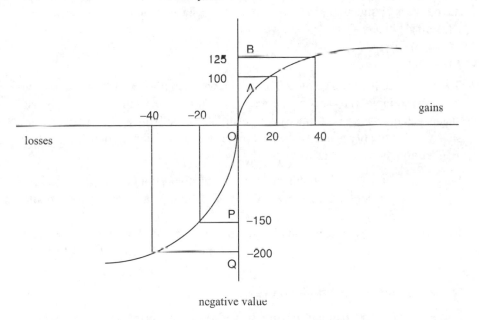

Figure 5.2 *The value function of prospect theory*

OA), whereas a loss of €20 brings a negative value of 150 (distance OP). Both gains and losses have a decreasing marginal rate of value. An additional gain of €20, over the €20 you already possess, will bring an additional positive value of 125 – 100 = 25 (distance AB). An additional loss of €20, over the €20 you already lost, will bring an additional negative value of 200 – 150 = 50 (distance PQ).

Gains and losses are judged from a reference point. If a person already has adapted to a gain or a loss, a new gain or loss will be judged from a reference point that includes that former gain or loss. The personal reference point will be adapted over time. For instance, people get accustomed to an annual bonus and their reference point has shifted to include the bonus. Removing the bonus will then be experienced as a loss.

People tend to take more risk to avoid a loss. Choosing between two options, a certain loss (losing €100) or a chance to avoid the loss (50 per cent chance to lose €200 and 50 per cent chance to lose nothing), most people will select the second option to avoid the loss, like the casino player. This implies that they accept the 50 per cent chance of doubling their loss.

Investors don't like to sell their stocks with a loss. Investors keep their losing stocks too long, hoping that the value will increase. And they sell their winning stock too early, as soon as they realize a profit. This is called the **disposition effect** and can be explained with prospect theory (Odean, 1998). Investors take the risk of not selling in order not to accept a loss. They also accept a small gain rather than taking the risk to wait for a possibly larger gain.

Whether an option is considered as a gain or as a loss may depend on how the question or situation has been framed, for instance whether it has been stated ('framing') in a positive or negative way.

Framing

The difference between gains and losses shows up in positive and negative framing. For example, the facts of the results of surgery and radiation therapy as a cancer treatment can be framed in a positive or negative way, respectively, in a survival or mortality frame with two options (surgery and radiation).

The survival frame is as follows:

Surgery: Of 100 patients having surgery, 90 live through the post-operative period, 68 are alive at the end of the first year, and 34 are alive after five years.

Radiation: Of 100 patients having radiation therapy, all live through the treatment, 77 are alive at the end of the first year, and 22 are alive after five years.

The mortality frame is as follows:

Surgery: Of 100 patients having surgery, 10 die during the post-operative period, 32 die by the end of the first year, and 66 are dead after five years.

Radiation: Of 100 patients having radiation therapy, no one dies during the treatment, 23 die by the end of the first year, and 78 are dead after five years.

Presenting people with the survival frame, most of them (82 per cent) prefer the surgery option, probably because more patients are alive after five years.

Figure 5.3 *Less worry through mental accounting*

Presenting people with the mortality frame, only a small majority (56 per cent) prefers the surgery option, probably because patients will die earlier in this option. This shows that the framing of choice options affects the choice.

Hedonic framing

Hedonic framing, based on prospect theory, is the tendency of individuals to increase the value for themselves and others by integrating and segregating gains and losses (Figure 5.3). **Integration** means here that the gains and losses are given or told at the same occasion without a time interval for the recipient to adapt to a new reference point, for instance a loss and a gain on the same day. **Segregation** means here that the gains and losses are given or told with a time interval long enough for the recipient to adapt to a new reference point. In principle, there are four cases of hedonic framing:

1. Segregation of gains.
2. Integration of losses.
3. Integration of a small loss with a large gain.
4. Segregation of a small gain from a large loss.

Segregation of gains

According to prospect theory, an integrated gain has a smaller positive utility (value) than two or more separate gains. Due to marginally decreasing utility, the first gain (distance OA) has a higher positive value than additional gains (Figure 5.4). The first gain of €20 has a value of 100. The second gain of €20 does not bring the value up to 200 (distance OC) but only to 125 (distance OB).

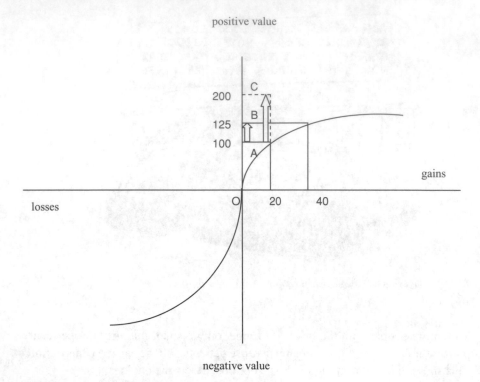

Figure 5.4 *Segregation of gains*

The recommendation is not to put all your Christmas presents in one box, but give them as separate presents with a time interval between the presents for the recipient to accommodate to a new reference point. The recipient will enjoy the separate presents more than one box filled with the presents.

Integration of losses

According to prospect theory, an integrated loss has a smaller negative utility (value) than two or more separate losses. Due to marginally decreasing utility, the first loss (distance OP) has a higher negative value than additional losses (Figure 5.5). The second loss of €20 does not bring the value down to –300 (distance OR), but only to –200 (distance OQ). A credit card, for instance, integrates a number of small losses (payments) into a large loss (total payment at the end of the month). People prefer to receive one credit card statement of payments rather than separate statements for each payment (Figure 5.6).

Integration of a loss with a larger gain

According to prospect theory, a loss of €20 has a negative utility of 150 (distance OP) and this is much larger than the decrease of positive utility (125 – 100 = 25) when subtracting this loss of €20 from the gain of €40 (distance BA) (Figure 5.7). The recommendation is thus to inform people about a loss in

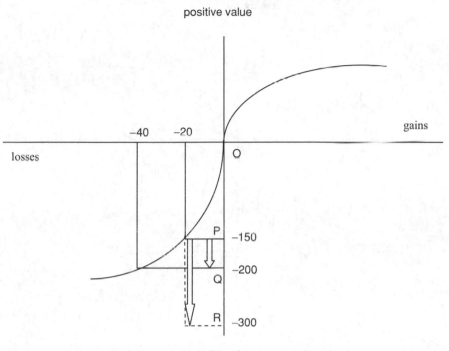

Figure 5.5 *Integration of losses*

Figure 5.6 *Paying by credit card is less painful*

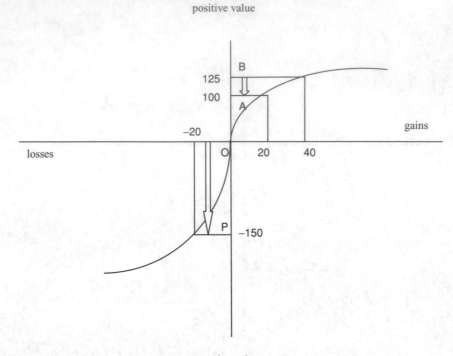

Figure 5.7 *Integration of a loss with a larger gain*

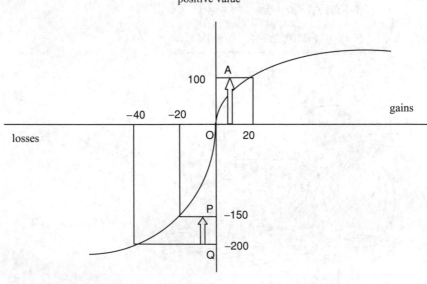

Figure 5.8 *Segregation of a gain from a larger loss*

combination with informing them about a larger gain. People will be less upset about the loss if the loss is perceived as a diminished gain. An investment broker may inform his clients about a rate/cost increase in combination with the good news that the stocks have increased in value.

Segregation of a gain from a larger loss

According to prospect theory, a gain of €20 has a positive utility of 100 (distance OA) and this is larger than the decrease of negative utility (200 − 150 = 50) when subtracting the gain of €20 from the loss of €40 (distance QP) (Figure 5.8). The recommendation is to facilitate the acceptance of a loss by also telling people separately about a smaller gain. This effect is also called 'silver lining', referring the silver line of the sun (good news) behind a cloud of heavy rain (bad news).

The rules and recommendations of hedonic framing provide an interesting description of how people would like to see the world be organized, trying to increase their positive utility/value and to decrease their negative utility/value. People try to organize their own world in a favourable way. With hedonic framing they also find ways to tell the good and bad news to other people, either in an integrated or segregated manner, in order to please others more or to upset others less. An application of hedonic framing is given in Box 5.2.

Box 5.2   Applying intervention strategies: Save More Tomorrow

Pension plans are changing, due to government and company policies. The traditional pension plans give all participants the same entitlement without considering how long they participated in the plan. This is called the 'defined benefit'. In the new pension plans the entitlement depends on the duration of the participation and how much has been saved ('defined contribution'). In many cases, the pension plan is a combination of defined benefit and defined contribution. Employees now have more responsibility for making decisions about how much to save for their retirement. It takes willpower and self-control to maintain an optimal level of saving. Some people may perceive saving as a loss, because it is deducted from their income. Thaler & Benartzi (2004) propose a prescriptive savings programme, called Save More Tomorrow™ (the SMarT programme). The essence of this programme is straightforward: people commit in advance to allocating a portion of their future salary increases towards retirement saving. Deducting the savings from a salary increase will not be felt as a loss but as a reduced gain, and thus will be more easily accepted (integration of a loss with a larger gain; Figure 5.7). The results are that (1) a high proportion (78 per cent) of those offered the plan joined, (2) the vast majority of those enrolled in the SMarT plan (80 per cent) remained in it through the fourth salary increase and (3) the average saving rates for SMarT programme participants increased from 3.5 to 13.6 per cent over the course of 40 months. The results suggest that behavioural economics and economic psychology can be used to design effective programmes for important economic decisions such as retirement saving.

Endowment effect

Last week I had to give a bottle of wine to a visitor who gave a presentation at our university. I have enough bottles in my cellar and could have taken a bottle from my cellar, but I preferred to buy a new bottle of wine for the visitor.

People feel discomfort giving up products they own and are less willing to sell or to give away these products. It may be that people get attached to these products and that they consider selling them or giving them away constitutes a loss. In general, people often demand a higher price to sell these products (**WTA**, willingness to accept) than they are willing to pay to acquire it (**WTP**, willingness to pay). In many experiments, the WTA is more than twice as large as the WTP (see Box 5.3).

Box 5.3   Research design on the endowment effect

Kahneman, Knetsch and Thaler (1991) report an experiment in which three groups of students were formed. The first group were given a coffee mug and asked whether they were willing to exchange the mug for a piece of chocolate. The second group were given a piece of chocolate and asked whether they were willing to exchange the chocolate for a coffee mug. The third group were only asked what they preferred, a coffee mug or a piece of chocolate. The results of this experiment are given in Table 5.1. The results show that students in groups 1 and 2 prefer the product they own over the other product. The results of group 3 show that the preferences for a coffee mug or a piece of chocolate do not differ significantly.

In an experiment with three similar groups, group 1 were asked for which price they were willing to sell their coffee mug (WTA). The average WTA price was $7.12. Group 2 were asked for which price they were willing to buy the mug (WTP). The average WTP price was $3.12. Group 3 were also asked for which price they were willing to buy the mug (WTP). Their average WTP price was $2.87. This means that there is a low volume of trade because of the unwillingness of the owners to sell and/or the high price they ask for the product. This difference is larger than the difference between selling and buying prices in transactions.

The results show that people want to keep what they possess (coffee mug or piece of chocolate) rather than exchange it for another product. This effect of keeping what you have is called the **endowment effect**. Giving up the endowment

Table 5.1 *Preference for a coffee mug or a piece of chocolate*

Group	Mug over chocolate	Chocolate over mug
1. Give up mug to obtain chocolate	89%	11%
2. Give up chocolate to obtain mug	10%	90%
3. No initial entitlement	56%	44%

Source: Kahneman, Knetsch & Thaler (1991).

is perceived as a loss, and this loss has a stronger negative effect on people than an equivalent gain. In this way, the endowment effect can be explained by loss aversion and thus prospect theory.

Does the endowment effect occur for all products? Van Dijk and Van Knippenberg (1998) found that there is less trade for different wines and more trade for similar wines. People are more willing to exchange a Spanish wine for another Spanish wine, and a Bulgarian wine for another Bulgarian wine, than to exchange a Spanish for a Bulgarian wine. The endowment effect proved to be stronger for dissimilar (less exchangeable) products. Giving up one item from a set of similar items (if one item still remains in possession) seems to be less painful than giving up a unique item.

Status-quo bias

The telecom market in the Netherlands has been 'liberalized' and now five or more telecom companies operate in this market with different options and prices. Still, 40 per cent of Dutch consumers have a subscription or prepaid contract with KPN, the former monopolist in the telecom market. Why?

If offered a number of options, most people prefer the standard or default option or the option they already possess (Samuelson & Zeckhauser, 1988). This is the **status-quo bias**, somewhat similar to the endowment effect. The difference is that the standard or default option is not necessarily owned. The status-quo bias may be caused by a lack of motivation or ability of consumers to process information about all choice alternatives. An easy way out for them is then to select the standard or default option. A default option is the option that is automatically given to consumers who did not make a selection themselves. Sellers could offer a default option that may be acceptable for most consumers, if consumers are unwilling or unable to make a selection themselves.

The states of New Jersey and Pennsylvania offer a choice between two options of car insurance: a cheap policy restricting the right to sue and an expensive policy maintaining the right to sue (Johnson, Hershey, Meszaros & Kunreuther, 1993). In New Jersey, the expensive policy is offered as the default, with the opportunity to opt for the cheaper policy. In Pennsylvania, the cheap policy is offered as the default, with the opportunity additionally to acquire the right to sue. In New Jersey

75 per cent choose the right to sue, whereas in Pennsylvania 20 per cent choose the right to sue. The default option has thus a clear impact on the choice. Is this only convenience, or lack of motivation and ability, or do consumers perceive the default option as the recommended option? All of these explanations may be valid. Choosing the default option is an easy way for consumers to solve a decision problem.

The status-quo bias and the endowment effect have a lot in common, for instance in the evaluation of **public goods**, that is, products or services for common use. Suppose that a firm wants to buy the Hofvijver (a pond near the government buildings) in The Hague, the Netherlands, to transform it into a large water park with the world's largest water slide. What is the minimum amount of money you want to receive to agree with this proposal? This is the WTA to compensate for the loss. And what is the minimum amount of money you want to pay to prevent the water park from being built? This is the WTP to prevent the loss. Both questions are being used to assess the value of a public good. The WTA (compensation) proves to be much larger than the WTP (prevention). This means that two different methods of assessing the value of a public good provide very different results.

Sunk-costs effect

Frances recently paid a large bill for the repair of her car. Then another repair is needed. Frances then also has the second repair done, rather than selling her car. She wants to recoup the costs of the first repair by using the car longer.

Sunk costs are the costs already invested in a project (account). Later we may discover that the project is less likely to be successful, for instance because a competitor comes on the market with a superior product. Are we going to invest additional money to complete the project? Some companies do invest, because they dislike 'writing off' the money they have already invested in the project and admitting that the project is a failure and the invested money is a loss. They would rather invest more money with the hope and expectation that the project will turn into a success in the end. This is an example of companies taking a large risk to avoid a loss (prospect theory). It takes a lot of courage for management to admit the failure and to stop investing in an unsuccessful project.

Patrons of the Ohio University Theatre received the option to buy season tickets. Some patrons (A) received the option to buy a regular ticket at $30. Other patrons (B) received the option to buy a ticket with a $4 discount. Still other patrons (C) received the option to buy a ticket with a $14 discount. They were told that the discounts were part of a promotion programme. The three types of tickets had different colours. Tickets were collected at the beginning of the theatre performance. Which group of patrons used the tickets most? Probably patrons A because they paid the most, had the largest sunk costs and were less willing to 'give up' the amount they paid.

Time preference

Suppose you win €500 in a lottery. They offer you the choice between getting the prize now or waiting a year. How much extra money do you want to receive the prize a year later? Is the extra money you require more than the interest rate? And if the prize is €5000, how high is the premium you require to wait a year for this prize?

In 1930 Irving Fisher published his book *The theory of interest: As determined by impatience to spend income and opportunity to invest it.* There is a clear distinction in this title between people who are impatient and impulsive in spending their money and those who are less impatient and invest their money. This distinction became known in economics as **time preference**.

People tend to ask a high premium (compensation or discount rate) for a delay in receiving their money, usually higher than the interest rate. The general pattern is that the demanded premium (percentage) is higher for a small amount of money and for a short time period. For a long period and a large amount of money the demanded premium is more reasonable. Discount rates are higher for gains than for losses. People want to be paid more for delaying a gain (e.g., a prize) than they want to pay for delaying a loss (e.g., a fine). People are less anxious to postpone a loss or debt. Many people want to pay off a debt quicker than they have to, simply because they dislike being 'in debt'.

Why do people want a larger compensation for a small amount than for a large amount? The perceived difference between €100 now and €150 in one year looks larger than between €10 now and €15 in one year. People are thus more willing to wait a year for €50 than for €5. Another possible explanation is that consumers consider small windfall income in terms of consumption and spending, and consider large windfall income in terms of saving. The opportunity cost of waiting for a small amount is then considered as foregone consumption, while the opportunity cost of waiting for a large amount is perceived as forgone interest. Foregone consumption is more vivid and tempting than foregone interest, and this may explain the higher opportunity costs for a small amount.

Similar to prospect theory, reference points matter. Receiving and paying money are perceived as gains and losses from a reference point. Loewenstein (1988) did an experiment in which participants could delay or speed up receiving a gift certificate of $7. Participants could receive their certificate in one, four or eight weeks. For instance, a participant with a four-week gift certificate could trade this in for an eight-week certificate and receive a premium for the delay. A participant with a four-week certificate could trade this in for a one-week certificate and pay a premium for the speeding up. The results are given in Table 5.2.

The results in Table 5.2 show that the premium for delaying the payment is always significantly larger than the premium for speeding it up. Obviously, a delay of eight weeks requires a higher premium than a delay of four weeks. A

Table 5.2 *Average amounts to delay and speed-up receiving a gift certificate of $7*

Time interval	Delay	Speed-up	Significance
One week versus four weeks	$1.09	$0.25	.001
Four weeks versus eight weeks	$0.84	$0.37	.005
One week versus eight weeks	$1.76	$0.52	.001

Source: Loewenstein (1988).

delay of one to four weeks requires a higher premium than a delay of four to eight weeks. The present is the reference point and delaying a period of four weeks from now is perceived as requiring a higher compensation than delaying a four-week period in the future. This is another case of loss aversion. The disutility of delaying (losing) money is larger than the utility of speeding up (gaining) the same amount of money.

Receiving money is a positive experience. What about negative experiences? Would people want to pay a lot to delay a negative experience, such as cleaning the house? And would people want to pay a lot to speed up a positive experience, such as receiving a bunch of flowers? No, it is quite the reverse. People like to delay the positive experience and keep the attractive anticipation of the positive experience (savouring). In a similar way, people like to speed up the negative experience in order to avoid the anticipation of it (dread). It seems that people prefer an increasing order of utility: first the negative experiences and then the positive ones, or first the pain and then the pleasure.

As said before, people require smaller premiums (compensation) for longer time periods. Thaler (1981) asked people to state the amount of money they require to receive $15 at a later time: one month, one year or ten years later. The median responses were, respectively: $20, $50 and $100. These are premiums of 345 per cent, 120 per cent and 19 per cent. The premiums decline when the periods become longer. A hyperbolic function fits these and similar data. This is the reason that the term **hyperbolic discounting** is used to describe these time preferences with the present as the reference point.

This section on time preference may be summarized as follows (Loewenstein, Read & Baumeister, 2003, pp. 27–28):

1. The **sign effect:** Gains are discounted more than losses. People want more compensation (WTA) for delaying a gain than they are willing to pay (WTP) for delaying a loss.
2. The **magnitude effect:** Small sums of money are discounted more than large sums of money. People want relatively more compensation (WTA) for delaying a small than a large sum of money.

3. The **delay–speed-up asymmetry:** People want more compensation (WTA) for delaying a gain than they are willing to pay (WTP) for speeding it up. People want more compensation (WTA) for speeding up a loss than they are willing to pay (WTP) for delaying it.
4. Preference for **improving sequences:** People prefer improving sequences with an increasing utility over deteriorating sequences with a decreasing utility. Duties first and then pleasure. Consumers want to take the regular restaurant first and then the best restaurant (savouring).

Towards a new 'rationality' of economic behaviour of consumers, investors and entrepreneurs

Economic psychology and behavioural economics meet each other in the study of heuristics and biases of economic actors and the explanation of economic behaviour of consumers, investors and entrepreneurs. The economic theory of utility maximization is a normative rather than a descriptive theory of economic behaviour. Economic actors do not behave according to this theory, but use heuristics and biases to make their decisions. Heuristics and biases usually make it easier and quicker for economic actors to find solutions and to make decisions. This is important in a period of information overload and time pressure. People use the heuristics to adapt to new and complex situations. Heuristics are simple search and decision rules. Economic actors, and humans in general, use these rules to 'survive' in a complex and uncertain world, involving multiple goals, in which utility maximization is not feasible and often impossible. From an evolutionary perspective, we may argue that heuristics and biases constitute a new ecological rationality, needed to make reasonably quick, efficient and effective decisions to survive in complex new environments.

Heuristics and biases may also be related to less conscious and unconscious thinking (van Raaij & Ye, 2005). A large part of our mental processes are outside our awareness and cannot be recalled or recognized, but nevertheless determine our preferences and choices. Conscious thought is only the tip of the iceberg. Heuristics and biases may largely be in the unaware and unconscious domain and interact, even interfere, with conscious judgement and decision making. Individuals may have the illusion that they make conscious decisions, but unconscious factors determine their decisions to a large degree. The unconscious seems to be more adaptive, less restrictive and more effective than we often realize, considering that our decisions are not that poor.

The use of heuristics and unconscious thought may point to a new 'rationality' of economic behaviour of consumers, investors and entrepreneurs. This is a 'bounded rationality' of making 'satisficing' rather than 'maximizing' decisions, taking the ability, motivation, effort, information load and time restrictions of decision makers into account.

Applied social psychology in context

More than two hundred years after Jeremy Bentham we focus again on experienced utility. Micro- and behavioural economists, economic and social psychologists meet each other to study economic behaviour and to provide a more realistic and valid theory of economic behaviour as a base for micro-economic theory. Results from cognitive, economic and social psychology on game theory, decision making and choice, social orientation and social reference are now applied to the economic behaviour of consumers, investors and entrepreneurs.

An anomaly for economic theory is not necessarily an anomaly for psychological theory. Economics is largely based on one dominant theory of utility maximization under conditions of complete information and stable preferences. Psychology has a richer base of theories, which is both a blessing and a curse. It is a blessing in the sense that theories are available to explain and predict behaviours in many domains and situations. It is a curse because of the incompatibility and even contradictory predictions of these theories. Social psychologists thus have to be aware of the boundary conditions of the applicability of social-psychological theories.

In any case, including social-psychological determinants to explain and predict economic behaviour will often improve the 'realism' and validity of the theories and models of economic behaviour. In economics, the focus is on predicting consumer behaviour at the aggregate level, for instance predicting how demand reacts to a price increase. In psychology, the focus is on the description and the prediction of behaviour, taking individual differences into account.

At the same time, we note that economic theory may not describe actual behaviour of consumers, investors and entrepreneurs, but it provides normative guidance and prescriptions for how to behave. Being an 'economic actor' and behaving according to economic theory will often bring personal profits and other desirable outcomes. Being a 'social actor' and behaving in a prosocial way will often bring better social relationships. The main focus of this chapter is thus to find the heuristics and biases that prevent people taking good decisions, either as an economic or a social actor. How can we teach and debias people to make fewer mistakes and sub-optimal choices or to act in a prosocial way (Arkes, 1991)?

Economic and social psychologists working in the domains of economic behaviour need to know the micro (consumer, investor, entrepreneur) and macro (consumer confidence) parts of economics, marketing and behavioural finance. In these domains, theories on social cognition, decision making and choice contribute to a better description, understanding and prediction of economic behaviour. Different from a few years ago, most micro-economists are now interested and convinced that the contribution of economic and social psychologists is valid and useful. Psychologists working in this area need to have knowledge on relevant economic issues and approaches, and need to assess whether their contribution improves the understanding and prediction of economic behaviour. Economic behaviour is also a fruitful domain to test the hypotheses of social-psychological theories in a realistic setting.

Conclusion

In this chapter, heuristics and biases are discussed in decision making and judgement regarding economic behaviour. Gradually, this approach tends to be accepted in (behavioural) economics. People make judgements about gains and losses not based on their final wealth, but from a personal, social or situational reference point. Losses have more negative impact than equivalent gains have positive impact. Thus, people try to avoid losses more than they try to get gains. This basic principle helps to explain heuristics and biases such as the endowment effect, status-quo bias, sunk costs effect and time preference.

Glossary

Altruism: a selfless concern and behaviour to improve the welfare of others.

Anomaly: deviation from economic theory in particular, and deviation from theory in general.

Cardinal utility: rating of the utility of an option.

Delay–speed-up assymmetry: the observation that people want more compensation for delaying a gain than they are willing to pay for speeding it up, and want more compensation for speeding up a loss than they are willing to pay for delaying it.

Disposition effect: the tendency of investors to keep losing stocks too long and to sell gaining stocks too early.

Endowment effect: the tendency of people to demand a higher price to sell goods in possession than one is willing to pay to buy these goods.

Entitlement: right to the terms of referent transactions using historical and posted prices and wages.

Fairness: evaluation of price and wage transactions based on historical changes and entitlements.

Framing: providing information in positive (gains) or negative (losses) terms or, more generally, the way of presenting a message.

Gain: increase of wealth, compared with a reference point.

Hedonic calculus: computation of utility as the net balance of benefits and costs (pleasure and pain).

Hedonic framing: the tendency of people to increase the value of gains and losses by integration or segregation.

Hedonic utility: the assumption that all human behaviour is explained by the pursuit of pleasure and the avoidance of pain.

Hyperbolic discounting: hyperbolic function fitting the time preferences of people with the present as the reference point.

Improving sequences: the observation that people prefer sequences with an ascending utility over sequences with a descending utility.

Integration: bringing gains or losses together, with a time interval short enough for the reference point not to change.

Loss: decrease of wealth, compared with a reference point.

Loss aversion: the motivation to prevent losses.

Magnitude effect: the observation that people want more relative compensation for delaying a small than for delaying a large gain.

Ordinal utility: ranking of the utility of two or more options.

Paradigm: scientific theories that are dominant during a particular period.

Personal reference: comparison of one's present welfare with welfare in the past.

Preference shift: change of reference point based on personal history.

Prospect theory: theory that posits that decisions deviate from expected utility theory outcome, in particular because decision makers are willing to take more risk to prevent losses.

Public good: a product or service for common use, such as a park or motorway.

Reference shift: change of reference point based on the position of relevant others.

Segregation: keeping gains or losses separate, with a time interval long enough for the reference point to change.

Sign effect: the observation that people want more compensation for delaying a gain than they are willing to pay for delaying a loss.

Situational reference: comparison of cases in different situations.

Social reference: comparison of personal welfare with the welfare of relevant others.

Status-quo bias: the tendency to select the present option or the default option.

Subjective expected utility theory (SEU): theory that posits that costs and benefits of options are multiplied by the perceived likelihood they occur and that the option with the best net balance of costs and benefits (highest SEU) will be chosen.

Sunk-costs effect: the tendency to take historical invested costs into account when making investment decisions.

Time preference: the preference for spending money now or delaying spending.

Ultimatum game: an experimental game in which a person (allocator) divides a sum of money between him/herself and another person (recipient), and the recipient may reject his/her offer.

Utility: value of an option for personal or common use.

Welfare function of income: functions derived from the assignment of income levels to evaluations such as excellent, good, sufficient, insufficient and poor.

WTA: willingness to accept (selling price).

WTP: willingness to pay (buying price).

Review questions

1. What are the basic determinants for decision making and judgement that run through this chapter? Describe them in your own words.
2. Why did eighteenth- and nineteenth-century economists try to develop hedonic calculus as a basis of micro-economics?
3. What should happen if a theory is confronted with a large number of anomalies (non-fitting cases)?
4. Why are economists now accepting behavioural sciences for their theory development and explanation of economic behaviour?
5. Are the use of heuristics and biases an indication of human deficiencies in decision making or are they an indication of a better adaptation to the environment?
6. Can all heuristics and biases be explained with the concept of loss aversion?
7. How can economic and social psychology contribute to a better explanation and prediction of economic behaviour?

Further reading

Belsky, G. & Gilovich, T. (1999). *Why smart people make big money mistakes – and how to correct them*. New York: Simon & Schuster.

Gigerenzer, G. & Selten, R. (2001). *Bounded rationality: The adaptive toolbox*. Cambridge, MA: The MIT Press.

Gilovich, T., Griffin, D. & Kahneman, D. (2002). *Heuristics and biases: The psychology of intuitive judgment*. Cambridge University Press.

Thaler, R. H. (1992). *The winners' curse: Paradoxes and anomalies of economic life*. Princeton University Press.

Tversky, A. & Kahneman, D. (1974). Judgment under uncertainty: Heuristics and biases. *Science, 185 (4157)*, 1124–1130.

(1981). The framing of decisions and the psychology of choice. *Science*, 211 (4481), 453–458.

References

Arkes, H. R. (1991). Costs and benefits of judgment errors: Implications for debiasing. *Psychological Bulletin, 110*, 486–498.

Bentham, J. (1789/2000). *An Introduction to the Principles of morals and legislation*. Kitchener, ON: Batoche Books.

Edwards, W. (1954). The theory of decision making. *Psychological Bulletin, 41*, 380–417.

Fisher, I. (1930). *The theory of interest: As determined by impatience to spend income and opportunity to invest it*. London, New York: Macmillan.

Güth, W., Schmittberger, R. & Schwarze, B. (1982). An experimental analysis of ultimatum bargaining. *Journal of Economic Behavior and Organization, 3*, 367–388.

Helson, H. (1964). *Adaptation-level theory*. New York: Harper & Row.

James, William (1890). *The principles of psychology*. 2 vols. New York: Henry Holt.

Jevons, W. S. (1871/1970). *The theory of political economy*. London/New York: Macmillan.

Johnson, E. J., Hershey, J., Meszaros, J. & Kunreuther, H. (1993). Framing, probability distortions, and insurance decisions. *Journal of Risk and Uncertainty*, *7*, 35–51.

Kahneman, D. & Tversky, A. (1979). Prospect theory. *Econometrica*, *47*, 263–292.

Kahneman, D., Knetsch, J. L. & Thaler, R. (1986). Fairness as a constraint on profit seeking: Entitlements in the market. *American Economic Review*, *76*, 728–741.

(1991). The endowment effect, loss aversion, and status-quo propensity. *Journal of Economic Perspectives*, *5*, 193–206.

Kuhn, T. S. (1962). *The structure of scientific revolution*. University of Chicago Press.

Loewenstein, G. (1988). Frames of mind in intertemporal choice. *Management Science*, *34*, 200–214.

Loewenstein, G., Read, D. & Baumeister, R. (eds.) (2003), *Time and decision: Economic and psychological perspectives on intertemporal choice*. New York: Russell Sage Foundation.

Odean, T. (1998). Are investors reluctant to realize their losses? *Journal of Finance*, *53*, 1775–1798.

Rubinstein, A. (1982). Perfect equilibrium in a bargaining model. *Econometrica*, *50*, 379–402.

Samuelson, W. & Zeckhauser, R. J. (1988). Status quo bias in decision making. *Journal of Risk and Uncertainty*, *1*, 7–59.

Thaler, R. H. (1981). Some empirical evidence on dynamic inconsistency. *Economic Letters*, *8*, 201–207.

Thaler, R. H. & Benartzi, S. (2004). Save more tomorrow: Using behavioral economics to increase employee saving. *Journal of Political Economy*, *112* (1, part 2), S164–188.

Trepel, C., Fox, C. R. & Poldrack, R. A. (2005). Prospect theory on the brain? Toward a cognitive neuroscience of decision under risk. *Cognitive Brain Research*, *23*, 34–50.

Tversky, A. & Kahneman, D. (1981). The framing of decisions and the psychology of choice. *Science*, *211* (4481), 453–458.

Van Dijk, E. & Van Knippenberg, D. (1998). Trading wine: On the endowment effect, loss aversion, and the comparability of consumer goods. *Journal of Economic Psychology*, *19*, 485–495.

Van Praag, B. M. S. (1971). The welfare function of income in Belgium: An empirical investigation. *European Economic Review*, *4*, 33–62.

Van Praag, B. M. S., Kapteijn, A. & Van Herwaarden, F. G. (1979). The definition and measurement of social reference spaces. *The Netherlands Journal of Sociology*, *15*, 13–25.

Van Raaij, W. F. & Ye, G. W. (2005). Conscious and unconscious processing in consumer motives, goals, and desires. In S. Ratneshwar & D. G. Mick (eds.), *Inside consumption: Consumer motives, goals and desires* (pp. 330–339). London, New York: Routledge.

6 Social psychology and immigration: relations between immigrants and host societies

JAN PIETER VAN OUDENHOVEN,
CHARLES JUDD AND COLLEEN WARD

Introduction

Globalization, migration and increasing cultural diversity within nations have resulted in a growing need to understand and enhance intercultural relations in plural societies. The purpose of this chapter on relations between immigrants and host societies is to highlight current trends and new advances in the study of acculturation and intergroup relations. To accomplish this, the chapter provides an overview of migration and cultural diversity across four major geographical regions; describes the evolution of acculturation theory, models and research; briefly reviews the developments in the application of social-psychological theory to the study of immigration and intergroup relations; discusses the convergence of these two approaches; offers suggestions how applied social psychology may help to solve intercultural problems; and makes recommendations for the course of future research.

Migration and cultural diversity in the twenty-first century

It is now estimated that there are almost 191 million international migrants on a world-wide basis. Europe currently hosts the largest number (64 million), which is about 8% of its population. However, relative to the total population, Oceania (15%) and North America (13%) are world leaders. Brief synopses of their immigration trends and issues are presented in the following sections.

- The United States (298 million inhabitants) has been culturally dominated by European Americans for centuries, while African-Americans formed the largest minority. Remarkably, African-Americans have recently been surpassed by Americans with a Hispanic background who – with 40 million – now form over 13% of the population. Hispanics keep going in and have a higher birth rate than Americans of European descent. After Mexico and Spain the US has the world's largest Spanish-speaking population. Within fifty years, Hispanics will form a quarter of the US population. We may safely predict that the US is becoming a country with two powerful cultures, the Anglo-western and the Hispanic culture, and two important languages, English and Spanish.

- In western Europe (311 million inhabitants) the situation is more diverse, because each country has its own language and its particular immigration history. In the 1960s, when economic growth in western Europe led to a scarcity of labour, many 'guest workers' from the Mediterranean countries moved to Germany, Belgium, France and the Netherlands. Roughly at the same time, the United Kingdom received many immigrants from Bangladesh, India and Pakistan. Most of them have settled there and have been reunited with their families. Many of them are Muslims. Later, refugees from Muslim countries such as Afghanistan, Iraq and Somalia strengthened the Muslim community. Nowadays, Muslims form 5 to 10 per cent of the population of western Europe. Their number is still growing whereas the native population is declining. Again, we may predict that – with respect to religion – western Europe is becoming more bicultural too: on the one hand it has had a long Christian tradition, on the other hand it is experiencing a vital and growing Islamic input.
- Canada (33 million inhabitants) is probably the most multicultural country. Canada used to be a bicultural country, consisting of an Anglo majority group and a strong French minority group. The Anglo part of the population, although still forming the largest part, has been decreasing over the last decades and has ceased to be the majority group. The percentage of Canadians of French-European descent is declining as well. In the early years after World War II, many other European nationals (Germans, Ukrainians, Italians and Dutch) immigrated to Canada. Subsequently, large numbers of refugees from Soviet-dominated Eastern Europe (Hungarians, Czechoslovaks and Poles) followed. Since the new Immigration Law of 1978, which eliminated some discriminatory elements, large groups of immigrants from Asia, Latin America, Africa and the Middle East were allowed to enter the country. Altogether they have transformed Canada into a true rainbow nation. This has been formalized by the adoption of the Multiculturalism Act in 1988. Although English will stay the dominant language, the dominant Anglo cultural identity will gradually be replaced by a pluralistic cultural identity.
- Australia (over 20 million inhabitants) has been the most Anglo-dominated immigration country. According to the 1971 census 83 per cent of the population originated from the British Isles. Other immigrants primarily were Italians, Greeks, Germans and Dutch. The dismantling of the White Australia policy in the early seventies opened the doors to immigrants from non-European countries. Immigrants from Asia, in particular from China and Vietnam, have benefited from this immigration policy change. At present, more than 7 per cent of the population of Australia originates from Asia. In 1986 Australia officially adopted a policy of multiculturalism. In view of the higher birth rate of Asians within Australia, and – more importantly – the proximity of densely populated Asian countries, it is to be expected that Australia will have an important Asian cultural input.

Original Culture $\Rightarrow$ Culture of host society (assimilation)

Figure 6.1 *One-dimensional model of acculturation*

Apparently, in the four major immigration areas immigrants are transforming the dominant culture. This leads in all four areas – in different forms – to a less western culture, which may mean less European, less Anglo-Saxon or less Christian. Because of these immigration streams and their impact, host societies increasingly become conscious of and start to care about immigrants' habits and needs. Therefore we will focus on acculturation strategies of both immigrants and members of the host societies.

Acculturation theory and research

Acculturation refers to the process of adapting to a different culture. Over the years, several theoretical models have been developed to assess the process of acculturation, including changes in attitudes, values, behaviours, language and cultural identity. These models of acculturation can be placed in one of two broad categories: (1) one-dimensional models – which see cultural change as a linear process, going from the heritage culture to the host culture – and (2) multidimensional models – where processes of cultural change are seen to take place independently in the original and host cultures. Most recently, acculturation researchers have emphasized the importance of the *receiving society* in the acculturation processes adopted by immigrants. The following section reviews a number of these models.

One-dimensional models of acculturation

Early studies of acculturation adopted a one-dimensional approach (see Figure 6.1), in which immigrants were seen as giving up their culture of origin and gradually moving towards identification with the host culture by adopting the cultural norms, values, attitudes and behaviours of the host society (e.g., Ramirez, 1984).

This model was more appropriate in the past than it is now, because circumstances were different. It is particularly applicable when host societies have a homogeneous culture; when immigrants are – relatively – welcome because of economic, ideological or moral reasons; when they form only a small proportion of the total population and when the cultural distance between immigrants' culture and host culture is small. Examples are Eastern European refugees fleeing to Western Europe during the Cold War period, or immigrants from the former European colonies who arrived immediately after the colonies' independence. Most colonies became independent in the two decades after the Second World War.

Immigrants from the colonies could easily assimilate to the host society, because they knew the culture of the colonizer and were admitted because the former colonizing countries had the moral obligation to let them in. The Eastern European immigrants were culturally not very dissimilar either; they came in small groups and were welcome for ideological reasons. At that time many European countries still were culturally very homogeneous. In general, immigrants conformed to the light pressures to assimilate and later generations tended to move spontaneously towards assimilation.

The US used to present another, related, example of a one-dimensional model with its **melting pot** ideology. In that ideology immigrants were free to a large degree to choose their own acculturation in private values, but there was a strong informal pressure on them to blend into the mainstream culture. By doing so, immigrants added a slightly different flavour to that mainstream culture. This ideology was realistic when the mainstream culture used to be relatively homogeneous. Although the US was an immigration country, its culture had a strong European character and most immigrants used to come from Europe. That changed in the twentieth century, most strongly after the Second World War, when large groups of immigrants from non-Western countries migrated to the US. For them it was much harder to blend into the mainstream culture, so that the melting pot became more of a mosaic in which each cultural group formed a little piece.

Despite the initial popularity of the one-dimensional, bipolar conceptualization of acculturation, it became apparent that one-dimensional models were too simplistic and that identification with home and host culture had come to be viewed as independent forces. To address this difficulty, more comprehensive models of acculturation emerged which began to consider the heritage and host cultures as independent influences.

Multidimensional models of acculturation

There are two assumptions underlying multidimensional models of acculturation (Ryder, Alden & Paulhus, 2000). The first one views acculturation processes as functioning in various separate domains, such as attitudes, values, behaviours, language and cultural identity. According to this view, immigrants may relate to their heritage and host cultures to different degrees in these various domains. For example, they may be fluent in the new national language, but still totally identify with the values that are predominant in their country of origin.

The second assumption frames orientations towards home and host cultures as independent domains, as in Berry's (1997) classification of acculturation strategies. According to Berry, immigrants are faced with two fundamental questions: the first, 'Is it of value to maintain my cultural heritage?' and the second, referring to relations with other ethnic or cultural groups, 'Is it of value to maintain relations with the host society?' On the basis of the answers to these questions four acculturation strategies may be distinguished: (1) **integration** (it is important

		Own culture is valuable	Own culture is not valuable
Contact with host	Yes	Integration	Assimilation
society is desirable			
	No	Separation	Marginalization

Figure 6.2 *A two-dimensional model of acculturation strategies (Berry, 1997)*

to maintain both cultural identity and to have positive relations with the host society); (2) **assimilation** (only positive relations with the host society are important); (3) **separation** (only maintaining one's own culture is of importance); and (4) **marginalization** (none of these outcomes is important) (Figure 6.2).

Berry proposed that immigrants undergo a process of change in at least six areas of psychological functioning (language, cognitive styles, personality, identity, attitudes and acculturative stress). As individuals acculturate, a number of behaviours are modified, together with attitudes, beliefs and values. Berry argued that the four acculturation strategies are not discrete, static strategies; individuals may switch from one strategy to another, and the host culture may consist of several cultures rather than a single majority culture. Berry's model definitely describes the current situation in the four immigration areas better, in which immigrants (mostly economic immigrants) come in large numbers and form considerable minority groups. Moreover, the cultural distance between the majority of the immigrants and the host cultures has widened. Examples are Turkish immigrants in western Europe, Mexicans in the US and Asians in Australia and Canada. Consequently, host societies are not totally culturally homogeneous any more, although generally they still have a dominant culture (Figures 6.3, 6.4, 6.5 and 6.6).

Although Berry's model has been extremely influential in the field, it has also received some criticism. Some researchers have argued that the concept of marginalization is not a viable one, since migrants do not choose to be marginalized, but rather may involuntarily be forced to adopt it as an outcome. Or alternatively, it is possible that some immigrants may not directly identify with either their heritage or host cultures because they have opted for a more individualistic acculturation strategy (e.g. Bourhis, Moïse, Perreault & Senécal, 1997). Immigrants who are more individualistic are often characterized by a high level of cosmopolitanism, selectively adopting elements from a number of cultures.

In most multicultural societies, the current discourse centres on the question whether immigrants should assimilate or integrate. Berry (1997) and many other

Figure 6.3 *Integration*

Figure 6.4 *Assimilation*

researchers (e.g., Horenczyk, 1996; van Oudenhoven, Prins & Buunk, 1998) have found that integration is the preferred and most 'adaptive' strategy for immigrants. Recent studies have demonstrated that it is also important to look to the acculturation expectations of members of the receiving society.

Based on Berry's model of acculturation, the interactive acculturation model by Bourhis *et al.* (1997) has provided a useful and inclusive framework by focusing on the role of both the acculturation expectations of the receiving community and the acculturation orientations adopted by immigrants. According to this model, host society members may endorse five acculturation orientations towards immigrants: integration, segregation, assimilation, exclusion and

Figure 6.5 *Separation*

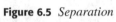

Figure 6.6 *Marginalization*

individualism. The first three orientations parallel Berry's (1997) notions of integration, separation, assimilation and the last two represent variations on marginalization. According to Bourhis *et al.* (1997), integration represents an accommodative approach in which host nationals believe that immigrants are entitled to preserve their heritage culture while simultaneously adopting aspects of the national culture. Those who endorse this strategy anticipate the gradual evolution of a multicultural society. Host nationals who espouse segregation believe it is in the best interest of the larger community to separate immigrant cultures from the mainstream society. Those who support assimilation express a desire to see immigrants relinquish their heritage culture in favour of the one from their adopted homeland. Exclusionism reflects the belief that immigration and immigrants are a threat to the national community and that the country would benefit most from a closed immigration policy. Finally, individualism is preferred by those who believe that individuals should be empowered to adopt any strategy that they see fit.

Convergence between host and migrant acculturation preferences do not always occur, and Bourhis *et al.* have argued that dissimilar attitudes result in problematic or conflictual outcomes. Horenczyk's (1996) research revealed that both Russian migrants and Israeli hosts preferred integration, but members of the receiving community had a stronger preference for assimilation than did migrants; they also believed that migrants were more willing to assimilate than was actually the case. Van Oudenhoven *et al.* (1998) noted that Dutch nationals strongly endorsed assimilation, but that they believed Moroccan and Turkish migrants favoured separation, whereas integration was actually preferred by both immigrant groups. The outcomes of host and migrant mismatches, however, have not been widely investigated.

In contrast to immigrants, who generally prefer integration, host society members have often adopted an assimilation ideology in which immigrants are expected to abandon their cultural and linguistic distinctiveness and adopt the core values of the host society. For instance, in Germany, Zick, Wagner, Van Dick and Petzel (2001) reported a preference for assimilation among nationals, while similar results were found in Slovakia (Piontkowski, Florack, Hoelker & Obdrzálek, 2000), Israel (Horenczyk, 1996) and the Netherlands (van Oudenhoven *et al.*, 1998). Generally, later generations tend to move spontaneously towards assimilation. However, when pressure on them to assimilate becomes too strong, some do assimilate, while others may show reactance, which may strengthen their need for separation or may lead them into marginalization. Admittedly, not all nations prefer assimilation. Exceptions are Canada and New Zealand, where hosts and immigrants tend to prefer integration.

It is clear from the research based on the current immigration climate that the process of acculturation can no longer be viewed solely in terms of the experiences of the immigrant, but must consider the mutual change that occurs when two cultural groups come into contact with one another.

Social-psychological theories and research

In addition to models of acculturation, social-psychological theories of intergroup relations are pertinent to the analysis of relations between immigrant groups and members of the receiving societies. It should be noted that social-psychological theories are often combined with individual differences measures (e.g., social dominance orientation) in intergroup research and that studies have been undertaken in both lab and field settings from a range of perspectives, including developmental and cross-cultural.

The **contact hypothesis** suggests that negative attitudes held by one group towards another are caused by a lack of knowledge about that group (see also Chapter 2). It is important that individuals of the two groups come into positive, personal and cooperative contact with each other, that the interaction takes place between individuals with equal status and that authorities support the contact. Under these conditions they will get to know each other, and mutual attitudes and interaction will become more positive, for instance through a growing recognition of similarities (Allport, 1954). As a consequence, prejudices will be eliminated or reduced.

According to the **similarity-attraction hypothesis**, similarity leads to attraction (Byrne, 1971). The hypothesis states that when one perceives another to be similar to oneself in various characteristics (for instance, attitudes and values), this other will be positively evaluated. In other words, we like people and groups who we think are like us and our own group. Therefore, the similarity-attraction hypothesis offers an easy explanation for why people do not appreciate cultural differences or dissimilar cultures (see Box 6.1). Similarity may reduce insecurity in interpersonal and intergroup relations. Therefore, cultural similarity may be rewarding because it suggests that our beliefs and values are correct. As a consequence, interactions between individuals and groups occur more smoothly.

Box 6.1   Testing the theory: the similarity-attraction hypothesis

Clear support for the similarity-attraction hypothesis was found in a large survey (van Oudenhoven, Judd & Hewstone, 2000) of Dutch-speaking citizens ($N = 2389$) of the Netherlands, who were asked to indicate their appreciation of several social categories, such as ethnicity, religion and employment. Respondents were given the following scenario: '*Suppose you got some new neighbours. You have a brief introductory chat with the man and the woman. You don't know whether they are married, but you do know that they are . . .*' Each respondent was then told that the couple was Dutch or Turkish, that the man was employed or unemployed, and that he was Muslim or did not practise his religion but celebrated Christmas, Easter, and

'Sinterklaas'. After reading the scenario, respondents were asked to indicate their liking of the couple. The results of this study showed that outgroup membership of each social category added to a decreased appreciation of the target. As long as the target did not share all characteristics of the ingroup, he or she was liked considerably less than the target that shared all characteristics of the ingroup. Respondents indeed felt most attracted to the employed Dutch 'Christian' neighbour, who was assumed to be most similar to themselves, and felt least attracted to the unemployed Turkish, Muslim neighbour (Figure 6.7).

The similarity-attraction hypothesis is further supported by a number of survey studies on attitudes towards immigrants in which acceptance of immigrants appeared to depend on their cultural distance from the host society. In Canada, British- and French-Canadians are seen as more acceptable than groups from northern, southern or eastern Europe, who are, in turn, viewed as more acceptable than those from south and east Asia and the West Indies (Berry, 2006). In a study by Ho, Niles, Penney and Thomas (1994), Australian respondents were more reluctant to accept immigrants from Asia and the Middle East than from Britain or southern Europe. This phenomenon of 'ethnic hierarchy', a sequence of preferences according to the cultural distance from the ingroup, appears to be a general phenomenon.

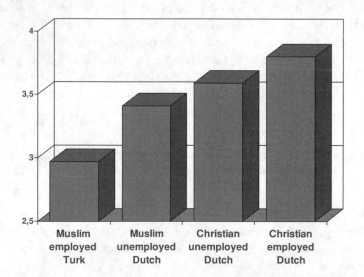

Figure 6.7 *Liking (1 = little; 5 = much) of 'neighbours' dependent on nationality, religion and employment status (N = 2389)*

Social identity theory (Tajfel & Turner, 1979) offers an even more pertinent perspective on the intergroup processes between immigrants and host societies. Social categorization and comparison are key features of the theory, which posits that: (1) individuals strive for a positive identity; (2) group membership forms an important component of their identity; (3) therefore individuals search for positive group distinctiveness; and (4) they may attain or maintain a positive self-image by engaging in comparisons between their ingroups and various outgroups in such a way that they favour their ingroup. Consequently, ethnocentrism is assumed to be an inevitable consequence of social identification. Ethnocentrism may manifest itself through ingroup favouritism or outgroup derogation, particularly in domains such as stereotyping and attributions. Social identity theory has been widely used to interpret intergroup relations from both host and migrant perspectives.

A more recent model which highlights the role of threat in the relations between hosts and immigrants is the **instrumental model of group conflict** (Esses, Dovidio, Jackson & Armstrong, 2001). Inspired by realistic group conflict theory (Levine & Campbell, 1972), the model identifies two determinants of intergroup antagonism. The first is resource stress, which may arise from limited resources, unequal access to resources, and the acceptance of unequal access based on a social hierarchy. The last factor is regarded as an individual difference variable and is often discussed under the rubric of social dominance orientation. Individuals who are high in social dominance orientation support group hierarchies and inequality in society, view the world as a competitive place in which only the toughest survive and express a willingness to discriminate against other groups in order to attain or maintain group dominance. The second determinant of conflict is the presence of a relevant outgroup. The outgroup should be salient, distinctive and a viable competitor for valued resources. Salience and distinctiveness can be accentuated by such things as the increasing numbers of outgroup members or by their distinguishable appearance. The combination of resource stress and a relevant outgroup results in intergroup competition and is accompanied by the cognitive and affective perception of threat. The cognitive component revolves around a zero-sum belief system, where there is a perception that any opportunities and benefits given to one group are regarded as directly reducing the opportunities and benefits of the others. The affective component encompasses the perceptions of fear and anxiety as a result of the challenges posed by outgroup competitors. Esses et al.'s (2001) work on attitudes towards migrants in the United States and Canada has given strong support for the instrumental model of group conflict.

A model that is oriented towards inclusion is the **common ingroup identity model** (Gaertner & Dovidio, 2000). The central idea of the model is that once some people are defined as part of an ingroup, they will be treated in a similar way to other ingroup members. Gaertner and Dovidio argue that by changing cognitive representations of ingroup and outgroup members to an inclusive social identity within a single group, more favourable attitudes towards former outgroup members may be produced. This happens through processes involving pro-ingroup bias (for an example of a study that manipulated a more inclusive identity, see Box 6.2). When members of a former outgroup come to be considered part of the ingroup, the cognitive and motivational forces that contribute to ingroup favouritism become redirected to improve attitudes towards the newly defined members of the ingroup. Common ingroup identity can be achieved by increasing the salience of existing superordinate memberships (e.g., a school, a company, a nation) or by introducing factors (e.g., common goals or shared fate) that are perceived to be shared between the original groups. The model does not necessarily require each group to give up its original, less inclusive, group identity completely. Individuals belong simultaneously to several groups and possess multiple identities (Brewer, 2000). Research demonstrating that national identity is linked to positive attitudes towards immigrants can be interpreted in terms of the theory of common ingroup identity.

Box 6.2   From theory to practice: how to promote a common ingroup identity

Esses, Wagner, Wolf and Preiser (2006) examined whether promoting a national ingroup that includes both immigrants and non-immigrants would improve attitudes towards immigrants among members of receiving societies. They also wanted to know whether one's nation of citizenship and individual differences in social dominance orientation would influence the effects. Participants were Canadian and German students, who completed a measure of social dominance orientation and were then asked to respond to a series of questions designed to heighten the salience of national identity (national identity) or promote a national ingroup that includes immigrants (common national ingroup), or were asked to respond to irrelevant questions (control). The dependent measures included attitudes towards immigrants. Results revealed that the manipulation of a common national ingroup successfully reduced negative attitudes towards immigrants among higher social dominance-oriented Canadian participants, but tended to strengthen negative attitudes of higher social dominance-oriented German participants. The study demonstrates the value of promoting a common national ingroup that includes both non-immigrants and immigrants, but also suggests that such a strategy cannot be applied indiscriminately. Rather, we must take into account the historical and contemporary demands within a nation.

Acculturation research and social-psychological theories

As we saw in the previous section, social psychologists have dealt with important topics that are all very relevant for acculturation research: contact, social identity, (cultural) similarity, intergroup threat, inclusion and exclusion. Remarkably, however, until recently, the two lines of research have evolved independently from one another in the study of host–immigrant relations. Social psychologists have too often developed and tested theoretical paradigms referring to isolated parts of intergroup relations (e.g., Tajfel's minimal group paradigm or the similarity-attraction hypothesis), whereas acculturation research has been very broad and in many cases largely descriptive (e.g., the great number of studies describing what adaptation strategies groups of immigrants prefer). Fortunately, however, acculturation researchers have inspired social psychologists to adopt a broader scope and to extend their research to the context of immigration, and social psychologists have encouraged acculturation researchers to formulate more precise theoretical explanations. A growing number of studies apply – to various degrees – social-psychological contributions to the study of immigration. In many cases they also demonstrate the merger of theories and frameworks from acculturation research with intergroup research. An interesting new concept in the field of immigration is **attachment**. The concept is pertinent to research on host–immigrant relations because attachment refers to the tendency to approach other people in novel situations. In Box 6.3 a study is presented on how attachment security can be experimentally induced.

Box 6.3   An innovative research method

Mikulincer and Shaver (2001) examined in a series of five studies the relevance of attachment theory, which deals with the sense of security in close relationships, for explaining intergroup attitudes. They focused on the connection between the attachment system and reactions to unknown and dissimilar people. Specifically, they examined the effects of activation of the sense of attachment security on the tendency to derogate and reject people who are different from oneself (outgroup members).

The secure base was primed, for instance, by subliminal presentation of words that exemplify this secure base (e.g., *love*, *support*). Or in another secure base priming condition, participants received the following instructions: 'Imagine yourself in a problematic situation that you cannot solve on your own, and imagine that you are surrounded by people who are sensitive and responsive to your distress, want to help you only because they love you, and set aside other activities in order to assist you.'

Overall, the findings indicated that the contextual activation of the sense of a secure base attenuates negative reactions to outgroup targets as well as negative reactions to people who express negative or critical opinions about certain aspects of a person's world-view (e.g., national identity). Having a sense of being loved and surrounded by supporting others seems to allow people to open themselves to alternative world-views and be more accepting of people who do not belong to their own group.

An important result was that in all five studies, secure base priming virtually eliminated any differential evaluation of ingroup and outgroup targets. This result was replicated using different priming procedures and different outgroups. The results also indicate that the effects of secure base priming on reactions to outgroups did not significantly depend on a participant's attachment style. In other words, contextual activation of the secure base schema attenuated negative reactions to outgroups without regard to attachment style. This finding implies that a situational, temporary activation of the secure base schema leads even chronically insecure people to react to outgroups in a more accepting and tolerant manner. Boosting attachment security increases cognitive openness and empathy, and fosters tolerance for outgroup members. No one knows, yet, whether repeated applications of secure base priming lead to a lasting change in attachment security, but this is a topic well worth exploring.

Social identity theory and social categorization theory, in particular, have been applied to the study of immigration, and, more importantly, have inspired scholars to formulate new theories, such as the common ingroup identity model, that are better tailored to the situation of immigrants. Another innovation comes in the form of comparative studies of the perspectives of both hosts and immigrants, of different groups of immigrants, cultures, nations and age ranges. Despite these advances, there is one important issue that merits further attention in future research: the refinement of core constructs, culture and identity, in particular. The imprecise and sometimes interchangeable use of 'culture' and 'identity' in the acculturation literature is problematic and should be remedied in future theory building and research. Culture is a complex construct and may be seen as encompassing artefacts, social institutions, language, customs, traditions and shared meanings. Cultural identity, however, refers to a sense of pride in and belonging to one's cultural group. Immigrants may easily adopt the language, the dress code and the working habits of the new country and even love the new food – all the external trappings of 'culture' – but they may still identify strongly with their nation of origin. This means that immigrants may give up parts of their cultural heritage without giving up their cultural identity.

The refinement of the definitions of culture and identity also has implications for social inclusion. Social inclusion is a normative concept in the sense that it is found to be desirable to promote conditions that favour the inclusion of individuals and groups into society (see, for instance, Abrams, Hogg & Marques, 2005). The concept is, however, not normative as to whether individuals and groups should maintain their culture or their identity. As such, social inclusion offers a valuable perspective on intergroup relations in culturally diverse societies.

Interventions

Social psychologists have always shown a strong interest in developing and testing methods to improve intergroup relations, in particular between ethnic groups. They are very relevant for the relations between immigrants and hosts. We will mention some of the most tested types of interventions.

1. Enhancing contact between members of the different groups. This implies non-segregated schools and participation of immigrants in the labour market. The contact should have a personal character; there should not be large differences in status between the participants; and it is important that authorities endorse the contact. The most important condition, though, is the presence of a common goal or a superordinate goal. Basically, the most effective instrument to improve intercultural relationships is cooperation. It helps if the cooperation has a good chance of success.

2. Reducing unnecessary social categorization. Social categorization is a normal and necessary cognitive process. Yet, when people are categorized as an out-group, self-serving distortions and negative stereotypes and prejudice appear on the scene. Many techniques which deal with these undesirable reactions are based on social identity theory. They all are focused on reducing unnecessary categorization, in many cases by creating superordinate memberships. Examples are organizations, the neighbourhood or the nation. One major step would be to avoid calling the new nationals 'foreigners'.

3. Acceptance of others' identity. An important part of one's identity is formed by the groups to which one belongs. People want to belong to respected groups. When their identity is threatened by the pressure to assimilate, people will show reactance towards the group that threatens their identity. Therefore, it is important that when intercultural contact takes place the cultural identity of others is accepted.

4. Training of competencies. Many educational and training programmes to enhance intercultural understanding and contact focus on learning cultural scripts. However, cultural scripts are culture specific and may get outdated. There is growing evidence that personal factors play an important role in intercultural contact. Some people are interculturally effective, whereas others are not. In the literature cultural empathy, open mindedness, social initiative, flexibility and emotional stability are mentioned as important intercultural competencies. Therefore it is more effective to develop training sessions in which people develop such crucial intercultural competencies. These competencies are useful in every culture and never get outdated.

Applied social psychology in context: the influence of globalization on host–immigrant relationships

Beyond issues pertaining to culture, identity and inclusion, attention should be paid to the influences of globalization on acculturation and intergroup relations. These influences, which have received earlier attention in the political and economical sciences, are elaborated in this final section. There are two related factors that are currently evoking changes in the lives and options of immigrants and their receiving societies: the unparalleled opportunities for transnational contact and the ever-growing number of immigrants on a world-wide basis. The consequences of these two factors have barely been investigated in cross-cultural and social-psychological research and should be incorporated into future research.

Transnationalism broadly refers to multiple ties and interactions linking people or institutions across the borders of nation-states. Although transnationalism may reflect international linkages across several countries, in many instances the term is used to refer to the process by which immigrants create and sustain multiple social relations that link together their societies of origin and settlement. An essential element of transnationalism is the great number and variety of involvements that immigrants sustain in both home and host societies. Examples are money remittances, commercial ties between the country of origin and the new country, intensive links with relatives and friends in the country of origin, branches of religious organizations that are set up in the new country, second homes in the country of origin and mutual visits. Transnationalism is facilitated by geographical proximity and good telecommunication services; some also argue that it is more likely to arise in conditions where immigrants form a considerable proportion of the nation, for example, North Africans in western Europe and Hispanics in the United States.

The emergence of these patterns suggests that we can add a new dimension – 'desire to be engaged in transnational contact' – to the dimensions 'wish to maintain contact with the host society' and 'wish to maintain culture and identity' in Berry's model of acculturation. This extends the within-society mechanisms referred to in the model to the international domain, reflecting current world-wide trends in globalization. The desire for transnational contact may combine with the four core acculturation strategies in different ways. For example, integrated migrants, who value both cultural maintenance and contact with the host society, may extend their means of cultural maintenance through association with their country of origin. On the other hand, immigrants who combine separation with transnational links may retreat from society and stay within 'ethnic enclaves' where they can keep living as they were accustomed in their country of origin. Such ethnic enclaves (e.g., Klein-Ankara in Berlin and Chinatowns in San Francisco and London) have multiple connections with the country of origin, such as trading companies, travel agencies, exchange of artists or students and sustained, frequent mutual visits. Indeed, withdrawal into ethnic enclaves may become an attractive option for immigrants when they experience discrimination or if the host society puts too much pressure on them to assimilate.

Transnationalism has provided immigrants with a wider range of alternatives for life in their new country. It also affords greater opportunities for immigrants to distance themselves from the host society when their identity is being threatened. Paradoxically, the availability of several options to deal with the new society may make immigrants also feel more at ease and more 'at home' in the new society.

The second factor that should influence developments in future research is changing demographics. Immigrants are evolving into members of established communities and now form a large proportion of many national populations. As a consequence, host societies are becoming increasingly culturally heterogeneous. These multicultural environments are likely to lead to new acculturation strategies and outcomes. Two of these are creolization and pluralism.

When a variety of cultural groups co-exist and there is no clearly dominant group, a process of **creolization** may take place. The concept of creolization refers to the mixing of two or more formerly discrete traditions or cultures. Examples of creolization include: spontaneous forms of youth language (ethno-language) or music (for instance, hip hop) in which elements from different ethnic groups are adopted, or food preferences (for instance, Cajun food, or New York pizza) that have become fashionable among a larger public. Creolization is specially to be found among transnational youth whose primary socialization has taken place in areas where different cultural influences come together. In the end, the implications of creolization are that immigrants shape the transformation of the host culture by adding elements from their own culture and, in doing so, find it easier and more appealing to identify with the evolving national culture.

Another plausible outcome in a multicultural society is **pluralism**. This approach encourages both cultural maintenance and intergroup contact; however, the cultural mixing, which is seen in creolization, does not occur. Pluralism arises from the relationships amongst a number of different groups that together form a new nation (or community). Although there may be status differences among the groups, each represents an important component of societies where no clear majority group is apparent. Pluralism is distinct from the common understanding of integration, which tends to refer to a dyadic relation between a subgroup of immigrants and a host society largely defined by its culturally dominant group. Furthermore, we may assume that marginalization and separation (including withdrawal into ethno-cultural enclaves) may occur in plural societies, but will do so relatively infrequently because these societies embrace cultural diversity.

Finally, the issue of national identity in multicultural societies is important and should receive greater attention in future research. Nations that support maintenance of cultural heritage while at the same time promoting a superordinate national identity show high levels of ethnic tolerance. Canada is a good example of this. As mentioned above, the Canadian policy of multiculturalism is very tolerant towards immigrants who want to express their own cultural identity. As a consequence, they identify more with the host society than immigrants in countries that stress assimilation. The tendency for migrants to identify by national label is higher in Canada than in the United States or Australia (van Oudenhoven, 2006). Similar trends have been observed in Singapore's multicultural society. There, research has shown that ethnic and national identity are strong and positively correlated in the four major ethnic groups, that Singaporeans typically refer to themselves in terms of a hyphenated identity (e.g., Singaporean-Chinese) and that stronger national identity is associated with more positive outgroup attitudes (DeRoza & Ward, 2008). These developments are in line with the common ingroup identity model of Gaertner and colleagues, who argue that intergroup conflict can be diminished by interventions that shift cognitive representations of membership in ingroups and outgroups to an inclusive social identity within a single group (Gaertner, Dovidio & Bachman, 1996).

Conclusion

Migration and cultural diversity have become key aspects of current societies. Models of adaptation of immigrants to their host societies are increasingly becoming models of mutual adaptation and take into account defensive reactions of majority groups, transformation of the majority culture and strongly expanding transnational contacts. The growing importance of the relations between immigrants and host societies has led to a strong interest of the social psychology of intergroup relations in immigration issues. Older theories, such as the contact hypothesis and social identity theory, are still useful, but new theories which focus on the role of threat and the positive effect of shared group membership lead to new insights.

At the individual level, there is abundant evidence that maintenance of heritage culture and adoption of aspects of the larger national culture are conducive to psychological and social well-being. This happens with the strategies of integration and pluralism, and, to some extent, with creolization. When such acculturation strategies are combined with the construction of a national culture as an inclusive superordinate identity, this leads to benefits not only for individuals and cultural groups, but also more broadly for plural societies. These strategies at the individual and group level, however, cannot be achieved without widespread acceptance of multiculturalism. It is the acceptance of multiculturalism and the evolution of a multifaceted, inclusive national identity that hold the promise for our future in an era of increasing globalization.

Glossary

Acculturation: the process of adapting to a different culture.

Assimilation: the abandonment of the heritage culture by immigrants in combination with a desire for contact with the host society.

Attachment: the nature of people's close relationships, thought to be formed in childhood.

Common ingroup identity model: the central idea is that once some people are defined as part of the ingroup, they will be treated in a similar way to other ingroup members.

Contact hypothesis: the theory that bringing members of conflicting groups together will reduce prejudice and improve intergroup relations.

Creolization: the mixing of two or more formerly different cultures.

Instrumental model of group conflict: a model which highlights the role of threat in the relations between hosts and immigrants. It identifies two determinants of intergroup antagonism: stress arising from limited resources and the presence of a relevant outgroup.

Integration: the maintenance of the heritage culture by immigrants in combination with a desire for contact with the majority group in the host society.

Marginalization: the abandonment by immigrants of the heritage culture in combination with a low desire for contact with the host society.

Melting pot: an ideology whereby immigrants are free to choose their own acculturation in private values, but experience a strong informal pressure to blend into the mainstream culture.

Pluralism: the combination of cultural maintenance with contact with several other cultural groups in the host society.

Separation: the maintenance of the heritage culture by immigrants in combination with a low desire for contact with the host society.

Similarity-attraction hypothesis: the theoretical and empirical principle that we like others who are similar to us in attitudes or other characteristics.

Social identity theory: theory which posits that group membership forms an important component of social identity, and that people strive to attain or maintain a positive self-image by engaging in favourable comparisons between their ingroups and various outgroups.

Transnationalism: the existence of multiple ties and interactions linking people or institutions across the borders of nation-states.

Review questions

1. Which acculturation strategy does your current government want from newcomers, and what would you personally want? Use both Berry's terms and Bourhis' terms.
2. Could you give some examples of creolization in your region/country which have not been mentioned in the text?
3. What kind of transnational ties do you have with people of your own nationality? Do they have any influence on your daily behaviour?
4. How could one prime a secure base schema in such a way that it has a long-lasting effect?

Further reading

Baumeister, R. F. (2005). *The cultural animal. Human nature, meaning, and social life*. Oxford University Press.

Matsumoto, D. & Juang, L. (2004). *Culture and psychology*. Belmont, CA: Thomson/ Wadsworth.

Sam, D. L. & Berry, J. W. (eds.) (2006). *The Cambridge handbook on acculturation psychology*. Cambridge University Press.

Smith, P. B., Bond, M. H. & Kagitcibasi, C. (2005). *Understanding human behaviour across cultures: Living and working in a changing world*. London: Sage.

Ward, C., Bochner, S. & Furnham, A. (2001). *The psychology of culture shock*. London: Routledge.

References

Abrams, D., Hogg, M. A. & Marques, J. M. (2005). *The social psychology of inclusion and exclusion*. New York: Psychology Press.

Allport, G. W. (1954). *The nature of prejudice*. Reading, MA: Addison-Wesley.

Berry, J. W. (1997). Immigration, acculturation and adaptation. *Applied Psychology: An International Review, 46*, 5–34.

    (2006). Mutual attitudes among immigrants and ethnocultural groups in Canada. *International Journal of Intercultural Relations, 30* (6), 719–734.

Bourhis, R. Y., Moïse, L. C., Perreault, S. & Senécal, S. (1997). Towards an interactive acculturation model: A social psychological approach. *International Journal of Psychology, 32*, 369–386.

Brewer, M. B. (2000). Reducing prejudice through cross-categorization: Effects of multiple social identities. In S. Oskamp (ed.), *Reducing prejudice and discrimination* (pp. 165–183). Hillsdale, NJ: Erlbaum.

Byrne, D. (1971). *The attraction paradigm*. New York: Academic Press.

DeRoza, C. & Ward, C. (2008). National identity, ethnic identity and intergroup perceptions in Singapore. Manuscript submitted for publication.

Esses, V. M., Dovidio, J. F., Jackson, L. M. & Armstrong, T. L. (2001). The immigration dilemma: The role of perceived group competition, ethnic prejudice, and national identity. *Journal of Social Issues, 57*, 389–412.

Esses, V. M., Wagner, U., Wolf, C. & Preiser, M. (2006). Perceptions of national identity and attitudes toward immigrants and immigration in Canada and Germany. *International Journal of Intercultural Relations, 30* (6), 653–669.

Gaertner, S. L. & Dovidio, J. F. (2000). *Reducing intergroup bias: The common ingroup identity model*. New York: Psychology Press.

Gaertner, S., Dovidio, J. & Bachman, B. A. (1996). Revisiting the contact hypothesis: The induction of a common ingroup identity. *International Journal of Intercultural Relations, 20*, 271–290.

Ho, R., Niles, S., Penney, R. & Thomas, A. (1994). Migrants and multiculturalism: A survey of attitudes in Darwin. *Australian Psychologist, 29*, 62–70.

Horenczyk, G. (1996). Migrant identities in conflict: Acculturation attitudes and perceived acculturation ideologies. In G. Breakwell and E. Lyons (eds.), *Changing European identities: Social psychological analyses of social change* (pp. 241–250). Oxford: Butterworth.

Levine, R. A. & Campbell, D. W. (1972). *Ethnocentrism: Theories of conflict, ethnic attitudes, and group behavior*. New York: Wiley.

Mikulincer, M. & Shaver, P. R. (2001). Attachment theory and intergroup bias: Evidence that priming the secure base schema attenuates negative reactions to out-groups. *Journal of Personality and Social Psychology, 81*, 97–115.

Piontkowski, U., Florack, A., Hoelker, P. & Obdrzalek, P. (2000). Predicting accultura-
tion attitudes of dominant and non-dominant groups. *International Journal of Intercultural Relations*, 24, 1–26.

Ramirez, M. (1984). Assessing and understanding biculturalism-monoculturalism in Mexican-American adults. In J. L. Martinez and R. H. Mendoza (eds.), *Chicano psychology* (pp. 77–94). Orlando, FL: Academic Press.

Ryder, A., Alden, L. & Paulhus, D. (2000). Is acculturation unidimensional or bidimensional? *Journal of Personality and Social Psychology*, 79, 49–65.

Tajfel, H. & Turner, J. C. (1979). An integrative theory of intergroup conflict. In W. G. Austin & S. Worchel (eds.), *The social psychology of intergroup relations* (pp. 23–48). Monterey, CA: Brooks/Coole.

Van Oudenhoven, J. P. (2006). Immigrants. In D. L. Sam & J. W. Berry (eds.), *The Cambridge handbook on acculturation psychology* (pp. 163–180). Cambridge University Press.

Van Oudenhoven, J. P., Judd, C. M. & Hewstone, M. (2000). Additive and interactive mod-
els of crossed-categorisation in correlated social categories. *Group Processes and Intergroup Relations*, 3, 285–295.

Van Oudenhoven, J. P., Prins, K. S. & Buunk, B. P. (1998). Attitudes of minority and majority members towards adaptation of immigrants. *European Journal of Social Psychology*, 28, 995–1013.

Zick, A., Wagner, U., Van Dick, R. & Petzel, T. (2001). Acculturation and prejudice in Germany: Majority and minority perspectives. *Journal of Social Issues*, 57, 541–557.

7 Applying social psychology to the classroom

PASCAL HUGUET AND HANS KUYPER

Introduction

The classroom is the core unit of our educational system. It also illustrates many common social-psychological concepts and phenomena. Whenever we bring groups of people together for the purpose of learning, we have the opportunity to apply social-psychological principles that will further our educational goals. Applying these principles to the classroom may help increase students' commitment to learning, make their attitudes towards school more positive, reduce their feeling of failure and related negative affects or emotions, improve their level of aspiration as well as their grades, and much more. Clearly, education is – at least in part – applied social psychology.

In the past three decades, more and more researchers contributed to bridging the gap between social psychology and education, resulting in the emergence of a new scientific area, the so-called 'social psychology of education', 'educational social psychology' or sometimes even 'social educational psychology'. Is this area merely social psychology applied to a particular domain of interest? Or is it a subdiscipline of the field of education, looked at from the vantage point of the social psychologist? As noted by Feldman (1986), the most appropriate answer is that it represents an amalgamation of the two fields; it is not merely social psychology, nor is it simply education. Whatever it is called, this new area represents an interface of the two fields, which has produced a broad range of theories, research and data that speak to the interests of educators and psychologists.

Our purpose here is not to describe all the current themes of interest that characterize this interface. This would be impossible in only one chapter. Instead, our purpose is to focus on a limited set of social-psychological concepts and phenomena in relation to a major component of the classroom: evaluation. Like it or not, evaluation is as much a part of education as is learning. The classroom, in particular, is a place for multiple evaluations, whether positive or negative. Many of these evaluations are provided by the teacher, but they can also be 'self-evaluations', based on interpersonal comparisons the students are constantly making with each other. Today, there is ample evidence that these social comparisons contribute to students' academic achievements. But exactly what does 'social comparison' mean, what do we know about it and about its consequences in the classroom?

Students' 'theories' of intelligence are of particular interest here as well. Over time, students come to believe that their performance in a wide range of tasks is or is not narrowly constrained by innate attributes, and that they can or cannot change their level of intelligence. Are such beliefs another significant determinant of students' academic achievement?

Likewise, over time, students develop positive or negative views about their abilities in such-and-such an academic domain (e.g., maths), which become an integral part of their 'academic self-concept'. Does this self-concept also make a difference, and how?

Students belong to social groups and may sometimes suffer from the negative stereotypes associated with these groups. Are these negative stereotypes a real problem for students, and why?

Finally, how students see themselves in the context of the classroom and how they behave in this context depend, at least in part, on the 'classroom climate'. But exactly what does 'classroom climate' mean, and exactly why does this notion also matter?

As we will see, each of these research lines provides convincing evidence that basic social-psychological principles play an important role in ordinary classroom circumstances. Their practical implications will be presented, and some recommendations will be made with regard to the struggle against academic failure and dropping out of school.

Social comparison

According to a widely accepted definition, **social comparison** is 'the process of thinking about information about one or more other people in relation to the self' (Wood, 1996, pp. 520–521). The theory itself was formulated in 1954 by Festinger. According to this famous social psychologist, most people want to evaluate their abilities and opinions, especially when there is no 'objective reality' (i.e., when a given ability or opinion cannot be measured or evaluated via objective means). In this case, people rely on 'social reality', by comparing their own abilities and opinions with those of others. In daily life, people are more or less free to engage in social comparison or not. In some cases, social comparison is almost forced. For instance, when the salary of a company manager appears in the news, it is difficult not to make a comparison with your own income. The class context clearly is a situation where social comparison is pervasive. Often grades are read out loud and clearly by the teacher, so that each student knows exactly where he/she 'belongs'.

Many studies have shown that social comparisons occur even in the preschool years, during which they facilitate children's adaptation to the rules at stake in their classroom. It is indeed through comparing the way the nursery school teacher reacts to their actions and to the actions of other pupils that young children learn how to obtain certain rewards (praise, encouragement) and how to avoid certain punishments (scolding, withdrawal of privileges). In doing so, children learn the prevailing norms and values of this new environment – their playgroup – and, more generally, their nursery school.

Ruble and her associates have done careful and detailed observational studies of the development of social comparison capabilities and interest in the primary school years and beyond. These have led Ruble (1983) to suggest that the capabilities necessary for making social comparison inferences about oneself (i.e., drawing conclusions about one's ability level in a given domain on the basis of comparison information) seem to be absent before the age of six or seven. After that, social comparison inferences become part of a pupil's self-knowledge. Children therefore pay an increasingly greater amount of attention to academic achievement and to the grades obtained by their peers, so they can rank themselves with respect to others in the various subject matters, a behaviour that becomes especially prominent at the age of nine to ten (Dumas, Huguet, Monteil, Rastoul & Nezlek, 2005).

Depending on what they discover, students may experience the classroom as a pleasant or a frightening place. There is indeed little doubt today that social comparison processes taking place in the classroom can trigger both positive and negative affects (e.g., pride vs jealousy; see Buunk, Kuyper & van der Zee, 2005). In his influential chapter on social comparison and education, Levine (1983) offered evidence that the potential for damage to children's self-esteem is high in the classroom setting, as is the potential for children to adopt artificially low conceptions of their own abilities. There are many cases in which students may even want to avoid social comparison. In the classroom, however, the norms frequently require disclosure of one's own achievements in a pattern of reciprocal disclosure with others (as in many other group settings). Fortunately, the discovery that another's achievements surpass one's own is not necessarily painful or negative. It can also have a beneficial impact on one's performance. Observing another person who masters a task can reveal useful information on how to improve, a phenomenon referred to as 'learning by observation' or '**observational learning**' in the psychological literature. Seeing another person succeed may also increase the motivation to improve. As noted by Blanton, Buunk, Gibbons and Kuyper (1999), however, this latter reason is not as straightforward as the first, because it may be motivating to see others doing better than oneself at a task for a variety of reasons. First, individuals may come to identify with their more successful comparison others, leading to imitation of their successful actions. Second, seeing others succeed may lead individuals to set higher personal standards for evaluating their own success, which can motivate efforts towards these new and more challenging goals. Finally, observing others doing well can endow individuals with a sense of their own potential, and this can raise self-confidence and feelings of **self-efficacy** (i.e., students' judgement of their own capabilities with regard to a specific task). There is evidence today that the belief that one is able to perform a certain (new) task plays an important role in academic achievement. Schunk and colleagues, for example, found that feelings of self-efficacy made unique contributions to increasing academic attainment over and above various task instructions (see Schunk, 1989).

Festinger (1954) stated that there is a preference for comparison with similar others. However, there has been much discussion among social comparison researchers about what exactly Festinger meant by 'similar'. Nowadays, it is widely accepted that one should consider similarity on '**related attributes**', that is, attributes that are related to the performance of the task at hand. If a young male adult wants to evaluate his running speed accurately, he should compare himself with a *male* of about *his own age* who has about an *equal* '*athletic posture*', because these three attributes are related to running speed. He should not compare himself with his grandmother. The preference to compare oneself with others who are similar on related attributes is at the core of the **similarity principle**. In the case of physical as well as intellectual abilities, Festinger suggested that social comparison follows a **unidirectional drive upwards**. Applied to the classroom, this suggests that most students prefer to compare their grades (among other things) with peers who generally are slightly better than themselves (while being relatively similar on related attributes). This is, in fact, exactly what happened in two field studies (Blanton *et al.*, 1999; Huguet, Dumas, Monteil & Genestoux, 2001b). As we shall see, these studies offered several results which we must recognize if teaching methods are to be optimized.

Upward social comparison in the classroom

In Blanton *et al.*'s (1999) field study, Dutch secondary school children (year seven, age thirteen years old) listed on a questionnaire their usual **social comparison target** in each of seven courses (maths, biology, geography, etc.) at the end of the second term (T2), and the schools provided the marks of all students. A score of 'comparison-level choice' was then assigned to each student on the basis of his/her comparison-target's marks, and the associations between this 'choice' and students' own grades at T2 and T3 (the end of the year school report) were tested. Several results are of particular interest here.

First, although all classes were coeducational, a vast majority of students (more than 90 per cent) deliberately compared themselves with students of their own gender. In a certain sense, this is another manifestation of the similarity principle. However, in this case, the similarity is on a dimension that is not necessarily related to grades.

Second, most students (around 60 per cent) compared themselves with classmates whose marks were just above them on the grading scale, exactly as Festinger (1954) would predict. From this other finding, it follows that a student whose grade-point average in maths is 5 out of 20 (the regular scale in some European countries) will typically pay more attention to classmates whose average is 6 or 7; a student with an average of 12 will focus on classmates whose average is 13 or 14, and so on. Students' inclination to make these slightly **upward comparisons** forces them to engage in a certain amount of mental gymnastics. Because their scholastic achievement usually differs across academic disciplines, at any given point in the school year students will have different comparison targets, which they will drop and replace whenever their own grades and/or those of their targets go up or down.

Finally, in Blanton *et al.*'s study, not only did students compare slightly upwards with their classmates, but higher comparison-level choices were associated with higher grades at T3. Furthermore, choosing to compare upwards did not lower students' **comparative evaluation** (i.e., how the children evaluated their relative standing in a given course in class).

Huguet *et al.* (2001b) replicated and extended Blanton *et al.*'s findings in a number of important ways in a study of French students of the same age. First of all, they offered a more detailed record of comparison choices. In Blanton *et al.*'s study, only the students' first nominations for each course were analysed. As the authors pointed out, however, students probably compared their grades with those of a variety of other students. It could be, therefore, that social comparison with more successful others did not lower students' comparative evaluation because they made up for a painful experience with a happy one, through the use of a **downward comparison** (i.e., comparison with worse-off others) in their second choice. For this reason, Huguet *et al.* (2001b) included two comparison choice measures in each of seven courses (resulting in 14 comparison choices). As expected, the vast majority of students (again above 60 per cent) compared slightly upwards on the two choices in most courses, higher grades were associated with higher comparison-level choices, and choosing to compare with someone who outperformed them in a course did not leave students feeling relatively less able in that course.

Blanton *et al.* (1999) reported indirect evidence that the individuals nominated as comparison targets were important in the lives of the students. Consistent with this, Huguet *et al.* (2001b) found that students engaged in upward comparison with psychologically close others (i.e., their best friends, as Mussweiler & Rüter, 2003 would also expect). According to Buunk and Ybema (1997), individuals generally avoid identification with worse-off others (with whom they contrast themselves – especially when their self-esteem is threatened) and try to identify with others doing better (and see these others as similar to themselves). Also consistent with this, and with the hypothesis that upward comparison is motivated by a desire for self-improvement (Wood, 1996), Huguet *et al.* (2001b) found that most students reported that their performance in almost all courses might become closer to that of their slightly more successful comparison targets in the future.

Box 7.1   Theory application: how to make use of social comparison principles.

Our knowledge of social comparison principles (see the previous section) leads towards at least two recommendations. First, recall that no matter what the subject is, cross-gender comparisons are relatively rare in the classroom setting, almost as if they were meaningless for most students. This suggests that if using a student as an example to stimulate other pupils has any effect, it generally does so only for students of the same gender. *If girls rarely or never compare themselves to boys, and likewise for boys, any given student in the class – no matter how brilliant – cannot serve as an example for everyone.* This should not be taken as an argument for separating the two sexes. This is just a matter of fact, suggesting that *teachers take one exemplar of each gender as comparison standards for their students* (especially when the comparison dimension is gender stereotyped, see the section on 'stereotype threat' later in this chapter).

Second, to compare themselves with others, most students choose peers not only of the same gender but also ones they judge to be within their reach (i.e., *slightly upward* comparison targets). On this basis, it is not surprising that the less capable students typically disregard the examples of excellence forced upon them by teachers applying some psychological technique that is at best naive, because it does not take the realities of students' comparison frameworks into account. But above all – and this breaks away from traditional teaching methods – our knowledge of students' spontaneous social comparison choices suggests that *even the less capable students can profitably be used as examples by teachers, not for the whole class, of course, but for those classmates who perform even worse.* It is truly amazing to find that, despite their attested failure, some less capable students continue to compare themselves slightly upwards. The least we can do is help them in this respect. Failure to take students' own standards into account, whether we like it or not, amounts to forcing them to compare themselves with the best students (as generally suggested by the teacher), and thereby run the risk of discouraging them. What happens then is quite simple: rather than comparing upwards, discouraged students focus on peers whose grades are even worse than their own. While reassuring, this downward comparison prevents all progress; and we have come full circle. Everyone remembers students stuck in the rut of failure, precisely because they were glad not to be the very worst in the class! As time passes, this situation feeds an **academic self-concept** (i.e., how the individuals self-evaluate in various academic dimensions) that is ridden with failure and has catastrophic effects on cognitive output (see next section).

Students' 'Theories' of intelligence and academic self-concept

So far, we have argued that maintaining slightly upward comparisons is a valuable advice for teachers. In order for upward comparison to be a resource for change, however, the students making the comparison obviously need to believe that they are able to change. Without a mutable self-image, students can respond to upward comparisons only by feeling inferior (see, e.g., Stapel & Koomen, 2000), or by defensively discounting the social comparison domain or target.

Entity versus incremental theory of intelligence

Dweck's impressive work on people's entity versus incremental theories of intelligence is of particular interest here (see Dweck, 1999, for a review). '**Entity theorists**', she reasoned, are people who believe that intelligence is an innate and stable property of a person. This typically leads the entity theorists towards the expectation that their general performance on a wide range of tasks is narrowly constrained by innate attributes. On the contrary, '**incremental theorists**' typically believe that performance can usually be improved by effort.

Consistent with this, Dweck and colleagues' research has shown that incremental theorists are much more resilient and optimistic in the face of failure than are entity theorists, including when failure comes from an upward social comparison episode. Dweck's research has generated robust effects simply by telling subjects about one of the two theories, either indirectly through stories or directly through bogus journal articles. Longer-term changes lasting several months have been produced merely by teaching subjects about incremental theories of intelligence and explicitly encouraging them to believe that their skills can improve.

Hendersen and Dweck (1990) assessed students' theories of intelligence and confidence in their intelligence as they entered year eight and before they had received any formal performance feedback. Students were asked to rate the extent to which they agreed or disagreed (from six-point scales ranging from 1, 'strongly agree', to 6, 'strongly disagree') with a series of sentences, such as, 'you have a certain amount of intelligence, and you really can't do much to change it', or 'no matter who you are, you can change your intelligence a lot'. On the confidence measure, students chose between series of paired statements, one expressing low confidence and the other high confidence, for example, 'I usually think I'm intelligent' versus 'I wonder if I'm intelligent'. Then, students' scores were examined in relation to their past grades (when they were in year seven) and performances as year eight pupils.

Among the students with an entity theory, those who had done poorly in year seven continued to do poorly in year eight, and many of those who were high achievers in year seven were now among the low achievers. More surprising, this decline from high to low academic standing was mainly due to the students

Figure 7.1 *Children doing a geometry or drawing test*

who had *high* confidence in their intelligence, indicating that confidence in intelligence is in fact problematic within an entity theory. In contrast, students with an incremental theory showed a clear improvement in their class standing. In general, those who had done well in year seven continued to do well. But many of those who had been among the low achievers in year seven were now doing much better, often entering the ranks of the high achievers.

These fascinating findings have some implications for our previous considerations on social comparison choices. They suggest that, in order to allow the poor or less capable students to learn from their more successful others (i.e., upward comparison targets), one should encourage them to see their abilities as malleable rather than fixed. Dweck has found that teachers can make a substantial difference by avoiding ability praise (e.g., 'you're very clever!'), which suggests the presence of innate attributes, and substituting effort praise ('you worked very hard on that!'). Students may also be exposed to the success stories of peers who initially struggled with a topic, but went on to master it.

These additional advices are of critical importance. Even students with high opinions of their ability would quickly disengage from a difficult task unless they also believed that their ability could be improved. Over time, the entity theorists may disengage from all activities that in fact simply require effort, and thus their academic self-concept may suffer. As reported below, an academic self-concept that is ridden with failure can, in turn, have huge negative effects on task performance.

Academic self-concept of failure and performance

In Huguet, Brunot and Monteil's (2001a) study, students in year seven and year eight who were either doing well or failing in mathematics were given 50 seconds to study a complex, rather abstract geometric figure. They then had to reproduce the figure from memory on a sheet of paper (see Figures 7.1 and 7.2). Before beginning the task, they were told that their ability in either geometry or drawing

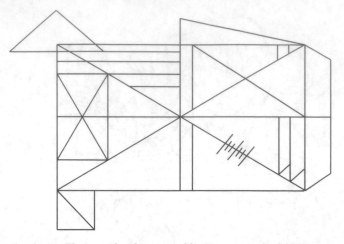

Figure 7.2 *The complex figure used by Huguet* et al. *(2001)*

was being evaluated. The children were randomly assigned to one or the other of these two conditions. Their performance was then assessed by judges who had no knowledge of the experimental conditions and of the students' ability level. The aim of this relatively simple study was to show that students' performance is closely tied to their self-representations in a given discipline. If simply mentioning geometry activates memories of failure, can this hinder their capacity to store and retrieve information?

The answer is a definite 'yes' (see Figure 7.3). In the geometry context, the poor students did far less well than the good ones, whereas in the drawing context, the poor students did so much better that they equalled the performance of the good students. Given that the task was exactly the same in the two experimental conditions (geometry vs drawing), it was the self-representations the children had constructed over time that proved to be the determining factor.

This study shows the strong impact of self-representations on cognitive output, which, as we can easily see, hinges on much more than just individual abilities. In our example, the required abilities rely on cognitive processes thought to be the expression of strictly neurobiological 'givens' (i.e., visual memory, visuospatial perception and organization). Neuroscience enthusiasts who advocate a 'hard' kind of science will see in these results a reason for avoiding a sometimes excessive 'biotropy' (i.e., an overly biological perspective; see also our section 'applied social psychology in context').

Let's take this a little further. If simply mentioning geometry suffices to lower the performance of students who do not excel in that area, then it follows, at a more general level, that a student's academic past can at least partially account for his/her present difficulties (Monteil & Huguet, 1999). The more often a student fails, the more the context of that failure (not only the subject matter but also the person teaching it) acquires an autobiographic significance for that student that interferes with achievement, causing a loss of interest over time that cannot

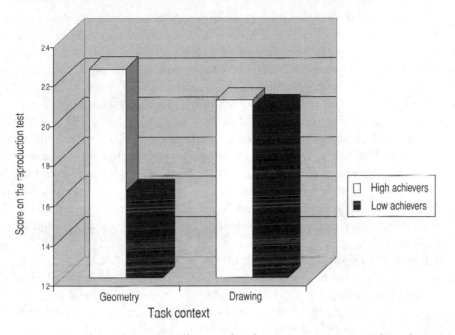

Figure 7.3 *Memory recall score of students (max = 44 points) by task context and academic standing*

be readily ascribed to a lack of motivation in the ordinary sense of the term. Very rapidly, all the necessary conditions are set up – again, right there in the classroom – for a situation in which poor students acquire a reputation of being stupid or of low ability, bringing them a little bit closer each day to dropping out of school early.

However, saying that bad reputations 'weigh heavy' is not enough to account for their impact. In reality, their effect on cognitive functioning resides in the fact that they lend 'instant accessibility' to a self-concept of academic failure and the string of negative emotions it entails. What does instant accessibility mean here? Try to remember what you ate for dinner two days ago. The answer doesn't pop right up. It's available in memory, so you can come up with it, but only after some effort; it is obviously not readily accessible. Try now to remember your date of birth. You've retrieved it even before you finish reading this short sentence. Not only is this basic piece of self-knowledge available in memory, it is always immediately accessible, just like your first or last name. In the same way, *once a student's poor academic reputation has been forged in the context of the classroom, it acts as an ongoing reminder of the student's weak points and other inadequacies.* This kind of self-knowledge is activated effortlessly and unwillingly every time a teacher proposes an activity associated with failure in the student's past (geometry or mathematics in our study). Unfortunately, the ongoing activation of such self-concepts engulfs these students in a sphere of failure, for at least two reasons.

First, because *it fosters within them pessimistic assessments of their chances of success and thus prevents them from getting involved to any serious extent in the proposed activity*. Second, because even when these students do attempt to apply themselves, *the highly accessible memory of their past failures, and their visions of getting lost again, use up so much of their attention that they are incapable of devoting themselves fully to the problem at hand*. Hence the well-known difficulty teachers have in getting their poor students to stop looking out the window (or even to stay in their seats!) and to concentrate on their exercises in order to prevent those 'same old mistakes'. The temptation is great for teachers to see the behaviour of these low achievers as the mark of their inability to do schoolwork, or at least as a reflection of what is often noted on students' reports as a 'genuine attention problem'. However, *the greatest obstacle generally lies elsewhere, namely, in the conditions under which cognitive abilities are expressed, not in the abilities themselves*.

Experimental results show (Huguet *et al.*, 2001a) that a student may have all the necessary skills and aptitudes for a given exercise but fail to implement them because the context is unfavourable. One must therefore proceed with caution before drawing the conclusion that so-and-so has such-and-such a learning disability. This problem is obviously a vital one for the schools, and for any educational system where the evaluation of knowledge is a common practice. It must be acknowledged – and this is fundamental – ability is not directly observable, it can only be inferred from performance. Yet, as we have seen, the latter is closely linked to the 'production' context. Hence the need to take the context into account if we hope to gain insight into the reasons why certain students fail, and thus to be in a position to apply that insight to improving the effectiveness of remedial techniques for lagging students.

Box 7.2   Application of a research technique

By this time, the reader will have understood that to enable poor students to progress, it is not enough to concentrate on the areas where they are lacking, even if carefully targeted. Granted, this step is mandatory. But to have any chance of success, it must be accompanied by close consideration of the actual learning context. School behaviour is like many other kinds of behaviour: it can be changed only if and when the conditions that contribute to its occurrence also change. If we ignore the fact that certain failures depend at least as much on the social and emotional setting (the classroom itself) as on the presumed low aptitude of the failing children, we are doomed to repeating the same things a thousand times, to giving the same advice over and over again, to reprimanding the same careless blunders time after time, without any noticeable consequences other than reciprocal annoyance and discouragement. Isn't this a daily experience of most teachers? One can hardly blame the teachers for it, given the difficulty of their occupation. *But the point is, to have an effective impact on poor students, one has to act upon the whole class. If failure in class is at least partly due to what other classmates think, then teachers should – rather, must – constantly pay attention to the reputation of poor students.* Several strategies are available for dismantling negative academic reputations, or, even better, for preventing them from being built up in the first place. For example, never publicly point out a student's inadequacies during oral testing or questioning in front of the class, or when handing back tests or having students write on the board. There is nothing worse for a poor student than to see or hear peers noticing or talking about his/her weaknesses or lack of ability. Eventually the day arrives when this scenario has become so familiar to poor students that they disregard it altogether. But by then the game is over, and lost. With time, as still other studies have shown (Monteil & Huguet, 1999, for a review), poor students' convictions about themselves fortify to the point where any success in a subject matter formerly associated with failure has the initial effect of troubling the child even more, especially if classmates find out about it. It is only when the teacher exercises a certain degree of discretion (when returning tests, for example) that this unusual event is sometimes followed by spectacular progress. On the other hand, students who are used to success or have developed positive views about themselves in such-and-such academic dimension want to be allowed to speak and to perform in front of others. They should be given this opportunity, otherwise their achievement level may decline. Deprive good students of the classroom visibility they are accustomed to – for example, by no longer calling on them in class – and it will not be long before their grades start dropping, sometimes falling even lower than those of poor students.

Academic self-concept of success and the BFLPE

Let us elaborate further on the good students. Educators and parents often assume that, for these students, there are academic benefits associated with attending higher-ability schools (or classrooms). After all, academic achievement, aspirations and subsequent attainment are typically higher in these schools. As demonstrated by Marsh and colleagues, however, equally able students have typically *lower* academic self-concepts in *higher*-ability schools than in lower-ability schools. This effect, which has been identified in many studies on thousands and thousands students all over the world (see Marsh & Hau, 2003), is called the '**big-fish-little-pond effect**' (BFLPE). While students' academic self-concept is positively influenced by their own academic accomplishments, the high ability levels of others in their immediate context negatively influence it (see Figure 7.4).

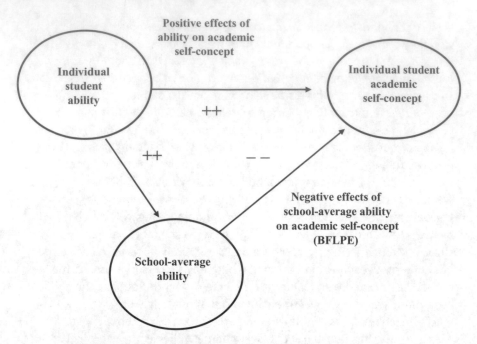

Figure 7.4 *The big-fish-little-pond effect (BFLPE): theoretical predictions (adapted from Marsh & Hau, 2003)*

There is now convincing evidence that the BFLPE also affects students' academic choices, academic effort and subsequent achievement. Likewise, it seems that the BFLPE represents the counterbalancing, net effects of two opposing processes, one based on contrast between oneself and others and the other on assimilation.

Contrast is said to occur when the self-evaluative judgement shifts away from the background or context. If students indeed use the other students in their academically selective schools or classes (i.e., schools or classes where the average ability level of students is especially high) as a basis of comparison, then participation in academically selective classes should result in lowered academic self-concepts, that is, a contrast or negative BFLPE (e.g., 'there are a lot of students better than I am, so I must not be as good as I thought').

Assimilation is said to occur when the self-evaluative judgment shifts towards the social context. For example, pride in selection for participation in academically selective settings might improve students' academic self-concept (i.e., 'if I'm good enough to be selected to participate in this prestigious programme with all these other very clever students, then I must be very clever').

Thus, attending higher-ability schools (or being placed in higher-ability classes) simultaneously results in a more demanding basis of social comparison for one's own accomplishments (leading to a stronger negative contrast effect), and a source of pride (leading to a stronger positive assimilation effect). Ironically, some educational programmes intentionally foster a highly competitive environment that is likely to exacerbate the BFLPE rather than to counteract it.

Stereotype threat: the role of negative stereotypes

Another critical phenomenon here is '**stereotype threat**' (Steele, 1997), or the threat that one's performance will confirm – to others, to oneself or both – a negative stereotype associated with one's own social group (e.g., for women and girls the stereotype that they are inferior to men and boys on maths-related tasks). This threat unfortunately leads to poorer performance and thus produces the expected negative outcome. In Spencer, Steele and Quinn's (1999) studies, for example, women with high maths ability performed less well (than equally qualified men) on difficult maths tests both when they were told that the test produced gender differences and when that information was not given, but performed as well as men when told that no gender differences had been found. There is now ample evidence that women and girls suffer from gender-stereotyped expectations on standardized maths tests (see Huguet & Régner, 2007, for a review). Huguet and Régner's (2007) findings indicate that girls in years seven–nine can exhibit a performance deficit in quasi-ordinary classroom circumstances *when they are simply led to believe that the task at hand measures mathematical skills.* In this new study, students (age eleven–thirteen) were faced with the same memory task as the one described earlier in this chapter (see Figure 7.2), which was characterized as a geometry test versus a memory game (Study 1) or as a geometry test versus a drawing test (Study 2). In both studies, whereas girls underperformed relative to boys in the relatively self threatening geometry condition, they outperformed them in the more neutral condition (i.e., when the task was characterized as a memory game or a drawing test). Furthermore, stereotype threat occurred in girls working alone or in mixed-gender groups (i.e., presence of regular classmates), but not in same-gender groups (i.e., presence of only same-gender classmates), which has several implications for educational practices.

Box 7.3   Application of a research method: should the two genders be separated in the school setting?

One implication of stereotype threat theory and research concerns the controversy about the merits of single-gender education over coeducation. The elimination of stereotype threat in the former setting may indeed be taken as a serious argument for separating the genders. After all, if such a separation could minimize the deleterious effects of gender stereotypes, why not make use of it? Several points must nevertheless be made here.

First, although single-gender education may help prevent stereotypes from taking effect downstream (i.e., in testing situations), it is ineffective if not detrimental upstream (i.e., stereotype formation and propagation), which is obviously not satisfactory. As indicated by numerous findings in the social-categorization literature, putting individuals into separate groups typically strengthens (or even creates) stereotypes rather than reducing them and the consequences they trigger. Clearly, if single-gender education leads to better performance in the classroom but generates tension and discrimination outside, it is undesirable or at the very least should be used with caution (i.e., temporarily rather than on a regular basis). In line with this argument, interventions designed to reduce separation and intergroup boundaries between the two genders undermine stereotype threat in women.

Second, Huguet and Régner's findings show that it is not the sheer presence of males that is problematic. In effect, girls worked alone in Study 1 (i.e., in the absence of any members of the opposite gender), yet this arrangement did not prevent their performance deficit from showing up in the threatening condition.

Finally, separating the genders is not the only way to proceed at the practical level. Teaching students about stereotype threat is an efficient means of reducing its detrimental effects in testing situations. This option is especially attractive, since it may also help people propagate counter-stereotypic views within their social network, including among their own children, which would be effective both downstream and upstream. Additional interventions can be found in Good, Aronson and Inzlicht (2003), who showed that adolescent females encouraged by university students to view intelligence as malleable and/or to attribute academic difficulties to the novelty of the educational setting earned significantly higher marks in maths standardized tests than females in the control condition (where these encouragements were not made). This interesting finding suggests that stereotype threat is the 'default mindset' for female students in maths classes, and shows how to change this mindset.

Classroom climate

Finally, although this chapter is necessarily very selective, it cannot be closed without mentioning phenomena related to the 'classroom climate' (Adelman & Taylor, in press). **Classroom climate**, another significant determinant of students' behaviour and performances, is the perceived quality of the classroom, also referred to as the 'atmosphere' or 'ambience' of this particular setting. As such, the classroom climate results from the combination of numerous factors (physical, material, organizational, economic, social and cultural factors, to name a few). It also ranges from hostile and toxic to welcoming and supportive, and can fluctuate daily and over the school year. Here, we simply focus on some of the teachers' practices, which can make this climate beneficial or a barrier to learning.

In a study in the Netherlands, one of us (HK) asked children at their very first day at secondary school to indicate how much they expected to like each one of ten different subjects (referred to below as 'expected liking'). About one month later, they answered another questionnaire, where they had to indicate how much they liked each subject, and also to judge each teacher on a number of aspects, which formed together a 'teacher-evaluation scale'. The 'expected liking' judgements can be considered to reflect the children's past history with the subjects. A child who liked maths at primary school will also expect to like it at secondary school. It appeared that the correlations between the expected liking and the expressed liking after one month were very low, rarely exceeding 0.30. On the other hand, the correlations between the expressed liking and the scores on the teacher-evaluation scale were much higher, up to 0.85. This means that teachers strongly determine whether their subject is liked. Or, in other words, one month being taught by a very good teacher (or a teacher perceived as such) can overrule all the six or more years of negative experiences with the specific subject. And vice versa, one month of lessons by a bad teacher (or one perceived as such) can overrule all the wonderful past experiences.

But the teachers themselves are rarely what pupils love or hate; it is rather the climate that they are partially or fully responsible for setting up in the classroom. We must acknowledge that classes where the atmosphere is highly unpleasant are ones where each child's scholastic standing is made conspicuous, for instance, when passing out tests that have been marked or when calling pupils up to the front, or, even worse, when students are systematically divided up into ability groups. In such settings, the risk of seeing the high achievers reject the low achievers is great, and the result is that both the former and the latter become irritable and aggressive, and less attentive to those around them.

The risk that the classroom climate will deteriorate can be substantially reduced if the teacher strives to minimize competition. This can be done in particular by scheduling activities where students can work collectively, without regard to their academic standing, where they can exchange opinions, reformulate problems together, and talk about the pros and cons of 'their' best solutions. At the same time, this kind of interactive pedagogy helps teach students some of the most fundamental social skills, such as taking contradictory points of view into account, a process that is now known to play a key role in cognitive development (Doise & Mugny, 1998).

Applied social psychology in context

In education, as in many other spheres of social life, social psychology generally offers a specific contribution to our understanding of relatively difficult theoretical or practical problems.

Take, for example, the origin of gender differences on standardized maths tests, which has frequently been a topic of debate in the past three decades. These differences have been sometimes attributed to ability differences, themselves rooted in biological mechanisms (e.g., prenatal testosterone exposure). But as we have seen (see the section on stereotype threat), a number of social-psychological findings clearly run against this biological hypothesis. In Spencer *et al.*'s (1999) series of experiments, the very fact that falsifying the gender stereotype about maths not only reduced the male advantage but eliminated it altogether runs counter to any biological account of gender differences in this domain. Consistent with this, Huguet and Régner (2007) offered evidence that girls can show a performance deficit when they simply come to believe that the task at hand measures mathematical skills (although it does not).

Taken together, such findings may prevent parents, teachers and policy makers from adopting a sometimes excessive biological approach. And this can make a huge difference regarding what should be done at the practical level: encouraging girls to see scientific disciplines and careers as self-relevant versus orienting them towards gender-'appropriate' occupations.

Final thoughts

The results briefly discussed here point out the strong interrelationship between student achievement and the social and emotional dynamics in the classroom as they are defined by how students compare themselves to their peers, how they perceive intelligence, how they self-evaluate in various academic domains, how they react to self-threatening stereotypes and how teachers conduct their classes. Yet, how much class time in teachers' colleges is devoted to these phenomena – and there are many others! – or more generally, to the behavioural sciences? Practically none in most cases, as a growing number of insightful teachers themselves have noted, complaining that as far as teaching methods are concerned, their training is inadequate (at least in some European countries). *By dogmatically treating the teaching profession as a sort of calling, we have ended up believing that being a good teacher requires no more than a love of teaching, a boundless passion discovered early. This is regrettable.*

Of course, most teachers do not have the luxury of being able to formulate and test relatively sophisticated theories and hypotheses about their classroom. They have to accomplish the practical task of teaching, which requires getting the job done through whatever conceptions and methods work best, under practical constraints that include physical resources, numbers and 'nature' of pupils, time pressure and so on. This is very clear. Most ordinary physicians everywhere in the world, however, are also faced with numerous constraints, and still their medical practices are scientifically grounded. Claiming that all the problems encountered in the teaching profession would vanish if we merely submitted them to scientific knowledge would be nonsensical. *But believing that they could be solved without the intervention of science would make even less sense.*

As Bruner (1990) noted, in spite of advances in the sciences, there remains the challenge of knowing when, where and how to apply our knowledge to the living context generated by 'the case' that we have before us (to borrow from medical jargon). And when education is at stake, that living context is a classroom, a classroom situated within a cultural whole that we must strive to understand and whose impact on student achievement and behaviour must be fully accounted for.

Conclusion

We argued that education is – at least in part – applied social psychology. We thereby showed how the understanding of basic social-psychological concepts and phenomena can help further our educational goals. The first phenomenon is 'social comparison' (i.e., the process of thinking about self-related information in relation to one or more other people), a basic process that occurs even in the preschool years. Then we showed how the findings of two recent field studies can be used in order to improve students' academic outcomes and inhibit negative social comparison inferences (i.e., concluding that one's ability in a given domain is necessarily inferior to that of others, given some self–other differences in that domain). Phenomena related to students' 'theories of intelligence' and 'academic self-concept' were also part of this chapter. We argued that students who have an 'incremental' conception of intelligence (i.e., who see their various abilities as open for change) have a better perspective than the students who seem to adhere to an 'entity' conception (i.e., who see their abilities as essentially innate and stable over time). In the same vein, we discussed a simple but important experiment which clearly shows how powerful the students' academic history and related self-concept (i.e., how students self-evaluate in various academic domains) can be in the determination of their actual performance. A paradoxical effect of schools' ability levels on students' academic self-concept, namely, the big-fish-little-pond effect (BFLPE) and the action of negative stereotypes were also described. Finally, throughout the chapter, we made specific practical recommendations about how teachers could and how they should not behave in order to facilitate a more optimal learning environment, especially for the less capable or poorer students. These recommendations rely on the idea that the social-psychological conditions under which students express their cognitive abilities matter as much as the abilities themselves. The conclusion is that the practical task of teaching in fact requires extensive scientific knowledge of social behaviour, especially the phenomena examined at the interface of social psychology and education.

Glossary

Academic self-concept: how the individuals self-evaluate in a number of self-relevant academic domains.

Assimilation effect (in the context of self-evaluation via social comparison): the self-evaluative judgement shifts towards the context, resulting in increased self-evaluation when comparison is made with more successful others or decreased self-evaluation when comparison is made with less successful others.

Big-fish-little-pond effect (BFLPE): the fact that the students in academically selective environments (i.e., schools or classes where the average ability levels of students is especially high) have lower academic self-concepts compared with students of equal aptitude who are educated in non-selective environments.

Classroom climate: the perceived quality of the classroom, also referred to as the 'atmosphere' or 'ambience' of this particular setting.

Comparative evaluation: the relative position attributed to the self on a dimension within a group.

Contrast effect (in the context of self-evaluation via social comparison): the self-evaluative judgement shifts away from the context, resulting in decreased self-evaluation when comparison is made with more successful others, and increased self-evaluation when comparison is made with less successful others.

Downward comparison: comparison with someone who is worse off or who performs worse on the dimension under comparison.

Entity theorists (about intelligence): people who believe that intelligence is an innate and stable property of a person.

Incremental theorists (about intelligence): people who believe that intelligence is malleable and open for change.

Observational learning: learning by observing how another person (model) performs a task.

Related attributes: the attributes that can be viewed as predictive for the positions on a given comparison dimension. 'Applying' the similarity principle, the comparison target can be similar on the core dimension (e.g., scores in tennis) or on dimensions that are related (or supposedly related) to the task at hand (attributes such as age, sex, level of practice, etc).

Self-efficacy (perceived self-efficacy): beliefs about one's own abilities to perform specific tasks.

Similarity principle: a preference to compare oneself with others who are similar on related attributes.

Social comparison: the process of thinking about information about the self (e.g., my marks in maths) in relation to one or more other people (others' maths marks).

Social comparison target: the person chosen for comparison in a given domain (e.g., maths).

Stereotype threat: the threat that one's performance will confirm – to others, to oneself, or both – a negative stereotype associated with one's own social group.

Unidirectional drive upwards: in the case of social comparison of abilities, a preference to compare oneself with others who perform (somewhat) better.

Upward comparison: comparison with someone who is better off or who performs better on the dimension under comparison.

Review questions

1. Exactly what do we know about social comparison principles and related consequences in the classroom?
2. How important is understanding social comparison principles in the struggle against academic failure?
3. Explain why students' conceptions about intelligence are a significant component of their academic achievement.
4. What do notions such as the 'BFLPE' and 'stereotype threat' mean, and exactly why are these notions important at the practical level?
5. Explain the notion of 'classroom climate' and why this notion is important for teachers.

Further reading

Ben-Zeev, T., Duncan, S. & Forbes, C. (2005). Stereotypes and math performance. In J. I. D. Campbell (ed.), *Handbook of mathematical cognition* (pp. 235–249). New York: Psychology Press.

Elliot, A. J. & Dweck, C. S. (2004). *Handbook of competence and motivation*. New York: Guilford Press.

Halpern, D. F. & Desrochers, S. (2005). Social psychology in the classroom. Applying what we teach as we teach it. *Journal of Social and Clinical Psychology, 24,* 51–61.

Smith, R. A. (2005). The classroom as a social psychology laboratory. *Journal of Social and Clinical Psychology, 24,* 62–71.

Suls, J. & Wheeler, L. (2000). *Handbook of social comparison: Theory and research.* Dordrecht: Kluwer Academic Publishers.

References

Adelman, H. S. & Taylor, L. (in press). Classroom climate. In S. W. Lee, P. A. Lowe & E. Robinson (eds.), *Encyclopedia of social psychology*. Thousands Oaks, CA: Sage.

Blanton, H., Buunk, B. P., Gibbons, F. X. & Kuyper, H. (1999). When better-than-others compare upward: Choice of comparison and comparative evaluation as independent predictors of academic performance. *Journal of Personality and Social Psychology, 76,* 420–430.

Bruner, J. S. (1990). *Acts of meaning*. Cambridge, MA: Harvard University Press.

Buunk, B. P. & Ybema, J. F. (1997). Social comparison and occupational stress: The identification-contrast model. In B. P. Buunk & F. X. Gibbons (eds.), *Health, coping and well-being: Perspectives from social comparison theory* (pp. 359–388). Hillsdale, NJ: Erlbaum.

Buunk, B. P., Kuyper, H. & van der Zee, Y. G. (2005). Affective response to social comparison in the classroom. *Basic and Applied Social Psychology*, *27*, 229–237.

Doise,W. & Mugny, G. (1998). The social construction of knowledge: Social marking and socio-cognitive conflict. In Uwe Flick (ed.), *The psychology of the social* (pp. 142–171). New York: Cambridge University Press.

Dumas, F., Huguet, P., Monteil, J.-M., Rastoul, C. & Nezlek, J. B. (2005). Social comparison in the classroom: Is there a tendency to compare upward in elementary school? *Current Research in Social Psychology*, *10*, 166–187.

Dweck, C. S. (1999). *Self-theories: Their role in motivation, personality, and development.* Hove, East Sussex: Psychology Press.

Feldman, R. S. (1986). The present and promise of the social psychology of education. In Robert S. Feldman (ed.), *The social psychology of education: Current research and theory* (pp. 1–13). Cambridge University Press.

Festinger, L. (1954). A theory of social comparison processes. *Human Relations*, *7*, 117–140.

Good, C., Aronson, J. & Inzlicht, M. (2003). Improving adolescents' standardized test performance: An intervention to reduce the effects of stereotype threat. *Journal of Applied Developmental Psychology*, *24*, 645–662.

Henderson, V. & Dweck, C. S. (1990). Achievement and motivation in adolescence: A new model and data. In S. Feldman & G. Elliott (eds.), *At the threshold: The developing adolescent*. Cambridge, MA: Harvard University Press.

Huguet, P., Brunot, S. & Monteil, J. M. (2001a). Geometry versus drawing: Changing the meaning of the task as a means of changing performance. *Social Psychology of Education*, *4*, 219–234.

Huguet, P., Dumas, F., Monteil, J. M. & Genestoux, N. (2001b). Social comparison choices in the classroom: Further evidence for students' upward comparison tendency and its beneficial impact on performance. *European Journal of Social Psychology*, *31*, 557–578.

Huguet, P. & Régner, I. (2007). Stereotype threat among schoolgirls in quasi-ordinary classroom circumstances. *Journal of Educational Psychology*, *99*, 545–560.

Levine, J. M. (1983). Social comparison and education. In J. M. Levine & M. C. Wang (eds.), *Teacher and student perceptions: Implications for learning* (pp. 29–56). Hillsdale, NJ: Erlbaum.

Marsh, H. W. & Hau, K. T. (2003). Big-Fish–Little-Pond effect on academic self-concept: A cross-cultural (26-country) test of the negative effects of academically selective schools. *American Psychologist*, *58*, 364–376.

Monteil, J. M. & Huguet, P. (1999). *Social context and cognitive performance: Towards a social psychology of cognition*. Hove, East Sussex: Psychology Press.

Mussweiler, T. & Rüter, K. (2003). What friends are for! The use of routine standards in social comparison. *Journal of Personality and Social Psychology*, *85*, 467–481.

Ruble, D. N. (1983). The development of social comparison processes and their role in achievement-related self-socialization. In E. T. Higgins, D. N. Ruble & W. W. Hardup (eds.), *Social cognition and social development: A socio-cultural perspective* (pp. 3–12). Cambridge University Press.

Schunk, D. H. (1989). Self-efficacy and achievement behaviours. *Educational Psychology Review*, *1*, 173–208.

Spencer, S. J., Steele, C. M. & Quinn, D. (1999). Stereotype threat and women's math performance. *Journal of Experimental Social Psychology, 35*, 4–28.

Stapel, D. & Koomen, W. (2000). Distinctness of others, mutability of selves: Their impact on self-evaluation. *Journal of Personality and Social Psychology, 79*, 1068–1087.

Steele, C. M. (1997). A threat in the air: How stereotypes shape intellectual identity and performance. *American Psychologist, 52*, 613–629.

Wood, J. (1996). What is social comparison and how should we study it? *Personality and Social Psychology Bulletin, 22*, 520–537.

8 Social psychology and environmental problems

LINDA STEG AND ROBERT GIFFORD

Introduction

Behaviour always occurs in the context of a physical environment. In many cases, the physical environment is crucially important to our thoughts, feelings, performance, behaviour and well-being. For example, many people feel uncomfortable in the heat, and are more easily annoyed by others when temperatures are high. Traffic noise may result in stress and cardiovascular diseases. Suburbanization causes people to commute for longer distances. The availability of recycling facilities increases recycling rates. Job satisfaction is higher if employees work in offices with windows that open rather than with windows that do not open. The presence of nature seems to improve health and well-being. Human activities also have an impact on the environment. For example, the use of fossil fuels produces carbon dioxide (CO_2) emissions, urbanization reduces farmland and natural landscapes and some species of animals become extinct by human activity. In fact, almost everyone lives in the built environment and many people never encounter an environment that has not been made or modified by human activity.

Environmental psychologists study such interactions between humans and their physical environments. Traditionally, environmental psychologists focused on how the physical environment (e.g., buildings, noise, pollution and the weather) affects us. More recently, much research is directed at the opposite relationship: how we affect the environment, for example, through our energy use, water use, vehicle use and land use. These two research directions are closely connected: individuals continuously change the environment, and, in turn, their cognitions, feelings, behaviour and well-being are changed by the environment. Our behaviour may affect environmental conditions that are crucial for our well-being. For example, car use increases local air pollution, which can result in health problems.

Why is the relationship between humans and their environment of concern to social psychologists? The reason is that many of the topics studied by environmental psychologists have social psychological aspects. For example, in order to be able to design human-friendly buildings, we need to know how people perceive and value various construction designs, and how they interact and perform in different physical settings. Similarly, to promote pro-environmental behaviour, we need to know which factors influence various types of environmental behaviour, and to develop and evaluate policies that successfully promote pro-environmental behaviour. Not surprisingly, various social-psychological theories, research methods and intervention techniques have been applied to the understanding and improvement of the relationship between humans and the environment.

This chapter offers a brief overview of how social psychology can be applied towards better understanding and management of human–environment relationships. The first part is devoted to the effects of the environment on cognition, feelings, performance, behaviour and well-being. In the second part, the consequences of human actions for environmental quality are discussed. To improve environmental quality through changes in human behaviour, two lines of research are of particular importance. First, we need to understand which factors cause the behaviour that affects environmental quality, because policies designed to promote pro-environmental behaviour will be more effective when they target important antecedents of behaviour. Second, we need to investigate the effectiveness of different policies in promoting pro-environmental behaviour, and to investigate which types of interventions will be most effective in various situations. This chapter discusses both approaches.

Environmental influences on well-being and behaviour

If you consider how the environment affects our well-being and behaviour, you will probably think of negative as well as positive influences. For example, you feel comfortable when the temperature in your room is about twenty degrees Celsius, and your work performance will improve if the work environment is properly illuminated. On the other hand, poor building design, noise, water pollution and toxic substances, to name just a few, all threaten health and well-being, performance and behaviour. For example, you wander around lost in a large building when no clear cues are given on how to find your way, and you are less inclined to move to a polluted area. The extent to which these environmental stressors affect us depends in part on social-psychological factors. For example, simple correlations between objective levels of noise and noise annoyance are generally small. The relationship between noise level and annoyance is moderated by social-psychological factors (Figure 8.1). For example, individuals tend to be less annoyed by noise when they have a positive attitude towards the source of the noise, or, people who have control over a source of noise are much less annoyed than those who do not control it, and people who believe the noise has an important purpose are less annoyed than those who do not. Thus, not only objective exposure to particular stressors, such as noise, or air pollution for that matter, should be considered, but also other factors influencing subjective annoyance.

That social-psychological factors affect annoyance levels has important policy implications. It means that annoyance from environmental stressors cannot

Figure 8.1 *The level of noise annoyance depends on social-psychological factors*

be reduced merely by lowering levels of objective exposure. We must also target relevant social-psychological factors that moderate the effect of stressors on annoyance. For example, noise annoyance from airports may be reduced if the neighbouring residents are consulted by planners and can be convinced that the noise is important, say, for the economics of the region.

Some environmental psychologists focus on solving problems with the built environment and have, through their advice to architects and designers, contributed to better adaptation of buildings to human needs. Environmental psychologists have been involved in the planning stages of construction, as well as in the formal design, and have a special role in evaluating completed buildings, to determine whether the goals envisioned in the planning and design stages were fulfilled in the completed building (e.g., Zeisel, 2006; see Box 8.1). One of the pioneers of **social design** is Robert Sommer (1972; 1974; 1983). Social design benefits the people who live or work in a building, or even visit it, by systematically incorporating their needs and ideas into the design of a building.

Box 8.1 Applying research methods: social design saves pain and improves moods in hospitals

The social designer's job is to advocate as many design considerations that benefit people who use a building as possible. A large hospital construction project can serve as one example of the way social design can help people – or, without it, harm them (Carpman, Grant & Simmons, 1986). Architects were asked to design a hospital courtyard. The architects planned to surface parts of the courtyard with brick. Brick is attractive and other hospitals had used it. But interviews by the social design team revealed that patients with recent injuries or surgery found it painful to be wheeled over brick surfaces, which are often bumpy. The aesthetics-minded architects had not thought of this. However, thanks to the social designers, portions of the courtyard over which wheelchairs were expected to pass were redesigned with a smoother surface.

In a second example, environmental psychologists acting as social designers were involved in the renovation of a hospital wing; they helped hospital users of all types (patients, staff and visitors) participate in the renovation decision making (Becker & Poe, 1980). The changes made to the building represented those agreed upon through a consensus-seeking process, although financial and administrative constraints restricted the changes slightly. Next, the effects of the changes were measured, using three methods (questionnaires asking about the organizational climate, questionnaires evaluating the changed physical environment, and behaviour mapping, in which the movements of people around a space are tracked and coded). The renovated hospital wing was compared with two similar but unchanged wings. The mood and morale of the hospital staff on the renovated wing increased dramatically after the design changes, in comparison with those on the unchanged wings. All the user groups rated the changed features of the renovated wing as better than comparable features of the unchanged wings, and conversation and social interaction increased in the renovated wing, but was essentially unchanged in the control wings.

This study's research method is called a quasi-experimental design (see Chapter 4): the experimental condition (the renovated wing) was systematically compared with a control condition (the unchanged wings). It would have been a true experimental design if the participants had been randomly assigned to the three wings, but often in everyday settings social scientists are unable randomly to assign participants to different conditions. On the other hand, people in similar settings (for example, the three hospital wings) probably are often not very different from each other, as groups, so the study qualifies as a quasi-experimental design, a study that uses 'presumably' randomized assignment to conditions.

Effects of behaviour on the environment

Environmental problems and human behaviour

Not only are our well-being and behaviour affected by the environment but human behaviour affects environmental quality as well. Environmental quality is seriously threatened all over the world. Some of the most important environmental problems are urban air pollution, noise annoyance, shortages in freshwater availability, over-fishing of the seas, loss of biodiversity and global warming (see, e.g., UNEP, 2002). **Global warming** refers to climate change, and, more specifically, to an increase in the earth's average temperature, caused in part by the emission of greenhouse gases, most of which can be attributed to the combustion of fossil fuels (EPA, 2004). In the twentieth century, global average temperature has increased by $0.7° \pm 0.2°C$, and in Europe by more than $0.95°C$ (EEA, 2007). The International Energy Outlook 2006 (EIA, 2006) foresees a rise of global energy consumption by 71 per cent between 2003 and 2030, and average US temperatures could rise another $3°$ to $9°C$ by the end of the century if global warming emissions are not reduced. The global average temperature is projected to increase by $1.4°$ to $5.8°C$ and by $2°$ to $6.3°C$ in Europe from 1990 to 2100 (EEA, 2007).

This will have far-reaching effects. Sea levels are expected to rise and flood coastal areas. Heat waves will be more frequent and more intense. Droughts and wildfires are likely to occur more often. Disease-carrying mosquitoes may expand their range. Ecosystems and food production will be disrupted, and some species may be pushed to extinction.

Despite various policy initiatives (such as energy conservation programmes or international agreements like the Kyoto Protocol), greenhouse gas emissions have steadily increased by about 1 per cent per year during the last decade, and are expected to continue rising in the next decades because consumption of fossil fuels like oil, natural gas and coal is still increasing (EIA, 2006; EPA, 2004; see Figure 8.2). Households significantly contribute to greenhouse gas emissions, by using electricity, natural gas and other fuels, and by the consumption of goods and services that require energy to produce. The latter is referred to as **indirect energy use**, that is, the energy needed to produce, transport and dispose of goods. Total residential electricity use in the OECD region is expected to increase by an average of 1.4 per cent per year from 2003 to 2020. In non-OECD countries, household electricity use is expected to grow even more, by 2.7 per cent per year on average between 2003 and 2030. This growth is mostly driven by economic growth and expanding populations in those countries.

Many environmental problems are rooted in human behaviour. For example, car use contributes to global warming (CO_2 emissions), the fragmentation of natural areas (caused by the construction of roads), noise annoyance and urban air pollution. By using water for cleaning, bathing, watering lawns, etc., the availability

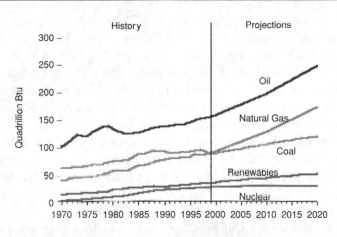

Source: EIA, International Energy Outlook 2001

Figure 8.2 *World energy consumption by fuel type, 1970–2020* (EIA, International Energy Outlook 2001)

of fresh water may be threatened, especially in arid regions. Through the consumption of fish or bushmeat, some species may become extinct. Consequently, environmental problems can be reduced through changes in human behaviour, and social psychologists can play an important role in this respect. Scientists realize that behaviour changes are badly needed because physical or technical measures (e.g., energy-efficient appliances) are not sufficient to resolve environmental problems. Efficiency gains tend to be partly overtaken by growth in consumption levels.

In order to design effective interventions aimed to reduce environmental problems through behavioural changes, we need to know (1) which behaviour significantly contributes to environmental problems, (2) which factors cause such behaviour and (3) which policy interventions are likely to promote pro-environmental behaviour. On the first point, social psychologists cooperate with environmental scientists to determine the environmental impacts of various behaviours. We return to this issue in the section 'Applied social psychology in context'. The second and third issues are of central interest to social psychologists. Below, we first elaborate on the second point: Which factors influence environmental behaviour? Then we elaborate on the third point: Which interventions successfully promote pro-environmental behaviour?

Understanding environmental behaviour

Environmental behaviour can be defined as behaviour that changes the availability of materials or energy from the environment or alters the structure and dynamics of ecosystems or the biosphere (Stern, 2000), and as such, influences human well-being, welfare and other things people value. Some argue that the environment should be valued for its own sake, regardless of its value for human beings. This rather broad definition implies that almost all human behaviour can be considered to be environmental behaviour. Individuals need not be aware of, or consider, environmental impacts of specific behaviours when making decisions. In fact, in many cases people do not know much about the environmental impact of their behaviour (Baird & Brier, 1981). Obviously, the extent to which behaviour affects the environment differs greatly. Driving a car has many more negative consequences than accepting a plastic bag in a grocery store. Ideally, social psychologists should focus their efforts on behaviour that most significantly affects environmental quality.

One might think that most or all social-psychological theories aimed at explaining behaviour would be useful in the environmental context. In principle, this is true. However, some theories are more useful than others. Pro-environmental behaviour is often associated with higher personal costs (more time, money or effort). For example, for many people, travelling by public transport is less convenient and attractive than driving a car. Organically grown food is more expensive, and recycling takes effort. Hence, theories that examine why people sacrifice personal gains in favour of the common good are especially promising in the environmental context. So, *under which conditions* are people willing to sacrifice individual advantages to protect the environment? In this section we briefly introduce three theoretical approaches that explicitly deal with this question: commons dilemmas, the norm activation model and theories on values and environmental concern. These theories have been often applied to explain environmental behaviour. Next, we elaborate on the role of habits. In many cases, individuals do not make conscious decisions. Especially in case of everyday behaviour (e.g., driving to work, cleaning the house, heating the house, buying groceries), habits are formed. We will briefly discuss how habits are formed, and why habits can inhibit behaviour change.

Commons dilemmas

Many environmental problems, such as resource depletion, global warming and pollution can be understood as **commons dilemmas**, situations that involve conflict between individual and collective interests. One example is urban air pollution resulting from accumulation of exhaust fumes from individual cars. In the short term, each individual may be better off driving a car than taking the bus, because the car is a much more comfortable, flexible and pleasurable vehicle. However, if everyone drives cars, urban air pollution will increase. In the long term, society would be better off if everyone reduced his or her car usage. Individuals do not need to be aware of the conflict between their individual and collective interests, for example, because they do not acknowledge or value the collective problems associated with their behaviour. Consequently, a distinction can be made between the perspective on environmental problems of an actor (consumer) and an observer (scientist or expert).

Typically, in large-scale commons dilemmas, individual contributions to collective problems and their solutions are futile. If one person reduces his or her car use while others do not, pollution is not reduced. The problems of car use will only be reduced when many other people do the same. Lack of trust in others' cooperation tempts individuals to act in their short-term self-interest, that is, to keep on driving. People are tempted to 'free ride', i.e., when they think that others will reduce their car use, they may decide to keep on driving, thereby continuing to enjoy the advantages of driving while pollution decreases. Thus, in the short term, the rewards for not engaging in pro-environmental behaviour often are greater than the rewards for engaging in it, no matter what others do. However, when most people act in their own interest, environmental problems will increase, which may harm present as well as future generations.

Commons dilemmas involve many people. In pursuing their own personal interests, many individuals tend to shift the relatively small negative impact of their behaviour onto their common environment. For example, almost every citizen in the developed world contributes to global warming, air pollution or resource depletion. However, individual contributions to environmental problems and their solutions are limited. Environmental problems will not be solved merely because one person stops driving, or lowers his or her thermostat settings in the home. They will be solved only if many other people do so as well. Because each individual's unhelpful choices have little impact, they seem to be excusable.

Fortunately, individuals do not always act in their own interest. Some use their car as little as possible or try to reduce their energy use, even though this might be less comfortable. Why do people engage in environmental behaviour when it has no direct benefits for them, at least not in the short term? In contrast to what is generally assumed in classical economics, people do not always choose the option with highest benefits against lowest costs (i.e., in terms of money, time or social approval). People also tend to consider what is the right thing to do, which means that they also consider moral costs and benefits. In other words, decisions are not just always made by cost-benefit analysis, but can be steered by morality as well. Traditional economic theory or cost-benefit models are less suitable to explain moral behaviour, because they do not consider moral costs and benefits. As a consequence, we need models that include morality in order to explain why some people give up personal benefits to safeguard environmental quality. A good example of such a model is the *norm activation model* (NAM) (Schwartz, 1977; Schwartz & Howard, 1981).

Norm activation model

The NAM was originally developed to explain pro-social behaviour, and has often been applied to explain environmental behaviour (which can be considered as a specific type of pro-social behaviour). According to this model, behaviour occurs in response to personal norms, that is, feelings of moral obligation. Personal norms are activated when individuals are aware of adverse consequences of their actions to others or the environment (awareness of consequences, or AC beliefs) and when they believe that they can reverse these consequences (ascription of responsibility, or AR beliefs). Imagine that you want to buy a new household cleaner. You can choose between a very cheap cleaner that contains dangerous solvents, or a cleaner that costs 50 per cent more, but does not contain any solvents. Which product would you purchase? According to the NAM, you will be more likely to choose the solvent-free cleaner if you are aware of the environmental problems caused by solvents (high AC), and when you think you could help reduce these problems by not buying products that contain solvents (high AR). When both AC and AR are high, you will feel a strong moral obligation to buy the solvent-free cleaner, and you will be more likely to actually choose this product. However, if you are not aware of the negative environmental effects of solvents, or do not see any opportunity to help reduce these harmful impacts, you will probably not feel a moral obligation to buy the solvent-free cleaner, and, consequently, will be more likely to purchase the cheaper product with solvent.

The NAM appears to be more successful in explaining environmental behaviour associated with relatively low behavioural costs (in terms of money, time or effort), such as recycling. It often has less explanatory power when the behaviour in question is more costly in terms of effort, money or time, such as reducing car use. Apparently, personal norms for acting in the common good are pushed into the background in favour of egoistic concerns when behavioural costs are high.

How can individuals deal with a decisional conflict between acting in the collective interest (following personal norms) and acting in their own interest (by choosing behavioural options with high individual benefits)? Such a decisional conflict can be reduced via **self-serving denial**, that is, denial of a moral obligation to act pro-environmentally in order to justify a choice to act in an environmentally unfriendly manner. Four types of self-serving denial may be distinguished. First, people may disregard, distort, or minimize environmental problems. Because the severity of some environmental problems is unclear and uncertain, and sometimes debated by scientists, people can selectively use scientific findings that support their position and behaviour. Second, people sometimes discount their liability for these problems, by believing that their own contribution to problems is small or undetectable, and by viewing environmental problems as the result of collective rather than individual decisions and actions. They may identify other parties, such as authorities or industry, as being responsible for environmental problems (Figure 8.3). Third, they can deny their personal ability or competence to perform the necessary pro-environmental actions. For example, they may indicate that they are willing to reduce their car use, but have no opportunities to do so because no public transport is available. Fourth, they can argue that their individual pro-environmental actions would not be effective in reducing environmental problems. This defence mechanism may be quite effective, especially in the case of large-scale environmental problems (such as commons dilemmas) where individual contributions to environmental problems do seem trivial.

Figure 8.3 *Self-serving denial*

From this, we can conclude that personal norms about the environment may play an important role when people make low-cost decisions, but are much less influential in the case of high-cost decisions. In the latter case, people are very creative at providing reasons why they ignore environmental concerns. Obviously, people do not only act out of environmental concerns. Other concerns, such as a desire for convenience, comfort, enjoyment, status or safety often play an important role in human decision making. In many cases, these concerns conflict with environmental concerns, making pro-environmental behaviour less likely.

The NAM was later extended to the *value-belief-norm theory of environmentalism* (VBN) (Stern, 2000; see Figure 8.4). The VBN model explicitly aims to explain behaviour resulting from pro-environmental intent. Like the NAM, VBN theory proposes that behaviour occurs in response to personal norms, and that personal norms are influenced by AR (ascription of responsibility) and AC (awareness of consequences), respectively. In addition, the VBN theory proposes that AC beliefs are rooted in general beliefs about human–environment relationships and on relatively stable value orientations. These concepts will be further elaborated below.

Values and environmental concern

Public concern for environmental issues is currently quite strong in many countries in the world. An opinion poll in 30 countries revealed that, across all countries, about 90 per cent say that 'climate change or global warming, due to the greenhouse effect' is a serious problem (World Public Opinion, 2006). One of the most influential measures of the extent to which people are concerned with the

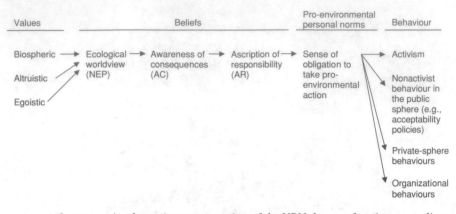

Figure 8.4 *A schematic representation of the VBN theory of environmentalism (adapted from Stern, 2000)*

environment is called the **new environmental paradigm (NEP)**. The NEP measures a person's fundamental beliefs about the relations between humans and the environment. Those who strongly endorse the NEP believe that there are limits to growth, that people cannot dominate and control the environment and that the balance of nature is easily upset by human actions (Dunlap, Van Liere, Mertig & Jones, 2000). Numerous studies have found significant relations between the NEP and behaviour-specific beliefs and norms, intentions and behaviour (which is also true of VBN theory). For example, NEP beliefs are positively related to concern about global warming, personal and social norms towards recycling, support for environmental policies, acceptability of energy-saving measures, willingness to pay for environmental protection, and buying environmentally friendly products. However, these relations generally are not very strong. As is true of personal norms, NEP support is particularly related to low-cost behaviour.

Values also can affect environmental behaviour. Schwartz (1992, p. 21) defines a value as 'a desirable transsituational goal varying in importance, which serves as a guiding principle in the life of a person or other social entity'. Values are concerned with important aspects of life, such as health, freedom and justice, and have four key features. First, a value is a belief about the desirability of a certain end-state, such as a good health. Second, values are abstract and therefore transcend specific situations. As such, they may affect a variety of behaviours at once. Third, values serve as guiding principles for the selection or evaluation of behaviour, people and events. Fourth, values are ordered in a system of priorities. This implies that when competing values are activated in a particular situation, choices are based on a person's most important values.

In the environmental literature, three general value orientations are usually distinguished (see, e.g., Stern, Dietz & Kalof, 1993). One is the **egoistic value orientation**, in which people try to maximize their own outcomes, that is, they particularly consider individual costs and benefits when making choices. This value orientation reflects values like power, material wealth and ambition. Another is the **altruistic value orientation**, which reflects concern for the welfare of other human beings. Related values include equality, social justice and helpfulness. Third, the **biospheric (or ecocentric) value orientation** reflects concern with non-human species and the biosphere. Related values include respecting the earth, preventing pollution and unity with nature. Research shows that people who strongly value concerns beyond their own interests, that is, altruistic or biospheric values, are more likely to engage in pro-environmental behaviour, whereas people who strongly endorse egoistic values are less likely to do so. Thus, people who endorse altruistic values and people who endorse biospheric values are both likely to act pro-environmentally, probably because both types of values reflect concern for others. However, when altruistic and biospheric values conflict (i.e., when acting pro-environmentally harms altruistic concerns), those who endorse altruistic values may be less likely to engage in pro-environmental behaviour than those who endorse biospheric values. This was illustrated in a study that examined to what extent values predict intention to donate to humanitarian or environmental organizations (De Groot & Steg, 2008). In this study, respondents first evaluated the relative importance of five egoistic values (social power, wealth, authority, influence and ambition), four altruistic values (equality, a world at peace, social justice, and helpfulness), and four biospheric values (respecting the earth, unity with nature, protecting the environment, preventing pollution) as 'a guiding principle in their life'. Next, respondents indicated whether they were more likely to donate money to a humanitarian or an environmental organization. They were presented with five pairs of organizations (e.g., UNICEF, a humanitarian organization, and Greenpeace, an environmental organization), including a short description of the mission of each organization. Organizations in each pair were comparable in their degree of (inter)nationalization of aid, publicity and aim. It appeared that respondents were more likely to donate to humanitarian organizations (and less to environmental organizations), the more they were altruistically oriented. In contrast, the more respondents valued the biosphere and environment, the less they intended to donate to humanitarian organizations and the more they preferred to donate to environmental movements. Egoistic values were not related to intention to donate. These results suggest that those endorsing altruistic values are less likely to act pro-environmentally when the particular behaviour conflicts with altruistic values.

Habits

The theories discussed earlier (i.e., the NAM, value theory and NEP) all assume that individuals think before they act. However, we often do not. Imagine getting up in the morning. Do you make reasoned choices about what to do first, and what to do next? What to eat for breakfast? How to travel to work or school? Most likely you do not. You simply do what you are used to doing. We cannot think through every choice we might make. In many cases, habits are formed to simplify our lives. Everyday behaviours in particular turn into daily routines.

That being said, frequently performed behaviour is not always a matter of habit. We may often deliberate about how to act, even though we have enacted the behaviour time and again. Thus, the frequency of engaging in behaviour is not a good indicator of a habit. Rather, habits refer to the way decisions are made. Habits have three important characteristics (Aarts, Verplanken & Van Knippenberg, 1998). First, they are activated in the presence of a specific goal. After all, people do not automatically take the bicycle to ride to the gym without having a goal to go there. Second, the same course of action will be repeated when outcomes are satisfactory. The more positive the outcomes of the action and the stronger the association between the goal (e.g., going to the gym) and the action performed to reach that goal (e.g., taking the bicycle) becomes, the stronger the habit strength. Third, habitual responses are mediated by cognitive processes. Although habits are automated behaviour, cognitions do play a role in the process. When people frequently act in the same way in a particular situation, the mental representation of that situation will be associated with the representation of the particular goal-directed behaviour. For example, if a person frequently cycles to the gym, he or she will associate going to the gym (the mental representation of the particular situation) with cycling (viz., the goal-directed behaviour). The more frequently a particular situation (going to the gym) is associated with a particular behaviour (cycling), the stronger the strength and accessibility of that association, and the more likely that an individual acts accordingly. This implies that habitual behaviour is triggered by a cognitive structure that is learned, stored in and retrieved from memory when we perceive particular stimuli.

Based on this, Aarts and colleagues conceive of **habits** as goal-directed automated behaviours that are mentally represented. They developed a response-frequency measure of habit strength that assumes goals are capable of automatically activating mental representations of habitual choices. When employing this measure for the strength of a car-use habit, respondents are presented with a set of different travel goals that widely vary in distance and destination, such as visiting the city centre, going to work or visiting a friend in a nearby town. They are asked to mention as quickly as possible the mode of transport that first comes to mind as the one they would use in response to each travel goal. They assume that the imposed time pressure and the instruction to respond with the mode that comes to mind first will facilitate automatic responses and rely on cognitively available structures. The frequency of responding with a particular travel mode is used as an indicator of habit strength.

When habits are strong, we no longer make reasoned choices. This implies that theories aimed at explaining reasoned actions, such as the theory of reasoned action (Fishbein & Ajzen, 1975; see Chapter 2), the theory of planned behaviour (Ajzen, 1985; see Chapter 2), or the norm activation model (Schwartz, 1977, described earlier in this chapter) are not particularly useful for explaining habitual behaviour. Indeed, research shows that when habits are strong, intentions are not related to behaviour (see Box 8.2).

Box 8.2   Applying theories: habit versus planned behaviour

Researchers compared two approaches to explaining travel behaviour choices, the theory of planned behaviour (Ajzen, 1985) and habits (Verplanken, Aarts, Van Knippenberg & Moonen, 1998). Travel behaviour is a good example of routine behaviour. Many trips are made frequently, which makes it quite likely that people no longer make conscious decisions about which travel mode to use. To test the theory of planned behaviour, the study first examined to what extent behaviour (i.e., proportion of car trips) could be explained by behavioural intention and perceived behaviour control. In addition, the researchers examined to what extent habit, and the interaction between intention and habit, were able to explain travel behaviour. They expected that habit would predict behaviour over and above behavioural intention. Moreover, with regard to the effect of the interaction between habit and intention on behaviour, the authors hypothesized that behavioural intention would be significantly related to behaviour only when habits were weak. In contrast, they expected that drivers would not make conscious decisions when habit was strong, and, consequently, that intention would not be significantly related to behaviour when habit was strong.

Respondents completed a survey that contained measures of attitude, subjective norm, perceived behaviour control and intention to use the car to destinations outside the village, as called for by the theory of planned behaviour. They also completed the response-frequency measure of general habit strength, as explained above. Following the survey, respondents kept a travel diary, in which they recorded all trips they made during a seven-day period. Based on the travel diary, the percentage of trips made as a driver to a destination outside the village was used as the dependent variable.

As expected, intention and perceived behaviour control were significantly related to the proportion of trips made by car. However, they explained only 5 per cent of the variance in behaviour, which suggests that the theory of planned behaviour is not very successful in explaining car use. Habit increased the proportion of variance explained by 5 per cent. Thus, also as being expected, habit predicted car use over and above variables from the theory of planned behaviour. In fact, habit appeared to be the strongest predictor. When the interaction between intention and habit was included in the regression analysis as well, the proportion of explained variance increased to 12 per cent (i.e., an additional 2 per cent was explained by this interaction). As hypothesized, behavioural intention was significantly related to car use when habit was weak. However, intention was not significantly related to car use when habit strength was moderate or strong.

In conclusion, the study revealed that habits set boundary conditions for the applicability of the theory of planned behaviour. People seem to be less likely to make reasoned choices when habits are strong.

Habits are highly functional for coping with daily life. They make it unnecessary to make repeated conscious decisions about how to act, because in many cases the circumstances are the same, and a person would come to the same decision anyway. However, habits may not always yield optimal outcomes; sometimes the circumstances of the situation have changed. For example, a new bus route can become available which makes the bus highly attractive compared with the car. Such changes may not be noticed when habits are formed. Habits result in selective attention: people may not pay attention to information that might change their choice. In general, habits are likely to be reconsidered only when the circumstances have changed significantly.

Promoting pro-environmental behaviour

In the previous section, we discussed various factors that influence environmental behaviour. This information is very important when interventions aimed at promoting pro-environmental behaviour are designed. Interventions will be more successful if they target factors that encourage or inhibit engagement in pro-environmental behaviour. For example, if a study shows that the level of recycling strongly depends on the availability of recycling facilities (e.g., curbside programmes, recycling bins), recycling can best be promoted by increasing the availability and quality of these facilities, but where studies show that a lack of information is related to a lack of recycling, education campaigns are more appropriate.

In general, two ways to change behaviour can be distinguished. First, interventions may target a person's perceptions, cognitions, motivations and norms. Second, interventions can be aimed at changing the consequences that follow behaviour.

Changing perceptions, cognitions, motivations and norms

Some interventions aim to change perceptions, cognitions, motivations and norms (see Abrahamse, Steg, Vlek & Rothengatter, 2005, or Schultz, Oskamp & Mainieri, 1995, for reviews). This approach expects that people will voluntarily change their behaviour in accordance with these interventions. For example, information campaigns can be developed to increase knowledge about recycling or to promote positive attitudes towards recycling. The approach assumes that increased knowledge or positive attitudes will result in higher recycling rates. Most of these strategies can be described as **antecedent strategies**, because they target factors that precede behaviour. An exception is feedback, which is a consequence strategy (see Chapter 3). In this section, we briefly discuss three kinds of interventions: provision of information, feedback and behavioural commitment.

Information campaigns can be aimed at increasing awareness of environmental problems, or knowledge about (environmental and other) consequences of various behavioural alternatives. This enables consumers to consider the environmental consequences of their behaviour. Alternatively, information may be provided about the behaviour and expectations of others, thereby increasing awareness of desirable social norms. In general, the effects of information campaigns have been disappointing. The information may be effective in increasing knowledge (thus priming change), but priming often is not followed by a change in behaviour. This is especially true for mass media campaigns. Tailored information, that is, highly personalized information, appears to be more effective (see also Chapter 10). A study on energy conservation revealed that households which received information on ways to reduce their energy use tailored to their own situation saved more energy than a control group (Abrahamse, Steg, Vlek & Rothengatter, 2007). Information tailored to the needs, interests and desires of the target group increase the likelihood that people will pay attention to and elaborate on the information provided, which consequently improves the chances that their attitudes and behaviour will change accordingly.

Feedback consists of giving individuals information about the extent to which their behaviour changes have been successful (see also Chapter 3). Feedback may be given about the extent to which one's behaviour changed (e.g., 'you reduced your showering time by ten minutes this week'), the consequences of this behaviour (e.g., energy or water savings), or on the environmental impact of behaviour changes (e.g., reduction of emissions of greenhouse gases). In this way, individuals become aware of the relation between their behaviour and environmental consequences. As described in Chapter 3, feedback is given after a particular behaviour has been performed. Feedback can be quite effective in promoting pro-environmental behaviour, especially when it is frequently and immediately provided (see Box 8.3).

Box 8.3   Applying intervention strategies: effects of feedback on household gas use

Researchers compared the effectiveness of different types of feedback and information in reducing household gas use (Van Houwelingen & Van Raaij, 1989) All participating households received information about ways to reduce gas use. Then respondents were placed in one of five experimental conditions. The first group received information only. The second group were taught how to read their gas meter, to enable them to monitor their own gas use over time. The third group received monthly feedback on gas consumption, while the fourth group received daily feedback. The last group served as a control group.

Daily feedback was most effective in reducing gas consumption. Households who had received daily feedback saved 12.3%. Households who received monthly feedback reduced their gas consumption by 7.7%. Those who were taught to read their meter and those who had received information only were the least successful in reducing their gas consumption (savings of 5.1% and 4.3%, respectively). All the experimental groups reduced their gas consumption, but no significant change was observed in the control group (0.3%). Unfortunately, interventions apparently must be maintained: one year after the intervention, gas use had increased for all groups, and the differences between groups disappeared.

Another intervention that can be quite effective in the environmental domain is **behavioural commitment**, that is, a written or verbal promise to perform a target behaviour (e.g., to recycle, or to reduce energy use by 5 per cent). This promise can be made privately or publicly. When made privately, the promise may activate a personal norm (see the section 'Norm activation model'), that is, people may feel obliged to engage in the particular behaviour. When the promise is made publicly, for example by an announcement in a local newspaper, people may act in accordance with their promise because they want to avoid the disapproval by others of their behaviour. As indicated in Chapter 3, commitment has been shown to have prolonged effects, and therefore may be superior to feedback.

Interventions often are more effective if they are combined. For example, feedback is likely to be more effective when people are provided with information on how to act pro-environmentally as well, or when people also commit themselves to act pro-environmentally. However, they do not guarantee change. Especially when habits are strong, these interventions may not succeed. Moreover, the strategies will have limited effects when people have few opportunities to change their behaviour, or when environmentally friendly behaviour is less attractive than their current behaviour. In these cases, stronger measures are needed, or measures that change the relative attractiveness of the behavioural alternatives. Some possible ways to do so are discussed in the next section.

Changing the incentives

In many cases, acting pro-environmentally is associated with greater costs to a person (in terms of time, money or effort), or difficult because of external barriers to pro-environmental actions. To put it differently, the incentives to act in one's self-interest often outweigh one's motivation to act pro-environmentally. Thus, changes in incentives may be needed in favour of pro-environmental behaviours, by means of **consequence strategies**. Pro-environmental behaviour is made more attractive or more feasible by rewarding it, and environmentally unfriendly behaviour is made less attractive by punishing it. For example, the attractiveness of cycling can be increased by the construction of cycle lanes, or car use can be made less attractive by increasing taxes related to driving. Advocates of this approach hope that attitudes and preferences eventually will change in the same direction, because behaviour changes are likely to be more robust when they are supported by changes in attitudes and preferences.

Three strategies may be considered. First, *pricing policies* can be implemented, to reduce the cost of pro-environmental behaviour or increase costs for environmentally unfriendly alternatives. This may be effective because currently many pro-environmental products are more expensive (e.g., organic food or heavier insulation) than regular products. Second, *legal measures* can be implemented. For example, laws can be implemented that prohibit the use of propellants in spray cans, or speed limits may be introduced to reduce emissions of exhaust gases and air pollution. Such measures will be effective only if the laws and regulations are accepted by most people and enforced, and violations are met with sanctions. Third, the *availability and quality of products and services* can be changed. For example, environmentally harmful behavioural options may be made less feasible or even impossible, such as closing off town centres to motorized traffic. Alternatively, new or better (pro-environmental) behaviour options may be provided, such as recycling bins or organic products. Also, environmentally friendly technologies aimed at reducing environmental impact per unit may be introduced. For example, energy-efficient washing machines or refrigerators provide the same service but use less energy.

In sum, strategies aimed at changing the incentives may be aimed at rewarding 'good' behaviour or punishing 'bad' behaviour. As explained in Chapter 3, penalties are believed to be less effective, because they are more likely to result in negative emotions and attitudes. In such cases, individuals engage in behaviour to avoid negative consequences. When enforcement is not consistent, or ceases, behaviours are likely to return to their previous state. Moreover, penalties can be difficult to implement when they evoke strong public resistance. Both rewards and penalties will be more successful when they are just sufficient to initiate behaviour change. In that case, people are more likely to attribute their behaviour change to their personal convictions, whereas when too-strong rewards or penalties are offered, people may attribute their change in behaviour to the rewards or penalties. Consequently, they may only have short-term effects (i.e., as long as they are in place), because people probably will not have changed their attitudes.

Applied social psychology in context

This chapter describes how social psychologists can significantly contribute to the understanding and improvement of human–environment relationships. However, the relationship between humans and their physical environments is affected by many factors, not only social-psychological ones. Therefore, input from other disciplines is needed to optimize human–environment relationships. For example, when studying negative effects of environmental conditions on health and well-being, input from epidemiology, medicine or health sciences is advisable. When studying the effects of pricing strategies, input from economists is advisable. When studying pro-environmental behaviour, one should be aware of the environmental impact of different types of behaviour to be able to decide which behaviour truly is pro-environmental, and so input from environmental scientists is needed. Environmental scientists can help social psychologists focus their efforts on behaviour that is most significant from an environmental point of view (see Chapter 1). For instance, when trying to reduce environmental impacts of households, we may do better to focus on reducing thermostat settings than on reducing showering time, because the environmental impact of the former is much higher. Such behaviour changes should of course be feasible and acceptable to those involved. Thus, the feasibility and acceptability of behaviour changes should be studied in conjunction with environmental impact. Social and environmental psychologists can play an important role in this respect.

However, as indicated in the introductory chapter, working in interdisciplinary settings is not easy. Understanding a problem from one's own disciplinary point of view is already difficult, but adding the perspectives and insights from other disciplines adds to the complexity. However, when researchers are willing to understand different perspectives, to clarify the background of their own perspective and to examine possibilities of integrating different views, interdisciplinary cooperation yields better and more comprehensive views on human–environment relationships and possible ways to improve them.

Conclusion

Environmental quality is essential for human health and well-being. Therefore, the built environment needs to be improved and the natural environment needs to be protected. Social psychologists have an important role to play in this respect. First, they can study how various environmental conditions affect social interaction, health, well-being, performance and behaviour how negative effects can be reduced and how positive effects may be enhanced. The extent to which environmental conditions threaten or enhance the quality of life depends on many social-psychological factors, including attitudes, norms and perceived control. These factors provide opportunities for interventions aimed at improving the well-being of people and other living things.

Second, social psychologists examine factors influencing behaviours that contribute to environmental problems. Social-psychological factors encourage individuals to act pro-environmentally or not. Because many pro-environmental actions have relatively high costs, moral considerations (i.e., concerns about what is the right thing to do) play an important role. Habits may inhibit people from acting pro-environmentally, but pro-environmental acts can become habitual as well.

Third, social psychologists can explore the effectiveness, acceptability and feasibility of policies aimed at reducing environmental problems through behavioural changes. Behaviour can be changed by changing perceptions, cognitions, motivations, goals and norms. If pro-environmental behaviour is unattractive, these interventions generally have limited effects. In those cases, interventions should be implemented in the form of societal-level incentives, to make pro-environmental actions an inviting option.

An interdisciplinary approach to all these topics is valuable, because substandard human–environmental relationships may be caused by a wide range of factors understood by multiple disciplines. Social psychologists should cooperate with other disciplines. Multidisciplinary research and collaboration enables social psychologists to take advantage of the knowledge and perspectives of other disciplines, and to create a comprehensive and integrated understanding of a problem that has a better chance of solving it.

Glossary

Altruistic value orientation: values that reflect concern for the welfare of other human beings.

Antecedent strategies: strategies that target factors that precede behaviour.

Behavioural commitment: a written or verbal promise to perform a target behaviour.

Biospheric (or ecocentric) value orientation: values that reflect concern with non-human species and the biosphere.

Commons dilemma: a situation in which individual and collective interests conflict.

Consequence strategies: strategies aimed to change the incentives following a behaviour.

Egoistic value orientation: values that reflect concern with individual costs and benefits.

Environmental behaviour: any behaviour that changes the availability of materials or energy from the environment or alters the structure and dynamics of ecosystems or the biosphere.

Global warming: an increase in the earth's average temperature, resulting in climate change.

Habit: goal-directed behaviour that is guided by automated cognitive processes.

Indirect energy use: the energy needed to produce, transport and dispose of goods.

New environmental paradigm (NEP): one's fundamental beliefs about relationships between humans and the environment.

Self-serving denial: denial of a moral obligation to act pro-environmentally in order to justify a choice to act in an environmentally unfriendly manner.

Social design: designing buildings in a way that benefits the people who live or work in the building, or visit it, by systematically incorporating their needs and ideas into the design.

Values: desirable trans-situational goals that vary in importance and serve as guiding principles in one's life.

Review questions

1. Why are correlations between objective noise levels and noise annoyance generally low?
2. Which three general value orientations are distinguished in the environmental literature? Briefly explain each of these.
3. What is meant by commitment? Which types of commitment can be distinguished?
4. Why are rewards often more effective than penalties for promoting pro-environmental behaviour?

Further reading

Bechtel, R. B. & Churchman, A. (eds.) (2002). *Handbook of environmental psychology*. 2nd edn. New York: Wiley.

Bell, P. A., Greene, T. C., Fisher, J. D. & Baum, A. (2001). *Environmental psychology*. 5th edn. Belmont, CA: Thomson Learning.

Gardner, G. T. & Stern, P. C. (2002). *Environmental problems and human behavior.* 2nd edn. Boston, MA: Pearson Custom Publishing.

Gifford, R. (2007). *Environmental psychology: Principles and practice*. 4th edn. Colville, WA: Optimal Books.

Nickerson, R. S. (2003). *Psychology and environmental change*. Mahwah, NY: Erlbaum.

References

Aarts, H., Verplanken, B. & Van Knippenberg, A. (1998). Predicting behaviour from actions in the past: Repeated decision making or a matter of habit? *Journal of Applied Social Psychology*, *28*, 1355–1374.

Abrahamse, W., Steg, L., Vlek, C. & Rothengatter, T. (2005). A review of intervention studies aimed at household energy conservation. *Journal of Environmental Psychology*, *25*, 273–291.

(2007). The effect of tailored information, goal setting and tailored feedback on household energy use, energy-related behaviors and behavioral antecedents. *Journal of Environmental Psychology*, *27*, 265–276.

Ajzen, I. (1985). From intentions to action: A theory of planned behavior. In J. Kuhl & J. Beckman (eds.), *Action-control: From cognition to behavior*. Heidelberg: Springer.

Baird, J. C. & Brier, J. M. (1981). Perceptual awareness of energy requirements of familiar objects. *Journal of Applied Psychology*, *66*, 90–96.

Becker, F. D. & Poe, D. B. (1980). The effects of user-generated design modifications in a general hospital. *Journal of Nonverbal Behavior*, *4*, 195–218.

Carpman, J. R., Grant, M. A. & Simmons, D. A. (1986). *Design that cares: Planning health facilities for patients and visitors*. Chicago: American Hospital Publishing.

De Groot, J. & Steg, L. (2008). Value orientations to explain environmental attitudes and beliefs: How to measure egoistic, altruistic, and biospheric value orientations. *Environment and Behavior*, *40* (3), 330–354.

Dunlap, R. E., Van Liere, K. D., Mertig, A. G. & Jones, R. E. (2000). Measuring endorsement of the New Ecological Paradigm: A revised NEP scale. *Journal of Social Issues*, *56* (3), 425–442.

EEA (2007). *Epaedía: Environment explained*. Available at: epaedia.eea.europa.eu/page.php?pid = 205

EIA (2006). *International energy outlook 2006*. Washington, DC: EIA. Available at: www.eia.doe.gov/oiaf/ieo/index.html.

EPA (2004). *Inventory of U.S. greenhouse gas emissions and sinks, 1990–2002*. Washington, DC: US Environmental Protection Agency (EPA), report no. EPA 430-R-04-003.

Fishbein, M. & Ajzen, I. (1975). *Belief, attitude, intention and behavior: An introduction to theory and research*. Reading, MA: Addison-Wesley.

Schultz, P. W., Oskamp, S. & Mainieri, T. (1995). Who recycles and when? A review of personal and situational factors. *Journal of Environmental Psychology*, *15*, 105–121.

Schwartz, S. H. (1977). Normative influences on altruism. In L. Berkowitz (ed.), *Advances in experimental social psychology*, vol. 10 (pp. 221–279). New York: Academic Press.

(1992). Universals in the content and structure of values: Theoretical advances and empirical tests in 20 countries. In M. Zanna (ed.), *Advances in experimental social psychology*. Orlando, FL: Academic Press.

Schwartz, S. H. & Howard, J. A. (1981). A normative decision-making model of altruism. In J. P. Rushton (ed.), *Altruism and helping behaviour: Social, personality, and development perspectives*. Hillsdale, NJ: Erlbaum.

Sommer, R. (1972). *Design awareness*. San Francisco: Rinehart Press.

(1974). *Tight spaces: Hard architecture and how to humanize it*. Englewood Cliffs, NJ: Prentice-Hall.

(1983). *Social design: Creating buildings with people in mind*. Englewood Cliffs, NJ: Prentice-Hall.

Stern, P. C. (2000). Toward a coherent theory of environmentally significant behavior. *Journal of Social Issues*, *56*, 407–424.

Stern, P. C., Dietz, T. & Kalof, L. (1993). Value orientations, gender, and environmental concern. *Environment and Behavior*, *25*, 322–348.

UNEP: United Nations Environment Program (2002). *GEO-3: Global Environment Outlook 3*. Nairobi: UNEP, and London: Earthscan.

Van Houwelingen, J. H. & Van Raaij, F. W. (1989). The effect of goal-setting and daily electronic feedback on in-home energy use. *Journal of Consumer Research*, *16*, 98–105.

Verplanken, B., Aarts, H., Van Knippenberg, A. & Moonen, A. (1998). Habit versus planned behaviour: A field experiment. *British Journal of Social Psychology*, *37*, 111–128.

World Public Opinion (2006). www.worldpublicopinion.org/. Consulted at 27 June 2006.

Zeisel, J. (2006). *Inquiry by design: Tools for environment-behavior research*. Cambridge University Press.

9 Gender issues in work and organizations

TINEKE M. WILLEMSEN AND
ANNELIES E. M. VAN VIANEN

Introduction

Gender stands for the expectations of an individual and others about what it means to be a man or a woman. Gender has been extensively studied in all fields of social psychology, for instance, in the psychology of health and mental health, education, criminality and political behaviour, to name just a few topics included in this book. The present chapter is about gender in work and organizational psychology. We first describe the societal context that gave rise to theories and research on gender and work. There are many differences between working men and women that often are disadvantageous for women. On average, women earn less than men for the same work, and have a lower probability of reaching top positions in organizations. We then focus on career-related decision making: women's own decisions and the decisions of others involved in selection and assessment. We pay special attention to women in management and leadership positions. After discussing the influence of the organizational context we finish by briefly discussing interventions that have been applied to change the relative position of men and women in organizations.

Women and men at work

Gender differences in the workplace concern both the amount of work and payment (quantitative differences) and the type of work (qualitative differences) that men and women perform.

Quantitative differences

Four quantitative differences characterize the working life of men and women. First, more men than women hold a paid job or earn an income. Second, men continue working throughout their lifetime, and their family situation hardly affects their working life, while women sometimes stop working or start working fewer hours when they get married, but especially when they become mothers. Third, men work, on average, longer hours than women. With few exceptions, men in general work full-time; women, and especially women with children, more often work part-time. Finally, women earn less than men. This is partly due to the fact that the job sectors women work in (see below) tend to have lower salary rates. However, even in the same job women often earn lower wages than men (International Labour Office, 2004).

Qualitative differences

Qualitative differences concern the type of jobs that men and women hold. First, men and women tend to work in different occupations. Women are relatively often found in healthcare and social services, education, public administration and retailing, while men work more often as technicians, engineers, finance professionals and managers. Second, men and women tend to work at different job levels: the higher the position in the organization, the lower the percentage of women. Women in higher managerial jobs are scarce, in top management even more so. This phenomenon is known as the '**glass ceiling**', a metaphor indicating that a hard but invisible barrier seems to hold capable women back from reaching the top of organizations. Box 9.1 illustrates these effects with statistics from the European Union (2005).

Box 9.1   Gender gaps: some statistics on women and men at work in the European Union (European Commission, 2005)

The difference between women's and men's participation or income is often called a **gender gap**. Below we present some of these gender gaps in the European Union.

Women's employment rate in the 25 member states that formed the EU in 2003 was 55%, while men's employment rate was 71%. The gender gap therefore was 16%.

Women more often work part-time than men. A total of 30% of female employees work part-time and only 7% of male employees. The largest differences occur in families with young children between 0 and 6 years old, where fathers work on the average 43 hours, and mothers 32 hours a week.

Of all managers, 31% were women and 69% men. Members of the daily executive bodies in the top 50 publicly quoted companies were 10% women and 90% men.

Women earn, on the average, 15% less per hour than men.

Early studies

At the start of the twentieth century, the general opinion among psychologists was that women were less intelligent than men, and physically unfit for many types of work. However, from the beginning these notions did not go unchallenged. As early as 1903, Helen Thompson published the monograph 'The mental traits of sex', in which she reported on a series of experiments with a group of male and female students on topics like motor ability, intellectual capacities and affective processes. Her conclusion was that only slight differences occur, sometimes demonstrating male superiority (e.g., in motor ability) and sometimes showing female superiority (e.g., in memory). Thompson concluded that 'according to our present light, the psychological differences of sex seem to be largely due, not to difference of average capacity, nor to difference in type of mental activity, but to differences in the social influences brought to bear on the developing individual from early infancy to adult years' (Thompson, 1903, p. 182).

In another early experimental study Leta Hollingworth (1914) reported on the mental and motor abilities of women during menstruation. It was generally believed that during menstruation women's work performance deteriorated. Hollingworth, however, concluded that: 'careful and exact measurement does not reveal a periodic mental or motor inefficiency in normal women' (Hollingworth, 1914, p. 94). The general conclusions of these two early experimental social psychologists are that (1) the differences between men and women are not as large as psychologists mostly assumed, (2) biology is not that important and (3) social influences play a large role in causing gender differences in work behaviour. These early studies made clear that many assumed differences reflect what we now call gender stereotypes rather than actual differences.

Stereotyping men, women and jobs

Gender stereotypes are expectations about the typical characteristics and behaviours of men and women. Every individual holds gender stereotypic ideas. However, most of the gender stereotypes are largely shared within a certain culture and even world-wide. Characteristics that generally are associated with women (*feminine stereotypes*) are kind, emotional and helpful, whereas characteristics that are associated with men (*masculine stereotypes*) are aggressive, decisive and independent. The feminine stereotype has been labelled as *communal* and the masculine as *agentic* or as *expressive* and *instrumental*, respectively.

Gender stereotypes also pertain to the types of behaviours one will perform and even the situations one will be in. For instance, men are associated with public space, women with being at home. Gender stereotypes are associated with occupations as well. Some occupations, for instance construction worker, are considered masculine, others, for instance nurse, feminine. Moreover, apart from the specific occupation or area of work, job level is also gender stereotyped. Because successful leaders are expected to have mainly masculine characteristics, women are not expected to be managers or leaders.

Gender stereotypes are not only *descriptive*, that is, indicating how we think men and women are, they are also *prescriptive*, that is, denoting how men and women should be and should behave. This dual nature of gender stereotypes can lead to two forms of bias in decisions about (and by) men and women. In the case of women, *description-based bias* occurs when gender stereotypes lead to the expectation that a woman does not have the (masculine) characteristics assumed to be necessary for a certain job, or that her feminine qualities will be unsuitable, for instance, that she will be too emotional and not rational enough to be a good manager (e.g., Van Vianen & Willemsen, 1992). *Prescriptive bias* occurs in reaction to counter-stereotypic behaviour, for instance, when a woman presents herself in a self-promoting manner. She is not considered 'nice' then and is therefore less likely to be hired than a woman who presents herself more modestly.

Gender stereotypes are, in general, rather good descriptions of the average man and woman. For instance, in personality tests men indeed score higher than women on agentic traits, especially assertiveness, whereas women score higher than men on communal traits, especially consideration. Note that no or negligible differences exist on most other personality attributes. Gender stereotypes can cause bias, however, when these expectations about the average man or woman are applied to an individual man or woman, such as an applicant or an employee, who, of course, is never completely average. Gender stereotypes and the associated occupational stereotypes cause substantial limitations both in the choices people themselves make, such as career choices, and in the decisions other people make, such as in hiring and promotion.

Women's choices and decisions regarding jobs and careers

In general, people's activities and (vocational) interests are determined by their capacities and traits, and their personal history of experiences. While on average, men are slightly better in mathematical and visual-spatial tasks like mental rotation, the fact that many more men than women are employed in jobs that involve technical, mathematical and spatial tasks cannot be traced back to these small gender differences in mathematical abilities. In a similar vein, while women score higher on verbal tasks and achievement tests in reading, spelling and literature, this cannot fully explain the large proportion of women graduating in the humanities and social sciences.

Gender differences in motivations and interests may provide a better explanation for gendered careers. Lent, Brown and Hackett (1994) propose that two types of beliefs determine people's vocational interests: self-efficacy beliefs and outcome expectancies.

Self-efficacy

Self-efficacy beliefs are task-specific judgements of one's capability to achieve a certain level of performance (Bandura, 1986). People may find themselves highly competent at one task, and not capable of performing well in another task. For instance, you may think you can write very well but are not at all good at mathematics. Gender differences in self-efficacy beliefs already start to develop at a young age. It was found that girls at the age of seven, nine and eleven years rated their maths competencies lower than boys did, even though no actual gender difference in maths achievement existed. Gender differences in self-efficacy beliefs seem most strongly linked to gender-stereotypic tasks and jobs, such as working with numbers or being a mathematician.

People may also generate *generalized* beliefs of self-efficacy, that is, a relatively stable, trait-like, generalized belief of competence, for instance the feeling that one is able to deal with the typical problems that come up in life. In many, but not all, cultures, women have on average more negative beliefs about their abilities than men. One study showed that female students in China and Germany obtained lower self-efficacy scores than their male counterparts, whereas no such gender differences were found in Costa Rica.

The extent to which individuals have challenging experiences during their (pre-) occupational years is of significant influence on their career development and success (McCauley, Ruderman, Ohlott & Morrow, 1994). Challenging experiences refer to situations in which there are unusual problems to solve, difficult obstacles to overcome and risky decisions to make. A study by De Pater (2005) showed that when they did not need actually to perform their chosen tasks, men and women had similar preferences for challenging tasks. However, in achievement situations, women tended to refrain from performing challenging tasks more than men did. Moreover, when women negotiated about the division of tasks with a male counterpart they ended up with a lower number of challenging tasks, although both partners had similar initial interests in performing these tasks. Women were also more motivated than men to avoid failure. These results suggest that women tend to focus on *doing things right* (i.e., to perform those tasks they are definitely capable of), while men tend to focus on *doing the right things* (i.e., to perform those tasks that will offer them optimal opportunities for career advancement). Women's task choices and behaviours may harm their career progression since the performance of challenging tasks is related to having better chances of promotion (De Pater, 2005).

Outcome expectancies

The imagined consequences of performing particular behaviours, termed '**outcome expectancies**', can also explain differences between men and women at work. Young women anticipate more educational and career barriers than men, and are more aware of the impact of having children and a family on developing an occupational career. Moreover, women, particularly, seem to be influenced by gender stereotypic expectations of their future occupational and job roles, especially when making the transition from school to university. As girls grow older they become more aware of the prevailing gender stereotypes. For example, at school they may see a career in mathematics as possible for themselves, but at university they have closed off that possibility.

Box 9.2 shows a different theoretical approach to the explanation of women's career behaviour.

Box 9.2   An application of the theory of reasoned action to women's career behaviour

The theory of reasoned action (Ajzen & Fishbein, 1980) posits that an individual's behaviour is best predicted by a person's *intention* to perform that particular behaviour. Behavioural intention is determined by (1) the person's attitudes (i.e., positive or negative evaluation) towards the behaviour, and (2) subjective norms, which concern people's perception of social pressure from significant others to perform the behaviour. Vincent, Peplau and Hill (1998) examined career-related intentions, that is, career orientations, gender-role attitudes and subjective norms of female college students (T1) and their career behaviours fourteen years later (T2). Career orientations concern women's ideas of what they would like to be in the future (e.g. homemaker, part-time employed, etc.). Gender-role attitudes concern women's attitudes towards traditional gender roles (e.g., 'in marriage, the husband should take the lead in decision making'). Subjective norms refer to their perceptions of others' wishes (father, mother and boyfriend) regarding their future career. Women's career behaviours were measured in a similar way as their career orientations. The results of this study are shown in the Figure 9.1.

The career orientations of these young women were strongly influenced by the expectations of important others, and to a lesser extent by their gender-role attitudes. Women's career orientations while at school directly predicted their actual careers fourteen years later.

Selection and assessment

Gender stereotypes affect selection decisions in several ways: **Gender typing** of applicants and their behaviours, and gender typing of jobs.

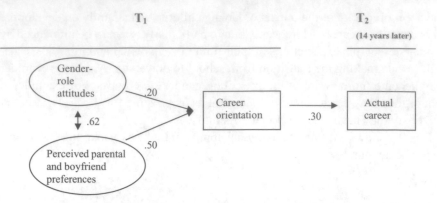

Figure 9.1 *Gender-role attitudes and subjective norms predicting career orientation and actual career. (Derived from Vincent, Peplau & Hill, 1998, p. 772.) The arrows reflect regression paths with standardized regression coefficients. The model could explain 42 per cent of the variance in career orientation and 9 per cent of the variance in career behaviour 14 years later*

Gender typing of applicants and their behaviours

Recruiters, like most individuals, have gender-stereotypic views on the characteristics and qualities of men and women. Moreover, they develop prototypes of 'ideal' candidates for a job. Gender typing of people is attributing gender-stereotypic characteristics and qualities to individual men and women. Gender typing of jobs refers to considering gender-stereotypic characteristics and qualities associated with the sex of the typical job incumbent as necessary qualities for every job incumbent.

If the characteristics of the ideal applicant do not match the characteristics associated with the gender of the applicant, the applicant's probability of being selected is reduced. This *trait-matching* explanation of **gender bias**, that is, the bias in selection decisions about (and by) men and women based on gender stereotypes, has received much empirical support (Davison & Burke, 2000).

Recruiters' selection decisions are, of course, also influenced by applicants' verbal and non-verbal behaviours, like smiling or hesitations in speech. Because the verbal and non-verbal behaviours of men and women are different, they generate a gender-stereotyped personality impression that in turn affects recruiter selection decisions. Gender bias is particularly evident if a woman applies for a masculine-typed job. Van Vianen and Willemsen (1992) found that 'if a female applicant made a feminine impression her chances of selection were reduced. However, a not so masculine (or even feminine) impression of a male applicant did not affect his chances of being offered a job. This implies the working of a double standard for men and women. Women should have the correct personality in order to get hired for the job, while for men a greater latitude of personality characteristics is allowed' (p. 488).

Gender-related expectations that recruiters have about men's and women's roles in society also affect their hiring decisions. Generally, people expect women to take responsibility for their family and, therefore, to be less committed to their job. Additionally, managers often assume women to be less interested in a career or to have fewer ambitions than men.

Gender typing of jobs

The *sex-matching* model suggests that jobs become gender typed according to the sex of the typical job incumbent. Thus, if one sex predominates in a job, then the image of a successful employee that comes most quickly to mind is that of the dominant sex and the associated stereotypic characteristics of that sex. For instance, most of us will think of a truck driver as a man, and of a secretary as a woman. Women who apply for male-dominated jobs evoke images of future success less easily than men.

Box 9.3 specifies the influence of gender stereotypes on parts of the selection process.

Box 9.3 Gender stereotypes and selection

The extent to which gender stereotypes affect selection decisions depends on the selection instruments employed during the selection procedure. An interview is almost always included and is often perceived as vital for the ultimate selection decision. Whether gender influences interviewers' judgement seems also to depend on, for instance, applicants' attractiveness. 'Women who are unattractive, obese, or dressed in a feminine manner are likely to be evaluated unfavorably' (Graves, 1999, p. 154).

Effects of gender stereotyping on selection decisions are more manifest if women are a minority in the applicant pool. This enhances the saliency of their sex, which in turn evokes information processing based on stereotypes. Moreover, gender stereotypes are more likely to be activated when little job-relevant information about the applicant is available (Davison & Burke, 2000). The selection method that provides the most job-relevant information about applicants is the assessment centre method, in which multiple selection instruments, such as tests, simulations, role playing, group exercises and interviews are used to assess multiple dimensions of job-relevant characteristics. Studies that compared the assessments of men and women indeed suggest that this technique is gender neutral.

Explaining the glass ceiling

Studies that explain the glass ceiling, that is, that study why women do not reach top positions as often as men do, have been carried out from different perspectives: (1) gender typing of leadership and management positions, (2) gender differences in leadership and effectiveness and (3) emergent leadership.

Gender typing of leadership and management

'Think manager, think male.' With this expression, Schein and co-authors (1996) summarized the results of a study on gender connotations of management jobs. The characteristics associated with successful managers are more similar to the characteristics associated with men in general than to characteristics associated with women in general. Even if people ascribe feminine characteristics to a successful manager, in general they think of a man when asked to describe a manager. Moreover, female leaders are often evaluated less favourably than male leaders, even if their performance is the same, especially when they lead in a way that is considered masculine, for instance if they use an autocratic leadership style. The 'lack of fit' between the requirements for a successful manager and the feminine stereotype results in a lower probability for women of being hired for such a job, even if they have the same competencies as men (Van Vianen & Willemsen, 1992).

However, the masculine image of management and leaders may be changing. Several authors have suggested that managers in modern organizations need traditionally feminine qualities such as the ability to support their employees, intuition, and a collaborative leadership style. Some authors have even claimed that women's characteristics such as their greater sensitivity in interpersonal relations make them superior leaders.

Gender differences in leadership style and effectiveness

Even after decades of research it is still not clear whether men and women have different leadership styles, and this topic remains the focus of heated scientific discussions. In the 1970s and 1980s, many studies used two-dimensional models of leadership that distinguish between task-oriented and interpersonal leadership. A **task-oriented leadership style** consists of behaviours like having subordinates follow rules and procedures and maintaining high standards of performance. An **interpersonal leadership style** includes behaviours like helping and doing favours for subordinates, explaining procedures and being friendly and available. A meta-analysis showed that in laboratory and assessment studies, men are more task-oriented and women more interpersonally oriented, whereas in studies in existing organizations these gender differences seem to have vanished and female and male leaders do not differ in leadership styles (Eagly & Johnson, 1990). In addition, women tend to adopt a more *democratic* or participative style by inviting subordinates to participate in decision making, whereas men more often adopt an *autocratic* style, not allowing subordinates to intervene in decision making (Van Engen & Willemsen, 2004).

More recently, studies on leadership styles use the distinction between transformational and transactional leadership styles. **Transformational** (or charismatic) **leadership** refers to the ability of leaders to inspire, stimulate and motivate subordinates (Bass, 1985). **Transactional leadership** refers to a more conventional style that includes rewarding subordinates for meeting objectives, monitoring and correcting performance. Evidence is growing that women more often use the transformational style than men (Van Engen & Willemsen, 2004). Interestingly, transformational leadership is often considered a better way of leading people than transactional leadership, as it is generally more effective. Therefore, one might be tempted to conclude that, according to these more recent meta-analytic studies, women are better leaders than men, although this would be a contestable conclusion as it is based on indirect evidence. On the other hand, one could argue that there are hardly any differences between men's and women's relevant leadership qualities so there is no reason to assume that women are better leaders than men, or the other way around.

The question whether female leaders are equally good as male leaders has also been investigated more directly by examining whether women and men are equally effective as leaders. The results of these studies are mixed. Women are less effective than men in situations where most of the leaders are men, or most of the subordinates are men, and especially in military organizations; women are more effective than men in educational, governmental and service organizations and in mid-level leadership positions (as opposed to line or supervisory positions). Together these results support the hypothesis that women fare better as leaders in roles defined in less masculine terms (Eagly, Karau & Makhijani, 1995).

Emergent leadership

Before one can get to a leading position, one must stand out as someone with leadership qualities and willing to compete for such a position. Women do not rise to leadership positions as easily as men do. This may be due to stereotypical responses, attributions and women's own behaviour.

If women act like leaders, that is, show dominant behaviour in a group, they violate the norms that are based on stereotypes, which causes negative affect in others. Women who use dominant language are less influential in groups. Women who act in a dominant and masculine way are not appreciated and even depreciated by others, as is shown in the verbal and non-verbal reactions to these women. A competent, assertive woman in a group receives fewer non-verbal expressions of positive affect, like smiling or nodding in agreement, and more expressions of negative affect, like a furrowed brow or tightening of the lips, than a similar male group member. These negative reactions by fellow group members result in the contribution being considered less valuable and thus diminish the woman's acceptance as a leader. They also are discouraging for the woman in question. See Box 9.4 for an example of experimental research into the negative reactions towards successful women.

Box 9.4   A series of experiments to refine the theory on gender bias in evaluations

Heilman, Wallen, Fuchs and Tamkins (2004) studied the effect of descriptive and prescriptive stereotypes on the evaluation of women in managerial jobs. In a first experiment, subjects evaluated male or female sales managers in an aircraft company (a job considered very masculine), who were either described as performing very well, or about whom no performance information was presented. In the latter, ambiguous, situation, women were seen as less competent than men, but when women were obviously successful, they were considered equally competent but less likeable and more hostile than men in the same job. To test whether this 'penalty for success' effect originates from breaking the prescriptive stereotype that women should work in feminine jobs, in a second experiment three types of jobs were studied: human resources manager in a male-typed (financial planning), female-typed (employee assistance) and neutral (training) job. All individuals described were obviously successful. Negative reactions towards women occurred only in the male-typed job, where women incurred less liking and more interpersonal hostility than men. A third experiment presented evaluation reports on a male or female manager who had just undergone a yearlong masculine-typed management-training programme. The likeability and competence ratings in these reports were manipulated. Both competence and likeability led to better overall evaluations, more recommendations for special career opportunities and higher salary recommendations. Not being liked can therefore have important negative effects.

Together, these results show that 'success in traditionally male domains can have deleterious consequences for women', but 'It is only when the success implies that gender stereotypic norms have been violated that it induces social penalties' (Heilman *et al.*, 2004, p. 426).

Successful behaviours are attributed to different causes. In general, if women succeed in a masculine task – and directing or influencing a group is stereotypically considered a masculine task – their success does not add as much to their status in the group as it does for men. Men's success is attributed to their skills and ability more than women's success, which is often considered to be caused by their efforts, or just by luck. Swim and Sanna (1996) summarized this effect as 'He's skilled, she's lucky'. The converse also holds true: in case of failures, lack of effort and bad luck is more likely attributed to men. For a man this may mean that he becomes more eligible as a leader after a successful performance, because he has demonstrated he's got what it takes. The success of a woman, however, does not make so much difference, because she may have made an extra effort this time, but that does not mean she will do so next time (Swim & Sanna,

1996). Moreover, a man's failure is more often attributed simply to bad luck, whereas a woman's failure can diminish her opportunity to become considered leader.

While it may be more difficult for women to be noted and appreciated for having leadership qualities, women themselves may also act in accordance with stereotypic expectations. They may, for instance, present themselves as being less competent than they actually are, in order to appear more feminine. Also, especially in mixed groups, women do not like to be openly competitive, whereas men seem to like competition. Gender differences in the propensity to choose competitive environments may explain part of the gender gap in higher management positions in competitive organizations.

Structure and culture of organizations

The structure and culture of the context in which work takes place also influence the way men and women behave.

Structure

Kanter (1977) emphasized a structural aspect of organizations that affect women's and men's power and ambition: skewed gender groups at upper organizational levels. These affect both men (the dominant group) and women (the *token* group). Differences between the groups are exaggerated, which impacts negatively on the token group, who suffer, for example, heightened visibility, performance pressure, bias in the assessment of their performance, and being viewed as women rather than as managers. There is, however, a certain asymmetry in these effects, as men in women-dominated contexts do not encounter them. Ott (1989) found that female police officers encountered all the difficulties Kanter predicted for a minority group, while male nurses benefited from their token status and were more easily promoted to supervisory positions. Moreover, while the male majority in police teams resisted women when their number reached a critical mass, the female majority in the nursing teams did not show a similar resistance to men. In fairy tale terms, men in feminine contexts are crown princes, women in masculine contexts Cinderellas (Ott, 1989). Power differences between men and women in the larger society may cause this asymmetry. Men are assumed to have a higher status and are considered benevolent when they are willing to do a feminine job. Women who hold a masculine job, however, are considered to do something above their approved status.

A minority group is often excluded from informal networks in organizations. Female executives report more often than men that they are excluded from informal networks. In higher management circles, the formal power structure is reflected in informal friendships and alliances, the 'old boy network'. Men feel threatened if women enter these networks. Exclusion from informal networks, which tend to consist of just one gender or ethnic group, is more difficult to fight than exclusion from formal groups. If decisions are made in the pub or in the sauna, it is a real disadvantage not to be part of the informal all-male network.

Organizational culture

Organizational culture is the pattern of basic assumptions that an organization has developed over time to cope with its problems, and that is taught to new members as the right way to perceive, think and feel in relation to these problems (after Schein, 1990). Organizational culture manifests itself at three levels: observable artefacts and practices, values and basic underlying assumptions. In a male-dominated organization such as a car repair shop, one of the artefacts may be the girlie calendar on the wall, one of the values may be towards strong male bonding, and one of the underlying assumptions may be that men are better suited to the jobs in question. In such a context, most women would probably not feel very comfortable.

Aspects of organizations can also positively affect the feelings and ambitions of male and female employees. In organizations with a supportive work–family culture, where managers support work–family balance and employees are not expected to take work home at night and weekends, both men and women are more attached to the organization and have lower intentions of leaving.

Men and women appreciate some other aspects of organizational culture differently. Men have a stronger preference for organizations with strong competition, and high work pressure and effort. These gender differences in preferences exist in career starters and tenured employees but not at higher management levels, where men and women have similar preferences. This probably indicates that only those women who feel at home in a more masculine, competitive context make it to the top.

Aspects of organizational culture that are typically associated with women are indeed related to women's position in organizations. If the shared values include a high humane orientation (being nurturing, sensitive, kind and generous) the percentage of women in management is relatively high. This percentage, however, depends mostly on organizational *practices* that relate to gender equity, such as encouraging both women and men to participate in professional development activities, placing women in non-traditional roles, and giving equal opportunities in promotion for men and women.

Interventions

How can gender gaps, glass ceilings and stereotyping be diminished in a way that is consistent with our social-psychological knowledge? Several suggestions can be made to improve women's situation in organizations without causing new problems of resistance or injustice.

Different problems call for different interventions. Organizations can take various measures to enhance women's participation in paid work, like providing or facilitating child care and other so-called family-friendly policies. For instance, flexible work hours, or flexitime, allow workers to determine, within certain boundaries, which hours of the day they work. Flexible work hours have advantages for organizations as well, like less absence, higher productivity and a slightly higher job satisfaction of employees. Moreover, family-friendly provisions help women to break through the glass ceiling: firms with the most generous work–family benefits tend to have the highest percentage of women in senior management positions. In order not to reinforce the stereotype that taking care of children and household tasks is a woman's responsibility, such facilities should be available to male and female employees alike.

A fundamental solution to many problems would be to get rid of the gender stereotypes that are so detrimental in the selection and assessment of women. Unfortunately, gender stereotypes are pervasive and tenacious and cannot easily be changed. People can learn, through extensive training and through the experience of counter-stereotypic examples, not to apply their stereotypes automatically, especially if they are motivated to make fair, unbiased judgements. Organizations could try to provide such training for all managers who have to make decisions about male and female employees, as well as for their human resources officers. At the same time, it is a good idea to make the selection and performance assessment procedures bias proof. The more objective selection and assessment processes are, the less biased they will be, as stereotypes cannot be expressed in the scoring of objective tests and measures. Assessment centres seem to diminish bias, due to their multi-method system (see Box 9.3). Installing a formal mentoring programme may help women who are already employed in the organization to break through the glass ceiling (see Box 9.5).

Box 9.5   The evaluation of mentoring programmes

Mentoring is characterized by a one-to-one relationship between a senior member of an organization (the mentor) and a less experienced one (the mentee), the latter often a newcomer in the organization. Mentoring involves both enhancing a mentee's feelings of competence, like giving support, counselling and role modelling, and career-oriented mentoring, like coaching, providing challenging work environments and enhancing visibility. A mentoring relationship can occur spontaneously, but often organizations install formal mentoring programmes, in order to help new employees integrate more smoothly into the organization, or to help women break through the glass ceiling.

The effectiveness of this intervention is generally studied by retrospective surveys, in which a cross-sectional comparison is made of the career or job progress of those that were mentored and those that were not. Recently, some meta-analyses of the effects of mentoring were published (Allen, Eby, Poteet, Lentz & Lima, 2004). In a meta-analysis, results from various studies are combined and analysed statistically, thus providing insight into the stability of effects found in separate studies.

In general, the meta-analyses show that being mentored has positive effects on mentees' subjective (career or job satisfaction, intention to stay in the organization) and objective (compensation, promotion) career outcomes. The effect on objective measures of career success is noteworthy for this rather informal and low-cost intervention. In general, little or no gender differences are found in the effects of mentoring. Same-gender mentoring often is to be preferred over cross-sex mentoring, as same-gender mentors like the mentees better and provide more role modelling. As women profit from mentoring as well as men, mentoring programmes for women are a cost-effective way to support women's careers.

Finally, what can women themselves do to break through the glass ceiling? They face a double bind: a competent woman risks being considered too feminine for a masculine job and too masculine if she acts as a real leader. This dilemma is difficult to break. The best general suggestion is to (continue to) act feminine in the daily aspects of communication, and especially in non-verbal communication such as smiling and nodding in agreement. At the same time a woman should show her competence and help others to attribute this competence to her capacities by claiming it in a not-too-assertive way. Quite a package!

We are not in favour of special training courses in masculine behaviour like assertiveness, as this may backfire, as explained above. However, a promising method may be the training of self-efficacy. Enhancing self-efficacy can help to support women to make more challenging career choices. Although by no means complete, this brief overview suggests that at all levels of the organization, from the broad level of the organization and its culture to the individual level of the employee or manager, interventions can be developed that are based on our current knowledge of gender processes in work and organizations.

Applied social psychology in context: what other disciplines say about gender differences in work

Economics: human capital theory

Economic theories are based on the assumption of rational decision making: people decide what to do in such a way that they maximize utility or efficiency (see Chapter 5). For instance, new home economics assumes that each household tries to get a maximum outcome from their efforts. Time is either spent in a job (in order to earn money) or in the household, according to the comparative advantage of each spouse in so-called 'human capital', the body of knowledge and skills of a worker (Schippers, 1995). Education and previous work experience are among the building blocks of human capital. Thus, in the average family situation, where a husband is a few years older than the wife, the husband will have more working experience and thus should specialize in work in the marketplace, whereas the wife should specialize in household work. In this way this theory explains why men work more often than women. As women more often have career breaks like parental leave than men and more often work part-time, they build less human capital during their working life. Moreover, their human capital suffers from depreciation due to non-use during career breaks, and therefore women have lower wages rates.

Although many studies have found that human capital does indeed explain a large part of the gender difference in earnings, at the same time it never explains the total difference, that is, generally it has been found that women earn even less than could be expected on the basis of their human capital (Schippers, 1995).

Economics: statistical discrimination theory

The theory of statistical discrimination (Phelps, 1972) tries to explain the gender differences in work and career opportunities from another viewpoint. It assumes that employers, who have to make decisions on hiring, promotion and payment under conditions of uncertainty, will prefer cheap and easy rules to make such decisions. To maximize their profit they will rather make decisions on the basis of characteristics that are easy to identify, like gender, age and race, than on characteristics that are more difficult to assess, like relevant work experience and ability. Decisions about hiring or promotion are based on expectations of productivity, which in turn are based on the characteristics of the group the (prospective) employee belongs to. In this way, statistical discrimination may lead to discrimination in earnings and in hiring and promotion.

Sociology: socialization theory

According to sociologists, values and norms regulate human behaviour, and these values and norms are internalized through socialization processes during childhood and adolescence. The norms and values regarding appropriate behaviour for men and women are internalized and form gender role expectations, a consistent and persistent system of norms and values indicating what is normal and appropriate behaviour for men and women. It is not only employees who base their choices on gender roles, employers also take them into account and will expect women to be less stable workers than men as they will probably leave the workforce when they start a family. As employers strive to minimize risk, they will therefore prefer men to women as employees.

Conclusion

Many differences exist in how much men and women work, and in the type of jobs they work in. These differences can only partially be explained by differences between men and women in personality or motivation. Men are more often in leadership positions than women, although they are about equally effective as leaders. Gender differences in behaviour cannot explain the existing 'glass ceiling' as women's preferred leadership style is at least as effective as men's. Expectations about gender differences, in the form of gender stereotypes and gender-related stereotypes of jobs, contribute to the differences in work situation through biases in the processes of hiring and promotion, which tend to continue the status quo. Women themselves also contribute to the persistence of gender differences through their career choices. Organizations can help men and women to reach a more equal work situation by interventions based on our knowledge of the causes for the gender differences, for instance, by offering family-friendly programmes for all employees and support for women through self-efficacy enhancement, training and mentoring.

Glossary

Gender: the expectation about what it means to be a man or a woman.

Gender bias: the bias in decisions about (and by) men and women based on gender stereotypes. *Description-based bias* occurs when gender stereotypes lead to the expectation that a woman does not have the (masculine) characteristics assumed to be necessary for a certain job, or that her feminine qualities will be unsuitable. *Prescriptive bias* occurs in reaction to counter-stereotypic behaviour, for instance, when a woman presents herself in a self-promoting manner.

Gender gap: the difference between women's and men's participation in work or income.

Gender stereotype: expectations about the typical characteristics and behaviours of men and women. Gender stereotypes are both *descriptive* (they indicate how people think men and women are) and *prescriptive* (they denote how men and women should be and should behave).

Gender typing: gender typing of people is attributing gender-stereotypic characteristics and qualities to individual men and women. Gender typing of jobs refers to the sex of the typical job incumbent.

Glass ceiling: a metaphor indicating that a hard but invisible barrier seems to hold capable women back from reaching the top of organizations.

Interpersonal leadership style: leaders' behaviours like helping and doing favours for subordinates, explaining procedures and being friendly and available.

Organizational culture: the pattern of basic assumptions that an organization has developed over time to cope with its problems, and that is taught to new members as the right way to perceive, think and feel in relation to these problems.

Outcome expectancy: the imagined consequences of performing particular behaviours and the value one places on the outcomes.

Self-efficacy: beliefs about one's own abilities to perform specific tasks. *Generalized self-efficacy* refers to a relatively stable, trait-like, generalized belief of general competence.

Task-oriented leadership style: leaders' behaviours, like having subordinates follow rules and procedures and maintaining high standards of performance.

Transactional leadership: a more conventional style of leadership that includes rewarding subordinates for meeting objectives, monitoring and correcting performance.

Transformational leadership (or charismatic leadership): refers to the ability of leaders to inspire, stimulate and motivate subordinates.

Review questions

1. What is meant by gender gaps, and which gender gaps exist in work?
2. What is, in your opinion, the most important cause for career differences between men and women, and why?
3. What are descriptive and prescriptive gender stereotypes, and what is their influence on the processes of hiring and assessment of employees?
4. What can women themselves do in order to improve their position in the labour market?

Further reading

Powell, G. N. (1999). *Handbook of gender and work*. Thousand Oaks, CA: Sage.

Wilson, F. M. (2003). *Organizational behaviour and gender*. 2nd edn. Aldershot: Ashgate.

The *Journal of Social Issues* has published two issues that together present a good overview of the current state of knowledge on gender and work: volume 57, issue 4 (2001) on gender, hierarchy, and leadership; and volume 60, issue 4 (2004) on women and work.

References

Ajzen, L. & Fishbein, M. (1980). *Understanding attitudes and predicting social behaviour*. Englewood-Cliffs, NJ: Prentice-Hall.

Allen, T. D., Eby, L. T., Poteet, M. L., Lentz, E. & Lima, L. (2004). Career benefits associated with mentoring for protégés: A meta-analysis. *Journal of Applied Psychology*, *89*, 127–136.

Bandura, A. (1986). *Social foundations of thought and action: A social cognitive theory.* Upper Saddle River, NJ: Prentice-Hall.

Bass, B. M. (1985). *Leadership and performance beyond expectations.* New York: Free Press.

Davison, H. K. & Burke, M. J. (2000). Sex discrimination in simulated employment context: A meta-analytic investigation. *Journal of Vocational Behavior*, *56*, 225–248.

De Pater, I. E. (2005). Doing things right or doing the right thing. A new perspective on the gender gap in career success. PhD Dissertation, University of Amsterdam.

Eagly, A. H. & Johnson, B. T. (1990). Gender and leadership style: A meta-analysis. *Psychological Bulletin*, *108*, 233–256.

Eagly, A. H., Karau, S. J. & Makhijani, M. G. (1995). Gender and the effectiveness of leaders: A meta-analysis. *Psychological Bulletin*, *117*, 125–145.

European Commission (2005). *Report on equality between women and men, 2005.* Luxembourg: Office for Official Publications of the European Communities.

Graves, L. M. (1999). Gender bias in interviewers' evaluations of applicants. When and how does it occur? In G. N. Powell (ed.), *Handbook of gender and work* (pp. 145–164). Thousand Oaks, CA: Sage.

Heilman, M. E., Wallen, A. S., Fuchs, D. & Tamkins, M. M. (2004). Penalties for success: reactions to women who succeed at male gender-typed tasks. *Journal of Applied Psychology*, *89*, 416–427.

Hollingworth, L. S. (1914). *Functional periodicity: An experimental study of the mental and motor abilities of women during menstruation.* Teachers College, Columbia University, Contributions to Education, no. 69. Retrieved 17 April 2006, from psychclassics.yorku.ca/Hollingworth/Periodicity/

International Labour Office (2004). *Breaking through the glass ceiling. Update 2004.* Geneva: International Labour Office.

Kanter, R. M. (1977). *Men and women of the corporation.* New York: Basic Books.

Lent, R. W., Brown, S. D. & Hackett, G. (1994). Toward a unifying social cognitive theory of career and academic interest, choice, and performance. *Journal of Vocational Behavior*, *45*, 79–122.

McCauley, C. D., Ruderman, M. N., Ohlott, P. J. & Morrow, J. E. (1994). Assessing the developmental components of managerial jobs. *Journal of Applied Psychology*, *79*, 544–560.

Ott, E. M. (1989). Effects of male–female ratio at work. *Psychology of Women Quarterly*, *13*, 41–57.

Phelps, E. S. (1972). The statistical theory of racism and sexism. *American Economic Review*, *62*, 659–661.

Schein, E. H. (1990). Organizational Culture. *American Psychologist*, *45*, 109–119.

Schein, V. E., Mueller, R., Lituchy, T. & Liu, J. (1996) Think manager – think male: a global phenomenon? *Journal of Organizational Behaviour*, *17*, 33–41.

Schippers, J. J. (1995). Pay differences between men and women in the European labour market. In A. van Doorne-Huiskes, J. van Hoof & E. Roelofs (eds.), *Women and the European labour markets* (pp. 31–52). London: Chapman.

Swim, J. K. & Sanna, L. J. (1996). He's skilled, she's lucky: A meta-analysis of observers' attributions for women's and men's successes and failures. *Personality and Social Psychology Bulletin, 22*, 507–519.

Thompson, H. B. (1903). *The mental traits of sex: An experimental investigation of the normal mind in men and women.* Retrieved 17 April 2006, from psychclassics. yorku.ca/Thompson/

Van Engen, M. L. & Willemsen, T. M. (2004). Sex and leadership styles: A meta-analysis of research published in the 1990s. *Psychological Reports, 94*, 3–18.

Van Vianen, A. E. M. & Willemsen, T. M. (1992). The employment interview: The role of sex stereotypes in the evaluation of male and female job applicants in the Netherlands. *Journal of Applied Social Psychology, 22*, 471–491.

Vincent, P. C., Peplau, L. A. & Hill, C. T. (1998). A longitudinal application of the theory of reasoned action to women's career behavior. *Journal of Applied Social Psychology, 28*, 761–778.

10 Social psychology of health and illness

ARIE DIJKSTRA AND ALEXANDER ROTHMAN

Description of problems in the field

The societal burden of unhealthy behaviours

When a baby is born, we can estimate the expected number of years the new individual will live. This **life expectancy** is calculated based on statistics regarding how many years people in a given population usually live. Life expectancy can be an important indicator of health and illness in populations. During the past forty years, life expectancy has increased all over the world (Table 10.1), although in some regions more than in others. Besides the number of years people live, one can calculate the number of healthy years in a person's life. The at-birth expected number of healthy years lived ranges from about forty years in African countries to about seventy years in developed countries (Mathers *et al.*, 2004).

Although the increase in life expectancy is a good sign, many factors continue to threaten health and life expectancy. In developing and in developed countries, different factors threaten life expectancy. In developing countries the relatively low life expectancy is largely determined by a high child mortality rate, often related to infectious diseases, bad housing and malnutrition. Most of the factors that underlie the high child mortality rate are more strongly determined by structural factors such as economic policy and the quality of the healthcare system than by individual behaviour. In developed countries life expectancy is largely related to lifestyle factors, such as smoking tobacco and dietary choices. Lifestyle factors are important causes of cancers and cardiovascular diseases. Thus, the more countries become developed, the lower their child mortality rate and the more life expectancy is determined by individual behaviours.

Smoking tobacco is one such behaviour. It is related to several types of cancers, to heart disease and to chronic lung disease. One in two smokers will die from smoking and smokers live seven years less on average and they live more unhealthy years. World-wide, about 1.1 billion people smoke, representing about one-third of the population aged fifteen years and older. About 3 million smokers die each year from smoking. Although the percentage of smokers in most developed countries continues to decrease, in many other countries the number of smokers is increasing. It is estimated that in 2030 this will result in 10 million deaths, of which 70 per cent will occur in developing countries (Fagerstrom,

Table 10.1 *Changes in life expectancy in years*
to live by world region

	1960	2000
Europe and Central Asia	68	76
East Asia and Pacific	42	71
Latin America and the Caribbean	56	70
Middle East and North Africa	48	69
North America	70	77
South Asia	44	63
Sub-Saharan Africa	41	46
Poorest countries	41	64
Richest countries	65	74

Source: Becker, Philipson & Soares (2005).

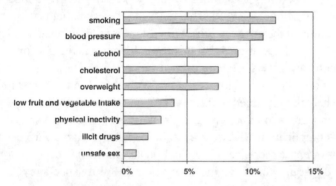

Figure 10.1 *Percentages of healthy years lost caused by health-related*
behaviours and risk factors (World Health Organization, 2002)

2002). Thus, smoking tobacco continues to threaten health and life expectancy.
Other threats are the global developments with regard to HIV/AIDS and obesity.
Future threats to health and life expectancy might come from infectious diseases
(e.g., avian flu) and climate changes.

To illustrate the importance of human behaviours in determining populations'
health, Figure 10.1 shows the percentages of healthy years of life lost due to
behaviours people engage in or risk factors that are closely related to behaviours
people engage in. For example, smoking and alcohol consumption influence the
risk directly by exposing the individual to high levels of potentially lethal com-
pounds, whereas blood pressure, cholesterol level and being overweight are risk
factors that can strongly be influenced by behaviours such as adhering to medical
treatment and, in the case of being overweight, losing weight. In developed countries these behaviour-related risk factors are together estimated to be responsible

for over 50 per cent of the loss in healthy years (WHO, 2002). Changing these behaviours could have a large impact on health and life expectancy.

The societal burden of chronic illnesses

Because in developed countries people live longer and effective medical treatments keep people alive, higher percentages of people end up suffering from chronic illnesses. One way to illustrate the magnitude of this problem is to add up the years that people live with disability or illness and look at the percentage of these years caused by different chronic illnesses. In developed countries, chronic conditions such as cancer, diabetes mellitus, neuropsychiatric disorders, cardiovascular and respiratory diseases are responsible for 86% of the total years that people live in disability or illness, whereas in developing countries this percentage is 65% (Mathers *et al.*, 2004).

One complicating factor related to the high prevalence of chronic illnesses is that, on average, one-third of patients do not adhere to the prescribed medical regimen (Myers & Midence, 1998). This means that these patients do not receive the medical treatment they need, which will compromise their health and increase healthcare use. It could be argued that this low adherence is typical for medicines that just promote lower risks in the long term; patients do not notice any immediate drawbacks of non-adherence. However, even with regard to immunosuppressive medications that are prescribed in the case of a renal transplant, up to 50 per cent of the recipients are non-adherent. This is associated with acute rejection and other serious complications (Weng *et al.*, 2005). Thus, because chronic illnesses are highly prevalent, adherence to medical prescriptions has become a relevant behaviour to target in attempts to increase health and life expectancy.

Contributions of social psychology to prevent and solve health problems

Social psychologists can contribute to improvements in health and life expectancy in three different ways. First, they can study ways to prevent healthy people from engaging in unhealthy behaviour and to persuade them to engage in healthy behaviours. This is considered primary prevention, in which the basic idea is that people should not engage in unhealthy behaviours in the first place. For example, with regard to smoking tobacco, the primary goal is to prevent youth from ever starting to smoke. Furthermore, people in general, but especially youngsters, can be socialized in school and at home to eat healthy food and to get sufficient physical exercise. Second, social psychologists can examine how people who behave unhealthily can be persuaded to change their behaviour. For example, obese people can be persuaded to lose weight and smokers can be persuaded to quit smoking. Third, social psychologists can study how to promote adherence to medical prescriptions in people who are ill. For example, patients with high blood pressure may be stimulated to use antihypertensive medication every day and not only contingent on their interpretations of the symptoms they think they can experience from high blood pressure. Thus, the extent to which medical treatment leads to desired (biological) changes depends on the patient's behaviour.

In sum, the pressures on health and life expectancy in developed countries are in large part related to not engaging in healthy behaviour, engaging in unhealthy behaviours and not adhering to medical treatments. Social psychology studies the social-psychological causes of these behaviours and investigates ways to influence these behaviours for the better.

Understanding health and illness behaviours

Motivation and self-efficacy expectations

Besides general models of behaviour, such as the theory of planned behaviour (TPB) (see Chapter 2), health-specific models have been developed to understand behaviours in the domain of health. For example, the health belief model (HBM), the protection motivation theory (PMT), and the health action process approach (HAPA) can be used to map the psychology of, for example, safe sex, maintaining physical exercise and taking medicines as prescribed. These health-specific models are developed to be complete psychological explanations of healthy or unhealthy behaviours. Although the models offer different sets of psychological constructs to understand behaviour in the domain of health, at a broad level they all refer to two general psychological categories: (1) **motivation** to engage in a behaviour, and (2) **self-efficacy expectations** with regard to a specific behaviour or task. Below, we present the social-psychological perspective on individual behaviour in the domain of health in these two main categories, motivation and perceived control.

Motivation

The most important reasons not to engage in unhealthy behaviours have to do with the state of our physical being: Nobody wants to be ill or hurt. One way this is captured is by assessing a person's **risk perception** for a given health problem (Weinstein, 2003). Risk perception refers to several different aspects of dangers. To answer the question 'how dangerous is it for me to have unsafe sex?', people combine their ideas about different aspects of health problems. One basic estimate that is used concerns one's **perceived vulnerability** (Brewer *et al.*, 2007), in this case, to contracting a sexually transmittable disease (STD). The perception of vulnerability may, first, be based on one's own disease history. People who have never had any STDs despite unsafe sex may come to conclude that they are not vulnerable, although it may actually be caused by luck or the selection of healthy partners. Second, people's perception of vulnerability may be based on family history. When they recall no infections of any type in family members, they may come to believe that they stem from a 'strong family' and therefore are not vulnerable to STDs. Third, to form a perception of their vulnerability, people may compare themselves to others. When in such social comparison they selectively recall a number of people with STDs, they may conclude they are relatively invulnerable. Such a conclusion based on biased social comparison is called **unrealistic optimism** (Weinstein, 1983).

Besides one's vulnerability to STDs, the **perceived seriousness** (Brewer *et al.*, 2007) of STDs may help to answer the question 'How dangerous is it for me to have unsafe sex?' The perceived seriousness of diseases, first, may be based on comparisons between diseases. When someone compares a chlamydia infection with an HIV infection, which can be lethal, they may conclude that the former is not as serious. Second, perceived seriousness may be based on how effective the treatment of the disease is thought to be. When someone understands that most STDs are easy to treat, they may conclude that an STD is not very serious. Third, and related to the former point, perceived seriousness may be based on estimates of how deadly a disease is. The more it is known that people do not have to die from AIDS any more because of successful pharmacological treatment, the less serious AIDS is perceived to be. Only the combination of high vulnerability and high seriousness may motivate a person to take action to prevent a certain disease.

Another perspective on the perception of dangers of unhealthy behaviours is that of fear. Fear is the basic emotion that is caused by the perception of danger; it signals danger and it motivates efforts to lower feelings of fear. When a smoker fears lung cancer, one way to lower the fear is to quit smoking. One specific aspect of fear is worry. **Worry** refers to uncontrolled repetition of thoughts about the danger (McCaul & Mullens, 2003). Although worry may be a disturbing experience, it can support efforts to change unhealthy behaviours; worrying thoughts are a continuous reminder of the dangers of the unhealthy behaviour, thereby sustaining the fear that comprises the basic motive to change the unhealthy behaviour. However, fear does not always motivate people to avert the external dangers; often they are just motivated to preserve their peace of mind. **Disengagement beliefs** of different types help to lower the fear without having to change the unhealthy behaviour (Bandura, Barbaranelli, Caprara & Pastorelli, 1996). For example, the belief 'If smoking is really that bad, the government would completely ban it', undermines the validity of information on the dangers of smoking, thereby lowering the motivation to quit smoking.

The motivation to behave healthily is primarily based on the dangers of unhealthy behaviour that people want to avoid. However, estimates of the benefits of healthy alternatives also are important; people may expect negative health effects of a certain unhealthy behaviour but this does not guarantee that they believe that changing the unhealthy behaviour will enable them to avoid these negative effects. For example, after thirty-five years of smoking the damage may already be done, thus, quitting might have a lowered benefit. These expectations of the benefits of changing an unhealthy behaviour are called **positive outcome expectations** (Bandura, 1986). Different outcomes can be distinguished. In the domain of health, first, expectations about the health outcomes are relevant. For example, a man may be motivated to use a condom because this has the positive outcome of not contracting an STD. Second, positive outcome expectations may refer to social benefits of the behaviour. The man may feel that by using a condom he can never be blamed by others for having transmitted an STD. Third, self-evaluative outcome expectations are another type of benefit that can motivate people to change their behaviour. For example a man may expect to feel good and consistent about himself because using a condom 'is a sensible thing to do'. If people expect no positive outcomes of healthy behaviour, the motivation to engage in that behaviour will be low.

Self-efficacy expectations

In addition to answering the question 'Are they motivated to engage in safe sex?' one must also consider the answer to the question 'Are they able to engage in safe sex?' **Self-efficacy expectations** reflect people's perceptions of their own ability to perform a particular behaviour (Bandura, 1997) (see Box 10.1). Estimates of self-efficacy are task-specific, for example, self-efficacy expectations with regard to the task of not drinking more than five beers may differ largely from self-efficacy expectations with regard to resisting social pressure to drink-drive. As argued above, people engage in healthy behaviour because they think this will lead to positive outcomes. A soccer player may be convinced that staying sober the day before playing a soccer game has huge benefits. However, when he knows that he will not be able to stay sober, he will also not be motivated to do so; why engage in a task (trying to not drink alcohol) in which you know that the chances of success are really small? Thus, a sufficiently high level of self-efficacy expectations is a precondition for the motivating power of expected positive outcomes of the healthy behaviour to manifest. Self-efficacy expectations determine whether people think it is useful to initiate a behaviour and whether they persevere in a behaviour, even when this is difficult. Only easy tasks (e.g., lift your hand) are not a matter of being able to (self-efficacy) but of wanting to (outcome expectations).

Box 10.1   Sources of self-efficacy

People's estimates of their self-efficacy stem from different sources (Figure 10.2). The question is: 'How do you know that you can do it?' The primary source is *enactive learning*. When someone has used a condom several times successfully, they have proved they are able to do it. However, this depends on the *attributions* of failure and success people make. People may attribute failures to their own efforts (lowering perceived self-efficacy) or

Figure 10.2 *Increasing self-efficacy*

attribute successes to their own efforts (increasing perceived self-efficacy). Furthermore, self-efficacy is influenced by interpretations of physical symptoms. For example, noticing that one's heart is pounding may be interpreted as a sign of anxiety and weakness (lowering perceived self-efficacy) but also as a sign of energy and readiness (increasing perceived self-efficacy). Another source is *social comparison* information. If a light smoker hears that a highly addicted fellow student was able to quit smoking, this might increase estimates of self-efficacy: When they can do it, I can certainly do it. However, this will only be the case when the other person is in a comparable range of efficacy to quit smoking, that is, there is a basic and relevant similarity. A last source of self-efficacy expectations is *vicarious learning* or *modelling*. By watching another person accomplishing a task, a person's self-efficacy expectations may increase, partly because the person gains knowledge on how to organize the behaviour to fulfil the specific task (what to do at what moment and how to do it) and partly because the person learns about the difficulty of the task.

Initiation and implementation of behaviour

From the above, we may conclude that different aspects of motivation and control are relevant to health and illness behaviours. However, according to most models, motivation and control do not influence behaviour directly; they result in the formation of *intentions* to engage in the behaviour, which in turn affects behaviour. Many studies have shown that intentions to engage in a specific behaviour are the best, although far from perfect, predictor of the actual behaviour. A review showed that across 40 measurements in 26 studies on health behaviours, intention explained 22.5 per cent of the variance in behaviour (Godin & Kok, 1996). Here we will address two issues related to this 'gap' between intentions and behaviour. The first issue has to do with the fact that people's intentions do not specify when, where and how they will initiate the planned behaviour. This means that there is an increased risk that the behaviour will be postponed because of motivational or circumstantial factors. For example, although the intention 'I intend to do exercise X' specifies the behaviour, it is uncertain when and where the person will start exercising. In other words, intentions do not specify the implementation of the behaviour. However, **implementation intentions** do specify when and where a person will act (Golwitzer & Schaal, 1998). For example, 'when I come home (where) on Wednesday (when), I will start exercising'. Explicit implementation intentions help people to engage in the behaviour when it is not a routine yet. At the specified time and place, implementation intentions are mentally activated and they lead to initiation of the intended behaviour. Research shows that when people formulate implementation intentions and write them down, the chance that the intended behaviour will indeed be executed strongly increases.

The second issue concerning the 'gap' between intentions and behaviour is related to the observation that people sometimes do engage in behaviours although they had no explicit intentions to do so. This is especially clear in behaviours that implicate taking some risk and that are under direct social control. Many behaviours youngsters experiment with fulfil these criteria. Typically, smoking tobacco and alcohol abuse often seem unintended. Engaging in such behaviours is not a matter of intending to do so but of the **behavioural willingness** to do so (Gibbons, Gerard & Lane, 2003). Behavioural willingness is the willingness to take a certain risk when a situation occurs, not a deliberate plan to take this risk. In youngsters, the willingness to get drunk refers to an inclination to act in a certain way in situations in which enough alcohol is available to get drunk. This willingness is strongly influenced by how youngsters want to present themselves socially. They have images, so-called **prototype images** (e.g., the image of the typical student who drinks a lot; Gibbons *et al.*, 2003), that they find more or less attractive. Wanting or not wanting to look like 'the typical student who drinks a lot' partly determines the willingness to get drunk.

Illness behaviour

Besides motivation and self-efficacy expectations with regard to specific illness behaviours, such as adhering to a medical prescription, psychological factors have been studied that are more specific for understanding patients' behaviours. Here we present some of the most important.

What makes people, healthy or ill, contact a doctor when they experience medical complaints? One factor is the way people perceive their physical symptoms. The **symptom perception** (the meaning given to symptoms) (Martin, Rothrok, Leventhal & Leventhal, 2003) is essential to whether the symptoms are ignored, cause anxiety, are discussed with the spouse or make the person contact a doctor. First, people are motivated to put a meaning to the symptoms: 'Does the symptom mean that I am ill?' Second, once someone has formed an opinion on what the symptom means, the question arises, 'Is it necessary to go to a doctor?' The perception of symptoms depends on the **illness beliefs** a person holds (Moss-Morris *et al.*, 2002). Illness beliefs are mental representations, for example, about what symptoms are typical for a specific illness. When the symptom is a headache and the sufferer thinks that a headache can be caused by high blood pressure, they may be alarmed and visit a doctor. In contrast, when the symptom fits the sufferer's ideas about a severe hangover, completely different actions will be taken, such as staying in bed, closing the curtains and waiting for it to vanish. When physical symptoms fluctuate, are moderate in intensity or are ambiguous (is it pain or pressure?), people may be uncertain about the meaning of their symptoms. In such cases, people typically use the strategy of 'wait and see' to gather information on the progress of symptoms, which lead people to postpone a doctor's visit.

The meaning people give to their symptoms and the subsequent actions they take and the adherence to a medical treatment must be viewed in their social context. First, they are influenced by the doctor–patient relationship (Myers & Midence, 1998). *What* the doctor tells the patient (e.g., about why and when to take a medicine, about the course of the illness) and *how* the doctor communicates (e.g., does the patient feel respected, does it invite the patient to listen carefully) influence how the patients will experience the illness and whether the patient will adhere to the medical prescriptions. Second, the patient's social environment is relevant. To be able to live with a chronic illness, adequate social support is important (Taylor, 2007). **Social support** is an extensive concept and it refers to the embedding of a person in an adequate social network in which the person is loved and valued. Different types of social support can be distinguished. With regard to adherence, social support can provide people with *emotional support*. For example, when the medical treatment is aversive, people may take time to listen and support the patient. Furthermore, social support may be in the form of *tangible assistance*. That is, friends and relatives may help patients to interpret and explain their experiences, thereby supporting the patient's behavioural decisions, for example, to discontinue or to continue the medicine. *Instrumental support* refers to doing something concrete for patients. For example, when the medical regimen takes time or a treatment demands recovery time, other people may temporarily take over the household. Or, more directly influencing adherence, others may remind the patient to take the medicines, prepare them for the patient or get them from the pharmacy.

Stage models

All social-psychological variables discussed above are thought to be causally related to health and illness behaviour. The idea is that behavioural changes may be elicited by changing one or more of these factors. However, in the process of behavioural change, these variables typically do not change instantly; change takes time. The perspective that **stage models** take stresses the temporal dimension of behavioural change. According to stage models, people move through different stages when they change their behaviour, and movement forward from each of the different stages into the next stage is caused by a different set of psychological factors.

The trans theoretical model (TTM) (Prochaska DiClemente & Norcross, 1992) is a general model of change that is most often used in the domain of health and illness. The TTM distinguishes between five successive stages that people pass through when they change a behaviour successfully. The five stages are as follows: In the *precontemplation stage*, people are not motivated to change their present behaviour; in the *contemplation stage*, they start to think about changing their behaviour but they postpone actual change; in the *preparation stage*, people plan to adopt the new behaviour on a short-term basis; in the *action stage* people start with the change in behaviour but still have actively to prevent relapse to the old behaviour; and in the *maintenance stage*, they have integrated the new behaviour into their lives. In this process of behavioural change, people cannot skip stages, but they can regress to former stages. For example, an ex-smoker in the action stage may start smoking again and may be very disappointed about the failed attempt to quit. This person may not be motivated to quit anymore and, thus, can be regarded as being regressed to the precontemplation stage. Another relapsing ex-smoker may immediately make new plans to quit and, thus, may regress to the preparation stage.

A basic premise of stage models is that in order to move forward from one stage to another, people have to finish stage-specific tasks. In the early stage, these tasks mainly concern the processing of information that can be used to change from one psychological state into the next. For example, for smokers in the precontemplation stage to move to contemplation they need to process information on the benefits of quitting, whereas for smokers in the contemplation stage to move to the preparation stage they need to process information that lowers their perception of the drawbacks of quitting. The ultimate consequence of this premise is that to stimulate the process of behavioural change, people in different stages need different types of interventions (Figure 10.3). There is some field experimental evidence that shows that people in different stages, indeed, benefit from different types of information (Dijkstra, Conijn & De Vries, 2006).

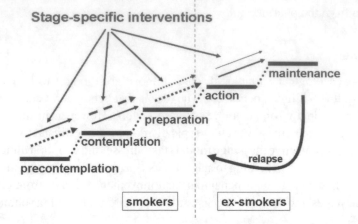

Figure 10.3 *A stage model of health behaviour change*

Research methods to assess changes over time

One of the contributions of social psychologists to healthcare lies in their analysis of the psychological causes of behaviour. Many of the above causes of behaviour are studied longitudinally, for example, positive outcome expectations assessed at T1 predict actual condom use at T2, four weeks later. However, people live in a dynamic world that can change minute by minute and contextual factors may influence behaviours. This means that the behaviour at T2 may not be governed by the psychological state four weeks earlier but, for example, by a psychological state that is activated in a specific situation one hour before T2. To deal with such challenges, investigators have been actively working to develop methods that are able to capture changes in individual situations and fluctuations in their physiological and psychological states and subsequent behaviours. In particular, they have been focusing on methods that provide frequent **momentary assessments** throughout the day.

Although momentary assessments can be conducted using diaries or paper monitoring forms, nowadays electronic devices are available with many possibilities. For example, palm-top computers, ambulant heart-rate monitoring devices or even cellphones can be used to gather individual psychological, behavioural and situational data. First, measurements can be objective or by self-report. For example, heart rate or social interactions can be recorded objectively or people may be asked to rate how they feel or what they think. Second, measurements can be situational or with time intervals. For example, a measurement may be initiated only in social situations or according to fixed or random time intervals (e.g., every fifteen minutes). Third, the initiation of the measurement may be determined by the apparatus or by the individual. For example, an ex-smoker may initiate a measurement when he feels the urge to smoke or when he enters a social situation. On the other hand, the apparatus may initiate measurement with a signal when the individual is actively involved in the measurement or secretly when no individual actions are needed for the measurement. Of course, many combinations are possible. Thus, momentary assessments provide a sophisticated way of studying psychological and behavioural processes in a dynamic environment (see Box 10.2).

Box 10.2   Near real-time versus retrospective recall

Shiffman, Hufford and Hickcox (1997) studied the causes of relapse in ex-smokers. Most of the existing data on the causes of relapse stem from self-reports of ex-smokers: in most studies they are asked to recall in what situation they relapsed. However, the accuracy of the recall is threatened by several psychological processes, including the person's current state and schemata that describe a prototypical class of events (e.g., smokers relapse because of withdrawal symptoms). Momentary assessments could circumvent these recall biases.

In Shiffman's study, ex-smokers were instructed to use a palm-top computer and they were asked to answer several questions each time they lapsed (smoked one or more cigarettes or had just one puff) or felt the urge to smoke. Thus, on the spot they reported their mood, the activity they were engaging in and the triggers of the lapse or urge. After about twenty-five days they were asked to retrospectively fill in the same questions with regard to (1) their first lapse or (2) their strongest urge to smoke. The main results are as follows. First, participants were confident that they could recall their lapses and strongest temptation; on average they scored 3.33 on a confidence scale from one to four. Second, of all the participants who reported a relapse using the momentary assessments, only 23 per cent recalled the correct day they relapsed, when asked retrospectively. Third, the correlations between the momentary assessment and recall (on mood, activity and the triggers) were .36, .24 and .28. This means that the recall data only captured a maximum of 13 per cent of the variance in scores assessed with the original momentary assessment data with regard to the first lapse. With regard to the strongest urge the correlations were lower, sometimes even negative. This study illustrates the limitations of retrospective reports and the strength of momentary assessments.

Promoting health behaviour

A fundamental part of almost every effort to promote healthy behavioural practices is to provide people with information that will persuade them to improve their behaviour (Rothman & Salovey, 1997). Although in some cases persuasive messages provide people with new information (e.g., information about a new health threat or about a new treatment), typically messages are designed to help people recognize and face up to issues they are aware of but have not yet dealt with. Given the challenges of persuading people to recognize that their behaviour may be putting them at risk, investigators have tried to develop strategies that make it difficult for people to ignore the health threat. Since the mid-1960s, investigators have been studying whether messages that elicit fear in the recipient can be an effective way to promote behaviour. Investigators have found that fear alone is not enough. In order to promote behavioural change effectively a **fear appeal** must also convince people that there is something they can do to reduce their risk and that they are able to perform the needed behaviour (e.g., safer sex practice can reduce the chance of HIV infection; see Witte & Allen, 2000, for a review). Although from time to time investigators have been concerned that too much fear might prove paralysing and prevent people from acting, there has been little evidence of this problem.

In situations where people face a clear health threat and there is something they can readily do to reduce their risk, fear appeals can be an effective intervention strategy. However, investigators have developed other communication strategies that have been shown to be effective for a wide range of health issues. Two of these strategies, message tailoring and message framing, are described in greater detail below.

Tailoring messages

Mass media messages are developed to persuade large audiences. Take a thirty-second television advertisement promoting safe sex among female students, showing a female student advocating safe sex. To be relevant for most female students, the student model in the advertisement should not have very specific characteristics. For example, one specific characteristic could be her argument that some sexually transmittable diseases increase the risk of infertility and that she wants to become pregnant in the future. The advertisement would become more relevant for students who also want to become pregnant, but for students who do not, the message may lose its persuasive power. Therefore, such an advertisement directed at female students in general should only contain the core of the message and as few specific characteristics as possible. The desired effect is that the message is not irrelevant for anyone. The problem is, however, that the message is not particularly relevant for anyone, either. Thus, in persuading large segments of populations, mass media try to reach everybody at the cost of personal relevance. Computer technology changed all this.

Computer technology and more specifically the Internet made it possible to adapt information to individual characteristics on a large scale. Through interactivity, computer systems can individually tailor information, based on individual input. In **computer-tailored persuasion**, a message for an individual might take into account the individual's name, gender, religion, past behaviour, motivation

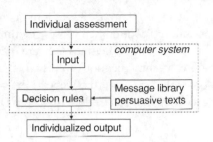

Figure 10.4 *Computer-tailored persuasion composes individualized output (on paper or on screen) based on an individual assessment*

to change the specific behaviour and situational self-efficacy expectations. For example, a tailored message might start like this: 'Dear Robbie, it seems from your answers you are not really motivated to practise safe sex. You may not be aware that the risk of . . .'. Then some content information follows to change Robbie's mind. All that is needed is (see Figure 10.4): (1) input on relevant individual characteristics; (2) decision rules that decide what (pieces of) information should be offered; (3) a library of different message pieces; (4) program to show the composed persuasive message (on screen or printed on paper). The more is known about the individual (input), the better the message will fit the individual (output). However, it is not yet known which and how many of all the possible individual characteristics a persuasive message should take into account to reach the optimum effectiveness (see Figure 10.5).

Figure 10.5 *Computer-tailored information*

Looking at the evidence, the current state of affairs is that tailored communications can be more effective than non-tailored communications; sometimes they are more effective than other communications and sometimes they are only more effective in subgroups. To develop tailored communications further it is essential to determine which elements are responsible for their effectiveness: the working mechanisms. Three tailoring working mechanisms can be distinguished (Dijkstra, 2005; see Box 10.3):

1. *Adaptation* refers to tailoring content information. For example, only a smoker with children will receive a tailored message in which the detrimental effects of smoking for children are presented. Adaptation makes the information more relevant and less redundant. Attention to the message may be enhanced (or not distracted), thereby leading to larger changes in the psychological factors that are targeted by the communication. One form of adaptation is the framing of the message (see the following section, 'Framing messages'). In their pure form, adapted messages are written 'as if' they are directing a general audience. The individual may not even be aware that the adapted message is especially selected for him or her.
2. *Feedback* refers to several methods of providing a person with information or interpretations of information in reaction to the input of the person. For example, the feedback may be literal: 'You tell us you are not motivated to change'; comparative: 'Compared to others your situation looks very good'; or evaluative: 'You think changing is not so important, that is a pity'. Feedback sometimes provides new content information (comparative and instructive), but it always signals that the message is directed at the person, thereby enhancing personal relevance.
3. *Personalization* refers to incorporating recognizable individual features in the content information. For example, a text for tobacco smoker Ben might start with 'Dear Ben' and it may mention at natural and expected places in the text the number of cigarettes he smokes, the number of years he has smoked, the brand he smokes but also his pet's name or the type of car he drives. Personalization does not provide any new information and some personalization items are more individual than others (e.g., first name versus brand of cigarettes) but together they may comprise a unique profile. Just like feedback, personalization signals that the message is directed at the person.

Box 10.3   Computer-tailored persuasive messages

Most tailored messages include all three potential working mechanisms, adaptation, feedback and personalization. Dijkstra (2005) dismantled such a message and investigated the effects of the three potential working mechanisms separately. The participants were smokers and the aim was to persuade them to quit. The following conditions were compared: (1) A condition with a *standard* persuasive message of about 800 words advocating smoking cessation; (2) A condition with an *adapted* text of about 800 words. For example, the long-term physical drawbacks of smoking were adapted to gender and the information on the social consequences of smoking and quitting were adapted to whether or not the participating smoker indicated that non-smokers inhale his or her secondary smoke; (3) A condition in which seven *personalization* items were incorporated in the 800-word standard text; the number of cigarettes smoked, the number of years smoked, the type of cigarettes smoked and the first name of the participant was mentioned four times; (4) A condition in which one sentence of *feedback* was incorporated four times into the 800-word standard text. For example, the text on the long-term physical consequences of smoking started with: 'From the questionnaire it seems you are not convinced that smoking has serious consequences'. Then the standard information followed.

Three results from this study stand out. First, the personalization and the feedback conditions were rated by smokers as being more strongly 'taking into account my personal situation as a smoker'. Second, after four months, in both these conditions the percentage of quitting activity was doubled, compared to the standard and the adapted condition. Third, a mediation analysis suggested that both tailored conditions increased the perception that the information was taking into account the smoker's situation and that this perception led to more quitting activity. Thus, the readers' experience that the information was directed at them *personally* seems to be one central psychological variable that is responsible for the sometimes higher efficacy of tailored communications.

One mechanism that might be responsible for the effects of computer-tailored persuasion is increased personal relevance. For example, the feedback and personalization working mechanisms both explicitly signal that the information is directed at the individual reader. Incorporating cues signalling that generic information is directed at a person may increase the perception of personal relevance of the generic information. According to the elaboration likelihood model this personal relevance may increase the involvement in the message and lead to more *central processing* of the information (Kreuter, Bull, Clark & Oswald, 1999). Thus, personalization may enhance the deep processing of information, leading to more cognitive reactions, which can lead to stronger persuasion (in the case of strong arguments). Another explanation is that personalization and feedback trigger *self-referent encoding*. In self-referent encoding information is processed against the background of the self; the information is actively related to memories about oneself, and to one's perceived self-attributes and values. Once self-referent encoding is triggered, the generic content of a tailored message is also more actively related to oneself.

Now that computers and the Internet are widely available, computer technology is increasingly used to persuade people. The question of how these modern environmental factors interact with the human brain, which has evolved since ancient times, is only recently addressed by social psychologists.

Framing messages

Message framing refers to the wording of persuasive messages. Messages designed to promote a health behaviour can be constructed to focus on the benefits of performing the behaviour (*a gain-framed appeal*) or the costs of failing to perform the behaviour (*a loss-framed appeal*). For example, a gain-framed brochure designed to promote HIV testing would emphasize the benefits afforded by testing, whereas a loss-framed brochure would emphasize the costs of failing to be tested. Research in cognitive psychology has shown that people respond differently to gain- and loss-framed information. People tend to avoid risks when considering the potential gains afforded by their actions (play safe), but are more willing to take risks when considering the potential losses afforded by their actions (little to lose) (Tversky & Kahneman, 1981).

Rothman and Salovey (1997) have been able to use this observation to predict how gain- and loss-framed health messages can affect people's health practices. Specifically, they found that when a health behaviour is perceived to involve some risk or uncertainty, loss-framed messages will prove more persuasive, but when a behaviour is perceived to afford a relatively certain outcome, gain-framed appeals will be more persuasive. Moreover, they observed that the function served by a health behaviour can operate as a reliable heuristic to predict whether people perceive the behaviour that they are engaging in to be risky.

Research in both laboratory and the field has provided strong support for this framework. Initiatives to promote the use of screening behaviours, such as mammography, have proved more effective when information is loss framed, whereas initiatives to promote the use of prevention behaviours such as the use of sunscreen have proved more effective when information is gain framed. A study by Rothman and his colleagues shows the most compelling evidence of the critical role the function of behaviour has in determining the effect of gain- and loss-framed information. In this study they manipulated whether people believed a mouth rinse was designed to prevent oral health problems or to detect oral health problems (Rothman, Martino, Bedell, Detweiler & Salovey, 1999). As predicted, people were more interested in a mouth rinse that prevents oral health problems (engaging in the behaviour keeps one safe) when they read a gain-framed brochure about the product, but were more interested in a mouth rinse that detects oral health problems (engaging in the behaviour may signal oral problems) when they read a loss-framed brochure.

To date, research has supported the thesis that gain-framed messages are more effective when promoting a prevention behaviour, whereas loss-framed messages are more effective when promoting a detection behaviour. However, it is important to remember that the distinction between prevention and detection behaviours rests on the premise that people perceive engaging in detection behaviours as posing some risk and engaging in prevention behaviours as posing little or no risk. Researchers are currently focusing on how people's perceptions of the behaviour can affect the persuasive impact of *gain- and loss-framed messages*. For example, there is mounting evidence that when people perceive engaging in a certain behaviour to be risky – regardless of its function – they will be more responsive to a loss-framed appeal.

In sum, message tailoring and message framing represent two new, innovative approaches to communicating health information. One thing that characterizes both of these approaches is that they emphasize that 'one size does not fit all'. In order to have an impact on the population health and life expectancy, the principles of computer-tailored persuasion and message framing must be diffused broadly into the healthcare system.

Applied social psychology in context

In the domain of health, social psychologists work with professionals in healthcare on a micro-level (e.g., doctors, physiotherapists and dieticians) and with professionals on a macro-level (e.g., epidemiologists and policy makers). First of all, from these professionals, social psychologists learn what the problems are that require psychological and behavioural solutions. For example, epidemiologists show the relation of certain behaviours with obesity in cohort studies or patient–control studies. This information provides social psychologists with the target behaviours they should analyse. For example, because obesity in children is related to the amount of time children spend watching television (data gathered by the epidemiologists), social psychologists have focused their attention on studying the social determinants of the children's behaviour.

On the other hand, social psychologists can provide other professionals with new angles to tackle the problems. First, social psychologists may develop persuasive communications in the form of leaflets, self-help books or mass-media advertisements to change the behaviours that are related to the problems. Second, social psychologists may educate and train other professionals to influence the problems. Third, social psychologists may advise policy makers how to shape the environment in order to stimulate the desired behaviour or to avoid undesired behaviours.

Conclusion

Health and illness are influenced in large part by individual behaviours, such as smoking tobacco, practising unsafe sex and low levels of physical exercise. Global developments with regard to these and other unhealthy behaviours maintain a threat to health and life expectancy in populations. Social psychologists are informed by other disciplines about the specific health problems that need attention and they provide other disciplines with means and knowledge on how to change individuals' behaviours in the domain of health. To be able to do so, they study the social-psychological factors that cause unhealthy behaviours and that support behaviour change.

Social psychologists recognize two main clusters of social-psychological causes of behaviour: the motivation (Why would I change this behaviour?) and self-efficacy expectations (Can I change this behaviour?). Furthermore, in the initiation of behavioural change, people formulate concrete plans about what to do at which moment: the implementations intentions. One way to organize the psychological factors that are involved in behaviour change is to apply a stage model. Stage models stress that behavioural change takes time. They assume people move through a series of psychological and behavioural stages from no motivation to change to long-term maintenance of the new behaviour. The complexity of behaviour and its causes has motivated psychologists to develop assessment methods that resemble the fluctuating and interactive nature of situations, psychological factors and behaviour more closely: the momentary assessments. In addition, social psychologists study how patients interpret physical symptoms and how the doctor–patient relationship and the social environment influence adherence to treatment. Social psychologists not only map all these psychological processes and factors, they also want to promote health by actually changing behaviours. In the domain of health and illness, there are two main developments in persuasive communications. To motivate people to change, information is offered on the outcomes of unhealthy and healthy behaviours that they can expect. These outcomes can be framed in terms of gains and in terms of losses and social psychologists study in whom and why the gain or loss frames are most effective. The large-scale use of computers in our society has stimulated the research on persuasive communication using computer technology.

Glossary

Behavioural willingness: the situational activated preference to engage in a certain action.

Computer-tailored persuasion: persuasion of an individual through a message composed by a computer taking into account information from an individual assessment.

Disengagement beliefs: beliefs that strategically lower the perception of negative consequences of an action in order to maintain peace of mind.

Fear appeal: a persuasive message that stresses the danger of a certain action to induce fear and that recommends a specific action to avert the danger.

Illness beliefs: ideas about the manifestation, the consequences of and the control over a specified illness.

Implementation intentions: intentions to engage in a specified action when a specific situation occurs.

Life expectancy: the number of years individuals can be expected to live in a certain population, computed on the basis of the observed age of dying in that population.

Message framing: the framing of outcomes in persuasive messages by stressing either the gains that follow an action or the losses that will follow in the case of no action.

Momentary assessments: the gathering of individual data on multiple occasions throughout the day.

Motivation: the drive that energizes a person's actions.

Perceived seriousness: one's perception of how negative it is to suffer from a certain disease.

Perceived vulnerability: one's estimate of the risk to contract a certain disease.

Positive outcome expectations: expectations of positive happenings or experiences (rewards) that will follow a certain action.

Prototype images: the mental representation of a prototypical member of a certain group or category of people.

Risk perception (with regard to illness): a general term for the threat of a certain illness based on perceived vulnerability to the illness and the perceived seriousness of the illness.

Self-efficacy expectations: beliefs about one's own abilities to perform specific tasks.

Social support: a general term for different ways people in the patient's social environment help the patient to adjust optimally to an illness.

Stage models: theoretical models that conceptualize the process of behavioural change as occurring in sequential stages over time.

Symptom perception: the processes of detection, interpretation and attribution of bodily events.

Unrealistic optimism: a subjective and strategically lowered personal estimation of the risk of a negative event, based upon a biased social comparison.

Worry: uncontrolled repetition of thoughts about dangers.

Review questions

1. What are the most important developments world-wide that indicate the importance of studying human behaviours that influence health and illness?

2. Explain the two main categories of psychological constructs that explain health and illness behaviours.
3. Give two reasons why intentions often are not good predictors of related behaviours.
4. Name two perspectives in social psychology that stress the importance of time in understanding or assessing psychological and behavioural change.
5. Describe two developments in persuasive communication with regard to health.

Further reading

Bartholomew, L. K., Parcel, G. S., Kok, G. & Gottlieb, N. H. (2006). *Planning health promotion programs: An intervention mapping approach*. San Francisco, CA: Jossey-Bass.
Conner, M. & Norman, P. (2005). *Predicting health behaviour: Research and practice with social cognition models*. Maidenhead, Berkshire: Open University Press.
Salovey, P. & Rothman, A. J. (eds.). (2003). *The social psychology of health: Key readings*. Philadelphia, PA: Psychology Press.
Suls, J. & Wallston, K. A. (2003). *Social psychological foundations of health and illness*. Oxford: Blackwell Publishing.
Taylor, S. E. (2003). *Health psychology*. New York: McGraw-Hill Higher Education.

References

Bandura, A. (1986). *Social foundations of thought and action; A social cognitive theory*. Englewood Cliffs, NJ: Prentice-Hall.
  (1997). *The exercise of control*. New York: Freeman.
Bandura, A., Barbaranelli, C., Caprara, G. V. & Pastorelli, C. (1996). Mechanisms of moral disengagement in the exercise of moral agency. *Journal of Personality and Social Psychology*, *71*, 364–374.
Becker, G. S., Philipson, T. J. & Soares, R. R. (2005). The quantity and quality of life and the evolution of world inequality. *American Economic Review*, *95*, 277–291.
Brewer, N. T., Chapman, G. B., Gibbons, F. X., Gerrard, M., McCaul, K. D. & Weinstein, N. D. (2007). Meta-analysis of the relationship between risk perception and health behavior: The example of vaccination. *Health Psychology*, *26*, 136–145.
Dijkstra, A. (2005). Working mechanisms of computer-tailored health education: evidence from smoking cessation. *Health Education Research*, *20*, 527–539.
Dijkstra, A., Conijn, B. & De Vries, H. (2006). A match–mismatch test of a stage model in tobacco smoking. *Addiction*, *101*, 1035–1043.
Fägerstrom, K. (2002). The epidemiology of smoking: Health consequences and benefits of cessation. *Drugs*, *62*, 1–9.

Gibbons, F. X., Gerrard, M. & Lane, D. J. (2003). A social reaction model of adolescent health risk. In J. Suls & K. A. Wallston (eds.), *Social psychological foundations of health and illness* (pp. 107–136). Oxford: Blackwell Publishing.

Godin, G. & Kok, G. (1996). The theory of planned behavior: A review of its applications to health-related behaviors. *American Journal of Health Promotion, 11*, 87–98.

Gollwitzer, P. M. & Schaal, B. (1998). Metacognition in action: The importance of implementation intentions. *Personality and Social Psychology Review, 2*, 124–136.

Kreuter, M. W., Bull, F. C., Clark, E. M. & Oswald, D. L. (1999). Understanding how people process health information: A comparison of tailored and nontailored weight loss materials. *Health Psychology, 18*, 487–494.

Martin, R., Rothrok, N., Leventhal, H. & Leventhal, E. (2003). Common sense models of illness: Implications for symptom perception and health-related behaviors. In J. Suls and K. A. Wallston (eds.), *Social psychological foundations of health and illness* (pp. 199–225). Oxford: Blackwell Publishing.

Mathers, C. D., Moesgaard-Iburg, K., Salomon, J. A., Tandon, A., Chatterji, S., Ustün, B. & Murray, C. (2004).Global patterns of healthy life expectancy in the year 2002. *BMC Public Health, 4*: 66.

McCaul, K. D. & Mullens, A. B. (2003). Affect, thought and self-protective health behavior: The case of worry and cancer screening. In J. Suls & K. A. Wallston (eds.), *Social psychological foundations of health and illness* (pp. 137–168). Oxford: Blackwell Publishing.

Moss-Morris, R., Weinman, J., Petrie, K. J., Horne, R., Cameron, L. D. & Buick, D. (2002). The revised illness perception questionnaire (IPQ-R). *Psychology & Health, 17*, 1–16.

Myers, L. & Midence, K. (1998). *Adherence to treatment in medical conditions*. Amsterdam: Taylor & Francis Books Ltd.

Prochaska, J. O., DiClemente, C. C. & Norcross, J. C. (1992). In search of how people change, applications to addictive behaviors. *American Psychologist, 47*, 1102–1114.

Rothman, A. J. & Salovey, P. (1997). Shaping perceptions to motivate healthy behavior: The role of message framing. *Psychological Bulletin, 121*, 3–19.

Rothman, A. J., Martino, S. C., Bedell, B. T., Detweiler, J. B. & Salovey, P. (1999). The systematic influence of gain- and loss-framed messages on interest in and use of different types of health behavior. *Personality and Social Psychology Bulletin, 25*, 1355–1369.

Shiffman, S., Hufford, M. & Hickcox, M. (1997). Remember that? A comparison of real-time versus retrospective recall of smoking lapses. *Journal of Consulting and Clinical Psychology, 65*, 292–300.

Taylor, S. E. (2007). Social support. In H. S. Friedman & R. C. Silver (eds.), *Foundations of health psychology* (pp. 145–171). New York: Oxford University Press.

Tversky, A. & Kahneman, D. (1981). the framing of decision and the psychology of choice. *Science, 211*, 453–458.

Weinstein, N. D. (1983). Reducing unrealistic optimism about illness susceptibility. *Health Psychology, 2*, 11–20.

(2003). Exploring the link between risk perceptions and preventive health behavior. In J. Suls & K. A. Wallston (eds.), *Social psychological foundations of health and illness* (pp. 22–53). Oxford: Blackwell Publishing.

Weng, F. L., lsrani, A. K., Joffe, M. M. *et al.* (2005). Race and electronically measured adherence to immunosuppressive medications after deceased donor renal transplantation. *Journal of the American Society of Nephrology, 16*, 1839–1848.

Witte, K. & Allen, M. (2000). A meta-analysis of fear appeals: Implications for effective public health campaigns. *Health Education & Behavior*, 27, 591–615.

World Health Organization (WHO) (2002). *The World Health report 2002: Reducing risks, promoting healthy life*. Geneva: World Health Organization.

11 Social psychology and mental health

ABRAHAM P. BUUNK AND
PIETERNEL DIJKSTRA

Introduction

Mental health disorders represent one of the most common problems facing adults: within a twelve-month period nearly 30 per cent of the population experiences some diagnosable mental health disorder. Mental health disorders pose an enormous emotional burden for the individuals suffering from them, as well as an economic burden for society, especially in terms of the incapacity to work. For instance, in the year 2000 in England alone, the total cost of adult depression amounted to over £9 billion of which £370 million represent direct treatment costs and more than £8 billion represent costs due to lost working days. Clinical psychologists are concerned with analysing the causes of mental problems from which people may suffer, and with helping people to deal with such problems. Mental health problems are of interest to social psychologists as well. Mental health problems are to an important extent rooted in how individuals perceive their social world, and in how individuals function in their interpersonal relationships. For example, depressed people are often socially isolated, which makes current work in social psychology on the 'need to belong' directly relevant to understanding depression (Baumeister & Leary, 1995). It is, of course, not possible to describe everything that social psychologists do in the field of mental health in just one chapter. Therefore, this chapter focuses on three mental health problems: a disturbed body image, depression and relationship problems. These three problems are highly relevant topics for social psychologists because of their high incidence and debilitating consequences for both the individuals suffering from them and their social context. For instance, marital problems may cause not only spouses to suffer from depression, anxiety and/or drugs and alcohol abuse, but also their children. In this chapter we discuss what social psychological factors may give rise to these problems, how social psychologists conduct research to understand these problems and how social psychology can contribute to their prevention and treatment.

Disturbed body image

The term **body image** is used to describe the internal representation we have of our appearance, that is, our own, unique perception of our body

Figure 11.1 *Disturbed body image*

(Thompson, Heinberg, Altabe & Tantleff-Dunn, 2002). Body image may best be conceptualized as a continuum model, with levels of disturbance ranging from none to extreme and most people falling near the middle of the range, experiencing mild to moderate dissatisfaction with their bodies. Yet, a substantial number of individuals are unhappy with the way they look. A large-scale questionnaire study, conducted in 1996 among the readers of *Psychology Today*, showed that 43% of men and 56% of women are dissatisfied with their overall appearance. Moreover, compared with the surveys conducted earlier by this magazine (in 1972 and 1985), men and women seem to have become more dissatisfied with their bodies over time. For instance, in 1972 only 15% of men and 23% of women reported feeling dissatisfied with their appearance. It is not so much our actual appearance that determines our body image, but our perception of how we look. Feingold (1992) found, for instance, that only 6% of one's own view of one's appearance is explained by one's actual attractiveness as assessed by objective raters. Several studies have illustrated the discrepancy between real and perceived appearance (Figure 11.1). In one study women who were free of eating disorders were asked to approximate the size of four parts of their own bodies, the cheeks, waist, hips and thighs. More than 95% of them overestimated the size of these body parts, on average by 25% (Thompson *et al.*, 2002).

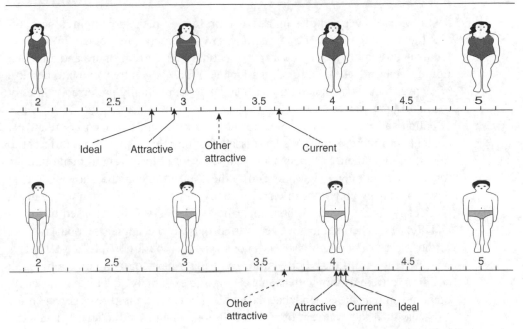

Figure 11.2 *Stimuli presented to the participants in Fallon and Rozin's study (1985)*

Box 11.1 Experiment: gender differences in weight dissatisfaction

Fallon and Rozin (1985) asked 475 undergraduates (227 women and 240 men) to fill out a one-page questionnaire during class. Participants were presented with nine figure drawings of each sex ranging from very thin to very heavy (Figure 11.2). Each figure corresponded to a number from 1 to 9 (1 = thinnest). Subjects were asked to indicate the figure (1) that approximated to their current figure (*Current*), (2) they would like to look like (*Ideal*), (3) that they thought would be most attractive to the opposite sex (*Attractive*) and (4) of the opposite sex that they found most attractive (*Other attractive*).

Gender differences in body image

In general, women feel more dissatisfied with their body than men. Gender differences in body image emerge somewhere between the ages of eight and ten years, with body dissatisfaction, particularly for girls, becoming more pronounced with increasing age. Although individuals may also be unhappy with their face or height, in general individuals, especially women, report most dissatisfaction with physical attributes that display fat, such as the abdomen, hips and waist. A classical study on gender differences in weight satisfaction was conducted by Fallon and Rozin (1985; see Box 11.1). When presented with figure drawings of each sex, men chose very similar figures as representing their ideal figure, their current figure and the figure they thought was most attractive to women. In contrast, women chose a heavier figure as representing their current figure and a thinner figure as their ideal. In addition, the female figure judged by women to be most attractive to men was much thinner than what men actually preferred, while for men the opposite was true.

Fallon and Rozin's study does not necessarily mean that men are relatively content with their weight. Weight dissatisfaction means something different to men than to women. Whereas many women want to lose weight, men often are interested in gaining weight. Several studies, for instance, have shown that men desire a heavier body, not in terms of body fat, but in terms of muscle mass, particularly with regard to their upper body. The set of figures used in Fallon and Rozin's experiment, however, varied only in the degree of body fat, not in the degree of muscle mass and, consequently, could not fully reveal men's dissatisfaction with their body build. By using a new set of figures, ranging in size from extremely thin with no muscle mass to extremely athletic and muscular, other researchers have found that male undergraduates want to be larger and more muscular than their current figure. In addition, when asked to select their ideal body build, male undergraduates tend to prefer a figure that is much bigger than what women find most attractive. Thus, whereas women want to be thinner than they actually are and overestimate the degree of slenderness men find attractive, young men desire to be more muscular than they actually are and overestimate the degree of muscularity women find attractive.

Consequences of disturbances in body image

Feelings of dissatisfaction and inaccurate perceptions of one's body are not necessarily problematic in nature. It seems more-or-less normal not to have an accurate image of our body and to feel somewhat dissatisfied with our appearance. Low to moderate disturbances in body image may even be beneficial and lead individuals to participate in healthy behaviour such as exercising and healthy eating habits. Nonetheless, the higher the level of body image disturbance, the more likely one will encounter clinical problems. The most frequent clinical problems that result from body image disturbances are eating disorders, such as anorexia nervosa and bulimia nervosa, and the body dismorphic disorder (BDD). Anorexia nervosa is characterized by an intense fear of gaining weight or becoming fat, even though one is underweight. To prevent themselves from gaining weight, anorexic individuals severely restrict their caloric intake and exercise excessively, even when they are already extremely underweight. Individuals suffering from bulimia nervosa eat a large amount of food in a limited time period, experiencing a lack of control over eating during that time. To compensate for their excessive food intake, they engage in inappropriate compensatory behaviours, such as purging and fasting. Individuals suffering from body dismorphic disorder (BDD) are preoccupied with an imagined or slight defect in appearance that they perceive as hideous and repulsive. Preoccupations commonly involve features of the face or head, such as the shape, structure or size of the nose, skin or hair. People with BDD believe that other people notice their alleged flaws in appearance, and, as a consequence, feel ashamed, unworthy, anxious and depressed. Between 7 and 24 per cent of BDD patients even attempt suicide and many seek cosmetic surgery for their perceived defects.

Theoretical explanations of disturbed body image

Which psychological mechanisms underlie disturbed body image? Below, we provide two theoretical explanations for a disturbed body image: social comparison theory and schema theory.

Social comparison theory

As discussed in Chapter 7, according to **social comparison theory** (Festinger, 1954), people have a fundamental desire to evaluate their opinions and abilities and strive to have stable, accurate appraisals of themselves. Although individuals prefer to evaluate themselves using objective and non-social standards, they will evaluate themselves by comparison with others when such objective information is unavailable. Individuals may compare themselves with others who are similar (**lateral comparisons**), better off (**upward comparisons**), or worse off (**downward comparisons**). Several studies (e.g., Thornton & Moore, 1993) have revealed so-called contrast-effects with regard to self-perceived attractiveness. These studies have usually exposed participants to stimuli (e.g., photographs or videos) of either highly attractive same-sex individuals (upward comparison) or not very attractive same-sex individuals (downward comparison). Following upward comparison individuals usually experience a decrease in body satisfaction, whereas following downward comparison individuals usually experience an increase in body satisfaction. Although social comparison processes may lead individuals to feel both less and more satisfied with their body (depending on the comparison target), in daily life social comparison processes more often have adverse than positive effects. Women, especially, tend to compare themselves upwards, particularly with beauty ideals, and focus on the differences between themselves and these ideals, feeling bad about themselves as a consequence. However, although everyone in our society is, at least to some extent, exposed to the beauty ideal, not everyone is influenced equally by societal beauty ideals. According to social comparison theory, individuals attempting to reduce feelings of insecurity and anxiety will especially compare themselves under conditions of uncertainty (Festinger, 1954). In support of this assumption, it has been found that individuals with low **self-esteem** (who suffer from uncertainty about themselves) are more likely to engage in social comparisons and are less satisfied with their looks than are individuals with high self-esteem.

Schema theory

Schema theory elaborates on social comparison theory by proposing that the schemas individuals use determine how they interpret information, and what information they acquire. According to the schema perspective, individuals have fundamental body image **schemas** that reflect their core, affect-laden assumptions or beliefs about the importance and influence of their appearance on happiness and success in life and organize and guide the processing of body image-related information. Examples of these schemas are 'Being thin is important' and 'My appearance is responsible for much of what happens to me in my life'. With regard to body image two important types of schemas can be distinguished. **Body image evaluations** refer to feelings of satisfaction or dissatisfaction with one's body whereas **body image investments** refer to the cognitive, emotional and behavioural importance of the body image for one's self-evaluation (Cash, 2002). When individuals are dissatisfied with their appearance (i.e., have negative body image evaluations), but do not feel their appearance is very important to their sense of self (low body image investments), the chance that they will develop clinical problems is low. Individuals suffering from eating disorders and BDD do not only negatively evaluate their body, but also attach extreme importance to their physical appearance. As a consequence, they are 'appearance schematic'. That is, they pay more attention to, place more importance on and preferentially process information relevant to appearance. In addition, because their body schemas are negatively laden, they often have irrational and negative thoughts and interpretations about their looks. They only compare their appearance to that of extremely attractive people, for instance, and tend to make overgeneralizations about their bodies (when someone criticizes their dress, they think: 'See, I am really ugly').

Preventing body image disturbances

As noted before, individuals who suffer from low self-esteem, in particular, are likely to compare themselves with beauty ideals and conclude that they are unattractive. Building self-esteem is therefore one of the best ways to prevent body image-related problems. Positive self-images make individuals become more satisfied with their bodies (and vice versa), largly because it reduces the need to compare themselves with others. Possible policies for preventing body image problems by means of enhancing self-esteem may include interventions such as government information campaigns and school programmes (for an example see Box 11.2). Interventions like these should, preferably, focus on children and adolescents, so that boys and girls reach adolescence with greater feelings of autonomy and self-confidence that buffer against socio-cultural influences on body image. Recent studies also indicate that, among adolescents, regular physical exercise, such as aerobic exercises, is effective in (temporarily) reducing body image dissatisfaction. Physical activity counteracts body dissatisfaction, both directly because of its weight loss benefits and indirectly by improving feelings of self-worth.

Box 11.2   Intervention: the 'Everybody's Different' programme

The Everybody's Different programme is executed in the classroom, in nine weekly lessons of fifty to eighty minutes. The programme consists of five components.

1. *Stress management.* Students learn, for instance, relaxation exercises that promote positive body awareness.
2. *Building a positive sense of self.* For instance, students are asked to identify positive self-attributes and learn to give and receive positive feedback.
3. *Exploring individuality.* In group discussions students examine and reject cultural stereotypes and beauty ideals.
4. *Acceptance of self and others.* For instance, students present art work on the theme 'everybody is different'.
5. *Communication skills.* Students learn to express their emotions by, for instance, role plays.

To examine the effectiveness of the programme O'Dea and Abrahams (2000) randomly allocated 470 students, between eleven and fifteen years of age, to an experimental group (participating in the programme) and a control group (not participating in the programme). On three occasions (before the programme, immediately following the programme and twelve months later) students filled in questionnaires about self concept, body satisfaction and eating attitudes. Compared to the control group (who only filled in the questionnaires), students in the experimental group showed improvements in body satisfaction, self-concept and eating habits immediately following the programme. Some of these effects were still apparent after twelve months.

Depression

Depression is a major mental health problem in Western society. It has been estimated that 17 per cent of all people become depressed at least once in their lifetime. Depression may be brought on by stressful life events (so-called reactive depressions), such as the death of a loved one or giving birth to a child, but may also surface apparently for no reason. People who feel depressed experience great sadness and apprehension, feel worthless and tired and withdraw from others. Despite these negative consequences, most depressions remain untreated. Only 28 per cent of the major depression sufferers have received any type of help during the past 12 months. An average untreated episode may stretch on for six to eight months or even longer.

Gender differences in depression

In response to the same events, women are more likely than men to experience stress and depression, especially in the interpersonal domain. Several theoretical explanations have been proposed to account for this sex difference. First, in most societies, women have less power than men. As a consequence, they experience more chronic strains, such as poverty, more constrained choices, either real or perceived, as well as a higher risk of childhood sexual abuse (e.g., Nolen-Hoeksema, 2001). A second explanation suggests that women's greater vulnerability to depression might be the result of biological characteristics unique to women, such as hormonal and genetic predispositions. Epidemiological studies, however, have found only limited support for this explanation (Nolen-Hoeksema, 2001). A third explanation is based on stress theory, and focuses on the way people cope with stress. In general, two major **coping** strategies can be distinguished: **problem-focused coping**, in which individuals try to alter the source of stress, and **emotion-focused coping**, in which individuals regulate their emotional responses to the stressor (Folkman, Lazarus, Gruen & DeLongis, 1986). In general, for both sexes, problem-focused coping is associated with less depressive symptoms over time, whereas emotion-focused coping is associated with more depressive symptoms and lowered self-esteem, especially when a stressor is appraised as changeable. Empirical evidence overwhelmingly shows that women are more likely to cope with daily stressors and stressful life events by means of emotion-focused coping – the less effective way of coping – whereas men more often use and are more proficient with the constructive problem-solving approach (e.g., Vingerhoets & Van Heck, 1990). Women are assumed to rely more often on ineffective, depression-enhancing coping strategies because of socialization experiences. In general, sadness is believed to be less 'natural' in boys, and therefore boys may receive more encouragement to utilize instrumental responses to alleviate stress. In contrast, girls may be less likely to receive such encouragement, which may leave them more vulnerable to brooding and depression. In support of this line of reasoning, several studies have shown that one's level of masculinity, regardless of one's biological sex, is negatively related to brooding and depression in both sexes.

Social comparison theory and depression

Social comparison theory is one of the social-psychological theories most frequently used to understand and explain feelings of depression. According to social comparison theory, social comparison processes are important links between the social environment and evaluations of the self. In several ways, negative social comparison processes are thought to give rise to and cultivate negative self-evaluations, feelings of inferiority and deprecatory thoughts about the self that are characteristic of depression. First, depressed individuals are more likely to seek negative social comparison targets. More specifically, compared to non-depressed individuals, depressed individuals are more likely to engage in upward comparisons that emphasize their inferiority. The tendency of depressed individuals to conclude that, relative to others, they are inferior and worthless may have serious consequences. When those around them are perceived to be better off than they are, the inclination of young men, especially, to commit suicide is increased. When depressed individuals do compare downwards they often identify with the comparison target, finding confirmation for their feelings of inadequacy. It has, for instance, been found that mildly depressed students, more than non-depressed students, tend to identify with someone with less positive attributes than themselves and less with someone with more positive attributes than themselves, causing them to engage relatively often in self-derogation (e.g., 'I am worthless/incompetent too').

In addition to seeking negative social comparison targets, depressed individuals tend to interpret social comparison information in a less self-serving way than non-depressed individuals do. For instance, whereas non-depressed individuals have a strong tendency to see themselves as better than most others (or the 'average' other) in regard to a wide range of traits and abilities, depressed individuals rate themselves, in comparison with others, as less attractive, less talented, weaker and less competent. These negative social comparison processes confirm depressed individuals' sense of inferiority and depression and make it hard for depressed individuals to take constructive actions to solve their problems and improve their mood.

There are indications that unfavourable social comparison strategies that make individuals vulnerable to depression may be activated early in life and reflect rearing (parent–child) patterns and early peer group experiences. For instance, memories of having to act in a submissive way during childhood have been found to be associated with adult depression. Unfavourable social comparison strategies may then, from childhood on, dominate the internal sense of self, making it more likely that individuals will respond with depression to negative life-events.

More recently, in explaining depression, scholars have linked social comparison theory to an evolutionary-psychological perspective, resulting in the so-called **theory of involuntary subordinate strategies** (ISS) (see Box 11.3).

Preventing depression

Compared to equally debilitating physical conditions, depression may start at a relatively young age. Therefore, as in the prevention of body image-related problems, depression prevention programmes and government campaigns should not only focus on high-risk adults, but also on adolescents. Several cognitive behavioural prevention programmes have been developed for adolescents that effectively reduce the risk of developing a depression, especially for girls. In these programmes, students usually meet after school once a week for twelve weeks in groups of nine to fourteen students. Adolescents learn to identify and evaluate pessimistic thoughts by considering alternatives and examining evidence

> **Box 11.3   The theory of involuntary subordinate strategies (Gilbert, Price and Allan, 1995)**
>
> According to ISS theory, when individuals perceive a defeat or a loss in rank, social comparisons with high status others will make them feel worthless, depressed and anxious. In this context depression can be seen as a so-called 'unconscious involuntary losing strategy' that causes the individual to accept his or her defeat or loss in rank, to suppress feelings of anger towards high status others and to accommodate to what would otherwise be an unacceptably low social rank. Support for ISS theory comes from studies among groups who have faced a loss in rank. For instance, among the unemployed, social comparisons have been found to be related to depressive symptoms: the more unfavourable differences unemployed individuals perceive between themselves and significant others, the more depressed they feel and the more their self-esteem suffers. However, it must be emphasized that the ISS perspective is somewhat unusual as it suggests that depression may be an adaptive response, by helping individuals suppress their feelings of anger, and helping them accommodate to an otherwise unacceptably low social rank. This would imply that individuals who don't respond to a perceived low social rank by getting depressed may be coping in a less adaptive manner, which seems difficult to justify. In general, psychologists would argue that depression is in most cases a non-adaptive response that may hurt the individual considerably. However, it might be that in our evolutionary past, when individuals were highly dependent on others for survival, depression was a more adaptive response than it is nowadays.

for and against their negative thoughts, and are taught skills for relaxation, emotion regulation, problem solving, assertiveness, decision making and successfully coping with conflict.

Fortunately, there are also indications that depressive symptoms among youngsters may dissipate with time. In a recent study of Sheffield *et al.* (2006), in which more than 2000 ninth graders (age fourteen) participated, researchers found that students at high risk of depression who followed an eight-week prevention programme did not improve more than high-risk students who did not follow such a programme. In fact, both groups of students showed a significant reduction of depressive symptoms and an improvement of social functioning in the course of the year.

Among adults at high risk of depression, such as single mothers, brief prevention programmes targeting negative thinking have been found to effectively prevent the onset of depression. Simple techniques such as positive self-talk ('I can do this!') and thought stopping (saying *Stop!* to oneself when one notices that one is brooding or having negative thoughts, for example, 'Others are better than I am', or 'I am worthless') may reduce, for instance, feelings of helplessness and inferiority resulting from unfavourable social comparisons. While in general social comparison is associated with a tendency to make, in particular, unfavourable social comparisons, some studies suggest that social comparison may (temporarily) alleviate feelings of depression (see Box 11.4). Finally, the societal costs of depression may also be reduced by government campaigns that inform the general public about the symptoms of depression and how and where to get help when people suspect that they are depressed. By lowering the threshold for help, more depressive individuals may seek treatment and, although short-term treatment costs may increase, in the long term the costs resulting from, for instance, job absenteeism will decrease.

Box 11.4   Experiment: temporarily alleviating depression

Buunk and Brenninkmeyer (2001) asked 122 participants, of which 40 were depressed, to read a scenario about a depressed target who overcame depression either through considerable work (high-effort condition) or without much effort (low-effort condition). Before and after reading the scenario participants were asked about their mood. The results of this experiment showed that depressed and non-depressed participants responded quite differently to the low- and high-effort targets. In non-depressed participants, the high-effort target evoked a positive mood change, whereas in depressed participants the low-effort target did. It must be noted that these changes were found only among those who had a strong tendency to compare themselves with others. It seems that depressed individuals who often compare themselves with other people perceive the high effort of the target as something that they might have to do as well, but cannot, whereas, due to their feelings of helplessness and defeat, they respond positively to the information that the target was able to get over depression without any special effort.

Relationship problems

The number of divorces is illustrative of the widespread nature of marital problems: between 2004 and 2005 155,052 divorces were granted in the UK (in comparison, in 2004 in the UK 313,550 weddings took place). Due to marital stress, spouses may suffer from mental and physical health problems, such as depression, anxiety, problems with drugs and alcohol and increased levels of suicide. In addition, children of divorced parents run similar health risks and, for instance, are more likely to drop out of school and to become delinquent. To shed light on the potential causes of marital (communication) problems, we will discuss two relevant theories: attachment theory and social exchange/interdependence theory.

Attachment theory

According to **attachment theory** (Bowlby, 1969) children, in response to the way they are treated by their carers, unconsciously develop a specific attachment style, that is, a relatively consistent way of responding to separation from a parent. The experiences in relationships with carers lead to the development of mental representations or 'internal working models', that is, a set of postulates about how close relationships operate, and about the extent to which one is worthy of love and support and others are dependable. Children who have carers who are always available for them, and responsive to their needs when they are in distress, will most likely develop a **secure attachment style**. That is, they will view others as trustworthy, dependable and helpful and develop a positive view of themselves. In contrast, children whose carers show rejection, a lack of responsiveness or physical and emotional abuse, are more likely to develop an **'avoidant' attachment style**, characterized by distance from others and a cynical view of others as untrustworthy and undependable. Children whose carers respond inconsistently to their needs are more likely to develop an **'anxious-ambivalent' attachment style**, characterized by a strong desire to be close to others, combined with a fear that others will not respond to this desire. According to attachment theory the effects of childhood attachment relationships extend into adulthood. Individuals tend to attach themselves to an intimate partner the way they attached themselves to their parents when they were children. As a consequence, the adult relationship may suffer because of attachment problems in childhood. Individuals may, for instance, respond with unreasonable jealousy, not because their partner is or desires to be unfaithful but because their parents responded inconsistently to their needs as a child, damaging their child's trust in others.

Attachment expert Bartholomew (1990) has argued that the avoidant attachment style is more complex than most researchers realized. She suggested that there are two ways in which individuals can be avoidant. First, individuals may want intimate relationships with others but avoid them because they are afraid of being hurt (the so-called **fearful attachment style**). Second, individuals may genuinely prefer freedom and independence to closeness with others (the so-called **dismissing attachment style**). As a result four attachment styles can be distinguished, which can be arranged along two dimensions, namely (1) global evaluations of self and (2) global evaluations of others (see Figure 11.3).

Attachment style and relationship quality

In examining the relation between attachment style and relationship problems, social psychologists usually present participants with questionnaires that assess the quality of relationship and attachment style. Attachment styles are often

Model of self

	positive	negative
positive	*secure* Comfortable with intimacy and autonomy	*preoccupied* overly dependent, preoccupied with relationships
Model of other		
negative	*dismissing* dismissing of intimacy, counter-dependent	*fearful* fearful of intimacy socially avoidant

Figure 11.3 *Attachment theory: the four-group model of attachment*

measured by means of the relationship questionnaire (Bartholomew & Horowitz, 1991), which consists of four short paragraphs describing the four attachment styles (see Box 11.5). These studies have found that individuals with secure attachment styles report higher levels of relationship satisfaction, relationship commitment and trust in their relationships than preoccupied or avoidant individuals. Preoccupiedly attached individuals perceive more conflict in their relationships, lack anger control, report a tendency for conflicts to escalate in severity and are ineffective support givers. Avoidantly attached individuals show high hostility and escapist responses during conflict and are more likely to sulk in an attempt to get support from their partner.

In addition to correlational studies, social psychologists have conducted experiments that demonstrate how attachment styles influence processes in intimate relationships. For instance, Collins and Feeney (2000) asked participants to prepare themselves to make a speech that later would be videotaped, while their partner was taken to a waiting room. The partner was then asked to copy a supportive or relatively unsupportive note in their own handwriting, which was delivered to and read by the participant preparing the speech. When the participants held their speech, they received another, equally supportive or unsupportive note from the partner. Results showed that, compared with secure participants, both preoccupied and avoidant participants responded much more negatively to their partner than securely attached participants: they appraised low-support messages

Figure 11.4 *Preoccupied attachment style*

more negatively, rated the interaction with their partner as less supportive and performed significantly worse at their speech.

Also the physiological consequences of marital stress may depend on an individual's attachment style. In response to relationship stress, preoccupied and fearfully attached individuals show higher blood pressure and pulse rate reactivity, whereas dismissingly attached individuals show lower blood pressure and pulse rate reactivity, making the former more vulnerable to diseases such as cardiovascular disease or hypertension. In addition, couples consisting of a preoccupied or fearfully attached wife and a dismissive husband, in particular, run a high risk of experiencing physical violence, with the wife being the victim.

Social exchange and interdependence theory

Social exchange and interdependence theory assumes that individuals form and continue relationships on the basis of reciprocity in costs and rewards in their relationships (see, e.g., Thibaut & Kelley, 1959). In evaluating the exchange between costs and rewards, individuals may consider a variety of inputs into and outcomes from the relationship, including love, sex, support, financial contributions and household tasks. Individuals will not only experience distress in situations where their partner is indebted to them, but will be upset in situations where they are

Box 11.5   Assessing attachment style

Which of the following descriptions best characterizes you?

Secure attachment style. It is relatively easy for me to become emotionally close to others. I am comfortable depending on others and having others depend on me. I don't worry about being alone or having others not accept me.

Dismissing. I am comfortable without close emotional relationships. It is very important to me to feel independent and self-sufficient, and I prefer not to depend on others or have others depend on me.

Preoccupied. I want to be emotionally intimate with others, but I often find that others are reluctant to get as close as I would like. I am uncomfortable being without close relationships, but I sometimes worry that others don't value me as much as I value them (Figure 11.4).

Fearful. I am somewhat uncomfortable getting close to others. I want emotionally close relationships, but I find it difficult to trust others completely, or to depend on them. I sometimes worry that I will be hurt if I allow myself to become too close to others.

indebted to their partner as well because of feelings of guilt, obligation and fear of being unable to repay the debt (Figure 11.5). As a consequence, relationship satisfaction often decreases. In addition, sexual satisfaction may be lowered when partners perceive inequity in the sexual domain, for instance, when they perceive their partner to be sexually less aroused during sexual activity than themselves. According to **social exchange theory**, therefore, relationships are most satisfying and stable when they are equitable, that is, when the outcomes for each partner (rewards, costs) are more or less equal.

Individuals who discover that they are in an unequitable relationship will try to restore the perceived balance between costs and rewards. These attempts may have various serious consequences for the relationship because they often take the form of conflict. A partner's attempt to change the unequal distribution of costs and rewards, for instance in the household or sexual domain, may lead to so-called demand–withdraw conflicts, a particularly destructive type of conflict (e.g., Gottman & Levenson, 2000). In an attempt to change their partner's behaviour, one spouse pressures the other with complaints, criticism or demands. The other spouse perceives these complaints as intrusive and withdraws with defensiveness or passive interaction. This, in turn, causes the complainant to intensify efforts to engage the other partner, which often causes the partner to become even more remote. In addition, extra-dyadic sex may be a way to restore equity: women (but not men) in inequitable relationships have a stronger desire to engage in extramarital relationships, and to have been involved more often in such relationships than women in equitable relationships. What and how strong

Figure 11.5 *Relationship inequity*

the consequences of inequity are is also determined by individual differences in the extent to which individuals are oriented towards exchanges (see Box 11.6).

It must be noted, that 'an unequal' distribution of, for instance, household chores, should not be equated with 'inequitable' or 'unfair'. For instance, although many women do more of the housework, the majority of women perceive the distribution of household chores as fair. Perceptions of fairness are not based on behaviour alone, but also on feelings of, for instance, mutual respect and supportiveness. For instance, the more individuals engage in tedious family chores and do their partner a favour – that is, the greater the costs – the greater the relationship satisfaction, but only when their efforts are appreciated by their partner. When their efforts are not appreciated, greater costs lowers relationship satisfaction.

Preventing relationship problems

From the perspective of attachment theory, which assumes that early parent–child interactions influence future marital interactions between partners, one might prevent marital problems by providing children with a stable and safe home environment and equipping parents with sufficient parenting skills. In several countries, such as Sweden and the Netherlands, all new parents are offered the possibility of parental training, a training that is provided by maternity and child healthcare, and initiated by central public authorities. Parental training may be especially

Box 11.6   Theory: individual differences in exchange orientation

Individual differences in **exchange orientation** can be arranged on a continuum: individuals at one end of the continuum (non-exchange-oriented individuals, NE) are insensitive to the exchange of rewards whereas individuals at the other extreme (exchange-oriented individuals, E) weigh their actions on a tit-for-tat scale. E individuals don't like others being indebted to them, or being indebted to others. E individuals agree with assertions such as 'If my spouse feels entitled to an evening out with friends, then I am entitled to an evening out with my friends, and 'It bothers me if my spouse is praised for a deed that he/she never did or did by accident', whereas NE individuals do not. Being highly exchange-oriented – that is, having problems with giving generously and receiving gratefully – contributes negatively to relationship satisfaction and commitment (Murstein & MacDonald, 1983).

relevant for parents in vulnerable socioeconomic or psychological conditions, such as teenaged or single mothers. In addition, in recent years the public awareness of the importance of a solid upbringing has grown tremendously due to the media. Television shows such as *Supernanny* and popular pedagogic books inform the general public about simple pedagogic principles such as 'consistency' and 'boundaries' and techniques to implement these principles, such as the 'naughty chair' and 'daily activity schedules'. Techniques like these may provide parents with the skills to discipline their children appropriately and decrease feelings of frustration due to a child's disobedience. Although governmental and commercial initiatives like these may not set out to increase the future marital satisfaction of children, in the long run they may benefit children's future marriages by improving childhood conditions.

From the perspective of social exchange theory the government may contribute to the restoration of equity in domains such as sexuality and household activities. For instance, in 2003 and 2004 in the Netherlands the government initiated a television show, TV spots and a website ('Men in the leading role') in order to encourage spouses to discuss the distribution of household activities and to distribute those activities (more) fairly between them. In twelve weekly one-hour television shows, called *Fathers*, couples discuss statements such as 'Men do not choose to become fathers, it just happens to them', and discuss how, in their home, they distribute tasks that involve paid work, the household and child care. Evaluation of this campaign has shown that, as a result of the campaign, spouses more often discuss the distribution of household tasks and make agreements about this distribution. In so doing campaigns like these may prevent marital problems. Other European countries, such as France, are considering initiating similar projects.

Applied social psychology in context

Social psychology has been applied quite fruitfully to mental health issues. In this chapter we could only give a number of examples, but there is now a blossoming literature on the interface of social and clinical psychology which has even led to the publication of a handbook (Snyder & Forsyth, 1991). Of course, the contribution of social psychology has been mainly theoretical and empirical. On the one hand, social psychologists have applied their concepts and methods to clinical problems; on the other hand, clinical psychologists have borrowed concepts and methods from social psychology to enhance their understanding of the problems their clients were reporting as well as their own role as therapists. Nevertheless, practising clinical psychologists in particular have a quite different way of thinking from research-oriented social psychologists. Whereas clinicians are mainly concerned with finding an effective therapy for a particular clinical problem, social psychologists are primarily interested in the theoretical background of clinical problems. For example, whereas clinicians are concerned with the treatment of pathological jealousy and conduct therapy effectiveness studies on pathological jealousy, social psychologists study the evocation of 'normal' jealousy, that is, the type of jealousy that everyone feels at times. Although findings on 'normal' jealousy may not directly contribute to the treatment of pathological jealousy, it may do so in the long run, by improving our understanding of pathological jealousy. For instance, knowing how individuals respond with 'normal' jealousy when someone else shows an interest in their partner may provide information on how pathologically jealous individuals respond to the delusion that another person is sexually attracted to their partner.

Conclusion

This chapter discusses the contribution of social psychology to the research, prevention and understanding of three clinical problems, i.e. body image-related problems, depression and marital problems. Body dissatisfaction is nowadays experienced by a majority of the Western population, although more so by women than by men. Consistent with social comparison theory, social comparisons in which individuals contrast themselves with the beauty ideal make individuals feel dissatisfied with their bodies. In addition, high body image investments, that is, finding one's physical appearance extremely important and perceiving it has highly connected to one's self-evaluation, contribute strongly to feelings of body dissatisfaction.

Like body image problems, depression is predominantly a problem among women. According to social comparison theory, unfavourable negative social comparisons may contribute to the development and maintenance of depression, especially among those suffering from a loss in societal rank. In addition, unfavourable social comparison strategies that make individuals vulnerable to depression may be activated early in life and reflect rearing patterns and early peer group experiences.

Marital problems were first discussed from the viewpoint of attachment theory. More specifically, preoccupied, fearful and dismissing attachment styles have been found to be connected with a range of marital problems, such as escalating conflicts and unreasonable jealousy. In addition, consistent with social exchange and interdependency theory, marital problems, such as infidelity and conflicts, often occur when the relationship is inequitable. This chapter discussed several social-psychological prevention programmes that may help individuals keep from developing body image-related problems, depressive symptoms and marital problems.

Glossary

Anxious-ambivalent attachment style: attachment to intimate others characterized by a strong desire to be close to others, combined with a fear that others will not respond to this desire.

Attachment theory: a theory that proposes that individuals possess an evolved adaptive tendency to maintain proximity to an attachment figure.

Avoidant attachment style: attachment to intimate others characterized by distance from others and a cynical view of others as untrustworthy and undependable.

Body image: the internal representation of one's appearance.

Body image evaluations: feelings of satisfaction or dissatisfaction with one's body.

Body image investments: the cognitive, emotional and behavioural importance of the body image for one's self-evaluation.

Coping: the process of managing stressful circumstances and/or solving problems.

Dismissing attachment style: attachment to intimate others characterized by the avoidance of intimacy based on the preference for freedom and independence to closeness with others.

Downward comparison: comparison with someone who is worse off or who performs worse on the dimension under comparison.

Emotion-focused coping: type of coping in which individuals regulate their emotional responses to the stressor.

Exchange orientation: the extent to which individuals expect an immediate repayment for benefits given.

Fearful attachment style: attachment to intimate others characterized by both a desire for intimacy and the avoidance of intimacy based on the fear of being hurt.

Lateral comparison: comparison with someone who is similar on the dimension under comparison.

Problem-focused coping: type of coping in which individuals try to alter the source of stress.

Schema: a mental set or representation that organizes and guides the processing of relevant information.

Schema theory: a theory that proposes that the schema an individual uses determines how he/she interprets information, and what information he/she acquires.

Secure attachment style: attachment to intimate others based on the view that others are trustworthy, dependable and helpful.

Self-esteem: an individual's subjective appraisal of him/herself as intrinsically positive or negative to some degree.

Social comparison theory: a theory that proposes that individuals think about information about the self (e.g., their grades or physical appearance) in relation to one or more other people.

Social exchange theory: a theory that proposes that social relationships are more satisfying and stable when they are equitable, that is, when the outcomes for each partner (rewards, costs) are more or less equal.

Theory of involuntary subordinate strategies (ISS): a theory that proposes that feelings of depression are adaptive in nature and the result of defeat or a loss in social rank.

Upward comparison: comparison with someone who is better off or who performs better on the dimension under comparison.

Review questions

1. What type of schema is typical for individuals suffering from severe body image concerns and why?
2. What is, according to social comparison theory, characteristic for individuals suffering from a depression? And, following this theory, what should mental health workers focus on in the prevention of depressive symptoms?
3. What attachment styles can be distinguished and how are they related to marital problems?
4. What type of contribution, in general, does social psychology make to the field of clinical psychology and the treatment of clinical problems?

Further reading

Bartholomew, K. & Horowitz, L. (1991). Attachment styles among young adults: A test of a four-category model. *Journal of Personality and Social Psychology, 61* (2), 226–244.

Buunk, B. P. & Brenninkmeijer, V. (2001). When individuals dislike exposure to an actively coping role model: Mood change as related to depression and social comparison orientation. *European Journal of Social Psychology, 31* (5), 537–548.

Maddux, J. & Tangney, J. P. (2008). *Social psychological foundations of clinical psychology*. New York: Guilford Publications (in press).

Snyder, C. R. & Forsyth, D. R. (1991). *Handbook of social and clinical psychology: The health perspective*. Elmsford: Pergamon Press.

Suls, J. & Wheeler, L. (2000). *Handbook of social comparison: Theory and research*. Dordrecht, Netherlands: Kluwer Academic Publishers.

Thompson, J. J., Heinberg, L. J., Altabe, M. & Tantleff-Dunn, S. (2002). *Exacting beauty: Theory, assessment and treatment of body image disturbances*. Washington, DC: American Psychological Association.

References

Bartholomew, K. (1990). Avoidance of intimacy: An attachment perspective. *Journal of Social and Personal Relationships*, *7*, 147–178.

Bartholomew, K. & Horowitz, L. M. (1991). Attachment styles among young adults: A test of a four-category model. *Journal of Personality and Social Psychology*, *61* (2), 226–244.

Baumeister, R. F. & Leary, M. R. (1995). The need to belong: Desire for interpersonal attachments as a fundamental human motivation. *Psychological Bulletin*, *117* (3), 497–529.

Bowlby, J. (1969). *Attachment and loss*. Vol. 1, *Attachment*. New York: Basic Books.

Buunk, B. P. & Brenninkmeijer, V. (2001). When individuals dislike exposure to an actively coping role model: Mood change as related to depression and social comparison orientation. *European Journal of Social Psychology*, *31*, 537–548.

Cash T. F. (2002). Cognitive behavioural perspectives on body image. In T. F. Cash & T. Pruzinsky (eds.), *Body image: A handbook of theory, research and clinical practice* (pp 38–46). London: The Guilford Press.

Collins, N. L. & Feeney, B. C. (2000). A safe haven: Support-seeking and caregiving processes in intimate relationships. *Journal of Personality and Social Psychology*, *78* (6), 1053–1073.

Fallon, A. E. & Rozin, P. (1985). Sex differences in perceptions of desirable body shape. *Journal of Abnormal Psychology*, *94* (1), 102–105.

Feingold, A. (1992). Good-looking people are not what we think. *Psychological Bulletin*, *111* (2), 304–341.

Festinger, L. (1954). A theory of social comparison processes. *Human Relations*, *7*, 117–140.

Folkman, S., Lazarus, R. S., Gruen, R. J. & DeLongis, A. (1986). Appraisal, coping, health status, and psychological symptoms. *Journal of Personality and Social Psychology*, *50* (3), 571–579.

Gilbert, P., Price, J. & Allan, S. (1995). Social comparison, social attractiveness and evolution: How might they be related? *New Ideas in Psychology*, *13* (2), 149–165.

Gottman, J. & Levenson, R. W. (2000). The timing of divorce: Predicting when a couple will divorce over a 14-year period. *Journal of Marriage and the Family*, *62*, 737–745.

Murstein, B. I. & MacDonald, M. G. (1983). The relationship of 'exchange-orientation' and 'commitment' scales to marriage adjustment. *International Journal of Psychology*, *18* (3–4), 297–311.

Nolen-Hoeksema, S. (2001). Gender differences in depression. *Current Directions in Psychological Science*, *10* (5), 173–176.

O'Dea, J. A. & Abrahams, S. (2000). Improving the body image, eating attitudes, and behaviors of young male and female adolescents: A new educational approach that focuses on self-esteem. *International Journal of Eating Disorders*, *28* (1), 43–57.

Sheffield, J. K., Spence, S. H., Rapee, R. M., Kowalenko, N., Wignall, A., Davis, A. & McLoone, J. (2006). Evaluation of universal, indicated, and combined cognitive-behavioral approaches to the prevention of depression among adolescents. *Journal of Consulting and Clinical Psychology*, *74* (1), 66–79.

Snyder, C. R. & Forsyth, D. R. (1991). *Handbook of social and clinical psychology: The health perspective*. Elmsford: Pergamon Press.

Thibault, J.W. & Kelley, H. H. (1959). *The social psychology of groups*. New York: Wiley.

Thompson, J. J., Heinberg, L. J., Altabe, M. & Tantleff-Dunn, S. (2002). *Exacting beauty: Theory, assessment and treatment of body image disturbances*. Washington, DC: American Psychological Association.

Thornton, B. & Moore, S. (1993). Physical attractiveness contrast effect: Implications for self-esteem and evaluations of the social self. *Personality and Social Psychology Bulletin*, *19* (4), 474–480.

Vingerhoets, A. J. & Van Heck, G. L. (1990). Gender, coping and psychosomatic symptoms. *Psychological Medicine*, *20* (1), 125–135.

12 Social psychology and modern organizations: balancing between innovativeness and comfort

KAREN VAN DER ZEE AND PAUL PAULUS

Introduction

Imagine that you have just obtained your master's degree in social psychology and that you are hired by a large company such as Shell or British Telecom. What would you be able to offer your company from your recent studies in social psychology? In this chapter we will approach important themes of modern organizations from a social-psychological perspective. We will first briefly describe the societal context in which modern organizations operate and its implication for the workplace. More specifically, we will focus on two important developments. In the dynamic world we live in nowadays organizations continuously have to adjust their strategies to new environmental demands, for example, by bringing new products on the market in response to changing needs of customers. In addition, globalization and migration forces, as well as the increased number of women and older employees in the workplace, cause the workplace to be more and more diverse. Both developments turn the workplace into an environment that has a higher potential for group creativity and innovation, but that at the same time is less likely to be a source of safety and provide a sense of belonging.

In this chapter, we will use theoretical perspectives from social psychology to explain why *change* and *diversity* promote creativity and innovation. Perspectives on cognitive stimulation are particularly helpful in this regard. Moving on from social identity theory, we will show that both change and diversity may at the same time also endanger feelings of safety and belonging. We will close the chapter by discussing how organizations can, in their policies and in group- and individually based interventions, build on these theoretical perspectives in trying to generate positive outcomes in the modern workplace. In addition, we will discuss how social-psychological insights can be combined with insights from different disciplines that address the same issues.

Social context of modern organizations

Nowadays, we live in a world where rapid technological developments and individualistic customers continuously challenge companies with new demands for products and services. Well-known examples of this are detection methods for explosive substances in response to terrorist threats, new computer technologies and mobile phones. As a consequence, organizations have to be flexible in redefining their goals and policies in order to respond effectively to new demands from the environment. This makes organizational life less predictable and stable. Consequently, employees are faced with organizational changes, and they have to deal with the uncertainties that these changes evoke. In order to remain effective in such a dynamic environment, organizations have come to rely less on bureaucratic and formal arrangements and more on collaborative processes, often organized in small and temporary project teams. The end of the traditional hierarchical approach to organization provides a work context that may be more positively challenging to employees, causing them to be happier and more productive, but it clearly has its price. More flexible and temporary forms of collaboration may not provide a social context where employees feel safe and at home. Modern work structures are therefore less potent in creating a sense of belonging and safety for employees. Thus, whereas rapid changes in the modern workplace may turn work into a more challenging and exciting experience, under some conditions it may also pose a threat to employees' well-being. It is therefore important for modern organizations to know under which conditions change goes with happiness and under which conditions it does not.

Another important aspect of the changing social context in which modern organizations have to operate concerns the composition of the workforce. Due both to migration and to a growth in international assignments, work units are more heterogeneous. The entry of women into managerial and professional careers has diversified the workforce (see also Chapter 9). Due to increasing life expectancies and the economic necessity for people to work longer, age also has become an important source of diversity for companies. The literature has repeatedly stressed the potential of diverse groups to be more creative and to generate better decisions (e.g., Mannix & Neale, 2005; Van Knippenberg, De Dreu & Homan, 2004; Williams & O'Reilly, 1998). With more ways of viewing a situation available, there is a greater potential for reaching the 'right solution'. Moreover, research has shown that multicultural groups develop more and better alternatives to a problem. They also seem to incorporate better criteria for evaluating those alternatives than do culturally homogeneous groups. It is not hard to imagine that this may be beneficial in a dynamic world that asks for continuous creativity and innovation. However, at the same time, being faced with norms and values that are different from one's own may be experienced as threatening. Hence, interactions among individuals with different norms and perspectives may easily create conflicts and tensions that may frustrate feelings of well-being and productivity.

In sum, modern organizations seem to be characterized by rapid changes, flexible and temporary work structures and by increased diversity of the workforce. Organizational flexibility and diversity allow for an exploration of new developments and mutual differences by co-workers. However, the literature on cognitive and social processes in groups suggests that there are strong psychological forces

Figure 12.1 *Intercultural working environment*

against such an exploration (Figure 12.1). These forces seem to result from the threat that open exploration poses to group members' positive sense of self and feelings of belonging at work.

Strengths of active exploration

In principle, organizational change may be beneficial to the satisfaction and performance of employees and work groups. Why is this the case? From a motivational perspective, being engaged in new developments may be challenging and enhance intrinsic motivation. The creativity that is evoked by the pleasure provided by new tasks and challenging goals will easily stimulate innovative activities. Moreover, being confronted with new tasks seems to evoke more thorough and active modes of information processing. When groups are confronted with routine tasks or the same tasks over a longer period of time, they may fall back on unconscious, automatic behaviours (Louis & Sutton, 1991). This may cause them to become rule-determined and insensitive to context. A typical example is an employee of a university housing office in a rural town who refuses to help an international student because she has neither a familiar student registration number nor a local address. Being used to the standard routine of dealing with

Table 12.1 *Stages of cohesion and locomotion in groups*

Cohesion too low	Cohesion too high	Optimal levels of cohesion and locomotion
Insecurity about behavioural expectations and norms	Sense of invulnerability	Reflection on goals and performance
Tensions and conflicts between group members	Issues are no longer discussed	Enthusiasm for learning
Subgroup formation	Group members agree easily	Disagreements are perceived as constructive and stimulating
Mutual stereotypes	Different problems are solved in the same manner	Ideas are put forward in the group
Disagreements are easily perceived as personal conflicts	Little new information is exchanged in the group	Original input is rewarded
Low satisfaction	Low curiosity for new information or newcomers in the group	Individuals feel free to express their views, even if these are controversial
Low performance and creativity	New initiatives are easily discouraged	High satisfaction
	High satisfaction	High performance and creativity
	Low performance and creativity	

registrations, the housing officer feels unable to handle such an exceptional case in filling out the standard application forms. In contrast, when employees encounter new events or perspectives on a regular basis, they are more likely to switch to more active modes of processing (Louis & Sutton, 1991). An officer who is employed at the housing office of an international business school in New York will more probably start trying to understand the specific situation of each student, focusing on a solution to the problem at hand. Cognitive and learning theories have pointed at the positive aspects of active processing in generating high quality decisions (Argyris & Schon, 1978). Thus, organizational change may promote active processing of information by employees or work groups, which seems beneficial to **group creativity** and **innovation**. Whereas group creativity refers to the fluency, flexibility and originality of thoughts that are produced by groups, innovation can be defined as the introduction of new and improved ways of doing things in organizations. Active processing is particularly important in dynamic and complex situations that require troubleshooting, environment scanning and complex decision making.

Effortful cognitive processes are motivated not only by change, but also by diversity of inputs. Hearing ideas from others that differ from our own may activate knowledge that has not been previously used. Models of cognitive processes in idea generation assume that knowledge is represented in **associative networks**. Associative networks are network structures of ideas in the brain in which the closest connections are between those ideas that are semantically related (e.g., toothpaste and toothbrush) and more indirect and distal connections are between ideas that are less closely related (e.g., toothpaste and lip gloss). Exposure to ideas is believed to lead to the activation of knowledge through a process in which activation of one knowledge area leads to activation of adjacent areas in the network and is subsequently spread out to other areas (see, e.g., Nijstad, Stroebe & Lodewijkx, 2002). In order for such a process to occur, ideas must actually be able to activate knowledge, or have associative value (Dugosh & Paulus, 2005). This requires that ideas do not overlap too much with the information that is already available. Too much overlap may be a wasteful duplication of knowledge and effort. In this regard, the necessity for a certain degree of inter-member difference seems obvious, and diverse groups do a better job in this regard than homogeneous groups. Indirect support of this view is provided by a recent study by Nakui and Paulus (2007) on group brainstorming. This study revealed that culturally diverse groups performed better than homogeneous groups. The authors instructed brainstorming groups to generate ideas on a specific topic. Although the multicultural groups generated fewer ideas, these ideas were of higher quality than those of monocultural groups. It must be noted that in order to have associative value, ideas should also not be too distal, because if they are they will evoke no further associations. For example, if a biologist comes up with a biochemical concept in a meeting with experts in medieval history, the historians may not at all be stimulated by the idea, since they have no sense of what the biologist is talking about.

To conclude, change and diversity both seem beneficial to exploration of problems and new ideas. Despite the necessity for work groups to explore new opportunities, ideas and products, the reality is conservatism in work approaches and a strong resistance to change the status quo (see, for instance, Dirks, Cummings & Pierce, 1996). Moreover, research on group decision making suggests that there is a strong tendency for group members to focus on ideas that are familiar to all group members. For example, research on the selection of ideas in brainstorming suggests that, as compared to conditions in which individuals select ideas from brainstorming on their own, groups have a preference for ideas that are less original and more feasible (Rietzschel, Nijstad & Stroebe, 2005). In a similar vein, other studies suggests that, even if diversity in perspectives is present in groups, there is a strong tendency for group members to focus on those knowledge elements that they have *in common*, rather than on the pieces of knowledge that are uniquely available to one or a few group members. If, for example, we communicate with colleagues about a destination for a field trip, we tend to share experiences about familiar destinations known to all, instead of exchanging information about less obvious places that may be more exciting to explore together. This decreases the quality of the decision-making process (see, for instance, Stasser & Titus, 1985). Finally, it has been suggested that too much novelty in ideas is threatening and may actually reinforce automatic and rigid forms of processing. This phenomenon is referred to as the **threat-rigidity effect** (Staw, Sandelands & Dutton, 1981) referring to a pattern of rigid thinking that is the result of feelings of threat, caused by stress, anxiety or physiological arousal. Threat-rigidity effects have also been linked to 'too much' diversity in work groups (Austin, 1997). What makes groups and individuals in organizations so reluctant to openly explore new ideas and developments?

Social identity theory

One theoretical perspective that may explain limited exploration in organisations is **social identity theory** (SIT). Individuals derive part of their identity from the social groups to which they belong, in SIT referred to as **social identity** (see, for instance, Tajfel & Turner, 1986). Moreover, SIT assumes that people have a need for positive self-esteem: they strive to feel good about themselves relative to others. In order to further strengthen the sense of self-esteem they derive from group membership, individuals tend to assimilate information about ingroup members (**ingroup assimilation**) and to contrast information about outgroup members (**outgroup contrast**). In other words, individuals tend to exaggerate similarities with ingroup members and they tend to exaggerate differences with outgroup members. This is illustrated by the example of employees of a sales department who regard employees of a research and development department (R&D) as less ambitious and less willing to work overtime. At the same time they perceive their sales colleagues as being just as ambitious and as just as willing to work extra hours as themselves. In fact, the two departments' attitudes to work may not differ strongly. However, to support their view, a sales colleague who leaves at half past four is perceived as having a late meeting, whereas an R&D colleague leaving at the same time is perceived as probably leaving to go home. These perceptions become a reality that reinforces existing boundaries between the two groups. The likely consequence is that sales employees feel good about their own sales department and keep identifying strongly with their sales colleagues.

Being a member of a work organization provides an important social identity: work organizations and work teams not only provide a context of belonging, but they also set goals and provide rewards for reaching those goals. Organizational identification is associated with increased efforts towards organizational goals, work satisfaction and commitment (see, e.g., Dutton, Dukerich & Harquail, 1994). Despite these positive effects associated with organizational identification, strong identification with the organization may become problematic if the organization aims to change. If planned change confirms the existing organizational identity, such as in the case of organizational growth due to new products or markets, individuals who strongly identify with the organization will be inclined to assist the organization in realizing its new goals (see, e.g., Dirks *et al.*, 1996). In many cases, however, organizational change can be seen as a threat to one's identity as a member of the organization. When the sales department from our earlier example has to merge with the R&D department, the sales people will be likely to try to maintain the 'good old sales identity'. This in turn may increase attachment to the status quo and a strong resistance to change.

Strong social identities may evoke resistance not only to organizational change but also to inclusion of members with non-shared characteristics in the team. Subgroup formation of members who share specific characteristics such as age, race or gender may harm constructive group processes, which may negatively affect group outcomes. Illustrative in this regard is a study by van der Zee, Atsma and Brodbeck (2004) who followed culturally diverse groups of business students who collaborated on a joint assignment over time. Among these students, strong identification with their own cultural background negatively contributed to satisfaction and commitment to the team, whereas identification with their team positively affected group outcomes. Apparently, if team members primarily stress their membership in a subcategory (e.g., being a white male), the emphasis in interactions will be on category values and perspectives, which differ for the different subgroups within the team (see Tajfel & Turner, 1979). Detectable differences will then result in fragmentation within the group and this may result in low trust among group members. Box 12.1 describes how organizations can use the insights from SIT in order to explain and reduce tensions between subgroups in diverse teams.

Box 12.1   Application of theory: a case example of principles from social identity theory

A large Dutch international bank struggled with problems in the collaboration between old and young employees. Team leaders were reluctant to accept older employees in the team and team members refrained from communication with their elderly teammates. This not only obstructed effective team functioning but also career possibilities for older employees. The company believed in the additive value of the older employees, bringing important experiences into the team and, in combination with their young colleagues, providing a richer perspective on important issues than would be obtained by a homogeneous age group. The bank asked for our help, and, departing from a social identity perspective, we decided to interview both age groups on their stereotypical views of 'the other group' and meta-stereotypes of their own group (e.g., 'Everyone thinks we are inflexible'). These stereotypes were brought back into the teams and related to each group's self-views in order to break down sharp 'us' versus 'them' distinctions. This process helped to improve openness between the groups and to each other's ideas, thereby improving the teams' effectiveness and sense of well-being.

In sum, threat to identity may result in a perception of group members in terms of 'us' and 'them', which may lower work satisfaction and may preclude group members from benefiting from the new perspectives that other subgroups bring into the team. In order to reduce this threat, group members in diverse teams may primarily focus on ideas of ingroup members. A preference for ingroup ideas was supported by recent findings by Dugosh and Paulus (2005) that participants in a brainstorming session who were presented with a large number of ideas were significantly more productive when they believed that these ideas had actually been generated by students with a similar creative aptitude than when they believed these ideas had been presented by a computer program. Prevention of ingroup threat may also explain the strong preference for shared information that was reported by Stasser and Titus (1985). Stressing those aspects that group members have in common rather than what divides them creates a shared group identity, which may serve important group needs and therefore enhance team satisfaction. Although we may eventually benefit more from dissimilar input, in many cases we feel more strongly motivated by ideas that confirm important social identities rather than those that provide the best source of exploration.

Dynamic organizational development: cohesion and locomotion goals

The processes described in the previous sections pose an interesting dilemma. Organizations need novelty to survive, but at the same time organizational members dislike and resist novelty, and they fall back on rigid functioning. This dilemma can be recognized in different theoretical paradigms both in the field of organizational change and in the areas of diversity research that focus on the *gains of new perspectives* in contrast to the *value of existing identities*. For instance, in research on diversity of the workforce, we can find perspectives that stress the importance of highlighting communalities between people from different social and cultural groups, as well as perspectives that focus on the gains of celebrating differences among such groups. As an example of the first perspective, Triandis, Kurowski and Gelfand (1994) presented a model in which they point out the importance of promoting *perceived communalities* in diverse groups. In their model the perception of communalities is reached by factors such as the presence of superordinate goals, knowledge of the other group and equal status contact (cf. contact theory as discussed in Chapters 2 and 6). More specifically, the assumption is that equal status contact helps in coping with diversity because it generates a focus on similarities between group members and hence stimulates positive outcomes in diverse groups. The similarity perspective can also be recognized in '**colour-blind perspectives**' to diversity management. Organizations that subscribe a model of colour-blindness are highly concerned not to discriminate between categories of employees and monitor and adjust their policies to ensure that this is the case. This focus on equal treatment makes them reluctant to stress or even actively use potential differences between groups. In contrast, value-in-diversity approaches to diversity management warn against ignoring differences between people (as in the colour-blind models) and suggest exploration of differences as an important strategic source for the organization (Harquail & Cox, 1993; Van Knippenberg & Haslam, 2003). For example, a consultancy aimed at promoting the welfare of children in different parts of the world may use the different cultural backgrounds of its employees to develop different versions of a child-support training module. Doing so enables them to be more effective across cultures. In this regard, Harquail and Cox (1993) argue that diversity is associated with positive outcomes in companies that are characterized by an **intercultural group climate**, that is, a climate in which diversity is positively valued, uncertainties are tolerated and only few behavioural descriptions exist. By making the positive value of diversity explicit, group members will start to like differences more and be more sensitive to them. This can be done either by the strategic choice to use diversity actively or by radiating a group norm that diversity is a positive thing. This may ultimately stimulate well-being and performance in diverse groups. Consistent with this view, Nakui and Paulus (2007) showed that the superiority of diverse brainstorming groups in generating higher quality ideas was particularly prevalent when participants were told that their fellow group members appreciated diversity.

We believe that both communality and difference-focused perspectives are useful and need to be on the agenda of companies. Lewin (1935) argued that all activities in groups evolve around two processes: cohesion and locomotion. Group members have a need for relational belonging and safety (**cohesion goals**) and a need to move towards the achievement of group goals (**locomotion goals**). According to Lewin, groups must have reached their cohesion goal in order to function effectively as a group; thus, the fulfillment of cohesion goals is a necessary requirement for the fulfilment of locomotion goals. We believe that the communality and differences perspectives that can be distinguished in the literature on innovation, organizational change and diversity that we have discussed differ in their focus on cohesion and locomotion goals. In order to deal effectively with processes of change and diversity, organizations have to switch between a focus on similarities and differences in a dynamic way, dependent upon aspects of the organizational and team context.

Figure 12.2 presents processes of cohesion and locomotion in organizations as a function of the organizational and team context. At the organizational level, as we have discussed already, an organizational climate characterized by colour-blindness primarily stimulates cohesion goals. In contrast, organizations who are more strongly oriented towards learning tend to emphasize locomotion rather than cohesion. Opportunities such as a sudden market for new products may also change the patterns of interactions of group members and their input in the group process, promoting locomotion. Moreover, both external and internal threats change the need for relational belonging and safety and thereby 'force groups' to switch from cohesion into locomotion and vice versa. On the one hand, a threat such as being faced with a common enemy (e.g., a competitor

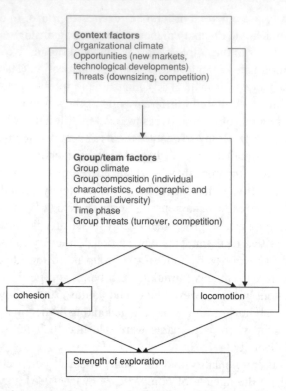

Figure 12.2 *Processes of cohesion and locomotion in organizations as a function of organizational and team context*

bringing a comparable product onto the market) may stop team members from an R&D department from focusing on their incompatibilities, which facilitates cohesion. On the other hand, an extra bonus for one of the teams may evoke competition and emphasis on mutual differences (locomotion).

In a similar vein, at the team level, the age of teams – that is, how long they have been in existence – seems to be an important context factor that influences which focus becomes dominant for effective functioning. It is well known that groups change over time, both in the way in which the group members relate to each other and in the activities that they perform. In this regard, recent formation seems to be related to a predominance of cohesion goals; over time locomotion goals become more important. It seems that group members first need some time to get used to each other and to form expectations and relations in order to be able to perform important aspects of group performance. In later phases they need to focus on locomotion in order to reach important performance goals. If teams in organizations fail to match their focus on either cohesion or locomotion to the requirements of the organizational and team context, sub-optimal functioning will be the outcome. If groups fail to reach reasonable trust in their earlier phases, focusing on differences in later phases is likely to result in emotional conflict. If groups are successful in reaching a similarity focus early on, but do not switch to a focus on differences later, groupthink occurs, also preventing groups from becoming creative. **Groupthink** refers to the tendency for members of highly cohesive groups to conform so strongly to group pressures that they fail to think critically, rejecting the potentially correcting influence of disconfirming information or alternative perspectives.

Interventions

How can work organizations intervene with the context factors mentioned in Figure 12.2 and the psychological processes that they evoke? How can they promote cohesion in periods of insecurity, tension and conflicts? How can they move their organization or teams within the organization from a cohesion to a locomotion focus in order to reach a healthy balance between comfort and innovation? Below we will discuss interventions aimed at changing the organizational or team *context* and interventions that are directly aimed at changing patterns of *behaviour, cognitions or affect* that are the result of characteristics of that context.

Promoting cohesion

Interventions that are aimed at promoting cohesion have predominantly departed from a social identity perspective. As we have already discussed, identity threat posed by organizational change asks for gradual changes in the definition of organizational or team identities, and confirmation of those identities. The 'new' identity of the team can be made salient, for example, by articulating group mission statements, or celebrating group achievements in the direction of new goals. In a similar vein, when organizational groups are united into one group (as in the case of mergers), or if diversity causes subgroup formation in diverse teams, it may be useful to stress common group membership by activities such as formulating a group dress code or creating a group logo, or by defining superordinate goals (such as adopting a school in a developing country as a team). Both in the case of organizational change and in the case of mergers, it may be important to be concerned about team stability, keeping the composition of groups similar over a certain period of time, in order to create a stable and identifiable context (Edmondson, 1999).

Cohesion may also be facilitated by changing the nature of the task. Whereas some tasks may foster a focus on communalities, others foster a focus on differences. This is an issue that has been largely neglected in the literature (for an exception see Postmes, Spears & Cihangir, 2001). In general, communality-focused tasks seem to be characterized by shared information and a joint solution that can be logically inferred from the information. A typical example is when all team members have a financial overview over the past year and have to compute the profit that was made. Moreover, tasks that facilitate a focus on communalities seem to be characterized by routine. When a task is simple and well understood, group members can rely on standard operating procedures. Under these circumstances, debates about task strategy are unnecessary and unlikely, and everyone shares the same approach to the task.

Promoting locomotion

An effective way of promoting locomotion is to take measures to stimulate group members to express their unique viewpoints in the group. In this regard, introducing a 'devil's advocate', who has the explicit assignment to stimulate creativity in the group, is sometimes also advocated. A way to achieve this is to invite an outsider into the group (for example, a colleague from another department, or an external advisor) to take this role in the group process. It is unclear if it is more or less effective when a devil's advocate criticizes existing viewpoints in the group than when the same criticism is simply put forward by a group member. The open and honest expression of disagreements that are naturally present in groups is usually referred to in the literature as **authentic dissent** (see Nemeth & Nemeth-Brown, 2003, for a discussion). There is evidence to suggest that a devil's advocate stimulates thoughts that confirm, rather than challenge, existing viewpoints. These studies suggest that groups with a devil's advocate are not motivated to explore the benefits of challenging views, nor do they display a stronger tendency to engage in **divergent thinking** (Nemeth & Nemeth-Brown, 2003). Divergent thinking refers to the process of reframing familiar problems in unique ways.

A way of promoting dissent in groups is to use *structured discussion and brainstorming methods* (see also Box 12.2). Groups using these methods are instructed to (Osborn, 1957):

1. Concentrate on the quantity of ideas.
2. Don't criticize others' ideas.
3. Elaborate and build on others' ideas.

A focus on locomotion goals may also be stimulated by specific kinds of tasks. Examples are divergent thinking tasks or tasks that require a joint solution which is optimized if group members combine individual information or different perspectives (e.g., deciding on a holiday destination under conditions where each group member has information on a different destination and there is no shared knowledge on a specific destination). In this regard, a study by Postmes et al. (2001) indeed showed that if group members first engage in a critical thinking task they will be more inclined to share unique information in subsequent decision-making tasks. In a more general sense, a focus on differences is likely to be evoked by complex tasks that require problem solving, have a high degree of uncertainty and have few set procedures. These tasks have in common that a wide variety of inputs is required in order to perform effectively.

A useful intervention based on social identity theory in this case is also **recategorization**, aimed at making subgroup identities salient. Identification patterns

> **Box 12.2   Interventions: application of structured brainstorming methods in practice**
>
> Sutton and Hargadon (1996) studied the effectiveness of brainstorming groups in IDEO, a company that specializes in design. The researchers intensively followed two design teams for a couple of months, performed retrospective interviews and also attended CEO meetings. In this company brainstorming rules were printed on the walls of the company. The study method did not allow testing of outcomes in terms of effective idea generation as a result of brainstorming. However, focusing on broader organizational outcomes, the brainstorming sessions had six important consequences for this firm, its design engineers and its clients: (1) it supported the organizational memory of design solutions; (2) it provided variety for designers' skills; (3) it supported an attitude of wisdom, facilitating designers to act on their knowledge while understanding its limits; (4) it created a competition for status based on technical skill; (5) it impressed clients; and (6) it provided income for the firm.

with subcategories can be enforced by recategorization procedures, such as using symbols or by paying explicit attention to the different backgrounds in a team, to make category memberships salient (Gonzalez & Brown, 1999). Introduction of 'threat' has also been advocated as a means of 'unfreezing' strong identification with the status quo (Lewin, 1958). For example, willingness to change among employees can be gained by presenting data that indicate that a serious problem exists in the organization, or by describing the negative consequences of not changing the status quo for the future of the team and its members.

Flexibility in cohesion and locomotion

It is obvious that organizations cannot continuously influence the focus of employee identities in different directions, in order to serve cohesion and locomotion purposes, or create different tasks dependent upon the stage at which they find themselves. Two aspects of organizational climate that have been mentioned in the literature and that may benefit both cohesion and locomotion goals are **psychological safety** and innovation. The first aspect, psychological safety, refers to a shared belief that well-intentioned interpersonal risks will not be punished (Edmondson, 1999). Psychological safety allows for the expression of concerns, without the fear of losing one's job or opportunities for advancement. Moreover, it promotes behaviours such as experimentation and help seeking that are important for learning and responding to organizational change. According to Anderson and West (1998) an organizational climate that stimulates innovation is characterized by:

- vision: a sense of valued outcomes represented by clear goals and motivating forces;
- participative safety: involvement in decision making occurring in an interpersonally non-threatening environment;
- task orientation: shared concern over excellence of the quality of task performance;
- support for innovation: stimulation of attempts to introduce new ways of doing things in the work environment.

All these dimensions share a concern with cohesion, as indicated by a sense of sharedness or organizational support as well as a concern with locomotion, as indicated by goal setting, standards of innovation and a concern with excellence.

Box 12.3   Research design: a case example of experimental evaluation of interventions

Brickson and Brewer (2001) report an unpublished laboratory analogue study of an organizational team. In this study a relationally oriented intervention was compared with a collectively oriented intervention of recategorization in promoting positive attitudes of males towards females. Two identity orientation manipulations were used. First, prior to the experiment, male participants received a questionnaire and were told that their responses would indicate whether they had a relational or a collective business orientation. Second, different versions of a role-play with two trained female confederates were used that were similar in terms of content, but varied in terms of context and instruction. Confederates behaved either in a relationally oriented or a collectively oriented fashion. Moreover, in the relational condition, the male participants were instructed to take turns in giving and seeking advice, to listen empathically and take the other's perspective. In the collective condition, the male participants were instructed to problem solve jointly and to assess current threats to team integrity and generate solutions for solving the problems at hand. Dependent measures were explicit and implicit attitudes towards the female interaction partner, distribution of credit points to fellow team members (including the female confederate) and selection of teammates for participation in a future study. Results showed that participants in the relational condition (1) were far more likely to give females an initiating role in a projective test that evoked character descriptions, (2) showed marginally less sex stereotyping on a reaction-type task and (3) allotted female team members marginally more credit points. No differences in the likelihood of selecting females as future teammates were found. These results provided preliminary support for the prediction that attitudes towards a female teammate and females in general were more favourable in the relational condition.

At the level of employees, a balance between a focus on communalities and differences may require identity orientations that are more flexible than the social category memberships that we discussed in the previous sections (team versus subgroups). It has been recognized only recently that the social self is not necessarily based on group identities but can also revolve around personal bonds with other individuals. Brewer and Gardner (1996) referred to the part of the social self that includes representations of (close) relationships with others as **relational identity orientation**. When a relational identity orientation is salient, the situation is defined in terms of mutual relationships rather than in terms of group membership and constituent norms. A focus on relationships with other individuals at work goes along with empathy and positive affect. Imagine the example of an employee who mentors a colleague in weekly meetings where they discuss the latter's uncertainties and problems at work. This promotes mutual understanding and enhances constructive collaboration. Interpersonal relationships may represent a better ground for cohesion and locomotion than groups: within relationships there seems to be a continuous switch between emphasizing communalities that form the relationship and empathizing with the unique needs and thoughts of the other person, while in larger, more impersonal collectives such as teams, there seems to be a strong pressure towards uniformity. A relational orientation within organizations is promoted by organizing work in small-scale and temporary work structures, creating opportunities for informal contact and mentorships (Brickson & Brewer, 2001; see Box 12.3 for experimental procedures).

Applied social psychology in context

Of course, issues of change or stability cannot be completely understood solely from social psychological perspectives. Economists, for example, have a longstanding tradition in trying to understand innovative endeavours from the economic advantages they bring. Since the driving force for companies will always be their need to survive and therefore to be profitable, strategic change in organizations cannot be understood simply from social cognitive and social motivational factors. Therefore, social-psychological analyses need to be complemented with rational analyses of expected utilities of strategic change in response to challenges or threats in the environment. An interesting example in this regard is the current economic growth in Asian countries, which is overshadowing that of Europe and the United States. The major response in the Western world has been one of fear of Asia 'taking over the world market' as well as fear of losing jobs as a result of outsourcing labour. This response can easily be understood from the identity and threat perspectives that we have discussed in this chapter. However, a recent economic analysis by Grant Thornton (*International Business Owners Survey*, 2006) suggests that the economic developments in Asia may promote rather than threaten business opportunities for Western countries. The Chinese economic boom, for example, is perceived by international companies in the United States and in Europe (e.g., Sweden, Germany and the Netherlands) to increase rather than to reduce their business opportunities. These opportunities include both import opportunities, particularly from China, and, to a lesser extent, export opportunities for commodities and machinery. Such economic analyses are undoubtedly of major importance and may in Lewin's (1958) terms eventually even work as a 'defreezing factor', reducing resistance to innovative responses to such developments on the global world market.

We have tried to clarify that also at the more detailed level of *actually producing* the creative ideas that underlie organizational innovations or change. Social psychologists tend to take a cognitive or social perspective, focusing on stimulating and inhibiting forces that influence idea generation and sharing in work groups (e.g., the presence of ideas that have associative value, group pressures or psychological safety). For example, in approaching the issue of psychological safety, social psychologists usually point at the importance of climate factors, collaboration or leadership behaviour. With this focus social psychology has tended to overlook the importance of more formal incentives or threats that are attached to being creative. What if your individual ideas are stolen by someone else? Or what if the company comes up with a new formula for shampoo that is copied by its competitors? Scientists in economics and law have paid much more attention to these issues. A rich literature can be found that deals with the issue of how to ensure recognition of creative ideas of single individuals while at the same time stimulating the sharing of knowledge that is necessary for innovation. This is usually done by analysing the outcomes of antitrust laws and different ways of protecting intellectual property. These formal protections have a strong impact on employee and company behaviour. We definitely need to take these issues into account when we put effort into changing cultures or leadership. In approaching problems of innovation and creativity, it is therefore important to seek collaboration with economists and law scientists and to integrate their perspectives with social-psychological approaches. The same openness to different viewpoints that benefits innovation also seems crucial to scientific progression in a complex world.

Conclusion

We have argued that the dynamics of modern organizations require continuous exploration of differences and new developments. From social identity theory we explained that individuals will strive for temporal stability of their identities, as well as stability in their perceptions of ingroups and outgroups. This may explain why in organizational practice resistance to change is strong, and diversity is surrounded by intergroup tensions. Up till now, social and cognitive approaches to issues of change and diversity have lived relatively separate lives (see also Van Knippenberg *et al.*, 2004). In order to benefit from the insights of social psychology, there is a strong need for such integrative endeavours. We have argued that effective functioning of modern organizations therefore requires that exploration activities that serve locomotion purposes of organizations need to be balanced with concern for group cohesion. For modern organizations this suggests that they cannot simply be as flexible as introductions to many textbooks on organizational developments (and also the first sentences of this chapter) suggest. Paradoxically, it is particularly in the face of changes that companies need to pay attention to communicating shared and stable organizational identities to their members.

Glossary

Associative network: network structure of ideas in the brain in which the closest connections are between those ideas that are semantically related, and more indirect and distal connections are between ideas that are less closely related.

Authentic dissent: open and honest expression of disagreements that are naturally present in groups.

Cohesion goals: goals in groups directed at serving members' need for relational belonging and safety.

Colour-blind perspective: approach to diversity management in companies characterized by a focus on communalities rather than differences, and on equal rights and opportunities for all employees regardless of their background.

Divergent thinking: the process of reframing familiar problems in unique ways.

Group creativity: fluency, flexibility and originality of thoughts that are produced by groups.

Groupthink: the tendency for members of highly cohesive groups to conform so strongly to group pressures that they fail to think critically, rejecting the potentially correcting influence of disconfirming information or alternative perspectives.

Ingroup assimilation: tendency to exaggerate similarities with ingroup members.

Innovation: the introduction of new and improved ways of doing things in organizations.

Intercultural group climate: climate in which diversity is positively valued, uncertainties are tolerated and only few behavioural descriptions exist.

Locomotion goals: goals in groups aimed at the achievement of central work outcomes.

Outgroup contrast: tendency to exaggerate differences with outgroup members.

Psychological safety: shared belief that well-intentioned interpersonal risks will not be punished.

Recategorization: enforcing alternative categorizations among individuals.

Relational identity orientation: part of the social self that includes representations of (close) relationships with others.

Social identity: part of one's identity that is derived from the social groups to which one belongs.

Social identity theory: theory which posits that group membership forms an important component of social identity, and that people strive to attain or maintain a positive self-image by engaging in favourable comparisons between their ingroups and various outgroups.

Threat-rigidity effect: pattern of rigid thinking that is the result of feelings of threat, caused by stress, anxiety or physiological arousal.

Review questions

1. A study by Van Knippenberg and Van Leeuwen (2001) showed that in the case of mergers, identification with the old organization was solely related to identification with the new organization, if employees felt that their old organization was represented in the merged company. Try to explain this finding from social identity theory and from a threat-rigidity perspective.
2. Try to link the four dimensions of an innovative climate (Anderson & West, 1998) with the three dimensions of an intercultural group climate (Harquail & Cox, 1993, see glossary). Do you recognize any similarities? How do you personally think these dimensions are related to the goals of cohesion and locomotion?
3. A company consults you because they are faced with low flexibility and lack of integration of older employees (see also Box 12.1). How would you diagnose this company in terms of a focus on cohesion versus locomotion? Which of the interventions (aimed at this focus) that are discussed in the chapter are applicable here? Which intervention would you preferably use in order to help this company?

Further reading

Hogg, M. A. & Terry, D. J. (2001). *Social identity processes in organizational contexts.* Hove: Psychology Press.

Leana, C. R. & Barry, B. (2000). Stability and change as simultaneous experiences in organizational life. *Academy of Management Review, 25,* 753–759.

Paulus, P. B. & Nijstad, B. A. (2003). *Group creativity: Innovation through collaboration.* New York: Oxford University Press.

Staw, B. M., Sandelands, L. E. & Dutton, J. E. (1981). Threat-rigidity effects in organizational behavior: A multilevel analysis. *Administrative Science Quarterly, 26,* 501–524.

Van Knippenberg, D., De Dreu, C. K. & Homan, A. C. (2004). Work group diversity and group performance: An integrative model and research agenda. *Journal of Applied Psychology, 89,* 1008–1022.

References

Anderson, N. & West, N. R. (1998). Measuring climate for work group innovation: Development and validation of the team climate inventory. *Journal of Organizational Behavior*, *19*, 235–258.

Argyris, C. & Schon, D. (1978). *Organizational Learning*. Reading, IN: Addison-Wesley.

Austin, J. R. (1997). A cognitive framework for understanding demographic influences in groups. *International Journal of Organizational Analysis*, *5*, 342–360.

Brewer, M. B. & Gardner, W. (1996). Who is this "We"? Levels of collective identity and self representations. *Journal of Personality and Social Psychology*, *71*, 83–93.

Brickson, S. & Brewer, M. (2001). Identity orientations and intergroup relations in organizations. In M. A. Hogg, & D. J. Terry (eds.), *Social identity processes in organizational contexts* (pp. 49–66). Hove: Psychology Press.

Dirks, K. T., Cummings, L. L. & Pierce, J. (1996). Psychological ownership in organizations: Conditions under which individuals promote and resist change. In R. Woodman & W. Pasmore (eds.), *Research in organizational change and development* (Vol. 9, pp. 1–23). Greenwich, CT: JAI Press Inc.

Dugosh, K. L. & Paulus, P. B. (2005). Cognitive and social comparison processes in brainstorming. *Journal of Experimental Social Psychology*, *41*, 313–320.

Dutton, J., Dukerich, J. & Harquail, C. (1994). Organizational images and member identification. *Administrative Science Quarterly*, *39*, 239–263.

Edmondson, A. (1999). Psychological safety and learning behavior in work teams. *Administrative Science Quarterly*, *44*, 350–383.

Gonzalez, R. & Brown, R. J. (1999). Maintaining the salience of subgroup and superordinate group identities during intergroup contact. Paper presented at the Small Group Preconference of the Annual Meeting of the Society of Experimental Social Psychology, St. Louis, MI, 14–16 October.

Grant Thornton (2006). *International Business Owners Survey*. www.international-businessreport.com

Harquail, C. V. & Cox, T., Jr (1993). Organizational culture and acculturation. In T. Cox, Jr (ed.), *Cultural diversity in organizations: theory, research and practice* (pp. 161–176). San Francisco: Berret-Koehler Publishers.

Janis, I. L. (1982). *Groupthink: Psychological studies of policy decisions and fiascoes*. Boston: Houghton Mifflin.

Lewin, K. (1935). *A dynamic theory of personality*. New York: McGraw-Hill.

(1958). Group decision and social change. In E. E. Maccoby, T. M. Newcomb & E. L. Hartley (eds.), *Readings in Social Psychology*, (pp. 197–211). New York: Holt, Rinehart & Winston.

Louis, M. R. & Sutton, R. I. (1991). Switching cognitive gears: From habits of mind to active thinking. *Human Relations*, *44*, 55–76.

Mannix, E. & Neale, M. A. (2005). What differences make a difference? *Psychological Science in the Public Interest*, 6, 31–55.

Nakui, T. & Paulus, P. B. (2007). *Diversity and outcomes of brainstorming teams*. Manuscript submitted for publication.

Nemeth, C. J. & Nemeth-Brown, B. (2003). Better than individuals? The potential benefits of dissent and diversity for group creativity. In P. B. Paulus & B. A. Nijstad (eds.), *Group Creativity: Innovation and collaboration in groups* (pp. 63–84). New York: Oxford University Press.

Nijstad, B. A., Stroebe, W. & Lodewijkx, H. F. M. (2002). Cognitive stimulation and interference in groups: Exposure effects in an idea generation task. *Journal of Experimental Social Psychology, 38*, 535–544.

Osborn, A. F. (1957). *Applied imagination: Principles and procedures of creative thinking.* 2nd edn. New York: Scribners.

Postmes, T., Spears, R. & Cihangir, S. (2001). Quality of decision making and group norms. *Journal of Personality and Social Psychology, 80*, 918–930.

Rietzschel, E. F., Nijstad, B. A. & Stroebe, W. (2005). Productivity is not enough: A comparison of interactive and nominal brainstorming groups on idea generation and selection. *Journal of Experimental Social Psychology, 42*, 244–251.

Stasser, G. & Titus, W. (1985). Pooling of unshared information in group decision making: Biased information sampling during discussion. *Journal of Personality and Social Psychology, 48*, 1467–1478.

Staw, B. M., Sandelands, L. E. & Dutton, J. E. (1981). Threat-rigidity effects in organizational behavior: A multilevel analysis. *Administrative Science Quarterly, 26*, 501–524.

Sutton, R. I. & Hargadon, A. B. (1996). Brainstorming groups in context: Effectiveness in a product design firm. *Administrative Science Quarterly, 41*, 685–718.

Tajfel, H. & Turner, J. C. (1979). An integrative theory of intergroup conflict. In W. G. Austin & S. Worchel (eds.), *The social psychology of intergroup relations* (pp. 33–48). Monterey, CA: Brooks/Cole.

Triandis, H. C., Kurowski, L. L. & Gelfand, M. J. (1994). Workplace diversity. In H. C. Triandis, M. D. Dunnette & L. M. Hough (eds.), *Handbook of industrial and organizational psychology* (Vol. 4, pp. 767–827). Palo Alto, CA: Consulting Psychologists Press, Inc.

Van der Zee, K. I., Atsma, N. & Brodbeck, F. (2004). The influence of social identity and personality on outcomes of cultural diversity in teams. *Journal of Cross-Cultural Psychology, 35*, 283–303.

Van Knippenberg, D., De Dreu, C. K. & Homan, A. C. (2004). Work group diversity and group performance: an integrative model and research agenda. *Journal of Applied Psychology, 89*, 1008–1022.

Van Knippenberg, D. & Haslam, S. A. (2003). Realizing the diversity dividend: exploring the subtle interplay between identity, ideology, and reality. In S. A. Haslam, D. van Knippenberg, M. J. Platow & N. Ellemers (eds.), *Social identity at work: Developing theory for organizational practice* (pp. 61–77). New York and Hove: Psychology Press.

Van Knippenberg, D. & Van Leeuwen, E. (2001). Organizational identity after a merger: Sense of continuity as the key to post-merger identification. In M. A. Hogg & D. J. Terry (eds.), *Social identity processes in organizational contexts* (pp. 249–264). Philadelphia, PA: Psychology Press.

Williams, K. & O'Reilly, C. (1998). The complexity of diversity: A review of forty years of research. In D. Gruenfeld & M. Neale (eds.), *Research on managing in groups and teams.* Greenwich, CT: JAI Press.

13 Social psychology and the study of politics

MARTIN ROSEMA, JOHN T. JOST AND
DIEDERIK A. STAPEL

Introduction

The application of social psychology to the study of politics is at the heart of the discipline called political psychology. Political psychology has been defined as the 'application of what is known about human psychology to the study of politics' (Sears, Huddy & Jervis, 2003, p. 3). Social psychology has been a more influential source of inspiration for the study of politics than any other subfield of psychology. Insights from social psychology have been of paramount importance in the study of both political elites and mass political behaviour. The many topics that have thus been studied include political socialization, public opinion, voting behaviour, collective political action, ideology, prejudice, political campaigns, presidential performance, policy making, conflict resolution, terrorism and genocide (see Jost & Sidanius, 2004). By providing insights about the psychological processes involved, social psychology has contributed to our understanding of all these aspects of politics. Several of those insights have been used in attempts to change political attitudes and political behaviour that are considered undesirable, such as racial prejudice, low voter turnout and political violence.

In this chapter we focus on three topics that have been central to political psychology: political leadership, voting behaviour and ideology. We discuss how different types of psychological studies have contributed to understanding these crucial aspects of politics. The field of political psychology comprises at least four different types of studies. First, some psychological studies are not directly about politics but contribute significantly to our understanding of political processes. A well-known example is Milgram's (1974) study on obedience. Asking subjects to deliver high-voltage electric shocks to other people in a learning experiment has little to do with politics per se. But the underlying principles that are uncovered – that most people obey when asked by an authority (in this case, the experimenter) – are crucial to understanding political behaviour, such as the loyalty of civil servants to their political leaders. These insights contribute, for example, to understanding how the tragedy of the Holocaust could have occurred.

The second type of research concerns studies by psychologists who select political topics as object of their research. An example that we discuss below is Ajzen and Fishbein's (1980) work on the theory of reasoned action. When applying their theory, one of the topics they focused on was voting behaviour. Ajzen and

Fishbein's aim was not to explain political phenomena as such. Politics was but one of many areas in which they could test their theory. So their work nicely illustrates the second type: psychological theories that are applied to politics, but that are not primarily concerned with explaining political phenomena in particular.

Studies that focus on political phenomena but that can also be applied outside the field of politics constitute the third type. A good example is work on the online model of candidate evaluations (Lodge, McGraw & Stroh, 1989), which we elaborate on below. This theory focuses on why people like or dislike political candidates, but there is no a priori reason to assume that those processes differ from those underlying evaluations of other persons or objects. On the contrary. Although the theory is formulated in terms of political concerns, the same psychological processes occur outside of politics.

The fourth type of research in political psychology is 'truly' political, which means that the work addresses the political sphere and has no meaning outside of this context. Research on the relationship between values and ideology nicely fits this category. Ideological labels like 'left' and 'right' are inherently political concepts. This implies that political psychology can be more than the mere application of general insights from (social) psychology to the field of politics. Political psychology is also concerned with developing theories that specifically and solely address political phenomena.

We now discuss how studies of the second, third and fourth types have contributed to our understanding of political leadership, voting behaviour and ideology (Figure 13.1). (We omit research on the first type because there is far too much of it to cover.) For more extensive reviews, which address many additional topics, we refer to the suggested readings at the end of this chapter.

Political leadership

In history individual political leaders have made great differences. Although it is impossible to predict with certainty what would have happened if other people had occupied the highest positions, there are good reasons to assume that things would have gone differently. One example is the role of Mikhail Gorbachev in the transformation of the Soviet Union, leading to the end of the Cold War and the abolition of the communist regime. Among the many factors that presumably contributed to his policies of perestroika (economic and governmental reform) and glasnost (openness) was his personality. He was presumably more open to new experiences, less likely to conform to others, and more willing to take risks. In light of this, several questions arise: how should the personalities of political leaders be conceptualized, how can their personality be measured, and when and how does leader personality affect behaviour in office? And once such questions are answered, can insights reached then help in selecting the best leaders? These questions have been central in political psychology.

Figure 13.1 *The relevance of politics to the young*

'Big Five' personality factors

Let us start with research of the type that applies general psychological theory to the political domain. One approach to studying political leaders is to take general theories of personality and apply them to an individual case. The five factor trait theory – also known as the **Big Five** – has become more widely accepted than any other theory of personality. According to this theory, personality is comprised of five major dimensions: neuroticism (or emotional stability), extraversion (or energy), agreeableness (or friendliness), openness to new experiences and conscientiousness. Research suggests that political orientation is consistently correlated with two of these dimensions. Specifically, people who are left of centre tend to score higher on measures of openness, whereas people who are right of centre tend to score higher on measures of conscientiousness (Jost, 2006).

It is customary to study individuals' personalities by asking them to complete questionnaires aimed at measuring such traits. If one would like to assess the personality of political leaders, the same questionnaires cannot be employed as easily. The chances are that most leaders would be unwilling to complete them – especially those politicians at the highest levels of government. This method is obviously even less well suited to investigate the personalities of dead political leaders, who are often the focus of research interest. Hence, other methods are required. One potential solution is to have other people complete the questionnaires 'for' the politician in question. This is what Rubenzer, Faschingbauer and Ones (2000) did. They assessed the personality of all American presidents on the basis of ratings provided by biographers and others who had closely studied or been in contact with these presidents.

After they had determined the personality of each president, Rubenzer *et al.* (2000) examined whether the trait scores were related to the perceived 'greatness' of the presidents (as judged by prominent historians). The strongest relationship found concerned openness. Key examples of presidents who scored high on openness as well as greatness were Thomas Jefferson and Abraham Lincoln. Another conclusion is at least as important, namely, that overall correlations were weak and most personality characteristics did *not* correlate with perceived greatness. On the whole, personality in terms of the Big Five contributed little to understanding why some presidents were more successful than others.

Profiling political leaders

A more widely used method to study political leadership is content analysis. Some researchers who employed content analysis focused on biographical sources, in particular passages that related to personality characteristics. Other researchers used content analysis to investigate speeches and interviews. Even if these are not fully written by political leaders themselves, they may still accurately reflect the leaders' characteristics because the leaders themselves select speechwriters, speechwriters 'know' their clients and leaders typically review drafts.

One of those scholars is Winter (1987). He analysed inaugural addresses of American presidents in terms of their motives, especially the achievement, affiliation and **power motive**. He coded each presidential address and standardized it by comparing it to scores for its contemporaries. Winter examined the impact of presidential motive profiles on popularity (indicated by margin of victory in the election) and perceived greatness (indicated by scores awarded by historians). He found that popularity was influenced by the match between motive scores of the president as compared to the society of that time, whereas presidential performance was influenced by leader characteristics (independent of the time period). Power motivation was positively correlated with perceived greatness, as well as with measures indicating crisis-oriented policy making.

Whereas the above studies focused on traits and motives, others adopted a more cognitive approach. The concept of **operational code** refers to leaders' belief systems about the world, such as whether the nature of political life is one of harmony or conflict, whether the future is predictable and can be controlled or not and how political goals are most effectively pursued. Such beliefs are presumed to influence political action in a predictable way. A study of the operational code of Russian president Vladimir Putin, for example, concluded that Putin would be unlikely to respond emotionally or impulsively, that he would reciprocate 'bad' as well as 'good' behaviour, and that breakdowns in cooperation would be recurring (Dyson, 2001).

Most research on personality and political leadership has focused on American presidents and leaders of authoritarian regimes (e.g., Nazi Germany, the Soviet Union and Iraq). An exception is a study by Kaarbo and Hermann (1998), who studied four European prime ministers: German chancellors Konrad Adenauer (1949–1963) and Helmut Kohl (1982–1998) and British prime ministers Margaret Thatcher (1979–1990) and John Major (1990–1997). They coded about one hundred press conferences and parliamentary question sessions in terms of five characteristics: conceptual complexity (openness to information), belief that one can control what happens, need for power, need for affiliation, and task orientation. This set of characteristics illustrates that many studies on political leadership compose profiles that combine factors like traits, motives, cognitive orientations and behavioural tendencies.

The first conclusion of this study was that the four leaders had different leadership styles.

> Adenauer and Thatcher were crusaders, taking charge and dominating the political system; they shaped, rather than were shaped by, their political environments and took advantage of opportunities to have influence. They interpreted any political constraints more as a nuisance than as limiting what they could do. Kohl is more the strategist, political timing is important and often is determined by the nature of the political context . . . Major was more pragmatic, taking cues from his environment about what needed to be done. He was interested in co-aligning the various important others around him toward a consensus position that would help to solve the problem or deal with the crisis. (Kaarbo & Hermann, 1998, p. 256)

Kaarbo and Hermann examined whether leadership style had an impact on foreign policy making. They argued that crusaders are more likely to opt for extreme, conflict-seeking activities in the international arena. This is indeed what they observed. Clear examples are Thatcher's decisions to respond with military force to the Argentinian invasion of the Falkland Islands (Malvinas) in 1982 and the Iraqi invasion of Kuwait in 1990.

Crisis decision making

Political leadership presumably matters most in times of crisis. Thatcher's response to the occupation of the Falkland Islands is an example of how leader personality may affect crisis decision making. However, leader personality is not all that matters. Political leaders do not operate in a vacuum. First, public opinion may influence the course of action that political leaders choose. Second, political leaders do not make their decisions on their own. Presidents and prime ministers are surrounded by ministers, civil servants, political advisors and sometimes military advisors. So to understand crisis decision making by political leaders, we also need insight into the ways in which they deal with public opinion and the group processes in which political leaders are embroiled.

Arguably the most important lesson from research on crisis decision making and the impact of public opinion is that it is easier to mobilize support for aggressive actions than for conciliatory actions. As a result, decision makers are more vulnerable domestically if they take steps towards compromise and accommodation than if they remain in the conflict situation. One of the theories in psychology (and economics) that can help us understand why this is the case is prospect theory (Kahneman & Tversky, 1979). This theory can be viewed as a response to **expected utility theory**. According to expected utility theory, possible costs and benefits of alternative decisions are multiplied by the likelihood they occur; the option with the 'highest utility' is chosen. According to **prospect theory**, decisions deviate from expected utility if decision makers are afraid to experience losses and when risk is in the moderate to high range: the decision maker is then willing to take more risk in order to prevent potential losses (see Chapter 5).

This theory has been applied repeatedly to the field of international relations. Because conciliatory actions by political leaders involve the risk of losing public opinion support, loss aversion causes leaders to embrace more conflicting positions than they otherwise would. Other studies have also shown that crisis decision making does not always conform to expected utility models derived from economic theory; prospect theory helps to explain these deviations (see Box 13.1).

Box 13.1   Prospect theory and the Cuban missile crisis

The Cuban missile crisis in 1962 was arguably the most dangerous period in world history. In spring of 1962 the Soviet Union's leader, Nikita Khrushchev, decided to send nuclear missiles to Cuba. If the operation had succeeded, it would presumably have prevented any possible attack by the United States on Cuba and would have strengthened Khrushchev's leadership position, both domestically and internationally. Apart from these considerable potential benefits, there were huge potential costs: the risk of a devastating war or, if forced to retreat, a weakened leadership position. US president John Kennedy found out about the missiles and decided to respond by blockading Cuba and giving Khrushchev an ultimatum to return the missiles. For Kennedy, the possible gains were obvious and great (restored American credibility, no missiles in Cuba), but so were the possible costs: if the Soviet Union refused to capitulate, war was the most likely result. Initially Khrushchev appeared willing to defy the blockade, but he eventually decided to retreat.

Haas (2001) examined whether the decisions by both leaders could be understood on the basis of expected utility theory and prospect theory. On the basis of information from Soviet archives and transcripts of secretly taped meetings of American officials, he determined the anticipated benefits, costs and probabilities of success. Haas concluded that Kennedy's decision to implement a blockade and Khrushchev's subsequent decision to withdraw the missiles could be explained on the basis of expected utility theory. However, Khrushchev's most crucial decision, namely, to send nuclear missiles to Cuba, could not. Whereas the possible benefits and costs of the whole operation were both very high, the perceived likelihood of success was low. Prospect theory, however, provides an explanation: the loss frame (the likely loss of Cuba and threats to domestic political goals) made Khrushchev willing to take more risk. Haas also identified two other decisions that conformed to expectations derived from prospect theory but not expected utility theory: Kennedy's decision to continue to threaten the Soviet Union after the blockade had been established and Khrushchev's decision to pretend to defy the blockade initially.

Groupthink

In addition to public opinion, political leaders are also influenced by those who surround them. The most important theory about political leadership and group processes is arguably that of groupthink, which was developed by Janis (1972). He studied several major political events in which the US government apparently made poor decisions (Bay of Pigs invasion, Pearl Harbor attack, escalation of the Vietnam War). Janis concluded that group processes were the key to understanding the poor decision making – later studies, based on new material on those decisions, suggested that Janis had overstated some of the effects and personal leadership styles also had mattered.

According to **groupthink theory**, particular circumstances can lead small groups to make poor decisions. These circumstances include ingroup cohesion,

" WHAT DOES EVERYONE
THINK OF MY IDEAS? "

Figure 13.2 *Psychological processes bring leaders support from their staff*

isolation from outside influences, directive leadership and stress. Janis (1972) identified several defects in the decision-making process that may result. First, group discussions will be limited to few alternatives (usually two) and initial decisions will not be critically assessed on the basis of new considerations (Figure 13.2). Furthermore, relevant expert information is not actively retrieved and information supporting initial decisions is given the most weight, rather than judging information on its merits. Finally, obstacles that might arise when the decision is carried out are not taken care of. Taken together, these processes lead to a situation in which poor decision making is, if not the rule, at least more likely than it needs to be – and certainly more likely than what citizens may expect from their government.

It is interesting to see that the psychological processes involved in groupthink are exactly the opposite of what we observed above concerning personality traits that contributed to the greatness of presidents. The personality factor that had the strongest impact on a successful presidency was openness. And openness is precisely what is lacking in groupthink.

There are at least two lessons that can be learned from Janis's (1972) observations. First, it may be wise to encourage ingroup members as well as others to challenge dominant views. Second, it makes sense to have a 'second round' after initial agreement has been reached. A telling example of this wisdom is a much-cited statement by Alfred Sloan, former chairman of General Motors, during a business meeting:

> Gentlemen, I take it we are all in complete agreement on the decision here. Then I propose we postpone further discussion of this matter until our next meeting to give ourselves time to develop disagreement and perhaps gain some understanding of what the decision is all about.

Although this may be counter-intuitive, politicians who adopt this approach presumably have better chances of becoming great leaders.

Voting behaviour

Probably the most important ordinary political action of citizens is selecting their representatives by casting a vote in elections. It should thus be no surprise that explaining why people vote the way they do has been an important topic in political psychology. The outcome of electoral research has important implications. To the extent that research reveals citizens to be well informed and paying close attention to politics, one would be more likely to assign citizens far-reaching responsibilities. On the other hand, if citizens turn out to be poorly informed and choose more or less randomly, or on the basis of, say, the physical appearances of the candidates, one would be more pessimistic about prospects for successful democratic governance.

To vote or not to vote?

Politicians and political scientists alike have emphasized that in a democracy it is essential that many citizens participate in elections (Figure 13.3). According to some, mass participation is a sine qua non of democracy. Others argue that the democratic ideal may or may not be violated by abstentions, depending on why citizens abstain and whether specific types of citizens abstain in larger numbers than others. The primary worry has been that those who are economically less well off abstain relatively often, and consequently their interests are not taken into account by politicians as seriously as the interests of people who do vote (and contribute to political campaigns). This would violate the democratic principle that each individual should have equal influence. High levels of turnout may mitigate such worrisome effects.

Although the decision to vote or not to vote has been studied by social psychologists, it has received more attention from economists. The primary reason is that the mere fact that so many people do vote poses a major challenge to rational choice theory. This leads to the expectation that citizens will not bother to vote, because the chance that an individual vote will make a difference is virtually zero. Quattrone and Tversky (1988) contrasted economic and psychological approaches and concluded that the latter clearly provides more insight into the

Figure 13.3 *Why some people do not bother to vote*

reasons underlying the decision to vote, because voters do not base their decisions to vote on expected utility. The main reason why people go to the polls is that they conceive of it as a civic duty. It is the existence of social norms, rather than influence on the election outcome, that drives the casting of a vote. So, the decision to vote is an excellent example of an act that is poorly understood on the basis of economic decision-making models, and social psychologists can contribute to its understanding.

Considering the importance assigned to electoral participation, it is no surprise that scholars have studied various means of increasing turnout. Research shows that such interventions have effects, albeit too small to prevent many voters from not going to the polls. One example is a field experiment about the impact of personal appeals to voters shortly before the election – a strategy adopted by governments and other organizations (see Box 13.2 and Figure 13.4).

Theory of reasoned action

Let us now focus on the electoral choices of those who do cast a vote. Why do people support a particular party or candidate? To answer this question, one research strategy would be to apply general psychological theories and make use of concepts that are central in social psychology. Few social psychologists would contest that attitudes are a fundamental concept (McGuire, 1985). What is more

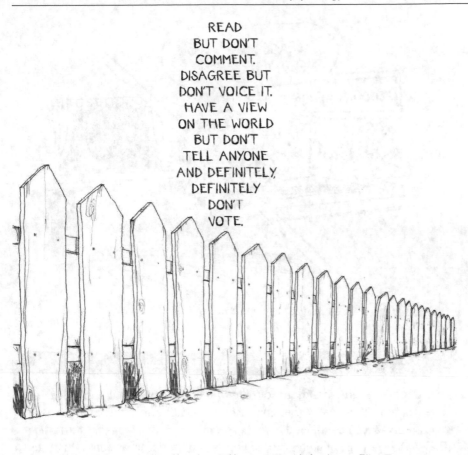

READ
BUT DON'T
COMMENT.
DISAGREE BUT
DON'T VOICE IT.
HAVE A VIEW
ON THE WORLD
BUT DON'T
TELL ANYONE
AND DEFINITELY,
DEFINITELY
DON'T
VOTE.

Don't sit on the fence. Vote May 5th The Electoral Commission
For information call 0800 3 280 280 or visit aboutmyvote.co.uk

Figure 13.4 *Poster used to encourage people to vote*

central to what you are than what you like and what you dislike? Furthermore, likes and dislikes strongly influence the decisions people make. Considering their central position in social psychology, it is no surprise that attitude-behaviour models have been applied to elections.

Ajzen and Fishbein (1980) developed the most influential theory about attitudes and behaviour: the **theory of reasoned action**, which in a slightly modified version is known as the theory of planned behaviour (see Chapter 2). According to the theory of reasoned action, the direct determinant of behaviour is the intention to perform that behaviour. An intention results from the combination of a person's evaluation of the consequences of the behaviour and the extend to which an individual complies with social influence. Ajzen and Fishbein applied their theory to several actions, including voting in a US presidential election, a British parliamentary election and a referendum in Oregon, USA. They concluded that the psychological processes in these elections were identical: salient beliefs

Figure 13.5 *Canvassing by phone is not effective*

Box 13.2   Effects of personal appeals on voter turnout

In order to examine the impact of different kinds of personal appeals on voter turnout (personal canvassing, telephone calls and direct mail), Gerber and Green (2000) conducted a field experiment in New Haven, Connecticut. They obtained a list of all registered voters and randomly assigned them to one of the treatment conditions or the control group. Personal canvassing was done by either making an appeal to a sense of duty or to a close election, prompting citizens to believe that their vote could make a difference (Figure 13.5). In both instances the appeal was made by a non-partisan organization. Similar messages were used in telephone calls, and direct mailings appealed to the sense of duty, neighbourhood solidarity, and/or the closeness of the election.

Actual turnout was determined on the basis of public records. The findings revealed that personal contact increased turnout by 9% on average. Furthermore, appealing to the fact that it was a close election had the strongest impact (12%) and the appeal to civic duty had the weakest (5%). Across the three modes of contact, differences were also observed: personal contact boosted turnout most, whereas telephone calls appeared to have an unanticipated negative effect. Later, the authors found that the negative result for telephone contact was in part the result of several errors made during the research. But after correcting these, phone calls still did not increase turnout.

resulted in attitudes towards voting options, which fairly accurately predicted voting intentions and hence vote choice (social influence was not very important). The content of the beliefs, however, differed. In the American case, beliefs about policy outcomes were important, whereas in Britain salient beliefs concerned the probability that voting for a particular candidate would increase the chances of a certain government.

Studies of voting on the basis of attitude-behaviour models have yielded valuable insights. For example, the distinction between attitudes towards objects (parties) and attitudes towards behaviour (voting for those parties), provides an excellent basis to study 'strategic voting', such as voting for a non-preferred party because the preferred party has no chance of winning the seat. However, in mainstream electoral research attitude-behaviour models have had very little influence. Electoral researchers have not been impressed by the conclusion that citizens vote for particular candidates because this helps to get their party into government. Such findings are considered tautological. Furthermore, theories such as the theory of reasoned action do not specify which beliefs determine attitudes towards parties and candidates and why beliefs are evaluated positively or negatively. Consequently, attitude-behaviour models do not provide answers to the kind of questions that electoral researchers would like to see answered.

The Michigan model of voting

The most important theory about voting behaviour, which does identify the kind of attitudes that influence vote choice as well as their origins, was developed by Campbell, Converse, Miller and Stokes (1960) from the University of Michigan. Their starting point was similar to that of attitude-behaviour models: political objects, such as candidates and issues, are not simply perceived, but evaluated as well. According to the **Michigan model**, the resulting orientations, whether positive or negative, comprise a system of forces that direct voters towards (the candidate of) one of the political parties (in the US: Democratic Party or Republican Party) (Figure 13.6).

Campbell *et al.* (1960) distinguished six such forces, so-called partisan attitudes. These concerned personal attributes of the Democratic candidate, personal attributes of the Republican candidate, issues of domestic policy, issues of foreign policy, groups involved in politics and parties' records in government management. These attitudes were influenced by voters' **party identification**: identification with one of the two major political parties that had been established in early adulthood through family influence and was reinforced through group memberships (see Figure 13.6). Party identification could directly influence vote choice, but primarily did so indirectly, through its impact on partisan attitudes. Because party identification appeared to be rather stable – albeit this has been questioned by other researchers – the model made it possible to distinguish between long-term and short-term factors.

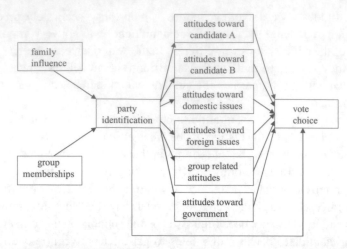

Figure 13.6 *The Michigan model of voting*

The concept of **partisan attitudes** differs from the concept of attitudes as commonly used in social psychology. Generally, attitudes are conceptualized as positions on a single dimension that ranges from very positive to very negative; they refer to liking or disliking certain things (but see McGuire, 1985, for a broader view). Partisan attitudes are positions on a dimension that ranges from, in the US context, strongly pro-Republican to strongly pro-Democratic. Furthermore, the partisan attitudes identified were not regarded as an accurate description of how the voter's mind is organized. The distinction was made for analytical purposes only, enabling the assessment of the impact of factors like candidate images and salient issues (Figure 13.7). Hence, the Michigan model is psychological in the sense that its explanation of voting behaviour is based on the information in voters' minds. However, it is not very psychological in the sense that it describes specific mental processes that underlie voting or that the concepts used are psychological entities.

The work by Campbell *et al.* (1960) has strongly influenced electoral research in Europe, theoretically as well as methodologically. Similar studies have been conducted, often on a regular basis in national election surveys, which are conducted around each national election (e.g., in Britain, Norway, Sweden, Denmark, Germany and the Netherlands). In some instances, scholars from these countries were enthusiastic about the explanatory power of the Michigan model, whereas other scholars have questioned its usefulness across the Atlantic (Thomassen & Rosema, in press). The most serious doubts concern the concept of party identification: in several European countries voters have been found to identify with the party they voted for and vice versa. Furthermore, the presumed stability of party identification was questioned. Consequently, in Europe it appears not possible to distinguish between long-term and short-term forces on the basis of the Michigan model. This shows that theories developed in one context cannot always be successfully applied to another context.

Figure 13.7 *Candidate differences determine level of electoral turnout*

Online model of candidate evaluations

The Michigan model and the theory of reasoned action build on the assumption that evaluations of relevant beliefs are integrated into attitudes, which in turn determine (voting) behaviour. This view of attitude formation has been challenged by Lodge *et al.* (1989). Their starting point is the distinction between memory-based judgements and online judgements. **Memory-based judgements** are made on the basis of information that is retrieved from memory. **Online judgements** are created and changed whenever information relevant to that judgement is processed and then stored in memory.

According to the **online model of candidate evaluations**, the process underlying candidate evaluations is that of online judgements. Whenever voters process information with respect to a candidate, they update an overall evaluation of the candidate, a so-called running tally. When casting a vote, the only thing voters do is to 'retrieve the online tally' (Lodge *et al.*, 1989, p. 416). The key point is that information underlying the formation and change of candidate evaluations may well be forgotten, while its impact lasts. Experiments in which individuals were asked to evaluate a brochure of a (fictitious) candidate with information about the person's party affiliation, policy preferences and biography supported the hypothesis. Another study (Lau & Redlawsk, 2006), which used innovative methodology, also provided (partial) support for the online model (see Box 13.3).

An important implication of this research concerns the intellectual abilities of voters. Since the introduction of modern electoral research, pessimism has existed about the ability of the electorate. The picture that emerged from the work by Campbell *et al.* (1960), for example, was not considered a positive one. Voters' choices appeared to be primarily an expression of 'blind party loyalty'. Earlier studies of voting had also found voters to be rather dissimilar to the ideal citizen. At the same time, other researchers have argued that voters are not as poorly informed as many assert. This whole debate has been based on the presumption that this matter can be assessed on the basis of what voters know. However, the work by Lodge *et al.* (1989) suggests that the information upon which voters base their choices is much more extensive than the information in their memory. This requires a fundamental shift in thinking about the role of political competence and sophistication in voting behaviour (see also Jost, 2006).

Box 13.3   The dynamic information board

According to Lau and Redlawsk (2006), the widely used survey questionnaires are ill suited to study the mental processes of voters. They developed an alternative method: the **dynamic information board**. This is a computer program that imitates the process of an election campaign in an experimental setting. Participants have to vote in an imaginary election and inform themselves about the competing candidates during the experiment. The computer screen continually presents several scrolling headings, which reveal information when clicked by the participant. The information board thus enables participants to select information about socio-demographic characteristics, party affiliation, policy preferences and endorsements received from particular groups. This process is occasionally interrupted by campaign commercials.

This method enabled Lau and Redlawsk (2006) to test the online model of candidate evaluations. They did this by comparing how well actual evaluations of the candidates (measured by asking participants to rate each candidate) could be predicted by taking the evaluation expected on the basis of the information individuals recalled (measured by asking everything they could remember about the candidate), and the evaluation expected on the basis of information individuals processed (which was registered by the computer). The analysis showed that candidate evaluations could be best predicted by combining both measures. This suggests that although memory does play a role – the authors argued this was caused by the requirement to make a choice – information forgotten does influence judgements, as suggested by the online model of candidate evaluations.

Ideology

Political attitudes are often studied in isolation. Some researchers focus on evaluations of political candidates, whereas others focus on racial attitudes. Some are interested in public opinion about capital punishment, whereas others explore how citizens think about foreign policy. One may expect, however, that all of these political attitudes are at least somewhat correlated. A central question in political psychology has been in which ways, and to what extent, such correlations do indeed exist (e.g., see McGuire, 1985; Jost, 2006). Are people's attitudes towards policies coherently structured, for example, in terms of ideological orientations such as left and right? Other hotly debated questions have been whether, and in what ways, the ideological orientations of the public at large have shifted across time (do citizens today adhere to different ideological beliefs and policy positions than previous generations did?) and whether ideology is still at all important today.

Has ideology come to an end?

In a classic paper, Converse (1964) argued that one may expect that opinions about individual issues are related to each other. The constraint between individual issue positions results from a person's underlying ideological position. For example, a person who is liberal on one issue is supposed to be liberal on another issue as well.

Converse's (1964) empirical analyses, however, suggested that only about ten per cent of the American electorate used ideological concepts, such as liberalism and conservatism or capitalism and socialism, to structure their opinions. Moreover, many individuals held beliefs that were not consistent. For example, they favoured reducing taxes and at the same time favoured increasing public spending. Another finding was that individuals' positions on issues were rather unstable over time. Converse concluded that although respondents generally politely answered questions about such issues, these did not reveal stable, well-founded opinions on those issues and social scientists were thus studying **nonattitudes** (apparent attitudes that have little meaning in the world outside the interview). Many scholars who have studied belief systems since then have come to similar, not very optimistic, conclusions about the political sophistication of the electorate.

These findings contributed to psychologists' general acceptance of the 'end of ideology' thesis, that is, the idea that after World War II left/right ideological differences no longer played an important role in mass politics (Jost, 2006). The thesis is based on four claims: (1) people's political attitudes lack logical consistency, (2) most people are unmoved by ideological appeals, (3) there are no fundamental psychological differences between proponents of left-wing (in the US, liberal) and right-wing (in the US, conservative) ideologies and (4) there are no substantive differences between left-wing and right-wing points of view. Jost

(2006) thoroughly examined these claims and concluded that each was problematic as a defence of the 'end of ideology' thesis. Let us briefly review some of the research that requires us to rethink earlier conclusions.

First, weak correlations between responses to questions concerning political attitudes were partly the result of methodological weaknesses. For example, the correlation between party identification and policy preferences increased substantially when scholars used parallel measures for both concepts. Second, although perhaps few voters are well informed about all topics, many are reasonably well informed about a subset. Moreover, increased levels of education have provided citizens with a better basis to process and structure political information, while the spread of mass media (first radio and television, today the Internet) has provided citizens with more information (as well as misinformation) about politics. Furthermore, voters' ideological self-placement along a left/right continuum remains a key factor in European (as well as American) electoral research, while on both sides of the Atlantic personality traits show clear relationships with party and candidate preferences (Jost, 2006). This leaves the question about ideological differences between major parties and candidates. It may be true that certain ideological differences are less pronounced than in earlier decades, when, for instance, communism existed in Eastern Europe. However, to suggest that today's politics are devoid of ideological differences seems unrealistic (see Jost, 2006). Ideology, it seems, has not (yet) come to an end.

Ideology and values

Although ideology is mostly studied without reference to the social-psychological concept of values, both concepts are clearly related. The most influential work on **values** is probably that by Rokeach (1973). His aim was to identify all major values across human cultures. Individuals' value orientations were assessed by asking them to indicate which from a list of values they personally considered most important. Rokeach argued that two of the values identified are closely related to left/right ideology, namely equality and freedom. Combining the importance assigned to equality (low vs high) and the importance assigned to freedom (low vs high) results in a two-dimensional space with four categories that match four ideologies: socialism (high equality, high freedom), communism (high equality, low freedom), capitalism (low equality, high freedom), and fascism (low equality, low freedom). Rokeach argued that if in a society virtually all assign high importance to one or both values, ideology becomes a one-dimensional concept. This nicely links up with the way ideology is often seen today, namely as a continuum with left and right (Europe) or liberal and conservative (United States) as opposite poles.

The concept of values is also central to Inglehart's (1977) work on materialism and **postmaterialism**. Inglehart argued that generational conflicts arise not (only) in terms of the left/right division, but in terms of 'materialism' and 'postmaterialism'. He posited that how much importance a person assigns to a particular value will depend upon, among other factors, the scarcity of goods required to satisfy needs. Things that are taken for granted will not be valued as highly as things that are scarce and would satisfy unmet needs. It is not difficult to see that Inglehart was inspired by Maslow's theory, which posits that needs can be ordered as a hierarchy and individuals will only seek to satisfy particular needs if more basic needs have to some extent been satisfied. Inglehart pointed out that once a basic character has been formed in childhood and youth, the person will retain the value hierarchy established throughout adult life.

These premises led Inglehart (1977) to hypothesize that across generations different value orientations could be observed. Those raised in times of economic security would assign less importance to values associated with bringing security than those who experienced economic hardship. Inglehart referred to the values that are assigned relatively high importance by recent generations as postmaterialist. These values include freedom of speech and participating in decision making as opposed to fighting price increases and maintaining order. This generational change, according to Inglehart, would be reflected in support for political parties and policies.

Empirical analyses have shown that across generations differences in value orientations have indeed occurred. Furthermore, value orientations are correlated with political preferences and vote choice. Green parties provide a clear example: they draw their support in relatively large numbers from voters who assign high importance to postmaterialist values. Inglehart's conclusions have, however, not remained uncontested. Several researchers have argued that value change comprises more dimensions than the one identified by Inglehart. Furthermore, the contrast between postmaterialism and materialism has not become as important as that between left and right. Issues related to the latter ideological positions have remained of paramount importance for understanding political behaviour.

Prejudice

Ideological orientations have also been shown to play an important role in prejudice. Research in this field has been strongly influenced by the seminal work of Adorno, Frenkel-Brunswick, Levinson and Sanford (1950) on **authoritarianism**. They argued that anti-Semitic attitudes were not held in isolation, but were part of more general psychological orientation that included ingroup glorification, prejudice against outgroups and pseudo-conservatism. Adorno *et al.* considered this orientation an expression of a particular personality structure, which they labelled 'authoritarian personality'. Several studies have shown that measures of right-wing authoritarianism indeed correlate with measures of prejudice. Another related measure that correlates with prejudice is **social dominance orientation**, which concerns whether a person prefers relations between ingroups and outgroups to be equal or hierarchical (Sidanius & Pratto, 1999).

Whereas right-wing authoritarianism and social dominance orientation have mostly been viewed as personality variables, Duckitt (2001) has argued that both scales are more appropriately viewed as measuring ideological belief dimensions, which are correlated with conservatism (see also Jost, Glaser, Kruglanski & Sulloway, 2003). Whereas right-wing authoritarianism is related to social conservatism, social dominance orientation is related to economic conservatism. Duckitt identified two world-views that supposedly underlie both orientations: right-wing authoritarianism is a response to a view of the world as dangerous, unpredictable and threatening, whereas social dominance orientation is a response to a view of the world as a 'ruthlessly competitive jungle' in which the strong win and the weak lose. He furthermore argued that these world-views are influenced by personality as well as social situations. For example, facing a threat will induce the world-view of a dangerous world and hence right-wing authoritarianism. This explains why right-wing authoritarianism and social dominance orientation measures are responsive to threat manipulations in experiments (see also Jost *et al.*, 2003). Considering the fact that social situations can be more easily manipulated than personality, this gives hope to those who wish to fight prejudice by means of interventions based on social psychology.

Applied social psychology in context

The topics discussed in the preceding paragraphs have not received attention in social psychology alone. Political leadership, for example, has also been studied by psychoanalysts and historians. Particularly when studying leaders from the past, taking into account the context, as historians do, can be highly relevant. In the field of voting behaviour, major contributions have been made in particular by sociologists (focusing on the influence of the social context) and economists (focusing on the decision-making process). Although psychological, sociological and economic models are frequently put forward as competing theories in this field, it would be more accurate to admit that each tells a part of the story. A question that has remained largely unanswered is how exactly these 'parts' relate to each other. Integrating sociological and economic models with psychological research is an important challenge. Self-evidently, political leadership, voting behaviour and ideology have also been extensively studied by political scientists. One challenge they face is to identify not only how social psychology can contribute to understanding politics, but also how insights reached in political science can contribute to social psychology.

When it comes to interventions, such as those aimed at increasing turnout, the contribution of social psychology has been modest. Although some measures that can be employed to increase turnout have been identified, the impact of the institutional context appears to be much stronger. Cross-national research by political scientists has identified several institutional factors that affect turnout, such as the day of voting (Sunday voting increases turnout) and the electoral system (the 'winner-takes-all' system, as used in Britain, decreases turnout). Not surprisingly, the single most important factor is compulsory voting. Countries in which voting is compulsory, like Belgium, have much higher levels of turnout than countries in which voting is not obligatory. So those who consider low levels of turnout a problem are more likely to promote institutional changes than interventions studied and proposed by social psychologists.

Another problem with interventions in the field of politics is that according to a widely accepted view, normative questions, that is, questions about what ought to be done, are by definition unanswerable on the basis of social scientific knowledge. Social scientists can only give answers to empirical questions, that is, questions about facts (but see Tyler & Jost, 2007, for a different view). This is also the main reason why political interventions by social scientists are rare. Whereas in many areas most people would agree what is desirable and what is not (e.g., few vs many traffic accidents, clean vs polluted environment and so on), in politics virtually all matters are value laden and involve complex trade-offs. What one politician or citizen considers desirable another may consider undesirable. From this perspective, influencing the decisions made by political leaders or voters would be considered unethical. The subfield that comes closest to being an exception in this respect is conflict resolution. But here, too, it would be a political decision to prevent the use of violence in a particular situation.

Conclusion

Social psychology has contributed to the study of politics not so much by developing intervention strategies, but by increasing our understanding of politics in many areas. Our review of studies in political psychology also tells us something about the usefulness of the types of studies that we distinguished in the introduction. When studying political leadership as well as voting behaviour, we identified general social-psychological theories that have been applied in these domains. Although such studies have resulted in several insights, their contribution to understanding political phenomena is clearly limited. Big Five ratings are related to political orientation and presidential performance, for example, but not very strongly. The theory of reasoned action has been applied to voting behaviour, but it cannot really specify in advance which attitudes will influence vote choice, nor explain why particular attitudes are held.

Studies in political psychology that have been more successful, at least in terms of how often they have been cited in research on politics, concern specific political phenomena. In electoral research, for example, the most important psychological theories explicitly concern vote choice and ideological commitment. This is not to say that the psychological processes involved in, say, voting behaviour differ qualitatively from behaviour in other areas of life. If that had been the case, social psychology would not have been such a rich source of inspiration for those who study political behaviour. But applying social psychology to politics apparently will require some fine tuning. This is one important reason why political psychology remains such a fascinating albeit challenging field of study.

Glossary

Authoritarianism: personality type that leads to ingroup glorification and prejudice against outgroups, such as anti-Semitism.

Big Five: theory that posits that personality consists of five traits: neuroticism, extraversion, agreeableness, openness to experiences and conscientiousness.

Dynamic information board: a computer program used in experiments to imitate the dynamic nature of election campaigns by giving participants many pieces of information about candidates.

Expected utility theory: theory that posits that possible costs and benefits of alternative choice options are multiplied by the likelihood they occur and that the option with the best net result is chosen.

Groupthink theory: theory that posits that ingroup cohesion, isolation from outside influences, directive leadership and stress lead small groups to make poor decisions.

Memory-based judgement: judgement that is made on the basis of information that is retrieved from memory.

Michigan model: theory that posits that vote choice is determined by voters' party identification, through its impact on attitudes towards candidates, policies, group benefits and government performance.

Nonattitudes: apparent attitudes expressed by respondents in survey questions that do not reveal any opinion relevant outside the context of the research.

Online judgement: judgement that is made at the moment that relevant information is processed and then is stored in, and hence can be directly retrieved from, memory.

Online model of candidate evaluations: theory that posits that voters update candidate evaluations whenever information about that person is processed, which implies that information in memory cannot accurately predict those evaluations.

Operational code: political leader's belief system about the world, in particular whether political life is one of harmony or conflict, whether the future is predictable and how political goals are most effectively pursued.

Partisan attitudes: psychological forces that direct voters towards a particular political party; these forces are the direct determinants of voting behaviour in the Michigan model.

Party identification: identification with a particular political party that voters develop early in their life, which influences their voting behaviour both directly and indirectly through its impact on political attitudes.

Postmaterialism: value orientation that emphasizes self-expression and quality of life over economic and physical security.

Power motive: the need of an individual (e.g., a politician) consciously or unconsciously to influence other people and let them do things they otherwise would not have done.

Prospect theory: theory that posits that decisions deviate from expected utility outcome, in particular because decision makers are willing to take more risk to prevent losses.

Social dominance orientation: personality characteristic that concerns whether a person prefers relations between ingroups and outgroups to be equal or hierarchical.

Theory of reasoned action: theory that posits that behaviour is directly determined by an intention, which is formed on the basis of a personal assessment of the consequences of the behaviour and the compliance with social influence.

Values: desirable trans-situational goals that vary in importance and serve as guiding principles in one's life.

Review questions

1. In this chapter we have distinguished four types of studies in political psychology. List these four types and provide one example of each.
2. What are the personality characteristics of *your* ideal leader? Do you expect other people to agree?
3. Is there any social-psychological theory that has been discussed in one of the preceding chapters that in your view could well be applied to explain mass political behaviour, for example, voting?
4. How are values and ideology related?
5. Is it appropriate for social psychologists to intervene in political processes in order to manage 'social problems'?

Further reading

Iyengar, S. & McGuire, W. (eds.) (1993). *Explorations in political psychology.* Durham, NC: Duke University Press.

Jost, J. T. & Sidanius, J. (eds.) (2004). *Political psychology: Key readings in social psychology.* New York: Psychology Press.

Kuklinski, J. H. (ed.) (2000). *Citizens and politics: Perspectives from political psychology.* Cambridge University Press.

Post, J. M. (ed.) (2003). *The psychological assessment of political leaders.* Ann Arbor, MI: University of Michigan Press.

Sears, D. O., Huddy, L. & Jervis, R. (eds.) (2003). *Oxford handbook of political psychology.* New York: Oxford University Press.

References

Adorno, T. W., Frenkel-Brunswik, E., Levinson, D. J. & Sanford, R. N. (1950). *The authoritarian personality.* New York: Harper & Row.

Ajzen, I. & Fishbein, M. (1980). *Understanding attitudes and predicting social behavior.* Englewood Cliffs, NJ: Prentice-Hall.

Campbell, A., Converse, P. E., Miller, W. E. & Stokes, D. E. (1960). *The American voter.* New York: John Wiley.

Converse, P. E. (1964). The nature of belief systems in mass publics. In D. E. Apter (ed.), *Ideology and discontent* (pp. 206–265). New York: Free Press.

Duckitt, J. (2001). A dual-process cognitive-motivational theory of ideology and prejudice. In M. P. Zanna (ed.), *Advances in experimental social psychology, 33* (pp. 41–113). San Diego: Academic Press.

Dyson, S. B. (2001). Drawing policy implications from the 'Operational Code' of a 'new' political actor: Russian President Vladimir Putin. *Policy Sciences, 34* (3–4), 329–346.

Gerber, A. S. & Green, D. P. (2000). The effects of canvassing, telephone calls, and direct mail on voter turnout: A field experiment. *American Political Science Review, 94* (3), 653–663.

Haas, M. L. (2001). Prospect theory and the Cuban missile crisis. *International Studies Quarterly, 45* (2), 241–270.

Inglehart, R. (1977). *The silent revolution.* Princeton University Press.

Janis, I. L. (1972). *Victims of groupthink.* Boston: Houghton Mifflin.

Jost, J. T. (2006). The end of the end of ideology. *American Psychologist, 61* (7), 651–670.

Jost, J. T., Glaser, J., Kruglanski, A. W. & Sulloway, F. (2003). Political conservatism as motivated social cognition. *Psychological Bulletin, 129* (3), 339–375.

Jost, J. T. & Sidanius, J. (eds.) (2004). See Further reading.

Kaarbo, J. & Hermann, M. G. (1998). Leadership styles of prime ministers: How individual differences affect the foreign policymaking process. *Leadership Quarterly, 9* (3), 243–263.

Kahneman, D. & Tversky A. (1979). Prospect theory: Analysis of decision under risk. *Econometrica, 47* (2), 263–291.

Lau, Richard R. & Redlawsk, David P. (2006). *How voters decide.* New York: Cambridge University Press.

Lodge, M., McGraw, K. M. & Stroh, P. (1989). An impression-driven model of candidate evaluation. *American Political Science Review, 83* (2), 399–419.

McGuire, W. J. (1985). Attitudes and attitude change. In G. Lindzey & E. Aronson (eds.), *Handbook of social psychology* (pp. 233–346). New York: Random House.

Milgram, S. (1974). *Obedience to authority.* New York: Harper & Row.

Quattrone, G. A. & Tversky, A. (1988). Contrasting rational and psychological analyses of political choice. *American Political Science Review, 82* (3), 719–736.

Rokeach, M. (1973). *The nature of human values.* New York: Free Press.

Rubenzer, S. J., Faschingbauer, T. R. & Ones, D. S. (2000). Assessing the U.S. presidents using the Revised NEO Personality Inventory. *Assessment, 7* (4), 403–419.

Sears, D. O., Huddy, L. & Jervis, R. (2003). See Further reading.

Sidanius, J. & Pratto, F. (1999). *Social dominance.* New York: Cambridge University Press.

Thomassen, J. & Rosema, M. (in press). Party identification revisited. In J. Bartle & P. Bellucci (eds.), *Party identification, social identity and political experience.* London: Routledge/ECPR Studies in European Political Science.

Tyler, T. R. & Jost, J. T. (2007). Psychology and the law: Reconciling normative and descriptive accounts of social justice and system legitimacy. In A. W. Kruglanski & E. T. Higgins (eds.), *Social psychology: Handbook of basic principles*. 2nd edn (pp. 807–825). New York: Guilford.

Winter, D. G. (1987). Leader appeal, leader performance, and the motive profiles of leaders and followers: A study of American presidents and elections. *Journal of Personality and Social Psychology*, 52 (1), 196–202.

Index

Aarts, H. 196
Abrahams, S. 255
Abu Ghraib prison 14
acculturation 143
  globalization and 155–158
  multidimensional models of 144–148,
    156
  one-dimensional models of 143–144
  theory and research 152–154
accuracy 10
action research model 32
adapted messages 240–241
Adenauer, K. 295
Adorno, T. W. 309
aggression 90, 91–92, 100–101, 105
Aitken, C. K. 69
Ajzen, I. 38–39, 49, 291–292, 301–303
Allen, M. 80
altruism 45, 121
altruistic value orientation 195
American Psychological Association, 'Ethical
    principles of psychologists and code of
    conduct' 10
Anderson, C. A. 76, 87, 90, 91–92, 94–95, 96,
    98, 100–101, 105–106, 111, 113
Anderson, N. 283
anomalies 118–119
anorexia nervosa 252
antecedent intervention strategies 59–62,
    198–199, 200
antecedent stimuli 58
anxious-ambivalent attachment style 260
applied behaviour analysis 57–59
applied social psychology 4–8
  and theories 8–9
Armstrong, T. L. 151
Aronson, E. 70, 71, 79, 80, 95–96
Aronson, J. 176
Asch, S. E. 13
ascription of responsibility (AR beliefs) 192,
    193
assimilation 145–148, 174
associative networks 274–275
Atsma, N. 277
attachment security 153–154

attachment styles 260
  and relationship quality 260–263
attachment theory 260, 264
attitudes 2–3, 34, 37, 38
  changing 69
  intergroup 153–154
  partisan 303–304
  towards immigrants 152
attributes, related 165
attribution theory 36–37, 74
Australia
  cultural mix 142
  intergroup relations 150
authentic dissent 282
authoritarianism 309–310
authority 75–76
availability heuristic 4, 74
avoidant attachment style 260, 261–262
awareness of consequences (AC beliefs)
    191–193

Bachman, B. A. 157–158
Bamberg, S. 38–39, 49
Bargh, J. A. 39
Bartholomew, K. 260
Bartholow, B. D. 105–106
Bedell, B. T. 242–243
behavioural change 1–3, 28
behavioural commitments 61–62, 200
behavioural intention 211
behavioural self-perception 70
behavioural willingness 233
Bem, D. J. 70
Benartzi, S. 129–130
Bentham, J. 117, 136
Berry, J. W. 144–148, 156
biases 42–43, 135, 137
  description-based 209
  prescriptive 209
big-fish-little-pond effect 163, 173–174, 179
Big Five trait theory 293–294, 311
biology, effect on behaviour and thought 15
biospheric value orientation 195
Blanton, H. 164, 166
block-leader approach 76–77

body dismorphic disorder (BDD) 252–253, 254
body image
  disturbed 249, 252–255, 266
  evaluations 254
  gender differences in 251–252
  investments 254
  schemas 254
Bohr, N. 50
Bourhis, R. Y. 146–148
Boyce, T. E. 78
brainstorming 275, 278, 279
  structured 282–283
Brehm, J. 60
Brenninkmeyer, V. 259
Brewer, M. B. 284, 285
Brickson, S. 284
Brodbeck, F. 277
Brown, S. D. 209
Bruner, J. S. 178
Brunot, S. 166, 169–170
bulimia 252
Burger, J. M. 76
Burn, S. M. 76, 77
Bush, G. W. 67
Buunk, A. P. 164, 166, 259
bystander apathy 45

Cacioppo, J. 40
Campbell, A. 303, 304
Canada
  inhabitants 142
  intergroup relations 150
  multiculturalism in 157
cardinal utility 117
Carlsmith, J. M. 95–96
causality 12
Chartrand, T. L. 39
Cheng, L. 42
Chinn, D. E. 61, 76
chronic illness, societal burden of 228
Cialdini, R. 40, 67, 70, 72, 73, 77, 79
Cihangir, S. 282
classroom climate 163, 176–177
cluster sampling 108–109
cognition, social
cognitive behaviour programmes 257–258
cognitive dissonance 4, 37–38, 68–69
cognitive processes 274–275
cohesion
  goals 279–281
  promoting 281
Collins N. L. 261–262
colour-blind perspectives 278–279
common ingroup identity model 151–152, 154, 157
commons dilemmas 190–191

comparative evaluation 166
compatibility principle 33, 38
compliance 40
computer-tailored persuasion 238–239
conflict 44–45
conformity 39–40
confound 90–92
consequence intervention strategies 62–66, 199–200
conservatism 310
consistency 61–62, 67
constructs 4, 34
consultant 23
contact hypothesis 43–44, 149, 158
content analysis 294–296
contrast 174
Converse, P. E. 303, 304, 307
coping strategies 256
correlational research 97–98, 112
  advantages of 99
  disadvantages of 99–100
countercontrol 60
covariates 100–103, 104–105
Cox, T., Jr 279
Craig, C. S. 75–76
creolization 157, 158
cultural identity 154
  acceptance of 155
cultural norms 15
cultural scripts 155
culture 154
  effect on behaviour and thought 15
  organizational 218
Cummings, N. 70

Daamen, D. D. L. 59
Darley, J. 45, 46, 51
Davis, A. 270
De Pater, I. E. 210
debriefing 11
deception 11
decision making
  crisis 296–297
  groups 275, 298–299
deductive approach 6, 7, 25
deindividuation 49
del Prado, A. 76
delay–speed-up asymmetry 134–135
dependent variable 89
depression 255, 266–267
  gender differences in 256
  preventing 257–259
  social comparison theory and 256–258
description 11
description-based bias 209
descriptive norms 72–75

Detweiler, J. B. 242–243
diffusion of responsibility 45
Dijkstra, A. 240
Dill, K. E. 90, 91–92, 94–95, 96, 98, 100–101, 105, 111
discrimination 43
disengagement beliefs 230
disincentives 63
dismissing attachment style 260, 262–263
disposition effect 124
disturbed body image 249, 266
    consequences of 252–253
    preventing 254–255
    and schema theory 254
    and social comparison theory 253
divergent thinking 282
diversity management 278–281
divorce 259–260
Dovidio, J. F. 151, 157–158
downward comparisons 9, 253, 257
dual concern model 44–45
Duckitt, J. 309–310
Dugosh, K. L. 278
Duke University 31
Dweck, C. S. 168
dynamic information board 306

ecocentric value orientation 195
economic theory 121, 220–221
Edison, T. 50
education
    to change behaviour 59–60
    single-gender 175–176
    social psychology of 162–163
education campaigns 30–31
egoistic value orientation 194–195
elaboration likelihood model 34, 40–42, 242
electoral participation 299–302
emotion-focused coping 256
emotional support 234–235
enactive learning 231–232
endowment effect 130–132
energy conservation 31
Engelen, M. 59
entity theorists 168
environment
    effect of behaviour on 184–185, 188–201
    influence on well-being and behaviour 184, 185–187
environmental behaviour 189–190
    effect of values on 194–195
    and habits 195–198
    and norm activation model 191–193
    see also pro-environmental behaviour

environmental problems
    commons dilemmas 190–191
    human behaviour and 188–201
environmental stressors 185–186
Eron, L. D. 101
Esses, V. M. 151, 152
ethical principles 10–11
ethnocentrism 151
Europe, Western
    cultural mix 142
    immigration from Eastern 143–144
Everett, P. B. 60
Everybody's Different programme 255
evolutionary psychology 15
exchange orientation 265
exclusion 146–148
expected utility theory 296–297
explanation 12

Fallon, A. E. 251–252
Faschingbauer, T. R. 294
fear 230
fear appeals 80, 238
fearful attachment style 260, 262–263
feedback 65–66, 199–200, 240–242
    normative 73
Feeney, B. C. 261–262
Feldman, R. S. 162
Festinger, L. 37, 163, 165
field studies 19–20
Finlayson, B. L. 69
Fishbein, M. 291–292, 301–303
Fisher, I. 133
framing 119–120, 124–125
    hedonic 125–130
Fraser, S. C. 68
Freedman, J. L. 68
Frenkel-Brunswick, E. 309
Freud, S. 47
Fuchs, D. 216
fundamental attribution error 36, 74

Gaertner, S. 151, 157–158
gain-framed appeal 8, 242–243
Gardner, W. 285
Gelfand, M. J. 278
Geller, E. S. 60, 61, 62, 71, 78, 80
gender 206
gender bias 216
gender differences
    and ability 208
    academic 177–178
    in body image 251–252
    in depression 256
    in leadership style 214–215

and self-efficacy beliefs 210
at work 206–207
gender gap 207
gender stereotypes 208–209
and job selection 213, 219
gender typing
jobs 212, 213
of leadership and management 214
people 212–213
Gerber, A. S. 302
Gibbons, F. X. 164, 166
glasnost 292
glass ceiling 206–207, 213–214
eliminating 219–220
global warming 188–189, 193
globalization 155–158
Goldstein, N. 40
Gonzales, M. H. 80
Good, C. 176
Gorbachev, M. 292
Grant Thornton 285
Green, D. P. 302
group conflict 151
group creativity 274–276
groups
age of 280–281
cohesion and locomotion goals 279–281
communality-focused tasks 281–282
dissent in 282–283
formation of subgroups 277–278
intercultural climate 279
groupthink 280–281, 297–299
Gupta, N. 64

Haas, M. L. 297
habits 195–198, 202
Hackett, G. 209
Haines, M. P. 46
Hargadon, A. B. 283
Harquail, C. V. 279
Harris, E. 87
Harvey, O. 43–44
Hau, K. T. 173
health action process approach (HAPA) 229
health belief model (HBM) 229
healthy behaviour, encouragement of 228
hedonic calculus 117
hedonic framing 125–130
hedonic utility 117
Heider, F. 36
Heilman, M. E. 216
helping 45
Henderson, V. 168
Hermann, M. G. 295–296
heuristics 135, 137
Hickcox, M. 237

Hill, C. T. 211–212
Ho, R. 150
Hollingworth, L. 208
Hood, W. 43–44
Horenczyk, G. 148
Hufford, M. 237
Huguet, P. 166, 169–170, 175, 176, 178
human capital theory 220–221
Huscmann, L. R. 101
hyperbolic discounting 134
hypocrisy effect 70, 71
hypothesis 33

identity orientations 284–285
identity threat 276–278, 281
ideology 307
end of 307–308
and values 308 309
Igartua, J. J. 42
illness beliefs 234
imitation 39
immigration 141–143
Immigration Law (1978) 142
implementation intentions 233
improving sequences 135
incentives 63–65
changing 200–201
incremental theories of intelligence 168
independent variable 89
indirect energy use 188
individual factors 12
individualism 148
inductive approach 6–7, 24, 25
information campaigns 30–31, 198–199
information processing 273–274
informed consent 11
Inglehart, R. 308–309
ingroup assimilation 276
ingroups 42, 309
ideas 278
injunctive norms 72–75
innovation 274, 283–284, 286
instrumental model of group conflict 151
instrumental support 234–235
intercultural group climate 279
integration 144, 145–148, 158
intelligence
incremental vs entity theorists of students' theories of 162–163, 166–168, 179
intention 211, 232–233
vs habit 197
interactive acculturation model 146
intergroup attitudes 153–154

intergroup relations 43–44
  globalization and 155–158
  methods for improving 154–155
  theories of 149–152
International Energy Outlook 188
interpersonal leadership style 214
intervention techniques 17
  antecedent strategies 59–62
  consequence strategies 62–66
intrinsic motivation 65
invasion of privacy 11
Inzlicht, M. 176

Jackson, L. M. 151
James, W. 117
Janis, I. L. 297–299
jealousy 266
Jefferson, T. 294
Jenkins, G. D. 64
Johnson, T. R. 68
Jost, J. T. 307–308

Kaarbo, J. 295–296
Kahneman, D. 119, 122, 130–131
Kaiser Family Foundation survey 109
Kalsher, M. J. 61, 62
Kanter, R. M. 217
Kapteijn, A. 120
Katzev, R. D. 68
Kelman, H. C. 39–40
Kennedy, J. 297
Kerry, J. 67
Khruschev, N. 296–297
Kitty Genovese case 45
Klebold, D. 87
Knetsch, J. L. 122, 130–131
knowledge-deficit model 30–31, 37
Kohl, H. 295
Kowalenko, N. 258
Kurowski, L. L. 278
Kuyper, H. 164, 166
Kyoto Protocol 188

Larimer, M. E. 73
Latané, B. 45, 46, 51
lateral comparisons 253
leadership
  style 214–215, 295–296
  women's qualities 215
  see also political leadership
learning, and classroom climate 176–177
Leckliter, I. N. 61, 76
Lefkowitz, M. M. 101
Lehman, G. R. 61, 62
Lent, R. W. 209
Levine, J. M. 14, 164

Levinson, D. J. 309
Lewin, K. 8, 279, 286
Lewis, M. A. 73
life expectancy 226–228
liking 76–77
Lincoln, A. 294
Lituchy, T. 214
Liu, J. 214
locomotion
  goals 279–281
  promoting 282–283
Lodge, M. 305–306
Loewenstein, G. 133
longitudinal designs 101–103
Lopes, O. 42
loss aversion 8, 122–132
loss-framed appeal 8, 242–243
Love, S. Q. 61, 76
Lundgren, R. E. 76

magnitude effect 134
Major, J. 295
Malone, E. L. 76
manipulation (of variables) 89
marginalization 145, 148, 157
marital problems see relationship problems
Marsh, H. W. 173
Martino, S. C. 242–243
Maslow's hierarchy of needs 309
materialism 308–309
mating preferences 15
McCann, J. M. 75–76
McClelland, D. 47
McGrath, J. 87–89, 107, 112
McGraw, K. M. 305–306
McLoone, J. 258
McMahon, T. A. 69
McMakin, A. H. 76
melting pot ideology 144
memory-based judgements 305
mental health 249
mentoring 219–220
message framing 240, 242–243
Messian, N. 76
meta-analysis 64
Michigan model (of voting) 303
Mikulincer, M. 153
Milgram, S. 13, 14, 40, 48, 75, 291
Miller, W. E. 303, 304
Mitra, A. 64
modelling 61, 232
models 33–34
Moïse, L. C. 146–148
momentary assessments 236–237
Monteil, J. M. 166, 169–170

motivation 43, 47, 229–231, 244, 273
  intrinsic 65
  lack of 30–31
  power 294–295
Mueller, R. 214
multi-method research 112–113
multiculturalism 141–143, 158
Multiculturalism Act (1988) 142
mundane realism 95

Nakui, T. 275, 279
national identity 157 158
negative thinking 258–259
Neighbors, C 73
new environmental paradigm (NEP) 193–194
noise 92–93
nonattitudes 307
norm activation model (NAM) 191–193, 196
normative feedback 73
normative prompts 73
norms 72–73
  correcting misperceived 73–75
  personal 191–193, 200

obedience 40, 48, 291
objectivity 10
observational learning 164
O'Dea, J. A. 255
O'Leary, M. 79
Ones, D. S. 294
online judgements 305–306
online model of candidate evaluations 292, 305–306
open-mindedness 10
operational code 295
ordinal utility 117
organizational change 273–277, 278–281
  and group stability 281
organizational climate
  and innovation 283–284, 286
  and psychological safety 283, 286
organizational culture 218
organizational identification 276–277
organizational structure 217–218
organizations
  cohesion in 279–281
  locomotion in 279–281, 282–283
  social context of 271–273
  workforce composition 272
Ott, E. M. 217
outcome expectancies 210–211
outgroup assimilation 276
outgroups 31, 309

Pallak, M. S. 70
parental training 264–265

Partain, K. K. 60
partisan attitudes 303–304
party identification 303, 304
Pasteur, L. 51
Patel, S. 76
Paulus, P. B. 275, 278, 279
penalties 62–63
Penney, R. 150
Peplau, L. A. 211–212
perceived behavioural control 2–3, 38
perceived communalities 278
perceived seriousness 230
perceived vulnerability 229–230
perestroika 292
Perkins, H. W. 46, 74–75
Perreault, S. 146–148
person-by-treatment quasi-experiment 104
person confound 91–92
personal norms 191–193, 200
personal reference 119–120, 124
personal relevance (of persuasive messages) 241–242
personal values 15–17
personality
  authoritarian 309
  five factor trait theory 293–294, 311
personalization (of messages) 240–242
persuasive communication 237–243, 244
Petty, R. 40
Petzel, T. 148
physical exercise 254
pluralism 157, 158
pluralistic ignorance 46, 74
policy advice 23–24
political leadership 292, 310
  Big Five personality traits 293–294, 311
  crisis decision making 296–297
  groupthink 297–299
  study of 294–296
  styles 295
political psychology 291–292
positive outcome expectations 231
positive reinforcement 63–64
postmaterialism 308–309
Postmes, T. 282
power motivation 294–295
prediction 11–12, 48
preference shift 120
Preiser, M. 152
prejudice 43, 309–310
preoccupied attachment style 261–263
prescriptive bias 209
principles 4, 33
pro-environmental behaviour 190
  promoting 198–201
problem-focused coping 256

procedural confound 92
prompts 60–61, 73, 79
prosocial behaviour 45
  decision-making model of 51
prospect theory 118–119, 122–124, 131, 132,
  133, 296–297
protection motivation theory (PMT) 229
prototype images 233
psychological realism 96
Psychology Today 250
public commitment 69–71
public relations 23
punishment 63–64
Putin, V. 295

quasi-experimental design 103–106, 112,
  187
  advantages of 106–107
  disadvantages 107
Quattrone, G. A. 299
Quinn, D. 175, 178

random assignment 89–90
random sampling 108–109
Rapee, R. M. 258
rational choice theory 34–35, 48, 299
reactance 79–80
recategorization 282–283
reciprocity 7, 77–79
  prompts 79
reference shift 120–121
Régner, I. 175, 178
related attributes 165
relational identity orientation 284–285
relationship problems 259–260, 267
  attachment style and 260–263
  preventing 264–265
  and social exchange theory 262–265
relationship questionnaire 260–261, 263
research 22–23
  design 18
  effect size 20–21
  field settings 19–20
  interdisciplinary 18–19
  multi-method 112–113
  selecting a method 87–89
  see also correlational research;
    quasi-experimental design; survey research;
    true experiments
reverse causality 99, 101–103
rewards 63–65
  pre-behaviour 78
Rhodes, M. U. 60
Rice, R. 46
right-wing authoritarianism 309–310
risk perception 229

Robber's Cave study 43–44
Roberts, D. 109
Rokeach, M. 308
role orientation 39–40
Rothman, A. J. 242–243
Rozin, P. 251–252
Rubenzer, S. J. 294
Ruble, D. N. 164
Rudd, J. R. 61, 62

Salovey, P. 242–243
sampling error 109
Sanford, R. N. 309
Sanna, L. J. 216
scarcity 79–80
scepticism 10
Schein, V. E. 214
schema theory 254
Schmidt, P. 38–39, 49
Schunk, D. H. 165
Schwartz, S. H. 194
scientific goals 11–12
scientific methods 10
scientific values 10
secure attachment style 260, 261–263
segregation 146–148
selection by consequences 58–59
self-concept, academic 166–179
  and the big-fish-little-pond effect 163,
    173–174, 179
  of failure and performance 169–173
self-efficacy 164–165
  beliefs 210
  expectations 229, 231–232, 244
self-esteem 253, 254, 276
self-perception, behavioural 70
self-referent encoding 241–242
self-serving biases 42–43
self-serving denial 192
Senécal, S. 146–148
separation 145, 157
sex-matching model 213
Shaver, P. R. 153
Shaw, J. D. 64
Sheffield, J. K. 258
Sherif, C. 43–44
Sherif, M. 43–44
Shiffman, S. 237
sign effect 134
similarity-attraction hypothesis 149–150
similarity principle 165
Singapore, multiculturalism in 157
situational factors 14
situational reference 121–122
Skinner, B. F. 57–58, 60
Sloane, A. 298

smoking 226–227, 237
    attempts to dissuade people from 31
social categorization 150, 155
    theory 154
social cognition
social comparison 6–7, 150, 163, 179, 232,
        259
    in the classroom 163–165, 179
    and depression 256–258
    disturbed body image 253, 266
    downward 166
    upward 165–167
    women with breast cancer 7–8, 9
social design 186–187
social dilemma perspective 7
social dominance orientation 151, 309–310
social exchange and interdependence theory
        262–265
social factors 12–14
social identity theory 150–151, 154, 155–156,
        158, 276–278, 286
social impact theory 45, 51
social inclusion 154
social influence 13–14
    principles 67–81
    theories 39–42
social norms 2–3, 72–73, 74
social problems, solving 1–3
social proof 72–75
social psychology
    definition 4, 35
social reference 120–121
social relationship theories 42–46
social support 234–235
social thinking theories 35–39
social utility 20–22
socialization theory 221
Sommer, R. 186
Spears, R. 282
Spence, S. H. 258
Spencer, S. J. 175, 178
Staats, H. 59
stage models 235, 244
Stahl, B. 61, 76
Stanford prison experiment 13–14
Stasser, G. 278
statistical discrimination theory 221
statistical interactions 93–94
status-quo bias 131–132
Steele, C. M. 175, 178
stereotype threat 175–176
stereotypes 42–43
    negative 175–176, 179
stimulus-overload theory 14
Stokes, D. 49–50, 303, 304
strategic voting 303

stress management 255
stress theory 256
Stroh, P. 305–306
subjective expected utility 118
subjective norms 38
sunk-costs effect 132
survey research 107, 112
    advantages of 110
    disadvantages of 110–111
Sutton, R. I. 283
Swim, J. K. 216
symptom perception 234

tailored messages 238–242
Tamkins, M. M. 216
tangible assistance 234
task-oriented leadership style 214
Taylor, S. 7–8, 9
Tertoolen, G. 69
Thaler, R. 122, 129–131, 134
Thatcher, M. 295–296
theories 4–5, 8–9, 32–33
    application of 47
    boundary condition of 47, 93–94
    complexity of 47–48
    development of 49–51
    and explaining behaviour 48
    and intervention 32, 48–49
    social influence 39–42
    social psychological 35
    social relationship 42–46
    social thinking 35–39
    testing of 32
    and understanding problems 29–31
theory of involuntary subordinate strategies (ISS)
        257–258
theory of normative conduct 17
theory of planned behaviour (TPB) 2, 6, 9,
        38–39, 196, 229, 301
    vs habits 197
theory of reasoned action 196, 291–292
    and electoral choice 301, 303, 311
    and women's career behaviour 211–212
third variable problem 99–101
Thomas, A. 150
Thompson, H. 208
threat-rigidity effect 275–276
three-term contingency 58
time preference 133–135
Titus, W. 278
training 59–60
trans theoretical model (TTM) 235
transactional leadership 215
transformational leadership 215
transnationalism 156
Triandis, H. C. 278

true experiments 88–90, 112
  advantages of 90–94
  disadvantages of 94–95
Tversky, A. 119, 299
2 × 2 factorial design 93

ultimatum game 121
unidirectional drive upwards 165
United States, cultural mix 141–142
unrealistic optimism 230
upward comparisons 253, 257
use-inspired research 51
utility maximization 117–118, 135,
    136
utility theory 119

value-belief-norm theory of environmentalism
    (VBN) 193
value-in-diversity approach 279
value orientation 40, 308
  altruistic 195
  biospheric (ecocentric) 195
  egoistic 194–195
values 194–195
  and ideology 308–309
  personal 15–17
  scientific 10
Van der Zee, K. I. 277
Van Dick, R. 148
Van Dijk, E. 131
Van Herwaarden, F. G. 120
Van Knippenberg, D. 131
Van Kreveld, D. 69
Van Oudenhoven, J. P. 148
Van Praag, B. M. S. 120
Van Vianen, A. E. M. 212

Verstraten, E. C. H. 69
vicarious learning 232
video games, violent 87, 90, 91–92, 100–101,
    105–106
Vincent, P. C. 211–212
vocational interests 209
voting behaviour 299–302, 310
  Michigan model 303–304
  online model of candidate evaluations 305–306
  and theory of reasoned action 301–303
  turnout 299–302, 310–311

Wagner, U. 148, 152
Walder, L. Q. 101
Wallen, A. S. 216
Wearing, A. J. 69
weight satisfaction, gender differences in
    251–252
welfare function of income 120
Werner, C. M. 60
West, N. R. 283
White Australia policy 142
White, J. 43–44
Wignall, A. 258
Wilke, H. A. M. 59
Willemsen, T. M. 212
Winett, R. A. 60, 61, 76
Winter, D. G. 294–295
Witte, K. 80
Wolf, C. 152
worry 230

Ybema, J. F. 166

Zick, A. 148
Zimbardo, P. G. 13–14